IMAGES
of America

WORCESTER
VOLUME II

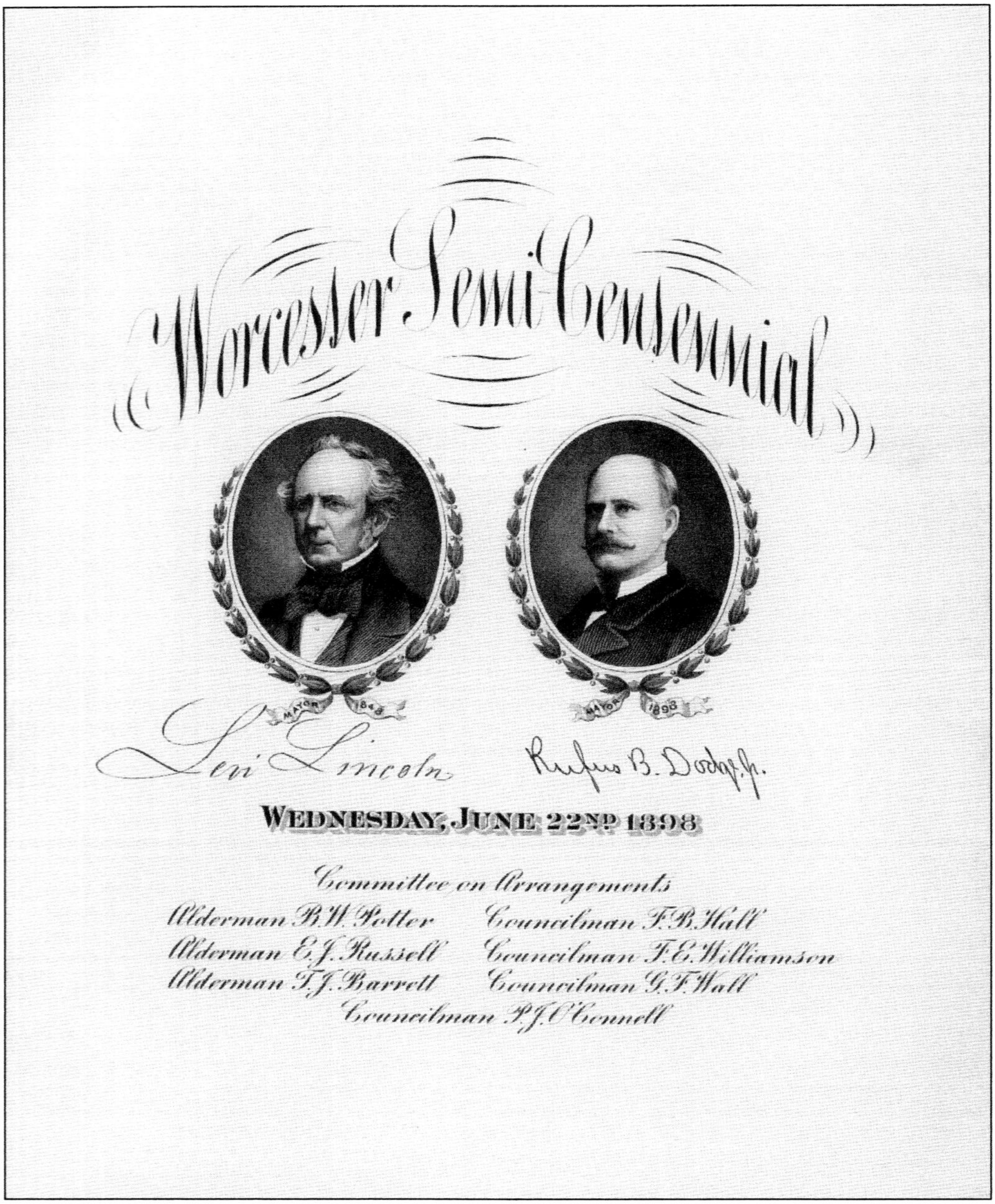

Worcester celebrated its 50th anniversary as a city in 1898. The front page of the program showed the city's first mayor, Levi Lincoln, and the then-current mayor, Rufus B. Dodge Jr.

IMAGES
of America

WORCESTER
VOLUME II

Barton Kamp

ARCADIA
PUBLISHING

ISBN 978-0-7385-6486-9

Published by Arcadia Publishing
Charleston, South Carolina

Printed in the United States of America

Library of Congress Catalog Card Number: Applied for

For all general information contact Arcadia Publishing at:
Telephone 843-853-2070
Fax 843-853-0044
E-mail sales@arcadiapublishing.com
For customer service and orders:
Toll-Free 1-888-313-2665

Visit us on the Internet at www.arcadiapublishing.com

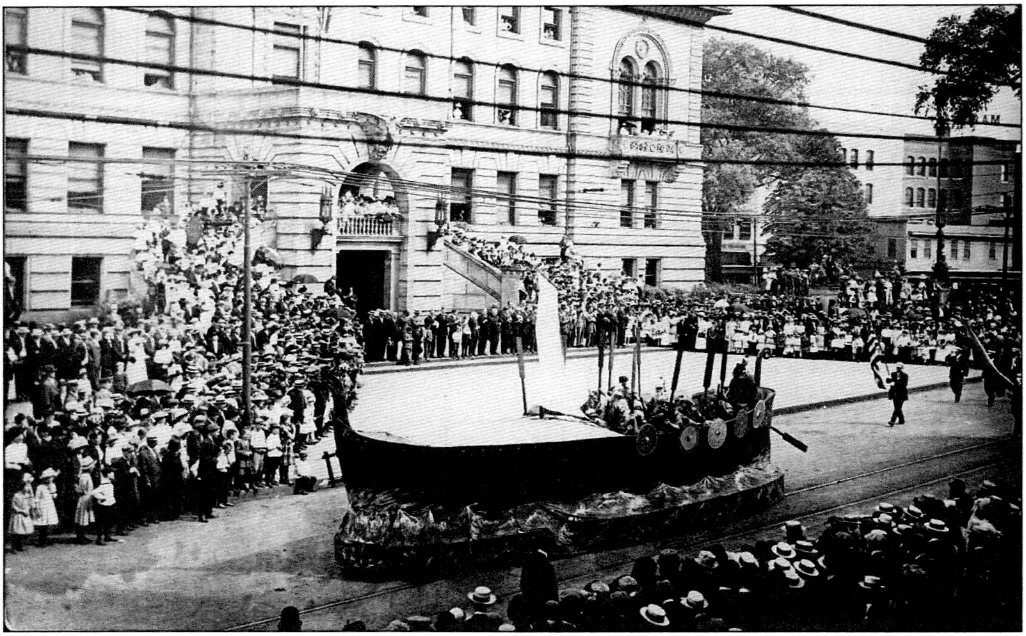

Over a hundred thousand people viewed the June 22, 1912 parade that was part of the city's Swedish Midsummer Festival. One of the floats was of the *Anno*, a re-creation of the longboat on which Lief Ericson sailed to America.

CONTENTS

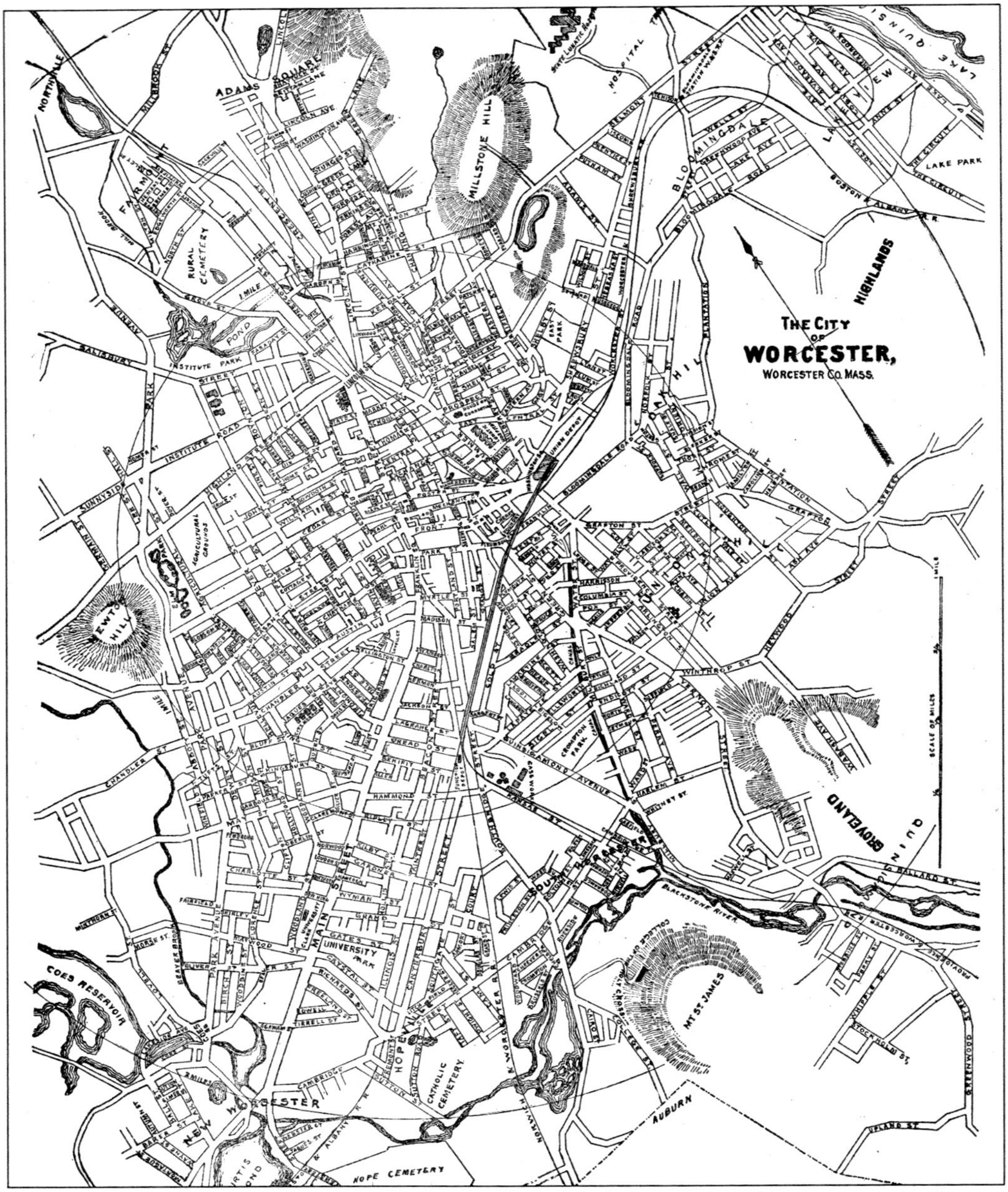

This 1898 map of the main part of the city was included in the *Pocket Guide to the City of Worcester*, published by George D. Monk.

INTRODUCTION

At the turn of the century Worcester was undergoing tremendous growth. Fortunately for us, it was at this time that the Golden Age of Postcards was in its infancy, because it is primarily through postcards that this growth was documented. The postcard craze had overtaken Europe by 1902 and by 1905 it had reached the United States in comparable proportions. In 1913 the United States, with a population of over 92 million people, recorded over 968 million postcards mailed. With Worcester's population over 160,000, it can be estimated that nearly 2 million postcards were mailed that year from the city.

The postcards were saved by the millions by placing them in albums, some of which held up to a thousand postcards. They were the cheapest and sometimes the only means of communication between businesses, friends, and families. Anyone with a camera could make a postcard. However, the majority of the postcards manufactured for the United States and the world came from Germany. The Germans had perfected the process to produce quality postcards. Prior to World War I the interest in postcards collecting began to diminish. The German companies that produced most of the world's postcards were destroyed during the war and their processes for producing postcards were lost. Changes in lifestyles after the war (i.e., more cars and telephones) reduced the need for and interest in postcards. Millions of postcards went into closets and attics to await the second postcard craze of the 20th century.

The growth of Worcester during the postcard era is best described in a book written by Donald Tulloch in 1914: "Few cities can show such tremendous growth in population. It has placed 3,000 people to its population every year on an average for 30 years. In the last 15 years it has added 50,000 people within its gates. Ah hour's ride by train, and Worcester can come in touch with 3,000,000 people, and that fact is true of one other city in the United States—New York."

The city is described also in Tulloch's book as follows: "Worcester is a unique city. There isn't anything just like it in the Western Hemisphere. First and foremost it is supremely a manufacturing and railroad center, and it is also a city of homes. It is a city of mechanics whose languages represent the nationalities of the universe, yet it is renowned as a center of music, art, culture, refinement."

It is the preceding paragraph that guided me in the selection of my images and how they would be presented. I visualized what a family would see and do upon arriving and settling in the city c. 1910. They would first encounter the city's streets and transportation. They would search for a job in manufacturing, in wholesale or retail, or in the services. They would become familiar with the city's buildings. They would join the church of their choice. They would make use of area schools. They would attend some of the many events that occur in the city.

This is the second book about Worcester in the Images of America series. It was prepared with the intent that it be a companion to the first Worcester book. Nearly all of the images in this volume are picture postcards covering the period from 1905 to 1930, though non-postcard images extend the coverage back to about 1890. Care has been taken not to duplicate any of the images of the first book.

One

STREETS AND TRANSPORTATION

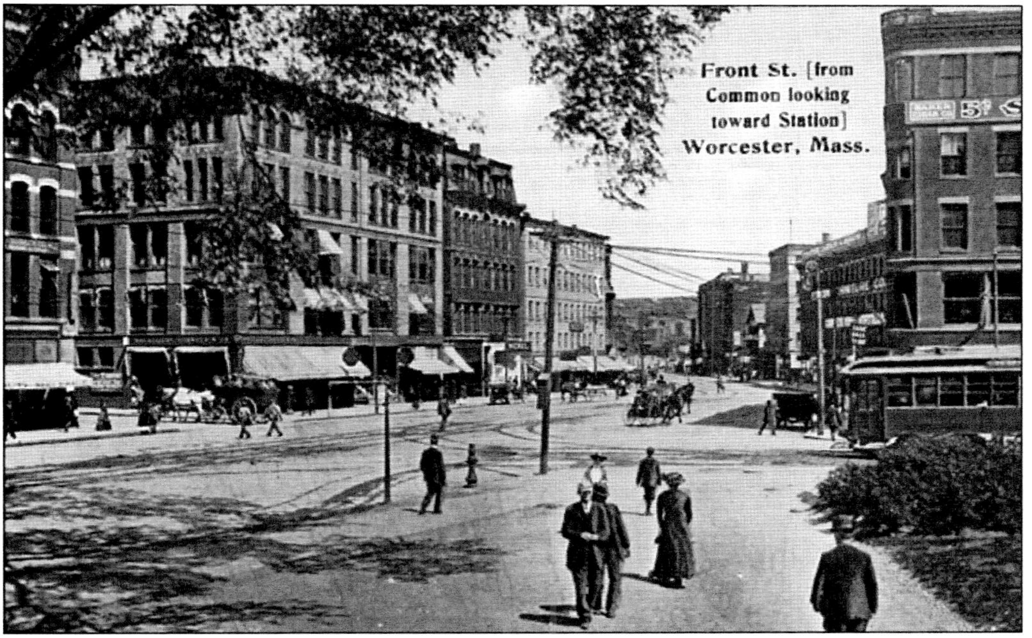

Salem Square met Front Street at the northeast corner of the common. The trolley is entering Front Street from Salem Square. Front Street was the main road to Union Station from the center of the city. Several hotels were located on the street to serve people arriving by train. The Essex, the Langdon, the Montreal, the Nashua House, New Sherwood, Sterling, and Warren Hotels were there *c.* 1910.

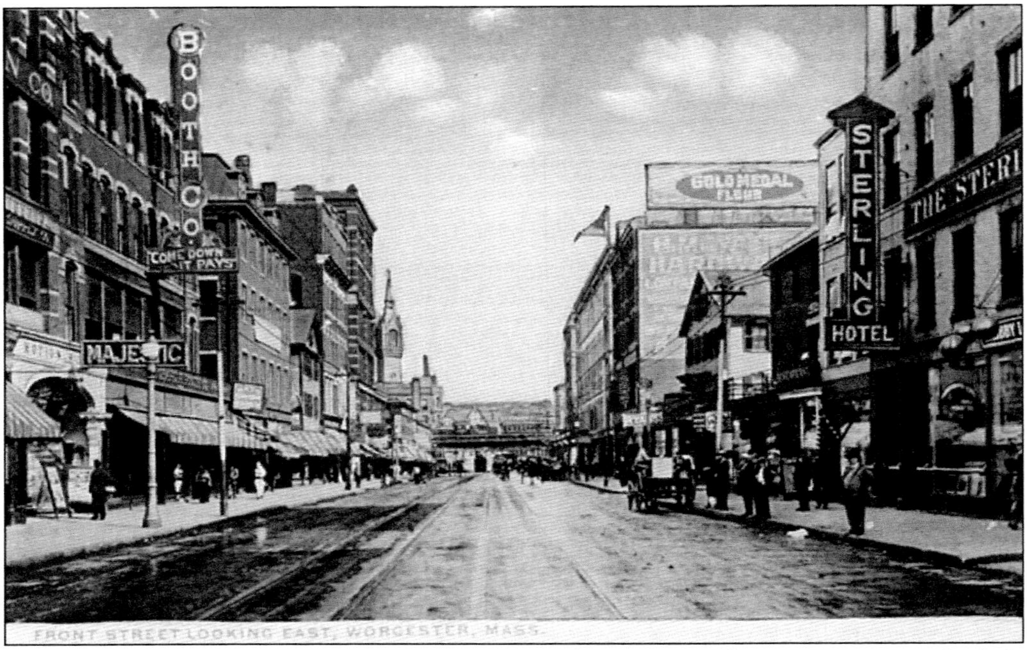

Lower Front Street, c. 1915, was the location of the Majestic Theater as seen on the left. Note the three-ball symbol of the pawn shop on the right at the entrance of Libby Loan Company. The loan company was one of the many pawn shops located on the street. The tower of the old Union Station can be seen in the distance. The Stars and Stripes flies on top of the Warren Hotel.

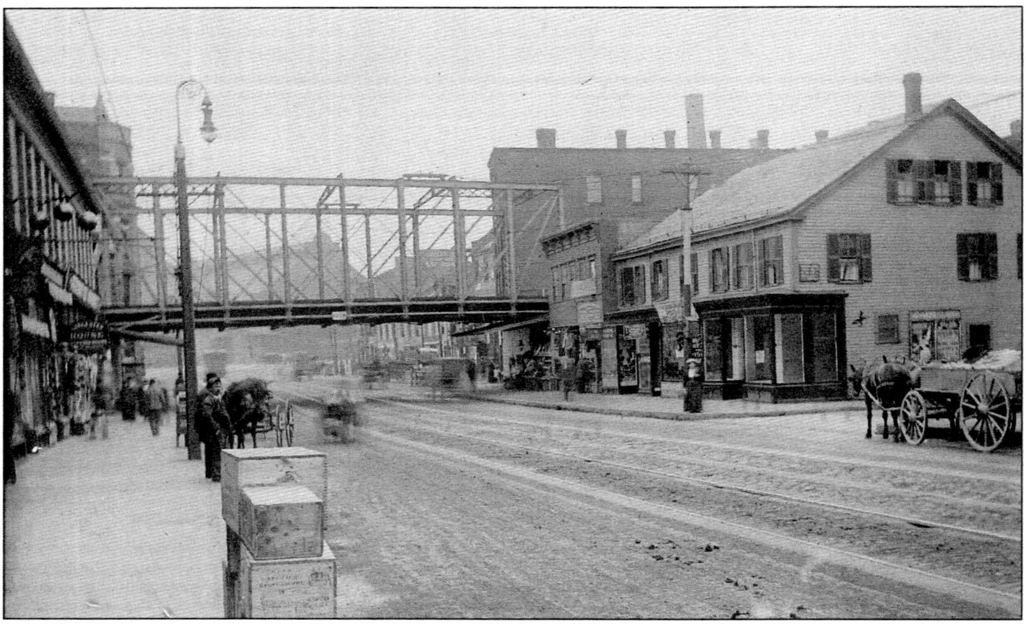

This is the end of Front Street, c. 1902. Washington Square began on the other side of the railroad viaduct. Canal Street was on the right. The wooden building on the right was a boarding house, and the Cape Cod Fish Company was located just before the viaduct.

Large American elm trees lined Front Street along the common. One of the trees had a growth in the shape of an elephant, which protruded from the trunk. It drew the attention of many passersby and was photographed extensively.

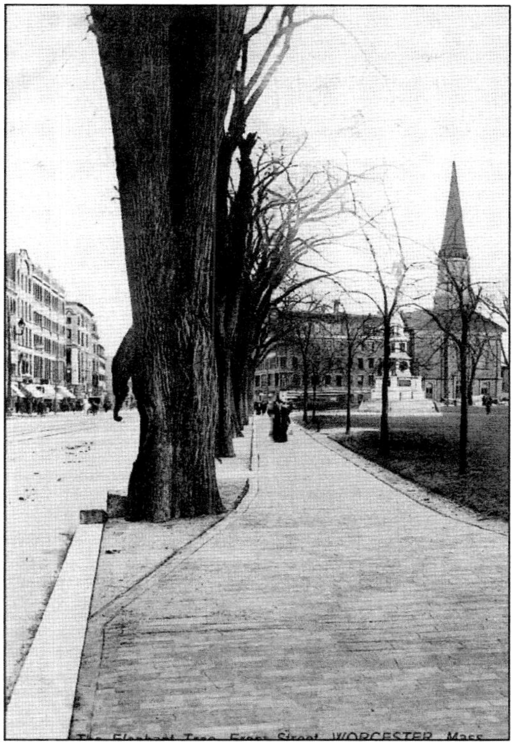

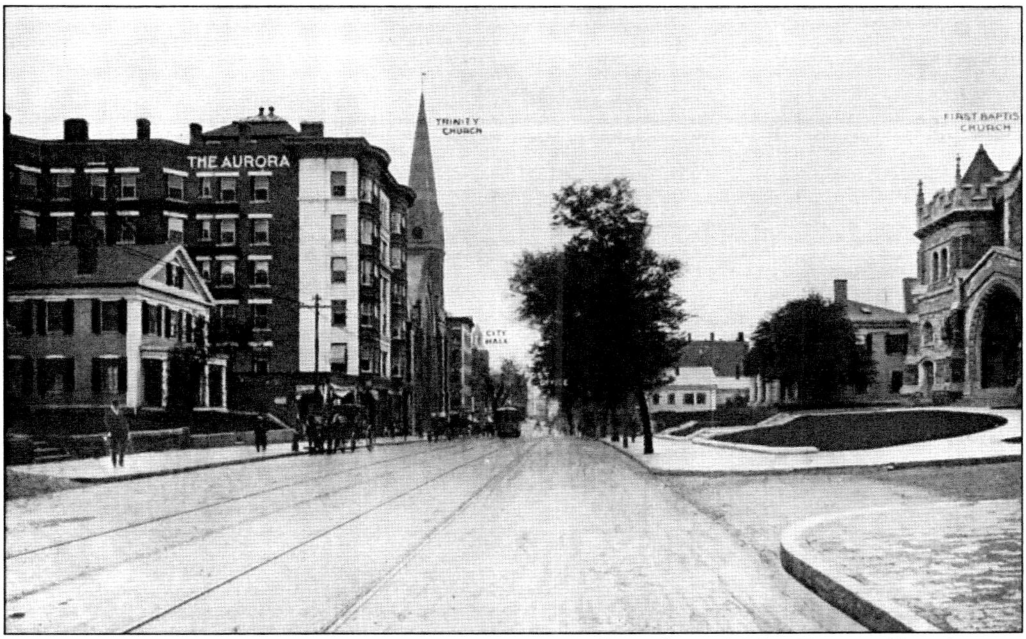

South of Chandler Street, Main Street, *c.* 1910, was still residential. The Trinity Church, seen on the left, was located at the corner of Main and Chandler Streets. On the right, at the corner of Mower (Ionic) Avenue, was the First Baptist Church. Next to the church was the home of Frank A. Leland, longtime owner of a piano and music store.

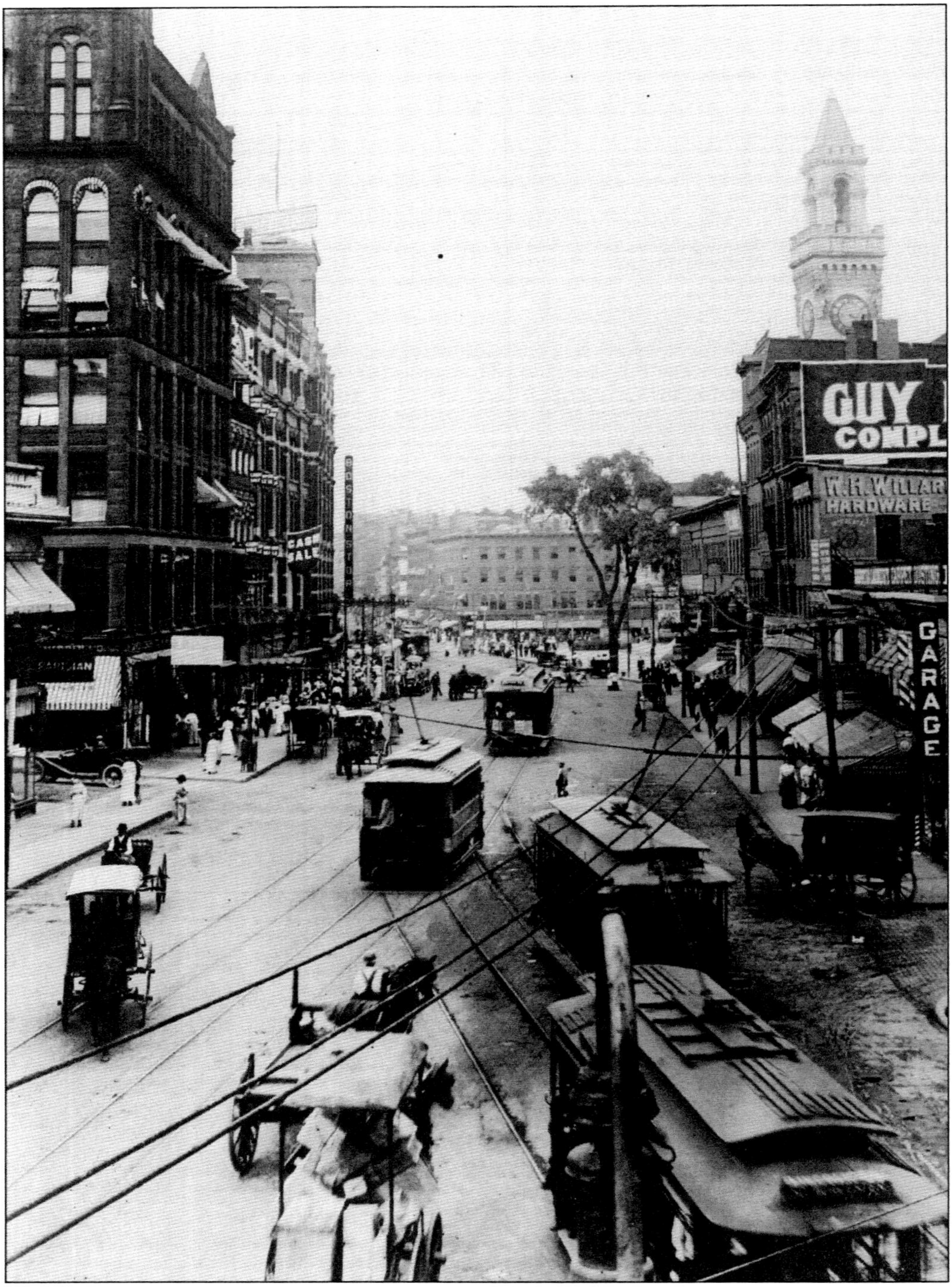

Trolleys from Southbridge Street merge with the Main Street trolleys at the intersection of Main and Southbridge Streets. Horse-drawn vehicles were the main means of transportation in this *c.* 1910 scene. A hard-to-find car heads up Chatham Street on the left. The tall building on the corner of Chatham Street was the Knowles Building.

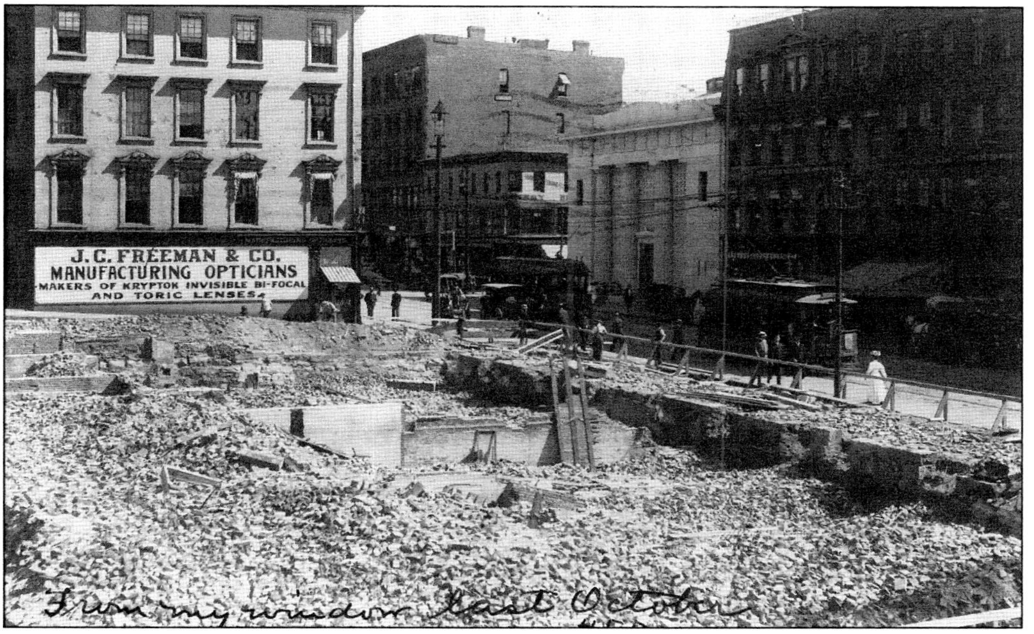

Site preparation has begun for the construction of the city's newest building, the Slater Building. This picture, taken in October of 1906, shows workers setting up the barriers that will guide the pedestrians around the construction site. The building was opened in 1907.

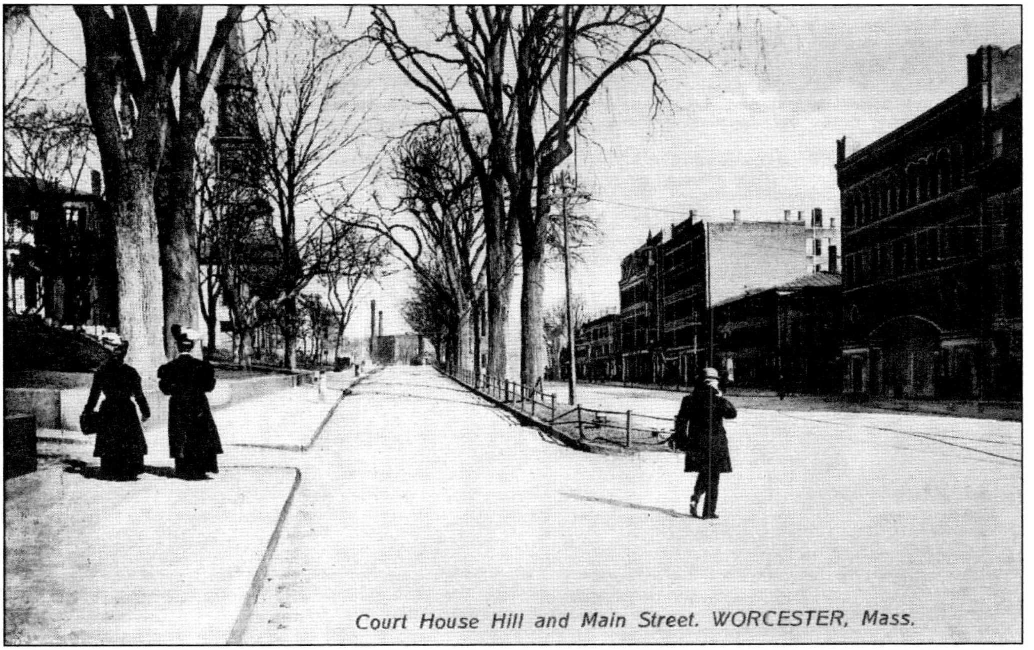

Not a car in sight as this gentleman attempts to jaywalk across North Main Street at Court House Hill in 1908. He's probably headed for the trolley barn or the Exchange Hotel on the corner next to it. The First Unitarian Church is visible on Court House Hill.

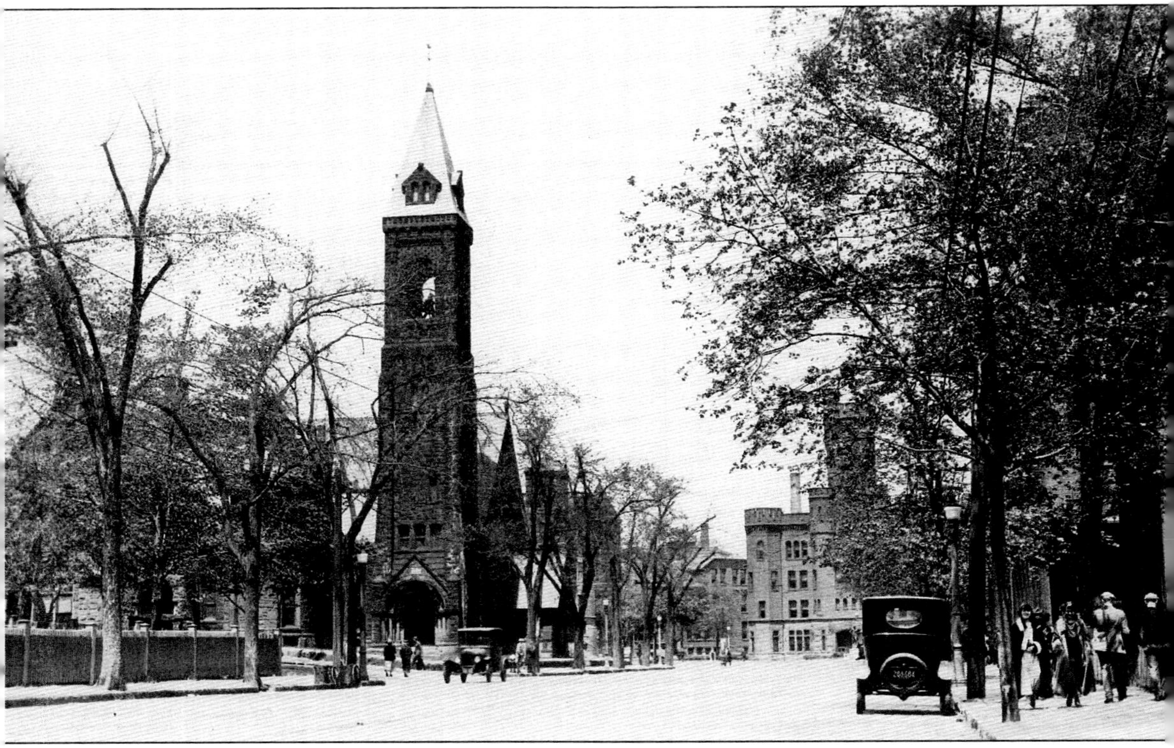

The traffic is light as it heads north from Lincoln Square in this c. 1920 scene of Salisbury Street. The Central Church is on the left at the corner of Institute Road. The State Armory is in the distance. The Whitcomb Envelope Company and the Hobbs Manufacturing Company were located along the right side of the street.

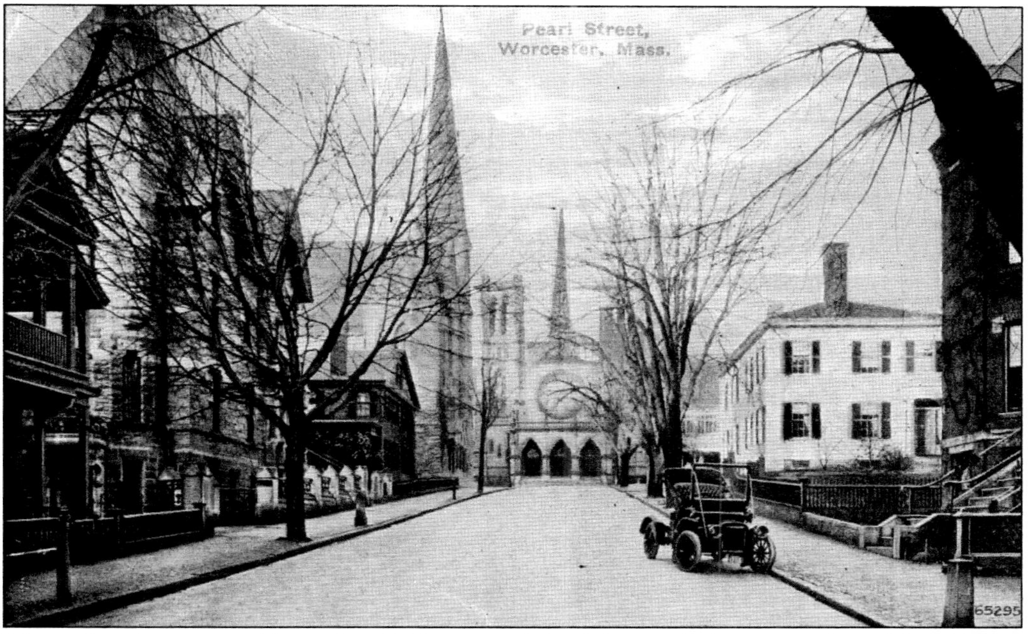

Three churches are visible in this 1910 scene of Pearl Street, looking west from Main Street. On the left is the Plymouth Church, located on the corner of Chestnut Street. In the center is the Chestnut Street Congregational Church, and the spire beyond that belongs to the Pleasant Street Baptist Church.

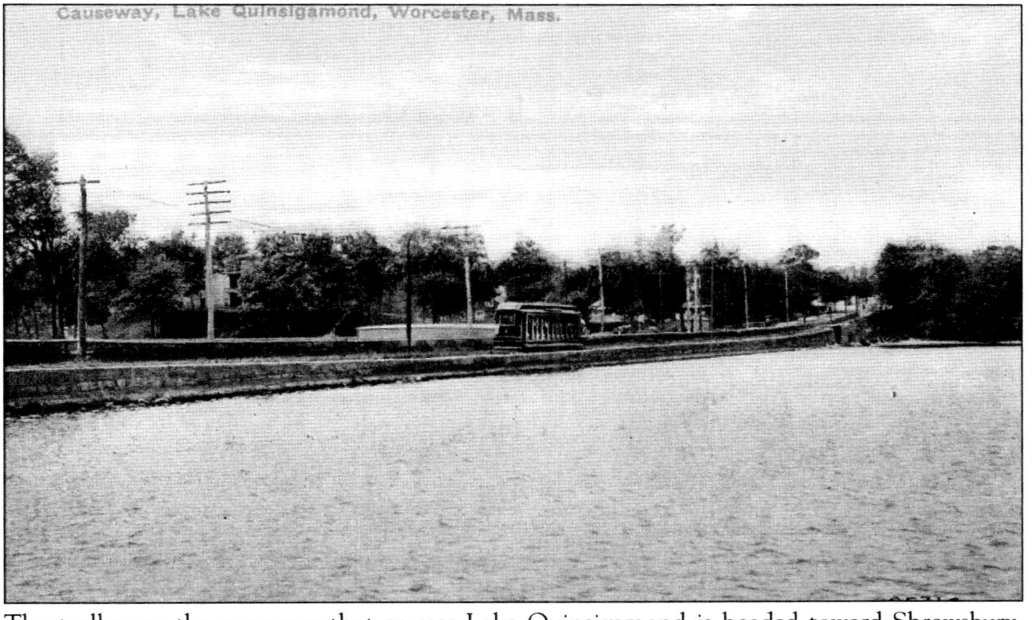

The trolley on the causeway that crosses Lake Quinsigamond is headed toward Shrewsbury. The two sides were originally connected by a floating bridge. On January 20, 1905, a bill was introduced in the state legislature to build a bridge over the lake to replace the causeway. The bridge was to cost $125,000 and be 30 feet above the water. When the bridge was finally completed in 1919 its total cost came to $325,000.

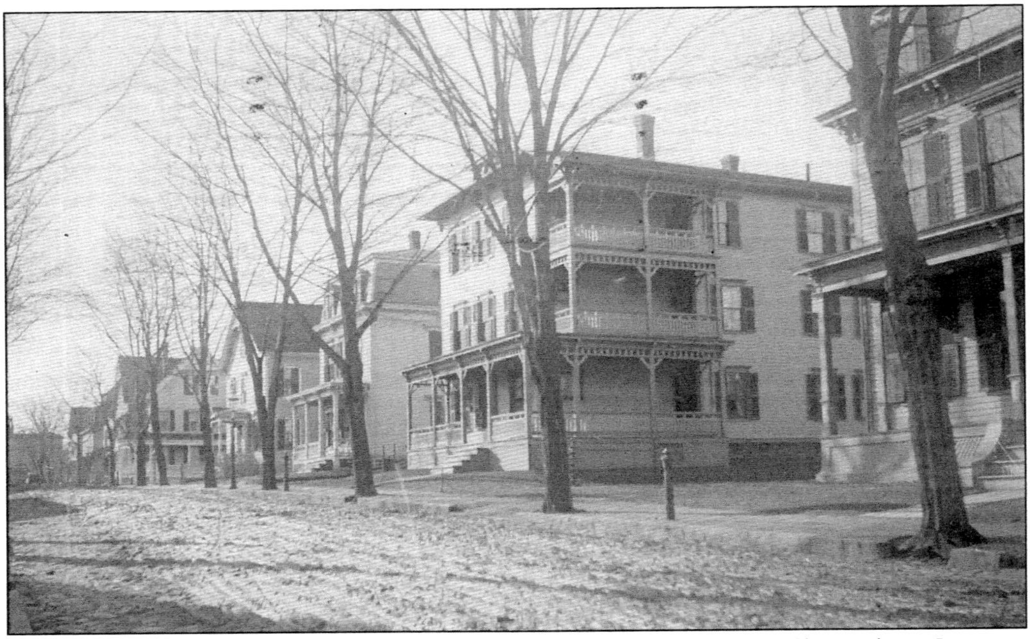

Russell Street, shown here in winter, extends from Queen Street, past Elm Park, to Institute Road. The portion of the street near the park was formally called Agricultural Street. The street was named after James W. Russell, who owned a greenhouse on Pleasant Street in 1842.

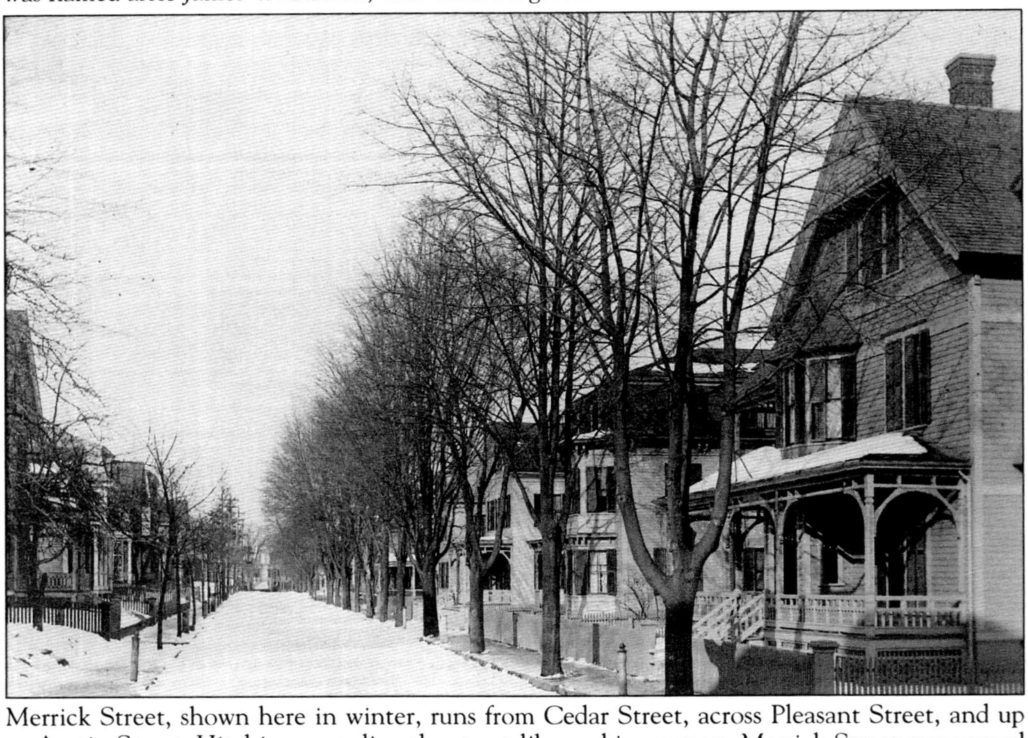

Merrick Street, shown here in winter, runs from Cedar Street, across Pleasant Street, and up to Austin Street. Hitching posts line the street like parking meters. Merrick Street was named after the family name of Mrs. D. Waldo Lincoln, wife of the former mayor of Worcester.

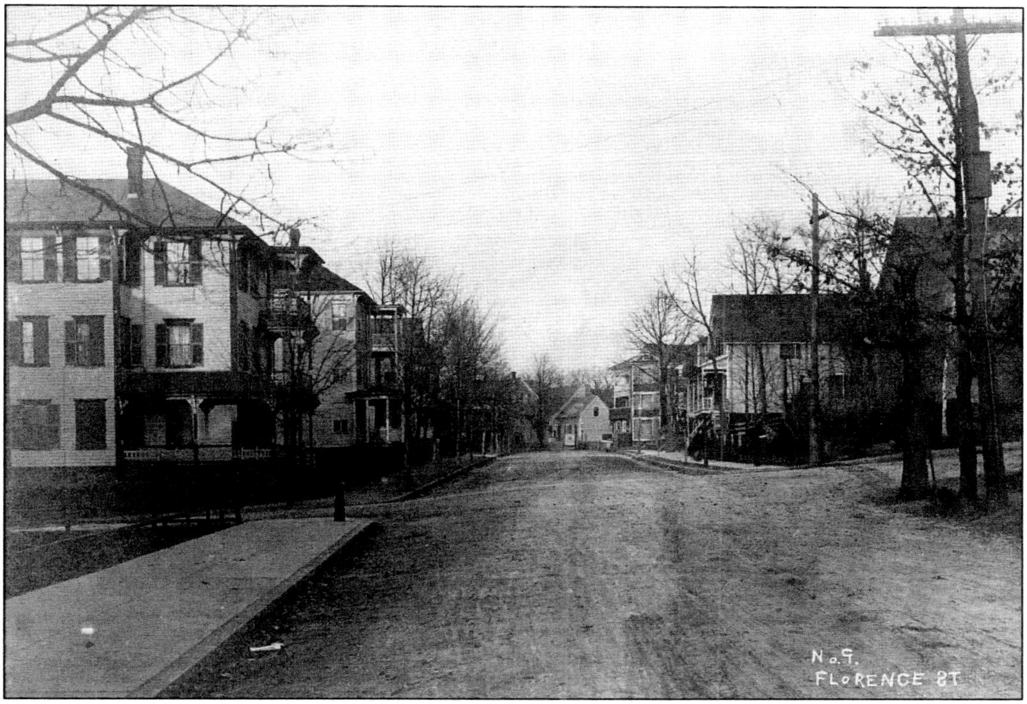

Florence Street is located off May Street near Park Avenue. It extends from May to Beaver Street. The east side of Florence Street runs along the campus of Clark University. The double- and triple-decker apartment buildings provided housing for many of the students of the university.

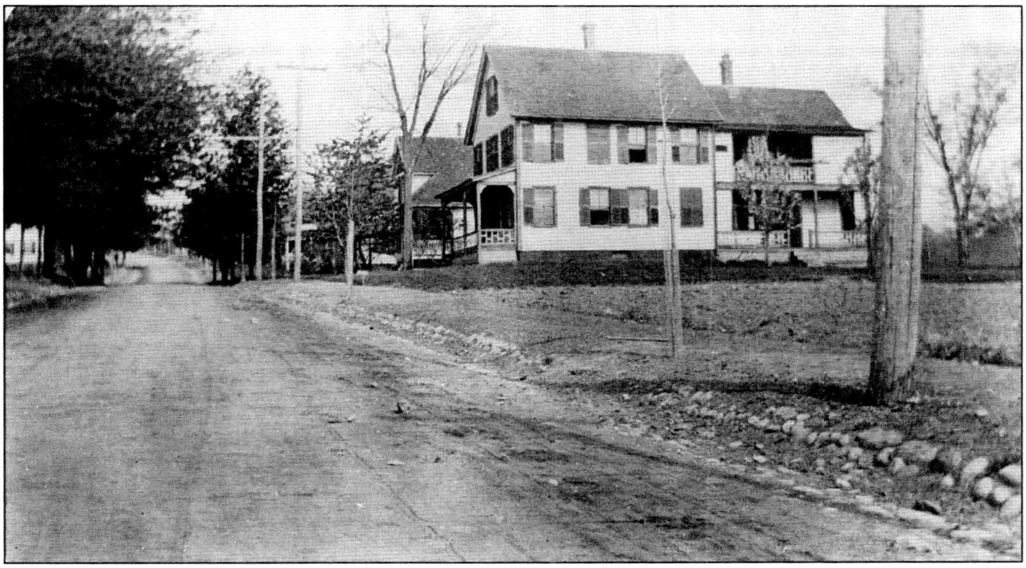

Fales Street is located in the Greendale section of the city. The street extends from West Boylston Street to Burncoat Street. The residents of the street worked at the many manufacturing companies, including the Norton Company and Bradley Car Works, which were located in this part of the city.

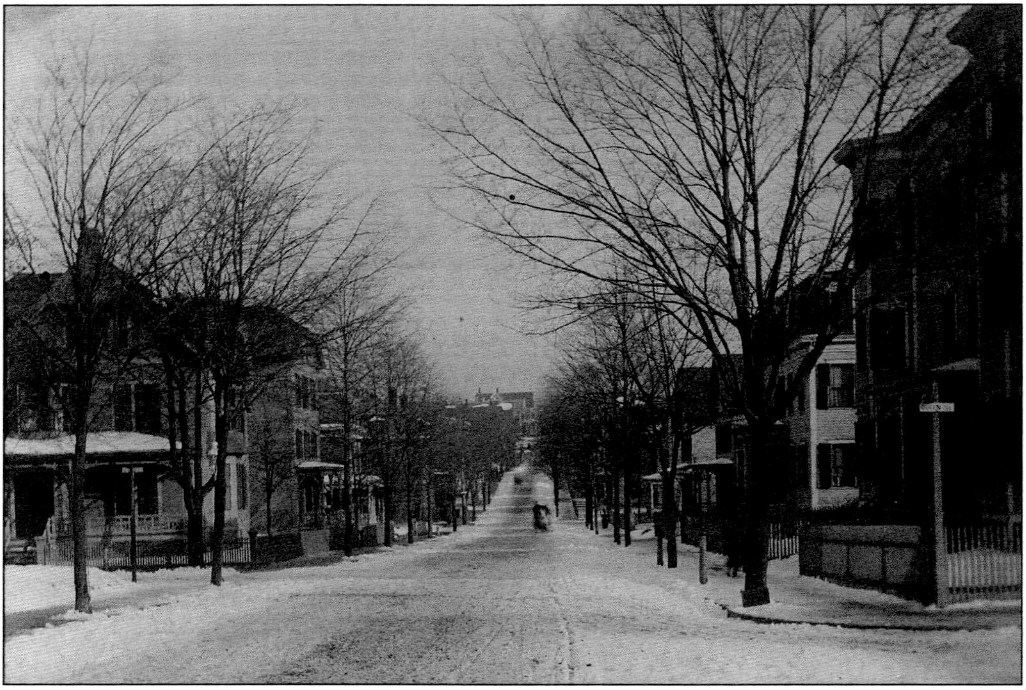

Austin Street, located near Queen Street, is pictured here in the winter months, c. 1910. Austin Street extends from Main Street to Dewey Street. It is named after Rev. Samuel Austin, the fourth permanent pastor of Old South Church.

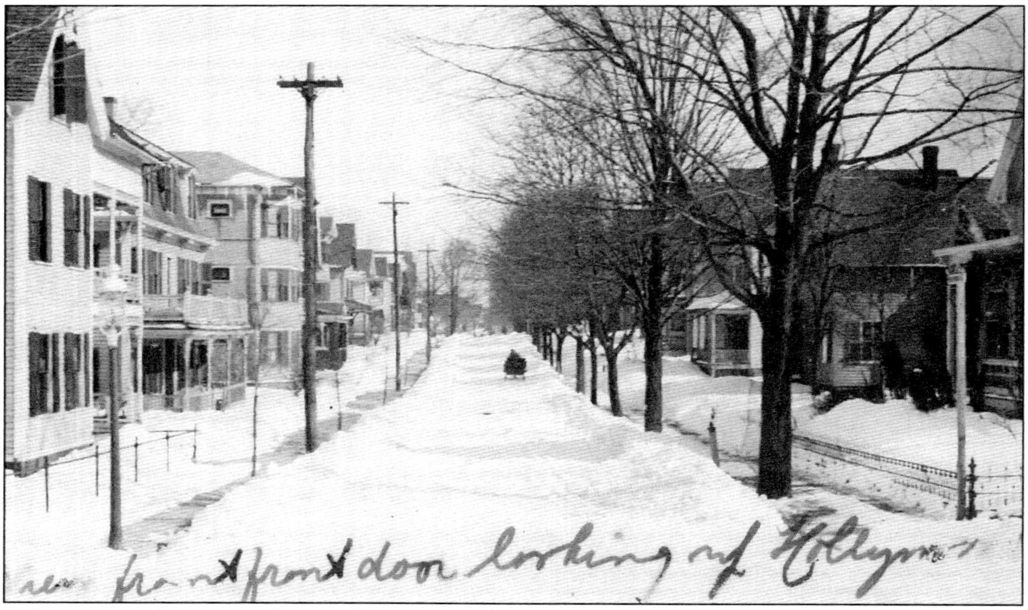

A lone horse-drawn sleigh travels down Hollywood Street in winter. Note the clear sidewalks and the snow-covered road. The main mode of transportation was the horse-drawn sleigh in 1910, so the streets were kept snow-covered for easy movement.

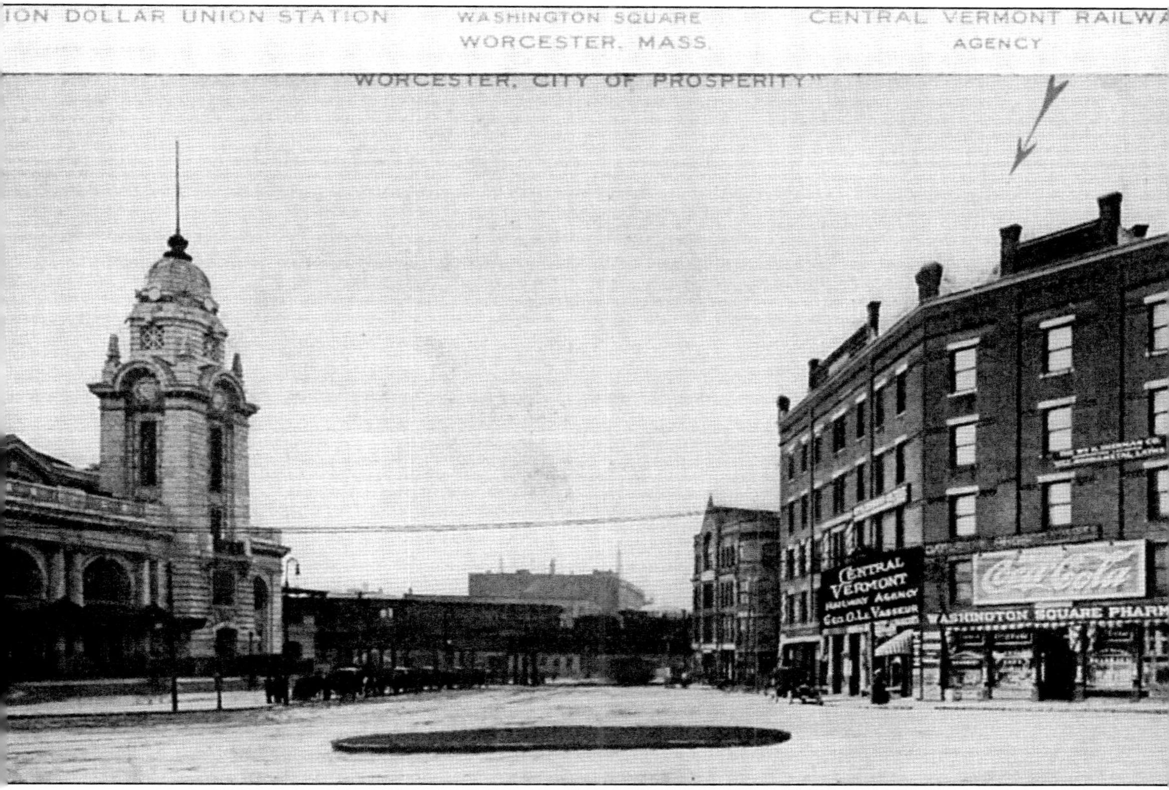

This is a view of Washington Square, c. 1912. The lower end of Front Street can be seen beyond the railroad viaduct. On the left is the new Union Station. On the right are the Washington Square Pharmacy and the Central Vermont Railway Agency.

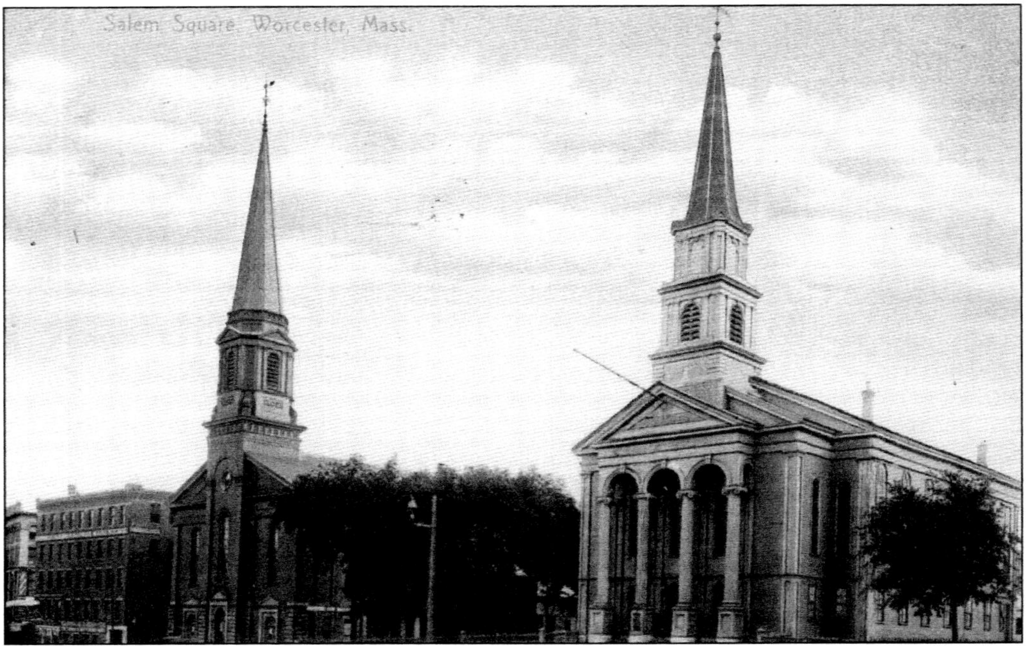

Salem Square was located at the east end of the common. It extended from Franklin Street to Front Street. The two churches, shown here in 1907, were the Swedish Congregational and the Notre Dame Churches. The Notre Dame Church was located on Franklin Street until it was destroyed by fire.

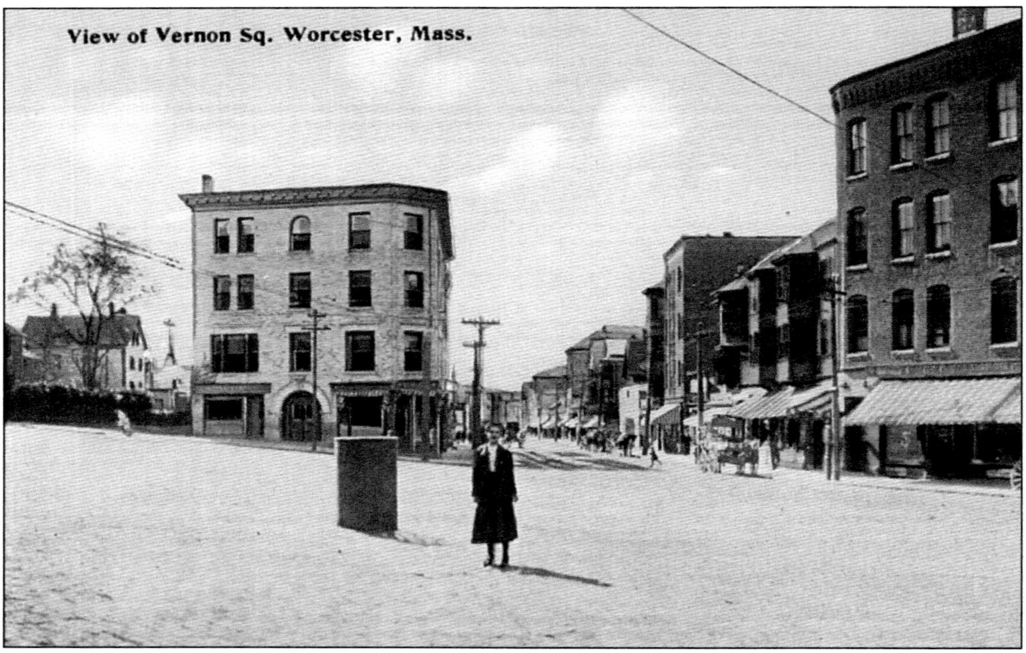

Vernon Square, now known as Kelly Square, doesn't look very busy here, c. 1910. Vernon Street is on the left and Millbury Street is on the right. Water and Green Streets also enter the square. The Hotel Vernon is at the corner of Vernon and Millbury Streets.

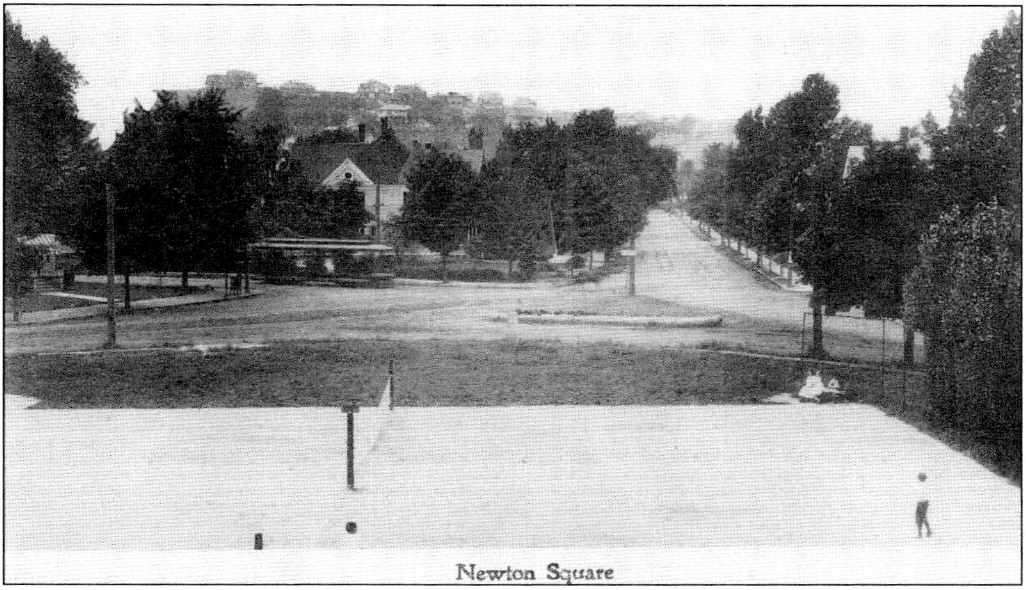

The trolley enters Newton Square from June Street. Pleasant Street enters the square from the left, exits the square, and heads northwest. Highland Street enters the square on the right. The public tennis courts are in the foreground.

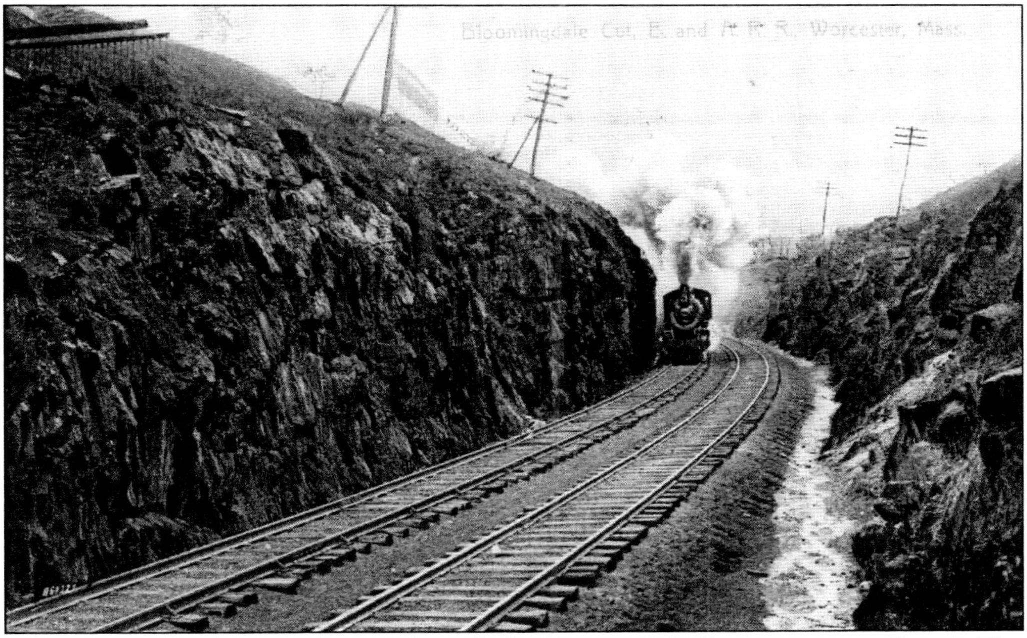

The Boston and Albany train passes through the Bloomingdale Cut on its way to Boston. The area around Plantation Street that runs from the fire station to Belmont Street was known as Bloomingdale. The cut can be seen from the bridge on Plantation Street that passes over the tracks.

Boston & Albany R. R. Restaurants

WORCESTER

Pittsfield ***Springfield***

MENU

Little Necks on half shell 20 Clam Cocktail 25

SOUPS

Clam Stew 30 Clam Bouillon 20 Chicken Broth with Rice 20
Tomato Soup 20 Consomme, hot or cold 15
Oyster Stew 30, with Cream 40

FISH

Broiled Fish 45 Broiled Live Lobster

RELISHES

Sliced Tomato 20
Gherkins 10 Queen Olives 15 Chow Chow 10

ROASTS

Roast Prime Ribs of Beef 60

STEAKS, CHOPS, ETC., FRIED OR GRILLED

Sirloin Steak 85 Tenderloin Steak 70 Porterhouse Steak $1.40
Small Steak 65 Broiled Lamb Chops (2) 50 Pork Chops 50
Broiled Chicken, half 70, whole $1.30
Hamburger Steak 40 Fried Chicken a la Maryland, half 75
Broiled Ham 40, with eggs 50 Broiled Bacon 40, with eggs 50
Roast Beef Hash with green peppers 40; dropped egg 50
Breaded Veal Cutlet, tomato sauce 50 Broiled Sausage 45
Welch Rarebit 35 Chicken Croquettes 40, with Green Peas 50
Minced Chicken with green peppers 50
Mushroom Sauce 30 Tomato Sauce 15 Smothered Onions 15

EGGS

Shirred Eggs (2) 20, (3) 30 Boiled (2) 20, (3) 30 Fried (2) 20, (3) 30
Scrambled (2) 20, (3) 30 Poached (2) on toast 25, (3) 35

OMELETS

Spanish 50 Plain 30 With Parsley 35 With Mushrooms 40
With Ham, Bacon, Tomatoes, Jelly, Cheese or Onions 35

VEGETABLES

Asparagus, Vinaigrette or drawn butter, (hot or cold) 30
Lima Beans 15 Corn 15 Succotash 15 String Beans 15
Domestic Peas 15 Tomatoes 15 Spinach 15, with egg 20

This is the second page of the menu of the Union Station Restaurant. The new station opened in 1911, after several delays. The restaurant was called the Boston & Albany Railroad Restaurant. The railroad also maintained restaurants at the stations in Springfield and Pittsfield.

POTATOES

Hashed Brown 15 French Fried 15 Hashed in cream 15 Saute 15
Lyonnaise 15 German Fried 15 Delmonico 20 O'Brien 20

COLD MEATS

Sardines, per order 25 Roast Chicken 65 Boiled Smoked Tongue 50
Boston Baked Beans 25 Boiled Ham 50 Roast Beef 50
Lobster boiled in shell Corned Beef, Potato Salad 50
Pickled Lamb's Tongue 30

SALADS

Chicken 50 Potato 20 Lobster Lettuce 25 Salmon Salad 40
Lettuce and tomato with French dressing 25

SANDWICHES

Tongue 15 Ham 10 Sardine 15 Chicken 20 Corn Beef 15
American Cheese Sandwich 10 Hot Roast Beef 30 Cold 20
Special Club Sandwich 35 Ham and Egg 25 Egg 15

GRIDDLE CAKES

Wheat Cakes with maple syrup 20

BREAD AND TOAST

French Bread 10 Home-made Bread 10 Bread with milk 15
Half and Half 25
Crackers with milk 15 Graham Crackers with milk 15 Dry Toast 10
Milk Toast 15 Buttered Toast 10 Cream Toast 25 Crullers 10
French Toast 35

DESSERT

Assorted Pies per cut 10 Ice Cream 15 Jelly Roll 10 Cup Cakes 10
Assorted Cake 10 Fruit Cake 10 Whole Grape Fruit 20
Cookies 10 Bananas with cream 20 Orange 10 Sliced Orange 15
Preserved Figs 20 Orange Marmalade 15
Pie a la Mode 20

American Cheese with crackers 15

Cup Coffee 10, pot 20 Small Pot Tea 10 Cup Cocoa 10 Instant Postum 10
Milk per glass 5 Horlicks Malted Milk 10

Tea Biscuits or Bread and Butter with all orders amounting to fifty cents or over.

White Rock	bottle 25	Imp. Ginger Ale (C.&C.)	25
White Rock	splits 15	Clicquot Club, per bottle,	15
		Domestic Ginger Ale, per glass,	10

Imported and Domestic Cigars

PLEASE PAY CASHIER

An extra charge of ten cents will be made where two persons are served from a single order.
No checks issued at table for less than twenty-five cents.

G. W. ANDREWS, MANAGER, WORCESTER, MASS. J. H. MARCY, SUPT DINING SERVICE, BOSTON, MASS

Page three of the menu lists lobster boiled in its shell. Like today's menus, it appears no price was printed for the lobster.

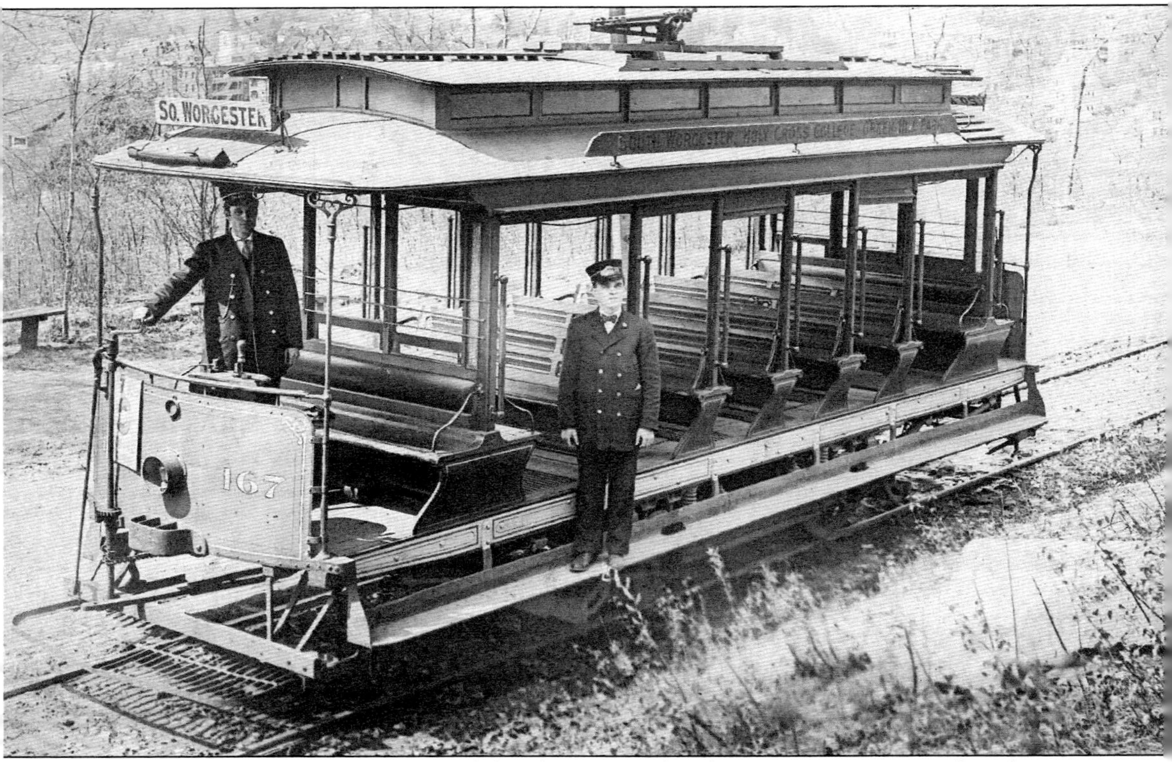

Car 167 of the Worcester Consolidated Street Railroad Company was a nine-bench, open car. The South Worcester Trolley, *c.* 1910, ran from Green Hill Park to Holy Cross College. The railway company was the oldest and largest railway system in the city. It was formed in 1887 by consolidating two horse-railway systems—the Citizens Street Railway Company and the Worcester Street Railway Company. In 1892 the company was granted the right to change from the slow-going, horse-car system to one of electric propulsion. By the end of 1893 all cars were run using electric power.

Two

HOME

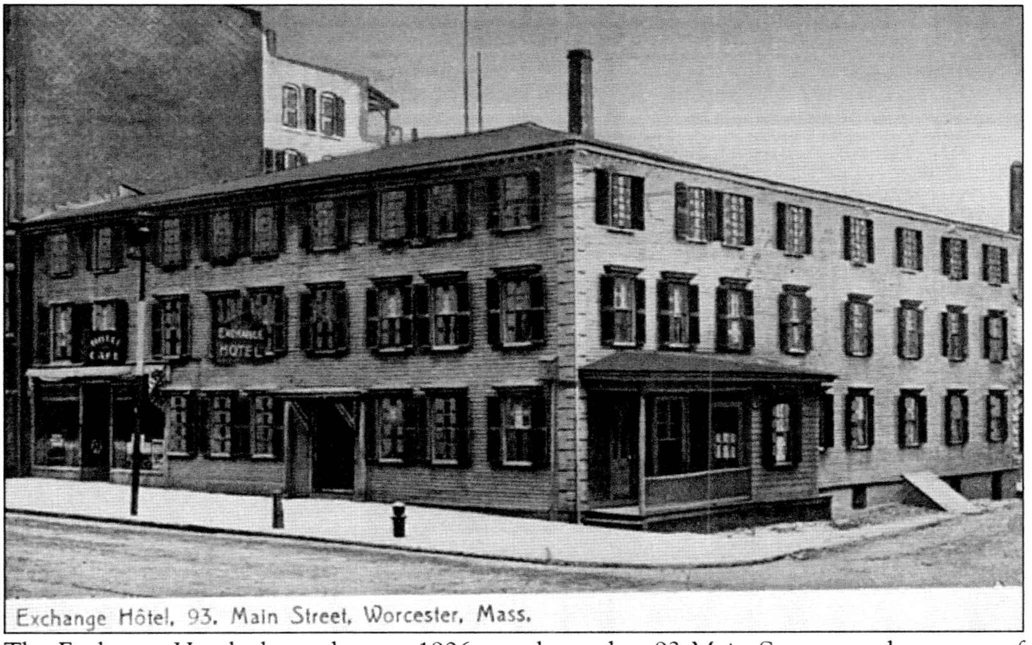

The Exchange Hotel, shown here *c*. 1906, was located at 93 Main Street, on the corner of Market Street. Known as the United States Arms Hotel at the end of the 18th century, this was the city's oldest hotel. George Washington stopped here for breakfast in 1789 while on his way to Boston. Lafayette was a guest at the hotel in 1825.

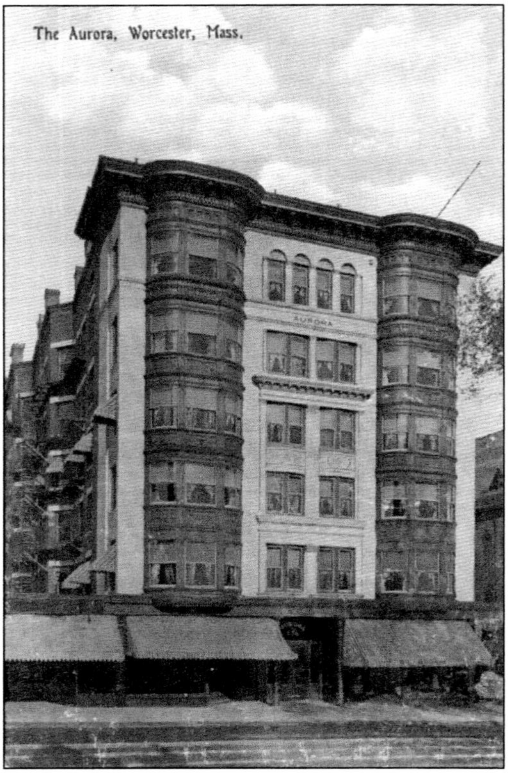

The Aurora Hotel was located at 656 Main Street, near Chandler Street. It was a select, high-grade, family hotel, with single rooms as well as suites. The rooms were either finished or unfinished, and there were special rates for prolonged stays.

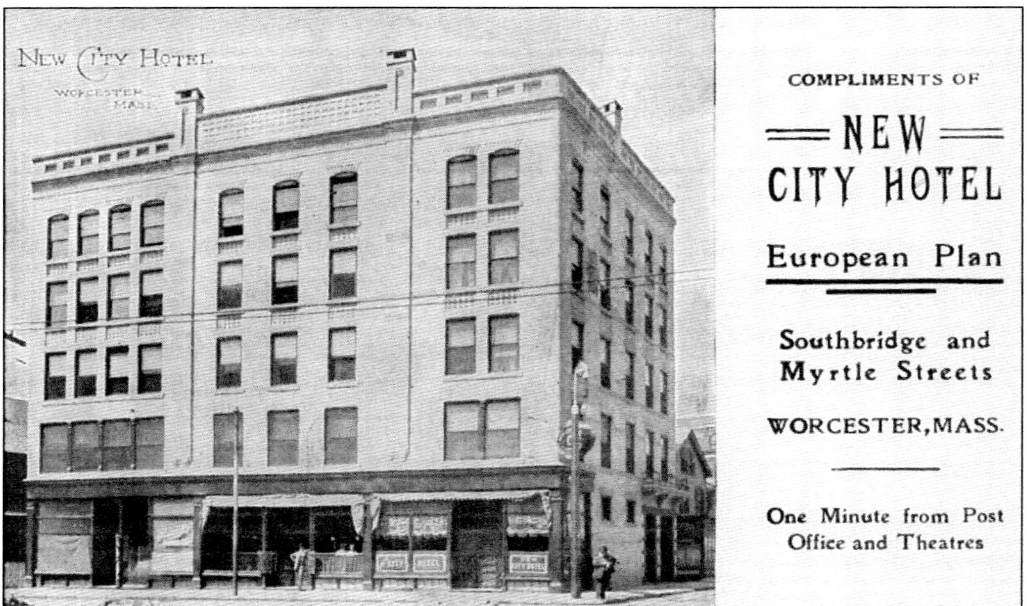

The New City Hotel was located at the corner of Myrtle and Southbridge Streets. Constructed in 1891, it contained 35 bedrooms.

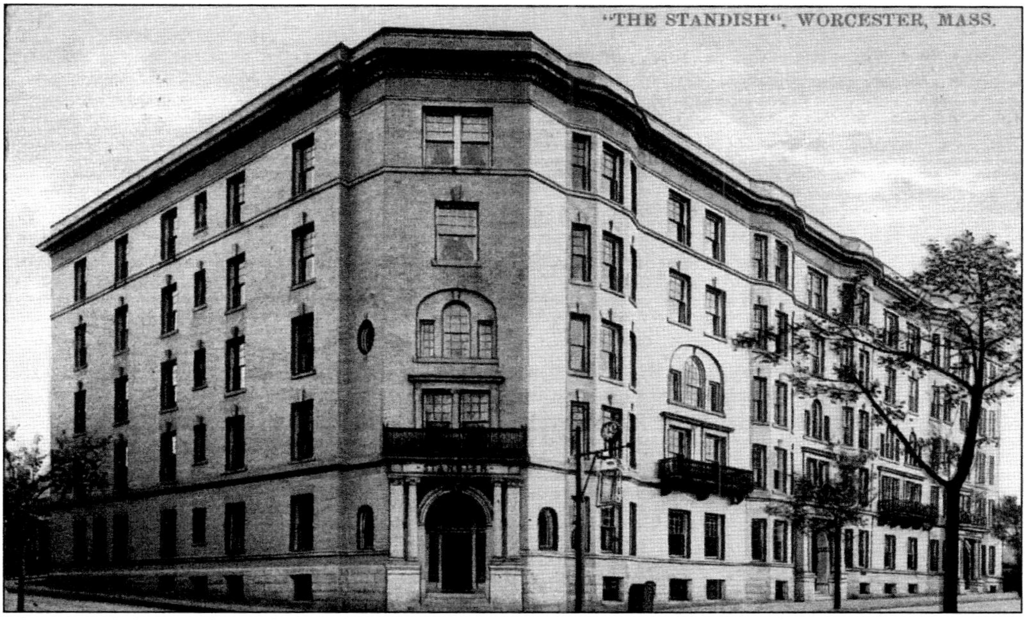

The Standish Hotel was located at 767 Main Street, at the corner of Jackson Street. In 1911 it offered accommodations for permanent and transient guests, with a first-class garage nearby.

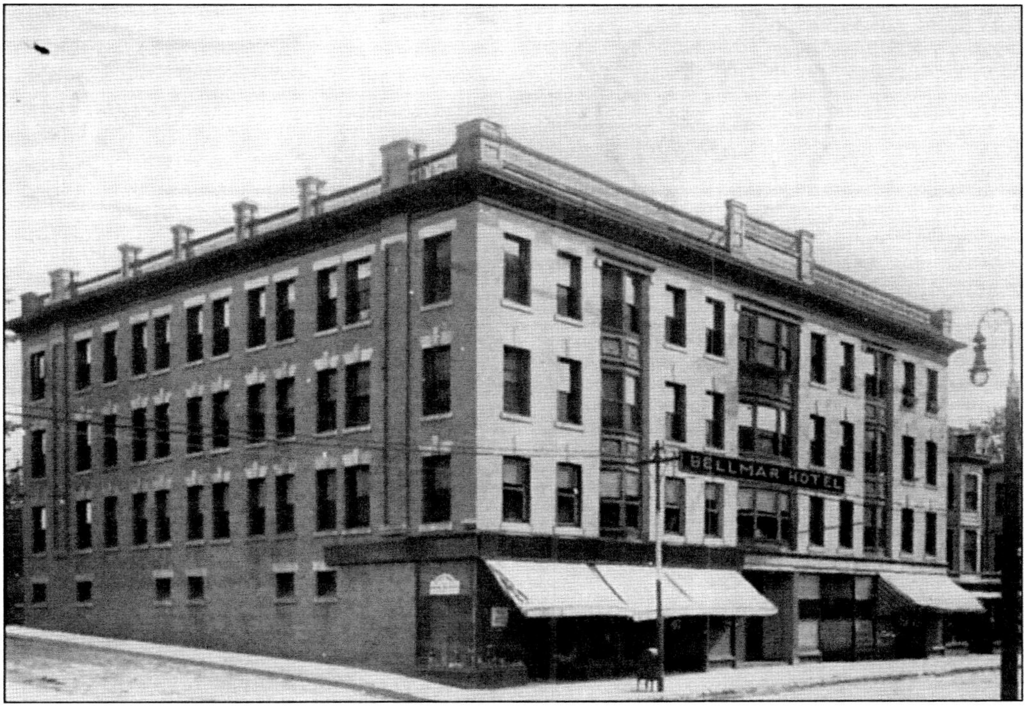

The Bellmar Hotel was located at 667 Main Street, on the corner of Mower (Ionic) Avenue. It was one of the city's private hotels, formerly known as fashionable boarding houses. The number of boarding houses in the city increased from 50 in 1870 to about 80 in 1920. People who rented their rooms planned to stay longer than just a few days.

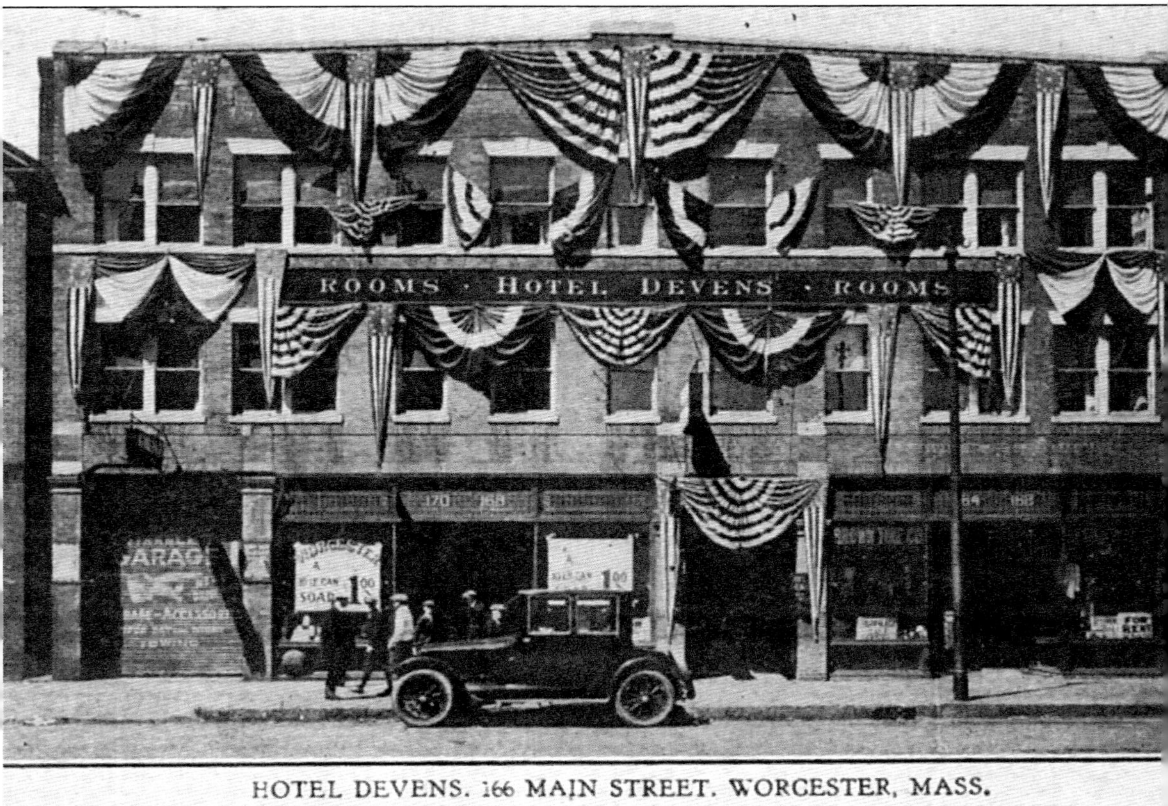

Decorated in honor of the end of World War I, Hotel Devens was located at 166 Main Street. This type of hotel, with stores on the street floor and rooms on the upper floors, catered to the visitors entering the city c. 1920. An average of ten thousand people entered the city daily, either by passenger train or by street railways. They preferred to stay in rooming or boarding houses, or private hotels, rather than lavish hotels like the Bancroft.

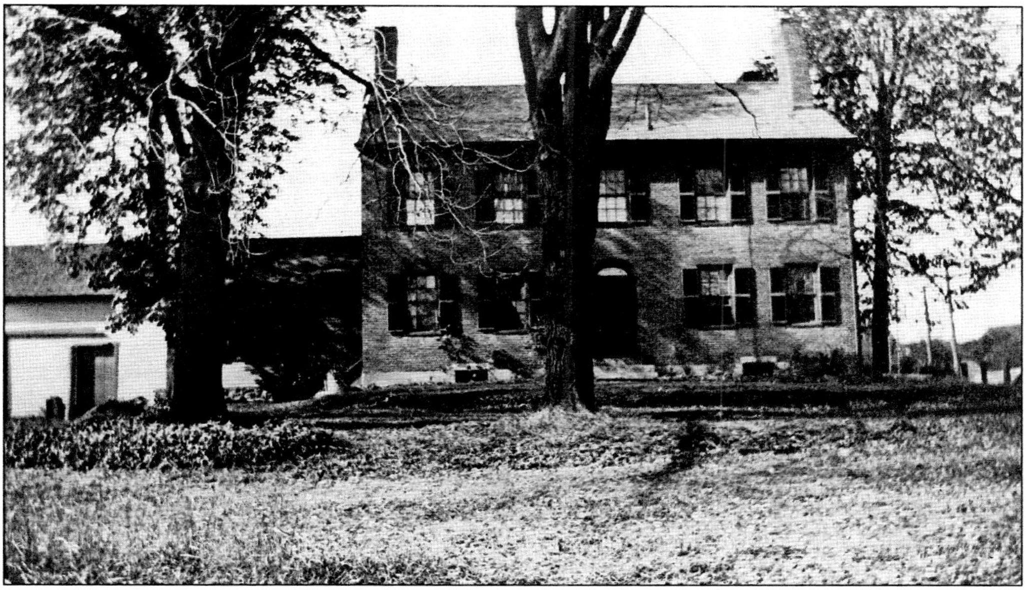

This large home was located at 1 Brooks Street in the Greendale section of Worcester. At the turn of the century this was the farmhouse of John A. Kendrick.

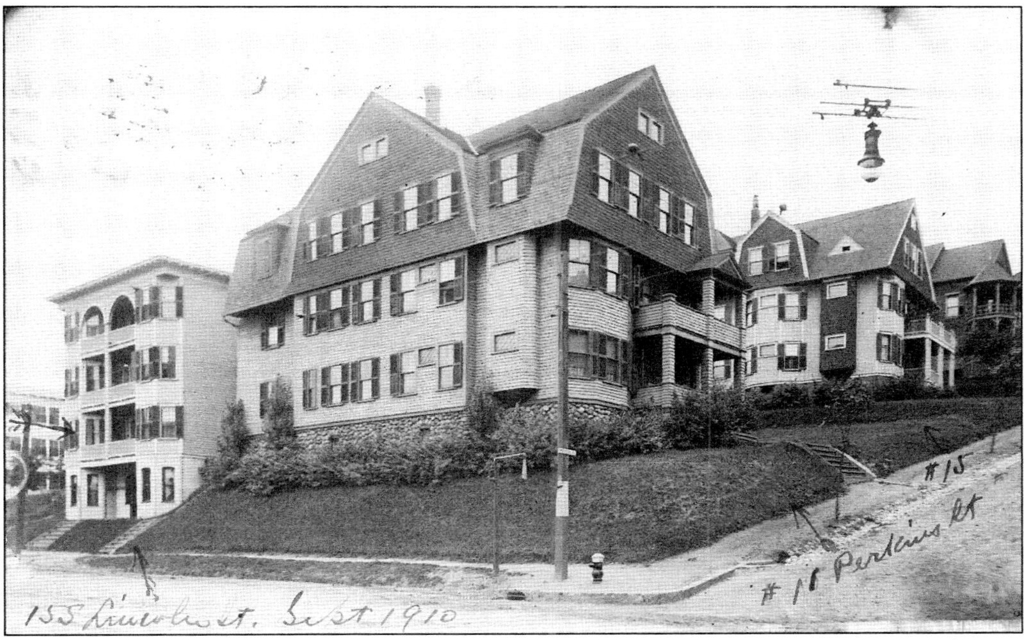

This large home is located at 155 Lincoln Street at the corner of Perkins Street. Around 1910, the house was occupied by a salesman, a nurse, an envelope maker, a wireworker, a lineman, and a carpenter.

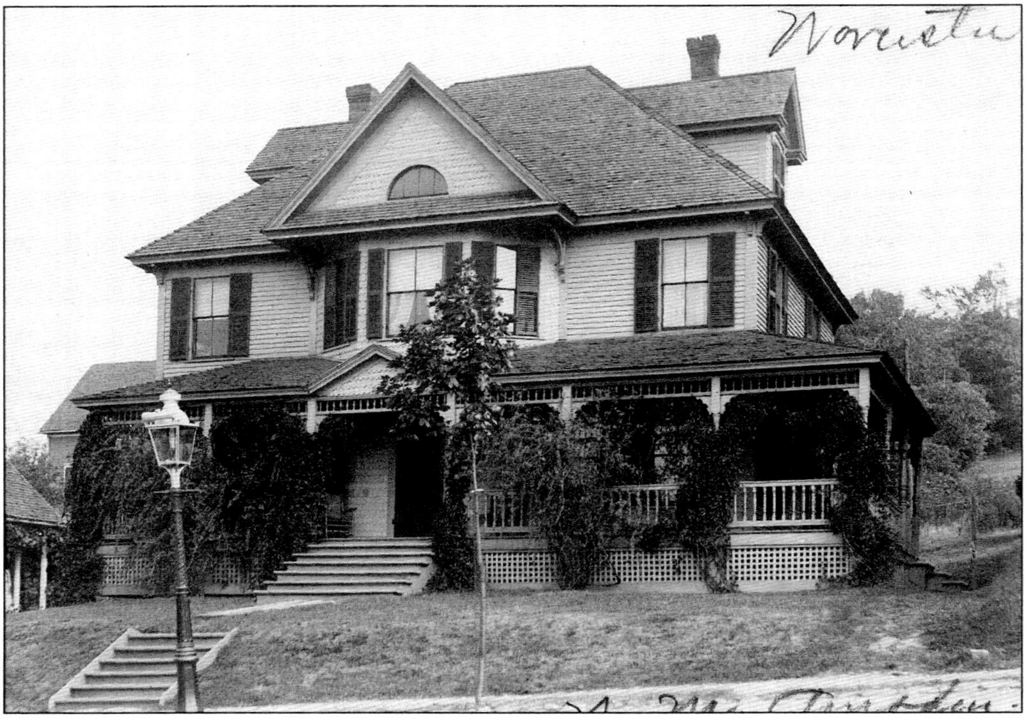

This was the 1910 home of Ward M. Amsden at 36 Uxbridge Street. Uxbridge Street is located near Lincoln Street. Mr. Amsden was a watchmaker whose place of business was at 418 Main Street.

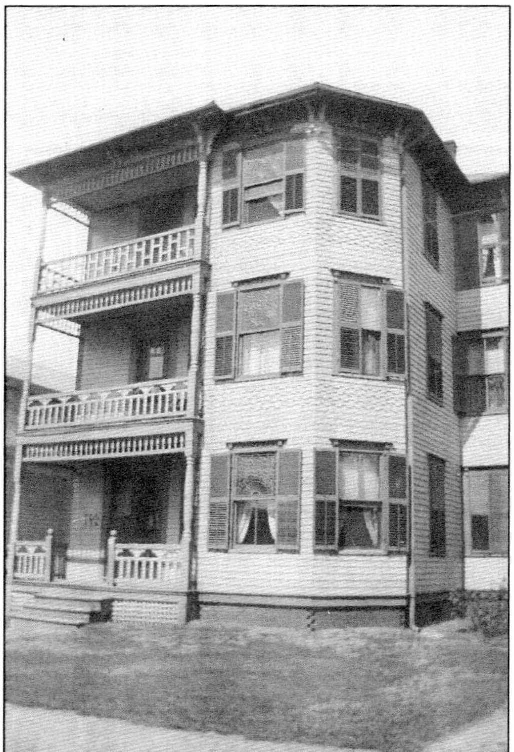

One of the many triple-deckers located in Worcester was located at 3 Shirley Street. That street is just off of Park Avenue. Around 1911, Walker Woodhead, a clerk at the Boston & Albany Freighthouse, lived on the first floor; William Gilbert, a repairer, lived on the second floor; and L. Gilbert Arnold, a bag maker, lived on the third floor.

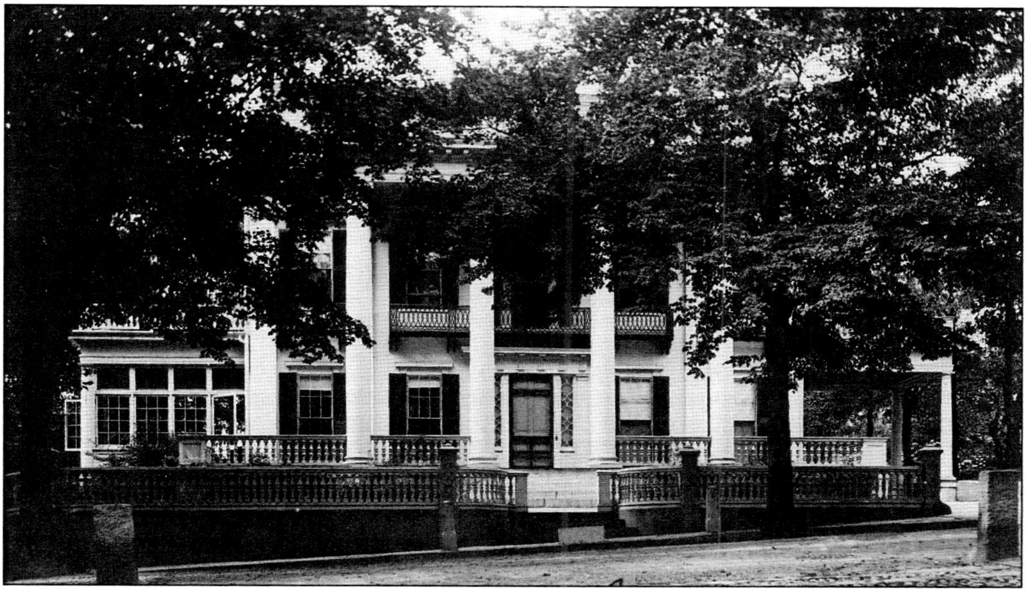

The picture of this beautiful home at 23 Chestnut Street was taken about 1907. The owners of the home were Mr. and Mrs. John C. Dewey. Mr. Dewey was a prominent lawyer in the city.

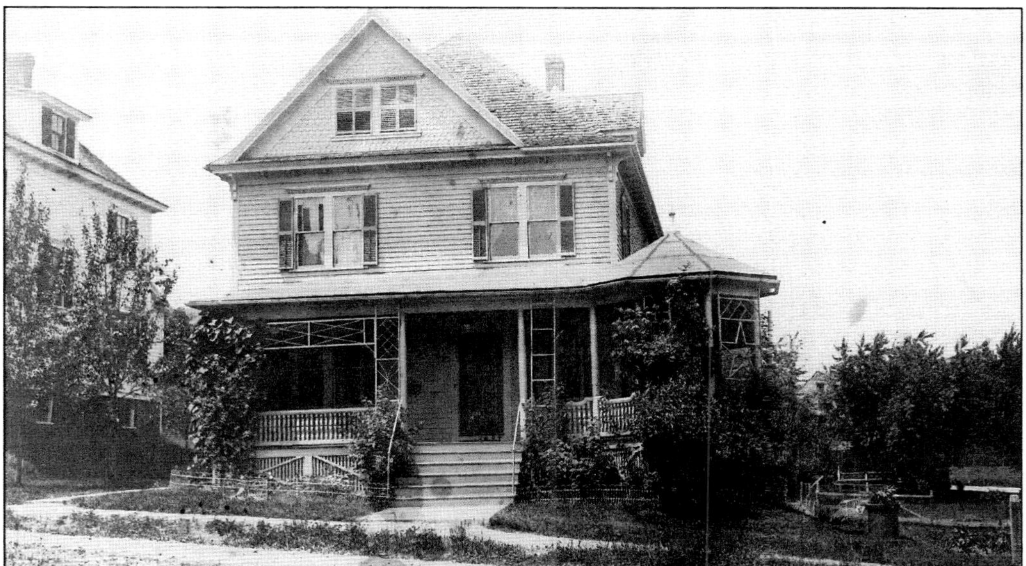

This home is located at 6 Lisbon Street near Coes Reservoir. Around 1912 it was occupied by Mr. and Mrs. Herbert Fisher. Mr. Fisher was an inspector for the city.

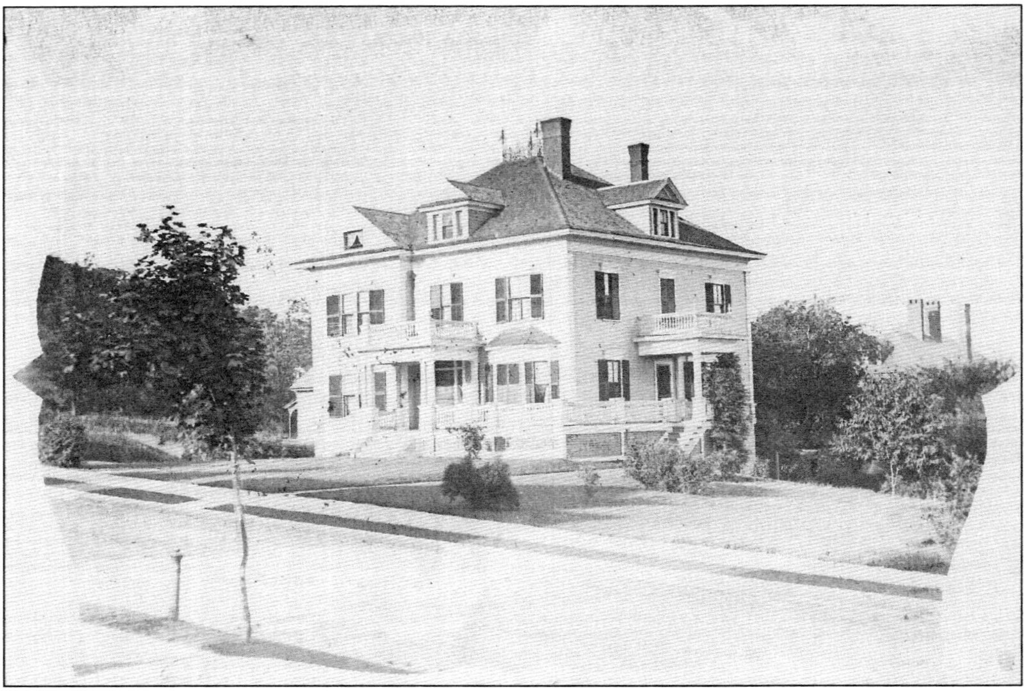

This large home is located at 32 Westland Street, which is off Highland Street near Elm Park. The home was occupied in 1911 by Allan B. Miller, who was a clerk at Worcester Mechanics Savings Bank.

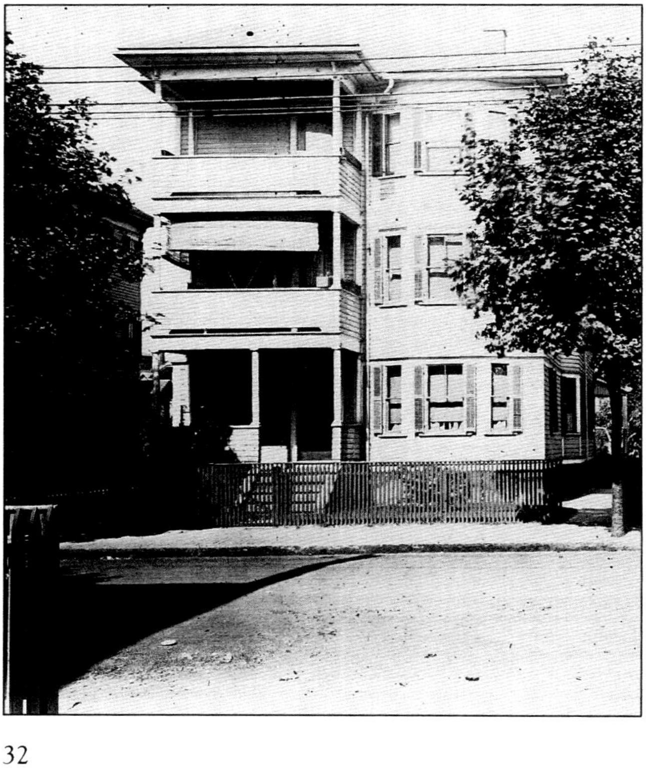

This picture of 523 Cambridge Street was taken in 1914. The house was located across the street from the Cambridge Street School, near Southbridge Street. In 1925 Harold Estabrook (a salesman), Joseph Westwood (a weaver), Earl T. Harper (president of Parker and Harper Mfg. Company), and Carl Hedberg (a packer), resided at the house.

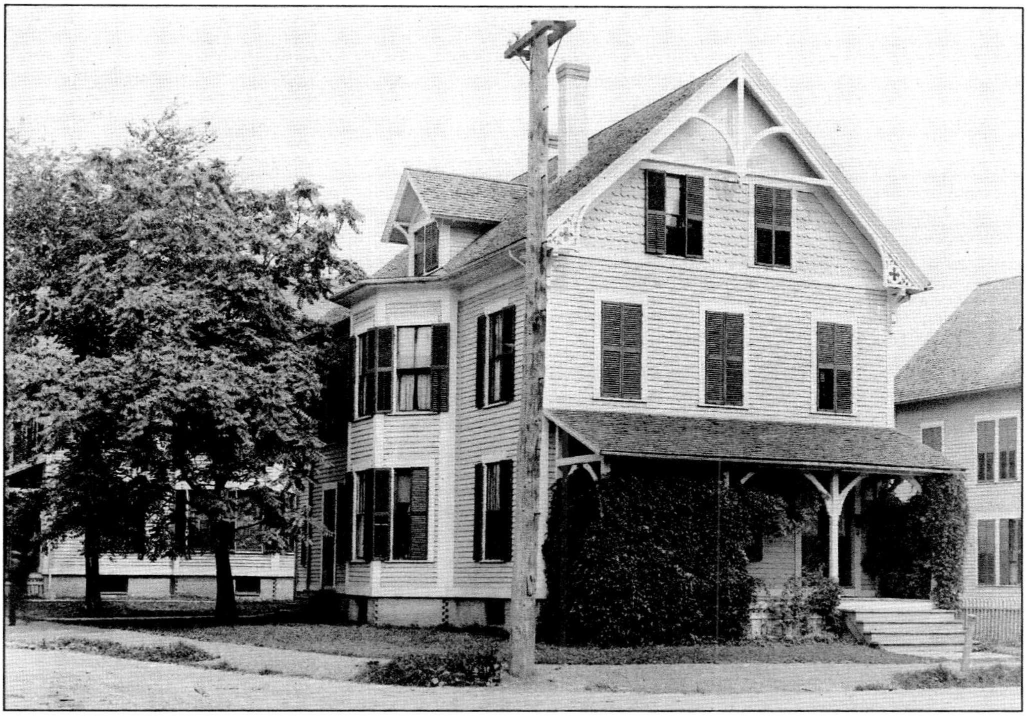

This home is located at 22 Kingsbury Street at the corner of Queen Street. In 1912 the first floor was occupied by John T. Sheehan, a mailman; the third floor was occupied by Arthur T. Church, a foreman at the Worcester Machine Screw Company.

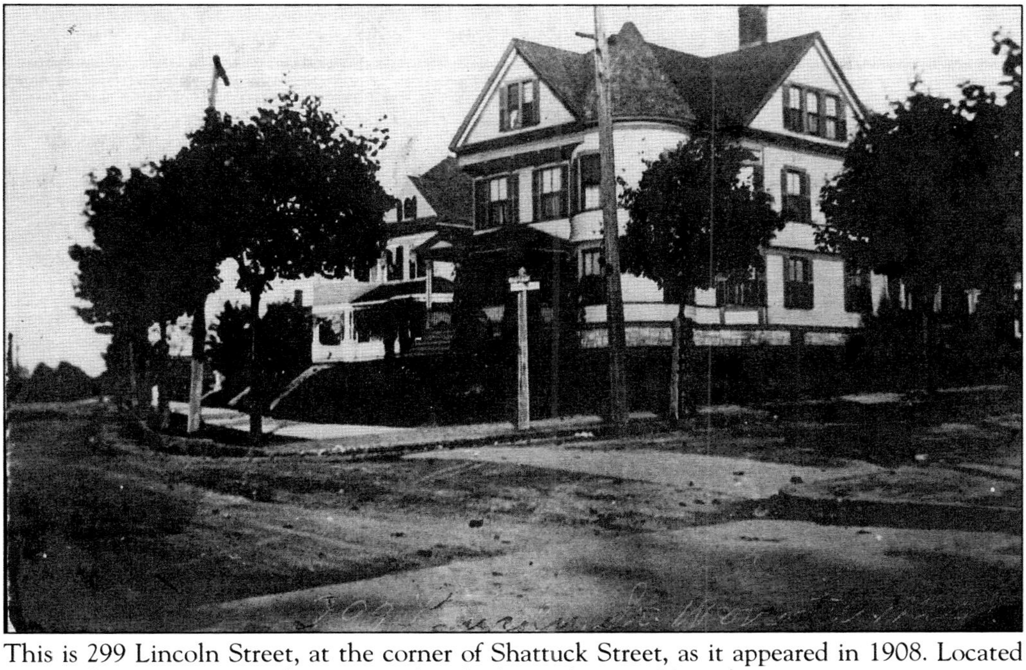

This is 299 Lincoln Street, at the corner of Shattuck Street, as it appeared in 1908. Located near Hahnemann Hospital, it was used as the home for over 20 graduate nurses.

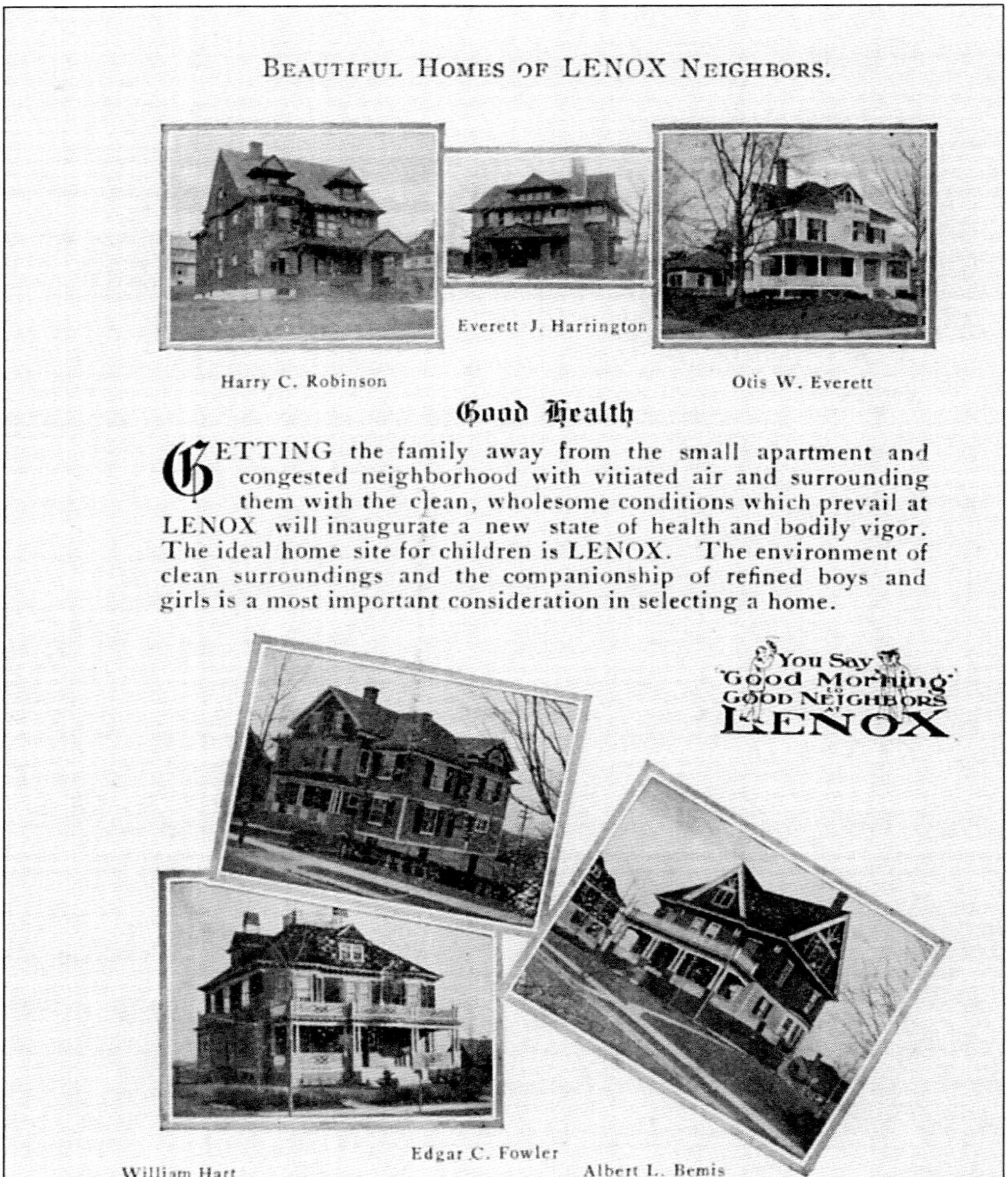

BEAUTIFUL HOMES OF LENOX NEIGHBORS.

Everett J. Harrington

Harry C. Robinson

Otis W. Everett

Good Health

GETTING the family away from the small apartment and congested neighborhood with vitiated air and surrounding them with the clean, wholesome conditions which prevail at LENOX will inaugurate a new state of health and bodily vigor. The ideal home site for children is LENOX. The environment of clean surroundings and the companionship of refined boys and girls is a most important consideration in selecting a home.

You Say "Good Morning" to GOOD NEIGHBORS at LENOX

Edgar C. Fowler

William Hart

Albert L. Bemis

LENOX IS THE BEAUTY SPOT OF WORCESTER.

Lenox was a housing development on the city's west side, *c.* 1910. It encompassed both sides of Pleasant Street, beyond Richmond Avenue, and included the following streets: Lenox, South Lenox, Berwick, Beeching, and Chamberlain Parkway. Pictured at the top pf the page are the homes at 25 Beeching Street, 46 Beeching Street, and 9 Beeching Street; at the bottom of the page are the homes at 26 Lenox Street, 6 Lenox Street, and 22 Lenox Street.

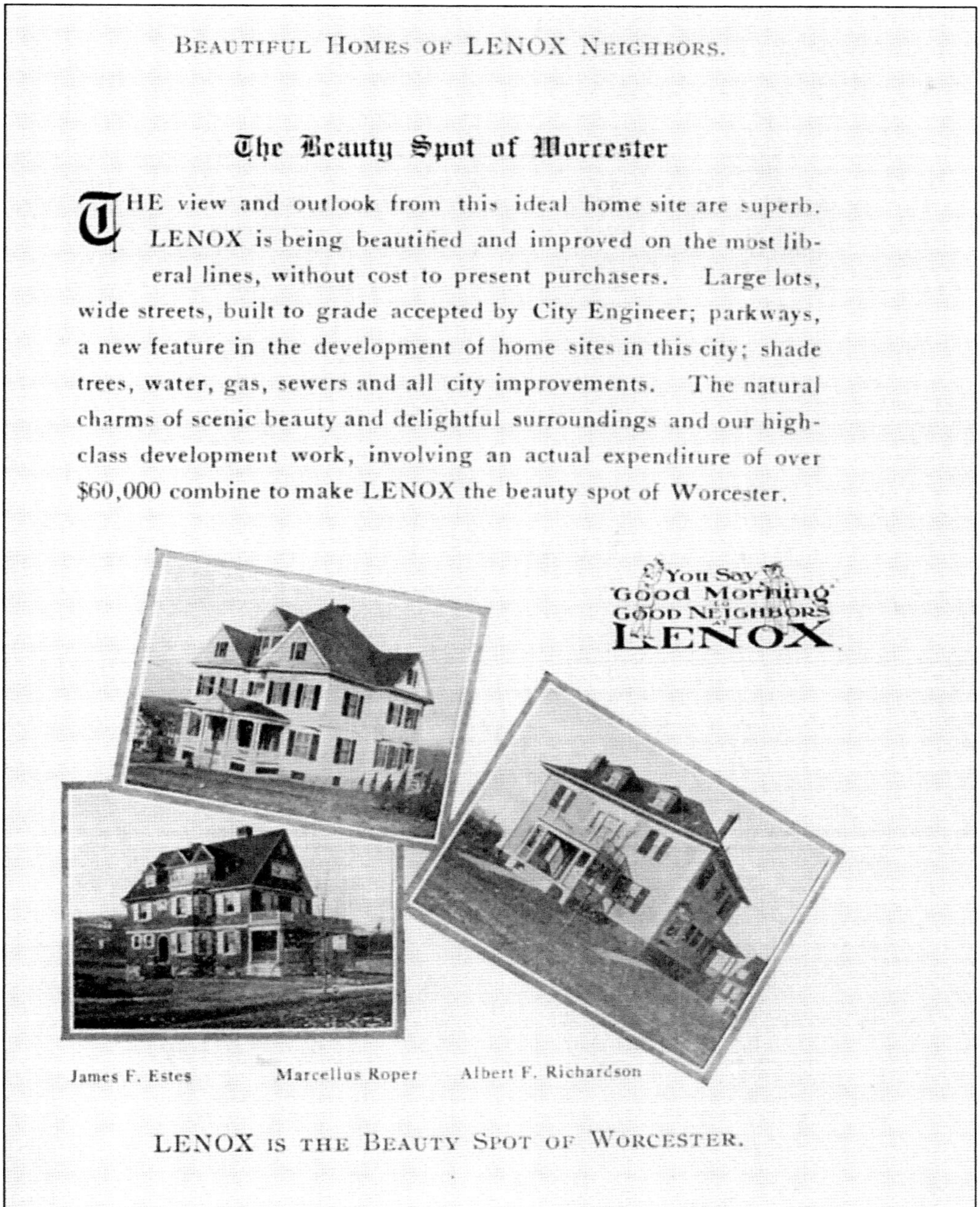

BEAUTIFUL HOMES OF LENOX NEIGHBORS.

The Beauty Spot of Worcester

THE view and outlook from this ideal home site are superb. LENOX is being beautified and improved on the most liberal lines, without cost to present purchasers. Large lots, wide streets, built to grade accepted by City Engineer; parkways, a new feature in the development of home sites in this city; shade trees, water, gas, sewers and all city improvements. The natural charms of scenic beauty and delightful surroundings and our high-class development work, involving an actual expenditure of over $60,000 combine to make LENOX the beauty spot of Worcester.

You Say Good Morning to Good Neighbors at LENOX

James F. Estes Marcellus Roper Albert F. Richardson

LENOX IS THE BEAUTY SPOT OF WORCESTER.

The city's population grew from about 58,000 in 1880 to 180,000 in 1920. With that growth came the need for more housing. Lenox offered single-family homes to the professionals and well-to-do living in the city. Pictured here are the homes at 15 Berwick Street, 11 Kensington Road, and 879 Pleasant Street.

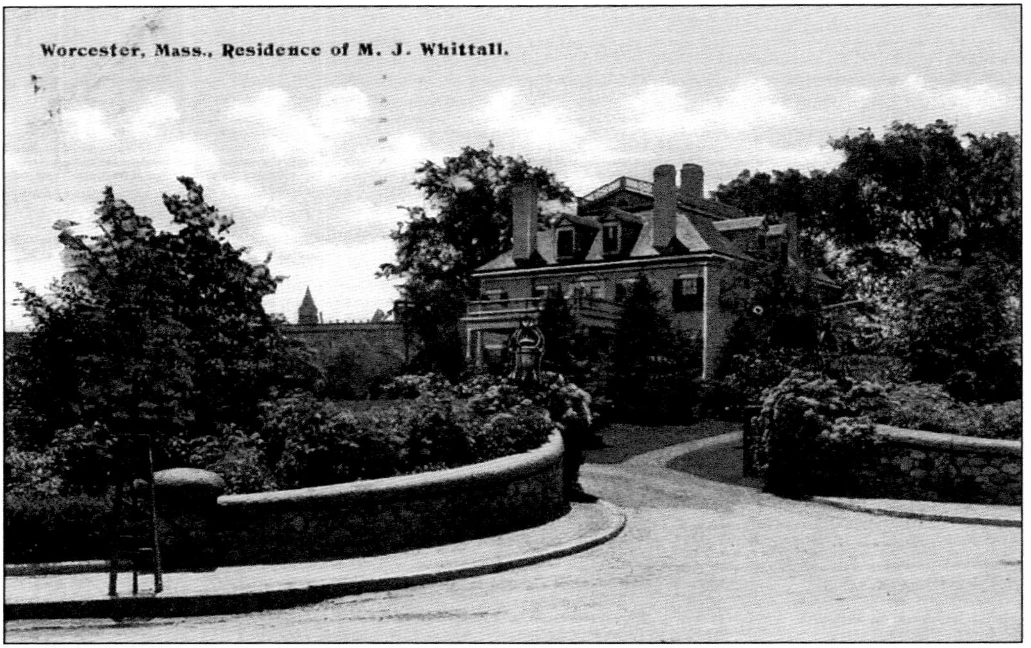

Pictured c. 1910, the home of Matthew J. Whittall was located at 692 Southbridge Street at the corner of Cambridge Street. He was a manufacturer of carpets with a plant on Brussels Street in South Worcester.

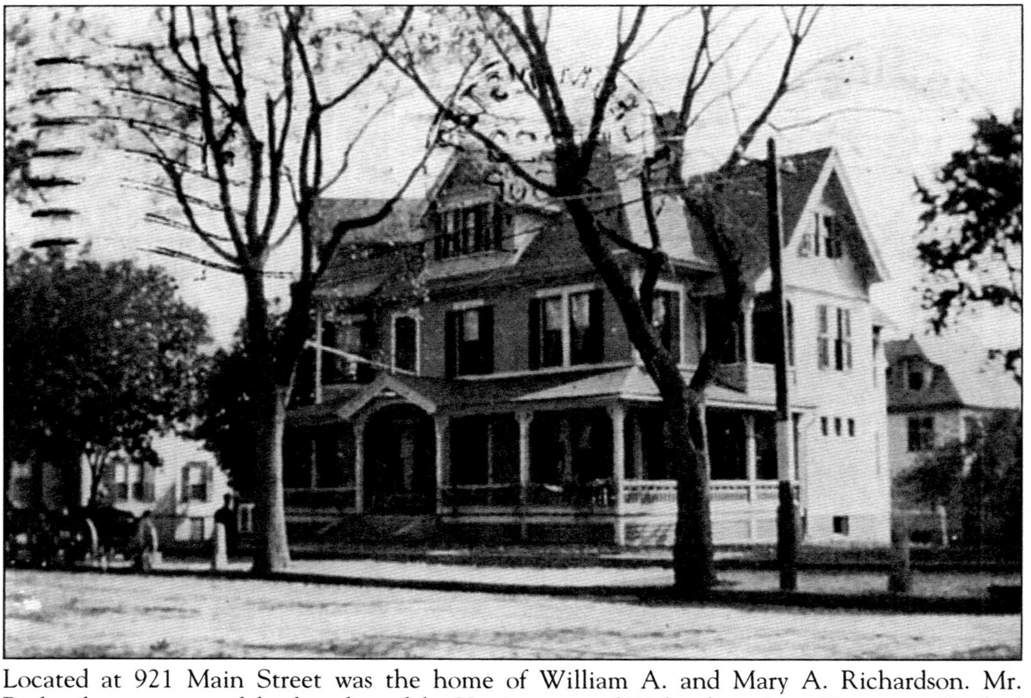

Located at 921 Main Street was the home of William A. and Mary A. Richardson. Mr. Richardson was one of the founders of the Harrington and Richardson Arms Company. He died in 1897. Mrs. Richardson died in 1910.

Three

MANUFACTURERS

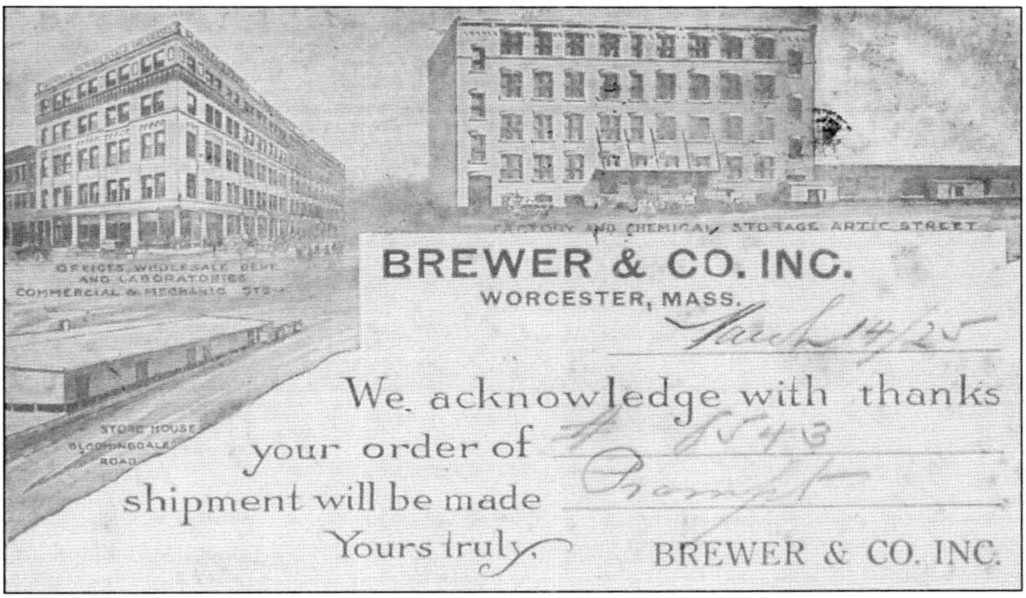

The Brewer Company, formerly Bush and Company, was the oldest drug company in Worcester County. It manufactured tablets and elixirs for physicians. Its offices, wholesale department, and laboratories were located on Mechanics and Commercial Streets, the factory and chemical storage building was located on Arctic Street, and the warehouse was located on Bloomingdale (Franklin) Road.

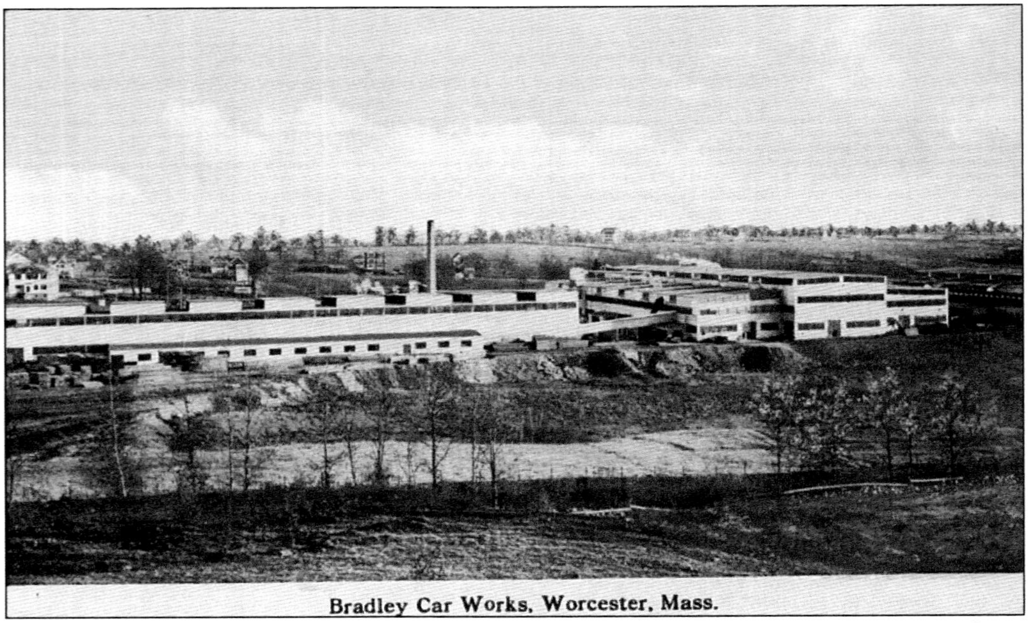

The Osgood Bradley Car Works was located on West Mountain Street, near West Boylston Street, in Greendale. Formerly located at Washington Square, in 1909 it had to move to make way for the construction of the new Union Station. In 1914 the company employed over 1,600 men. It was capable of turning out six hundred all-steel railroad cars per year.

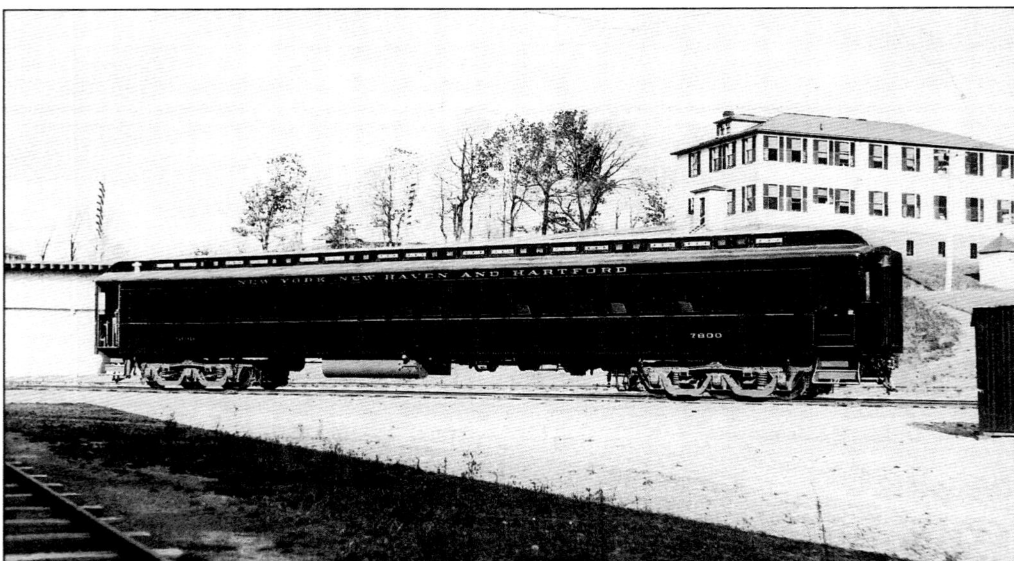

This is one of the products of the Osgood Bradley Car Company—a passenger car built for the New York, New Haven, and Hartford Railroad. In 1822 the company began by building carriages and state coaches. With the coming of the railroad, the company sold the carriage business and devoted its time to making railroad cars. The company also built trolleys and buses.

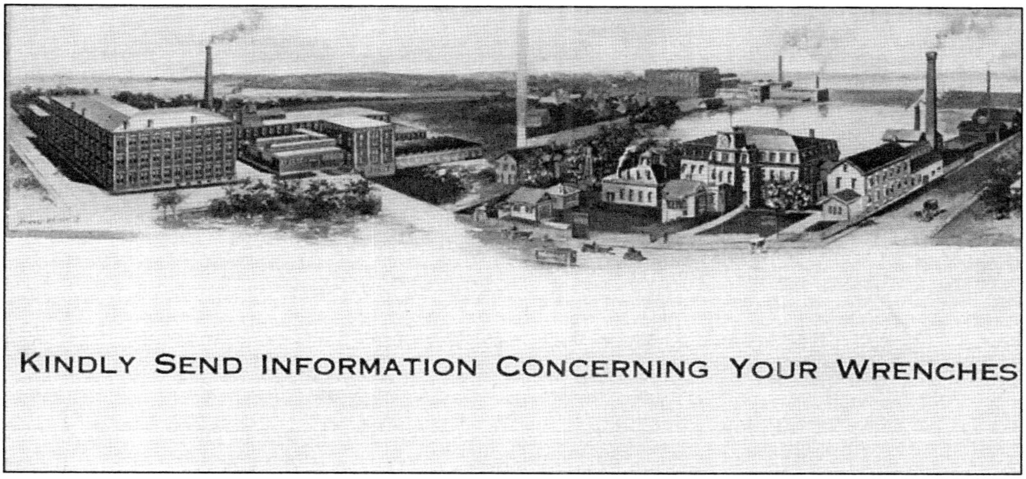

The Coes Wrench Company, shown here on the left, was located at Coes Square. The Loring Coes Company, a division of Coes Wrench Company, was located at the corner of Mill and Coes Streets, on the shores of Coes Reservoir and Coes Pond. The Coes's residence is shown in the right foreground. Upon completion of the new city hall, the old town hall was torn down and the hall clock was placed in the clock tower of the residence.

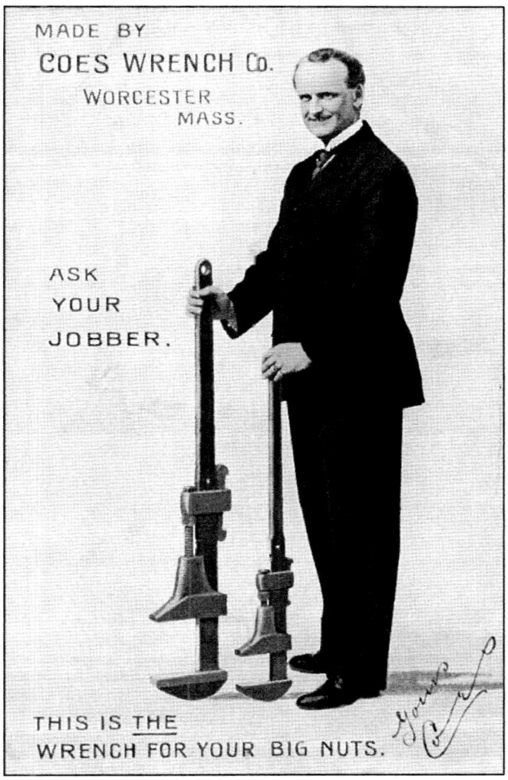

Mr. Coes shows off his wrenches. The key model Coes's screw wrench is the heaviest, strongest, largest-capacity screw wrench made. It comes in four sizes—28-inch, 36-inch, 48-inch, and 72-inch.

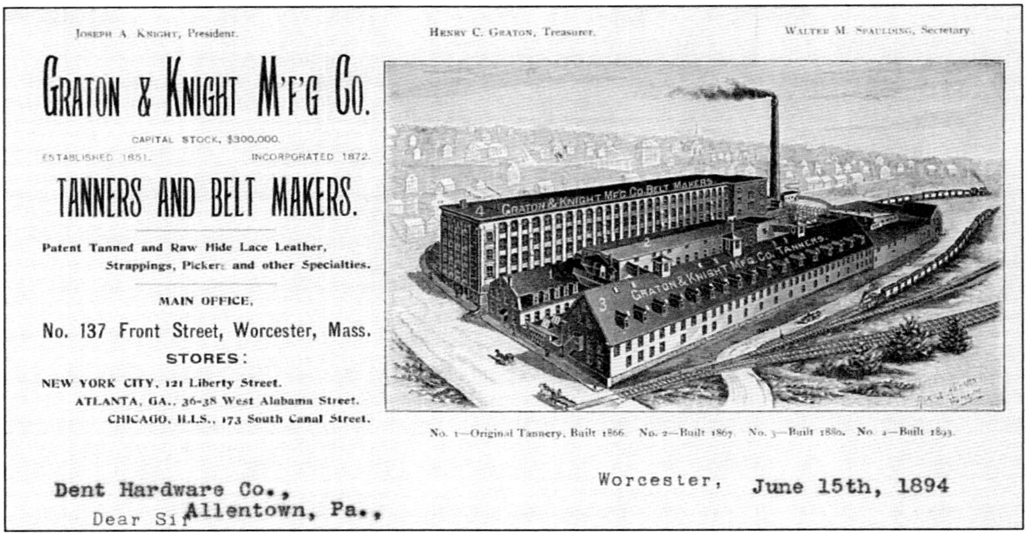
Joseph A. Knight, President. Henry C. Graton, Treasurer. Walter M. Spaulding, Secretary

GRATON & KNIGHT M'F'G CO.

CAPITAL STOCK, $300,000.

ESTABLISHED 1851. INCORPORATED 1872.

TANNERS AND BELT MAKERS.

Patent Tanned and Raw Hide Lace Leather, Strappings, Pickers and other Specialties.

MAIN OFFICE,

No. 137 Front Street, Worcester, Mass.

STORES:

NEW YORK CITY, 121 Liberty Street.
ATLANTA, GA., 36-38 West Alabama Street.
CHICAGO, ILLS., 173 South Canal Street.

No. 1—Original Tannery, Built 1866. No. 2—Built 1867. No. 3—Built 1880. No. 4—Built 1893.

Worcester, June 15th, 1894

Dent Hardware Co.,
Allentown, Pa.,

Dear Sir

The Graton and Knight Manufacturing Company was located on Bloomingdale Road. The company tanned leather and manufactured belting from it. Manufacturing plants needed belting for the transmission of power.

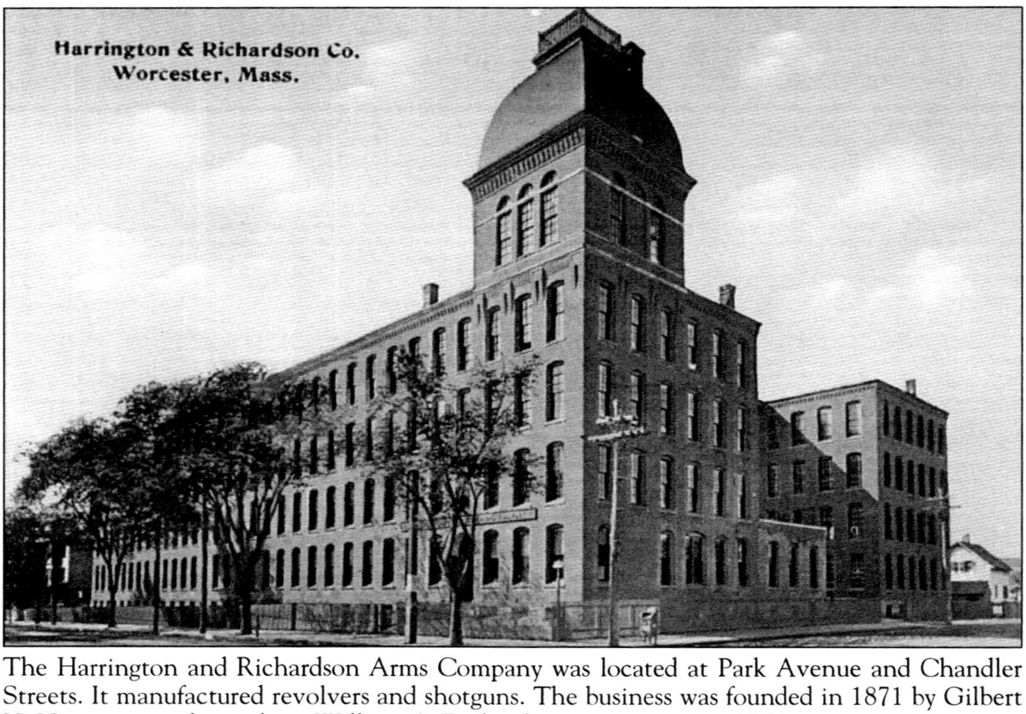

The Harrington and Richardson Arms Company was located at Park Avenue and Chandler Streets. It manufactured revolvers and shotguns. The business was founded in 1871 by Gilbert H. Harrington, who took on William A. Richardson as a partner in 1874.

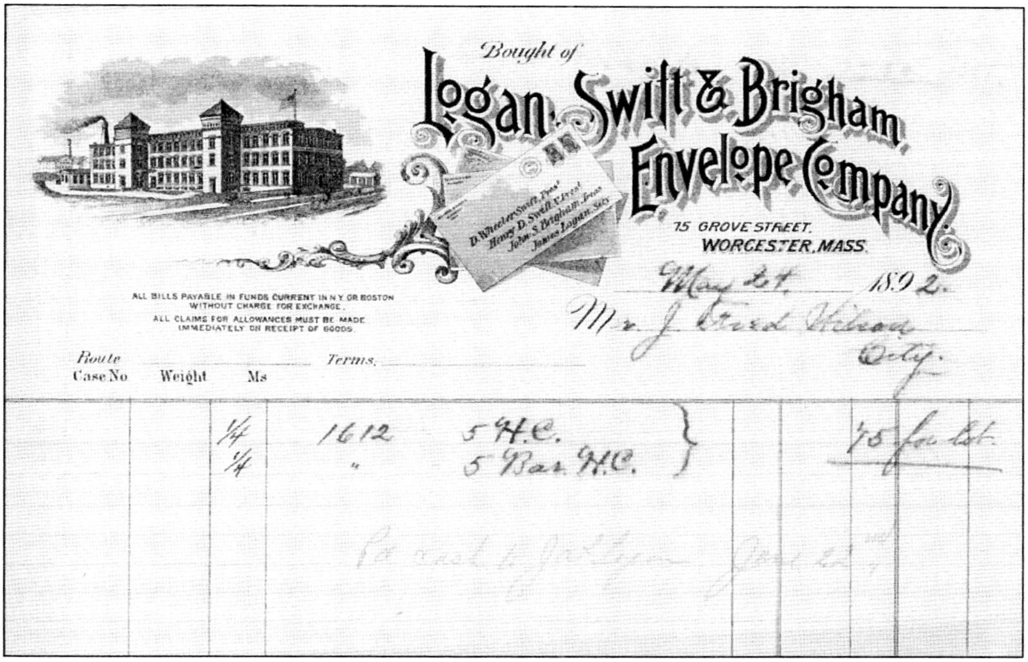

The Logan, Swift, and Brigham Envelope Company was located at 75 Grove Street. All of the machinery in the factory was invented and built by the Swifts. The company made envelopes in every conceivable size and shape.

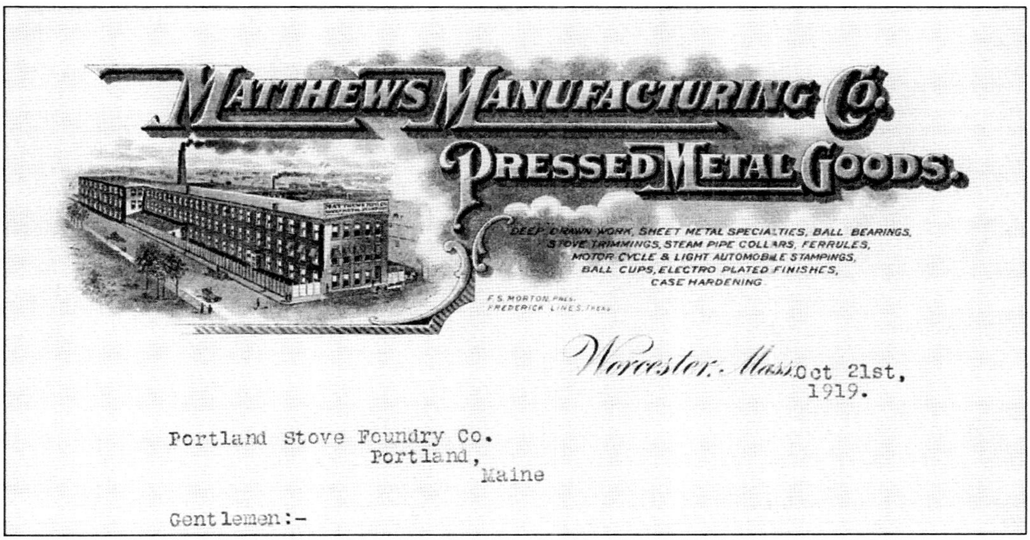

The Matthews Manufacturing Company was located at 116 Gold Street. The company manufactured all kinds of furnishings for heating apparatus and light-weight, cold-rolled steel for the manufacture of bicycles.

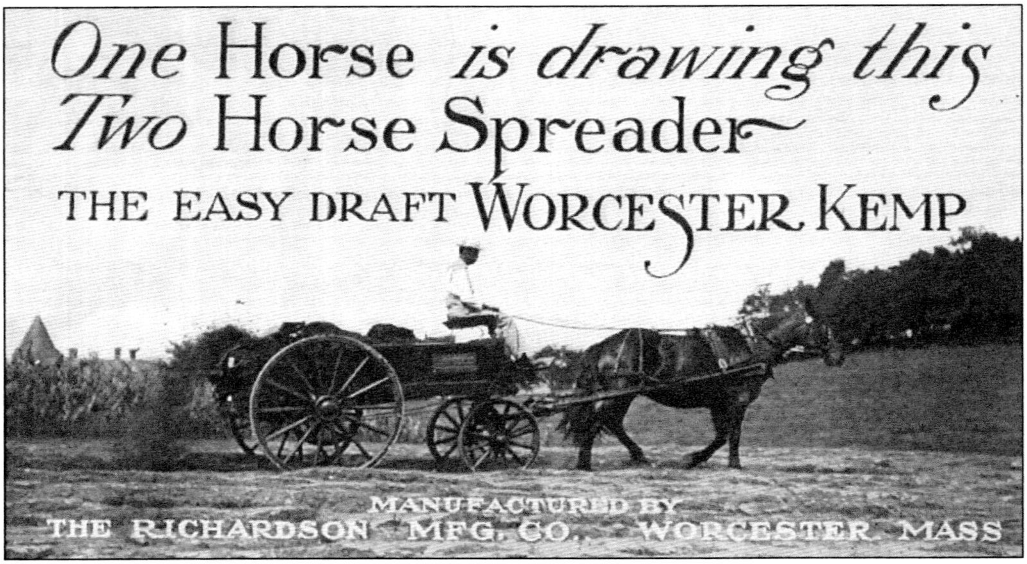

The Worcester Kemp Manure Spreader was one of the many products manufactured by the Richardson Manufacturing Company. The company, located at 84 Prescott Street, also manufactured the Worcester Buckeye Mower, the Bullard Hay Tedder, and the Worcester Horse Rake. In 1910 Edwin P. Curtis was president and John D. Curtis was vice-president of the company, which manufactured many kinds of agricultural implements.

Stephen M. Sargeant, president, and S. Mortimer Sargeant, treasurer, were the officers of the S.M. Sargeant Company in 1910. The company manufactured extracts and toiletries and its laboratories were located at 107 June Street.

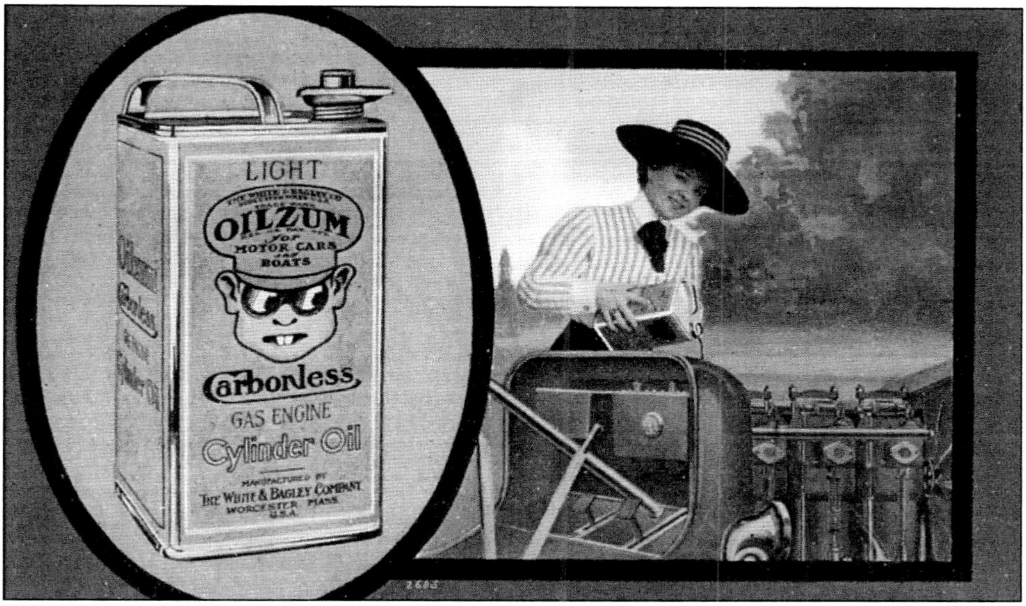

Oilzum, a carbonless, gas-engine-cylinder oil, was manufactured by the White & Bagley Company, which had offices at 100 Foster Street and a factory on Manchester Street. The White & Bagley Company started business in 1889 in a small, frame building on Woodland Street with Herbert P. Bagley as president and Fred W. White as treasurer. The company was an extensive manufacturer of oils and greases for lubricating purposes.

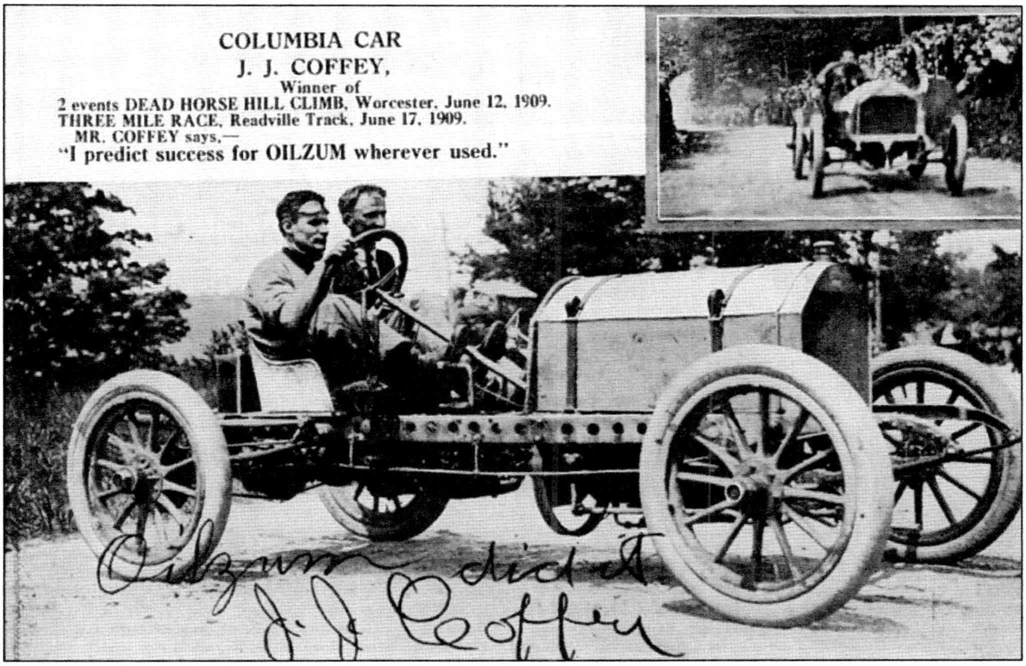

J.J. Coffey, racecar driver, gives testimony to the benefits of Oilzum. He won the Dead Horse Hill climb on June 12, 1909. The Dead Horse Hill climb took place on Stafford Street for several years at the beginning of the 20th century. The race has been revived in recent years.

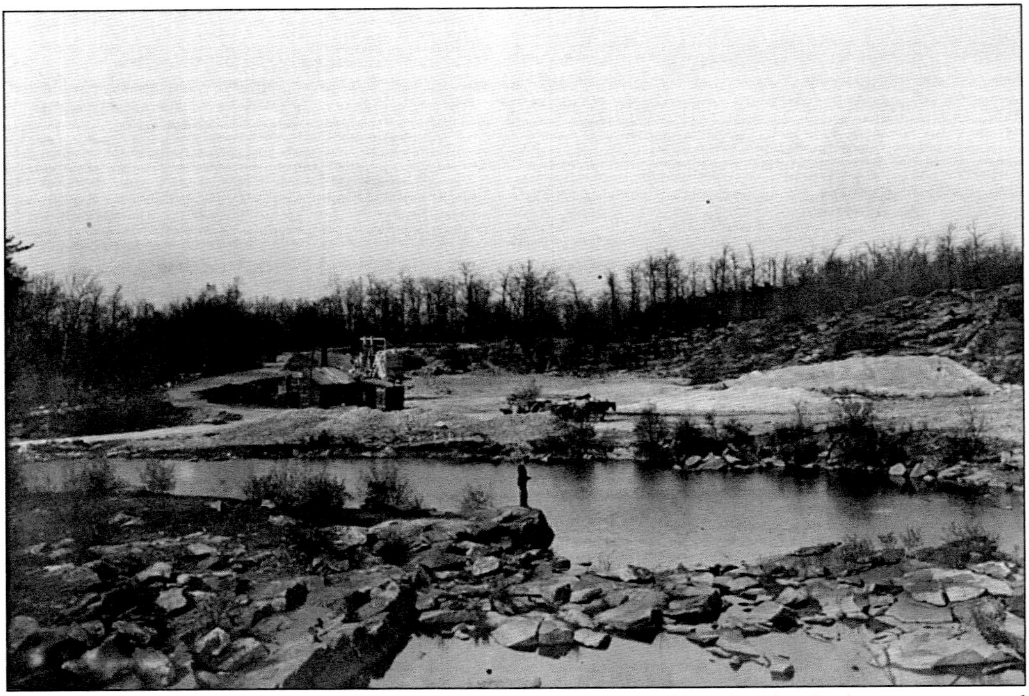

This quarry on Millstone Hill was located in part of Green Hill Park. The facility was operated by George B. Webb, a general contractor. The granite mined was used in buildings, monuments, curbing, and paving. George D. Webb died on December 28, 1910.

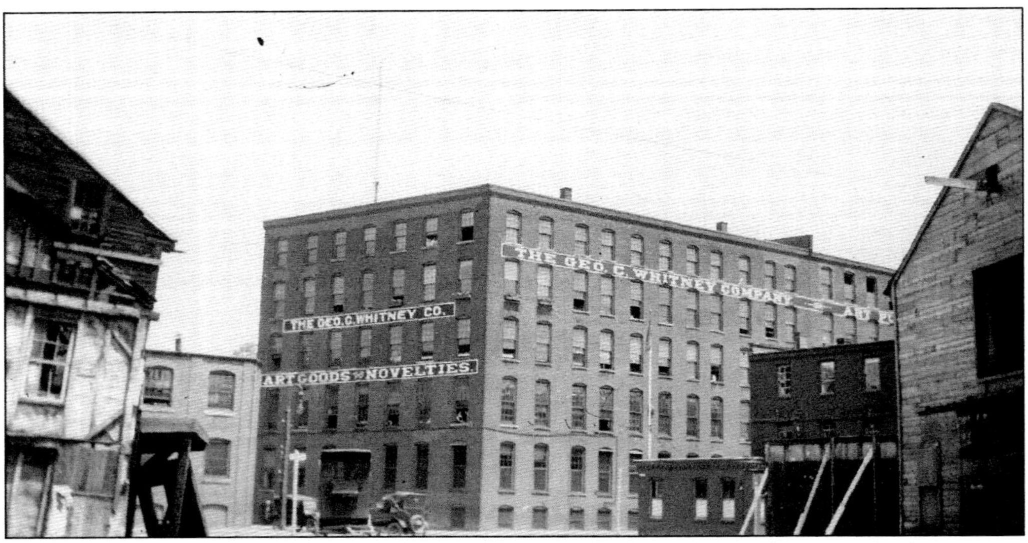

Pictured here is the George C. Whitney Company—the largest manufacturer of valentines in the world, *c.* 1910. It also manufactured postcards, art goods, and novelties. On January 12, 1910, starting at 9 p.m., the company's five-story factory at the corner of Union and School Streets was burned to the ground. On January 22, 1910, the company purchased buildings nearby on Union and School Streets and resumed manufacturing with little interruption, despite the recent fire.

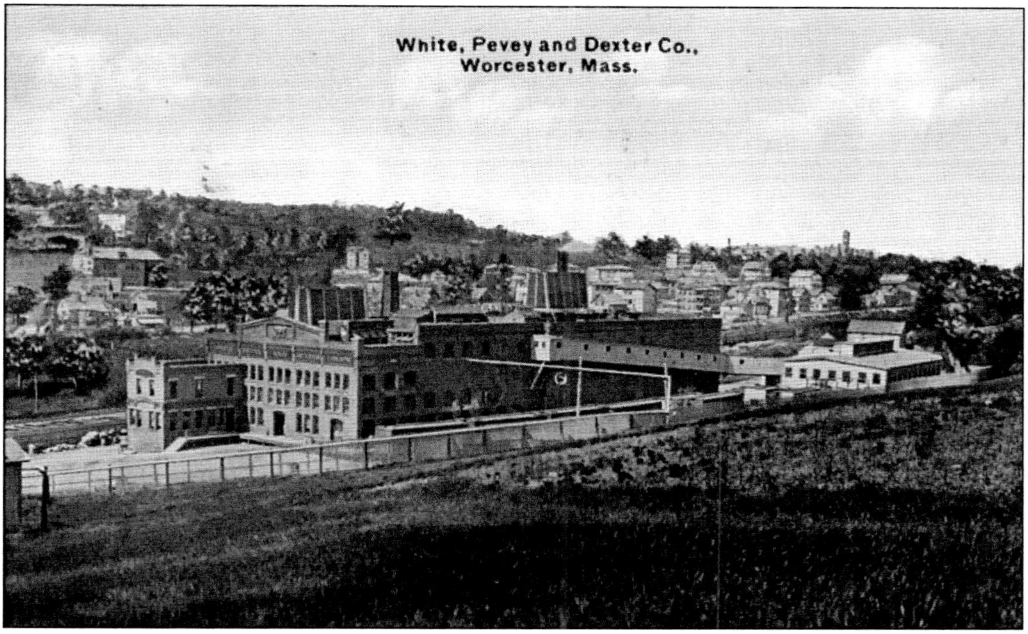

The White, Peavey, and Dexter Company packed pork. Their factory, shown here, was located on Putnam Lane off of Shrewsbury Street.

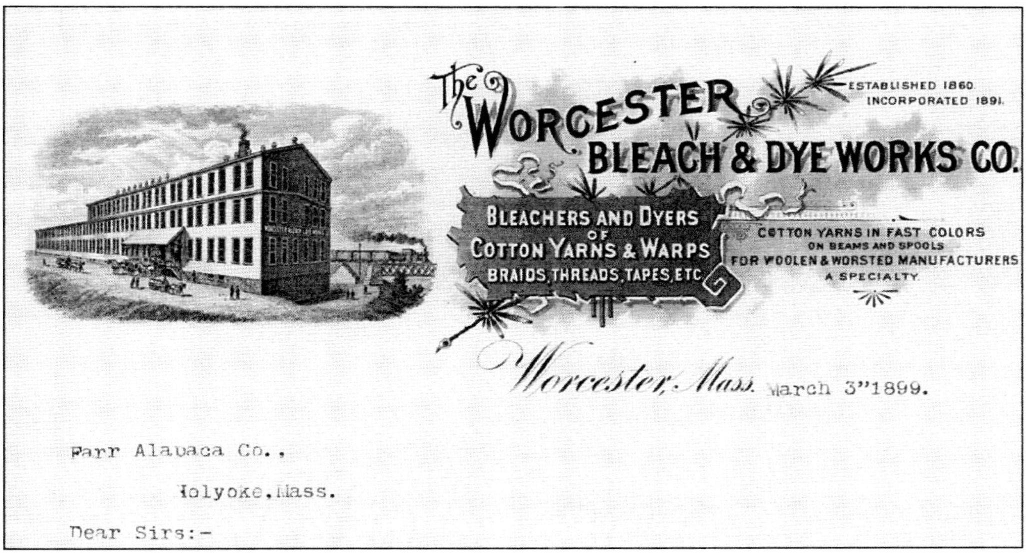

The Worcester Bleach & Dye Works Co.

Established 1860. Incorporated 1891.

Bleachers and Dyers of Cotton Yarns & Warps Braids, Threads, Tapes, Etc.

Cotton Yarns in Fast Colors on Beams and Spools for Woolen & Worsted Manufacturers a Specialty.

Worcester, Mass. March 3"1899.

Farr Alapaca Co.,

Holyoke, Mass.

Dear Sirs:-

The Worcester Bleach and Dye Works was located on Fremont Street. The companies that manufactured fabrics in the city were the customers of this dyeing company—the leading company in the industry.

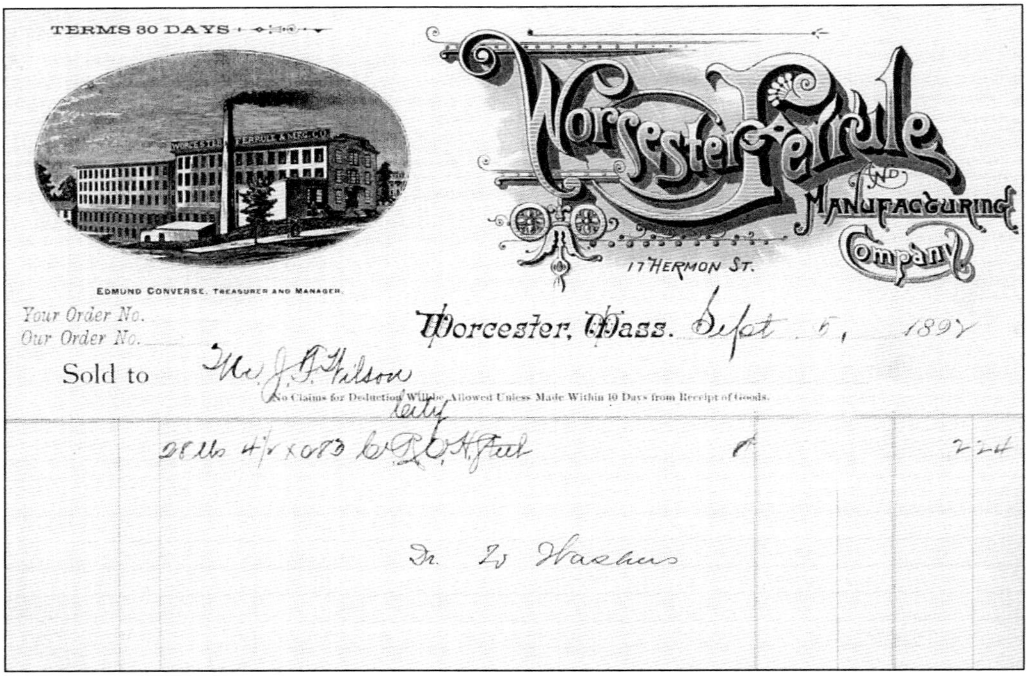

TERMS 30 DAYS

WORCESTER FERRULE & MFG. CO.

Worcester Ferrule and Manufacturing Company

17 HERMON ST.

EDMUND CONVERSE, TREASURER AND MANAGER.

Your Order No.

Our Order No.

Worcester, Mass. Sept 5, 189

Sold to

No Claims for Deduction Will be Allowed Unless Made Within 10 Days from Receipt of Goods.

The Worcester Ferrule and Manufacturing Company, located at 17 Hermon Street, was the pioneer in the manufacture and sale of ventilated stove knobs. The company also manufactured steel and brass ferrules, bicycle bearing cases, and other specialties.

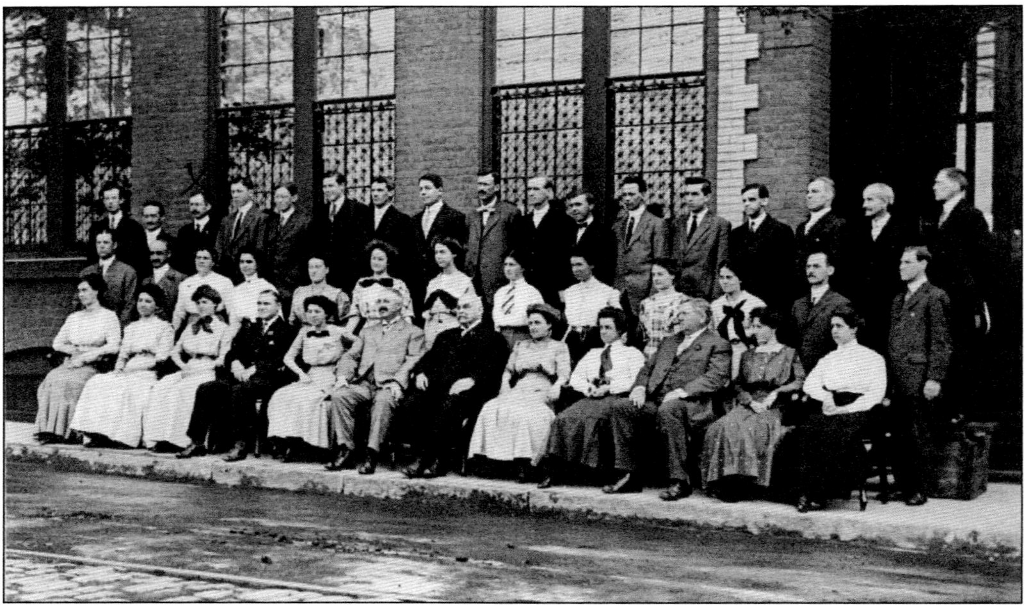

The office staff of the Wright Wire Company posed for this picture *c.* 1910. The company, located at 69 and 71 Hammond Street, manufactured copper, brass, galvanized, tinned, steel, and iron wire cloth. There were more wire manufacturers located in Worcester than any other city in the country at the turn of the century.

Four

BUSINESSES

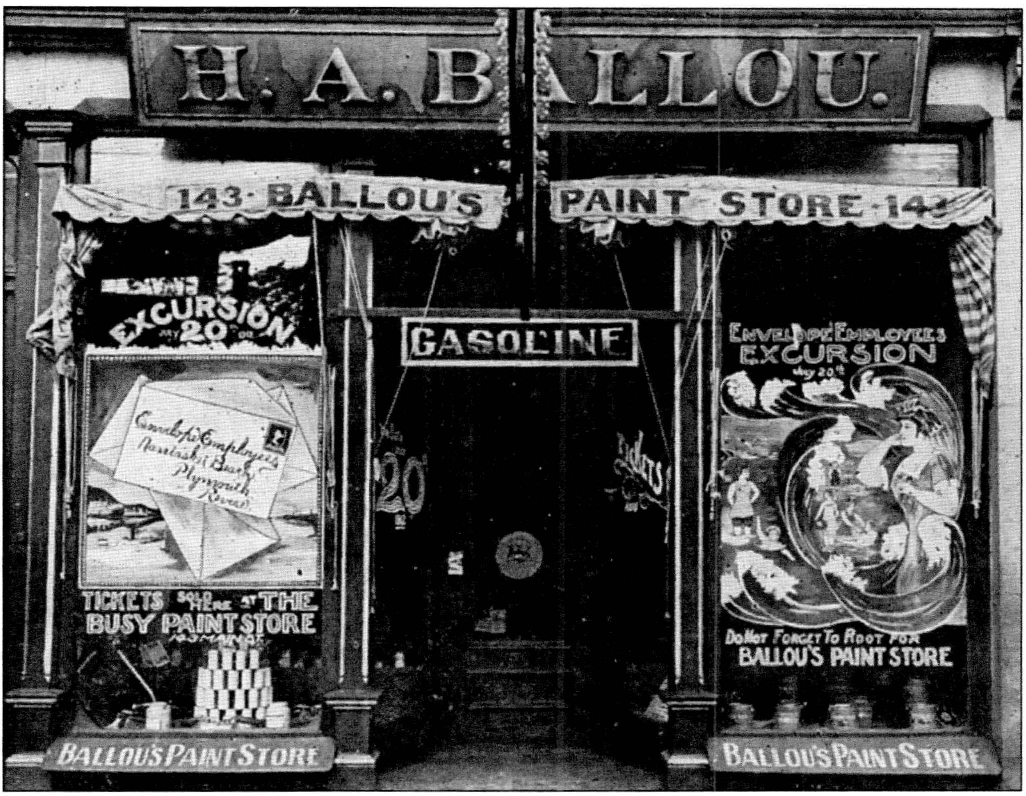

The H.A. Ballou Pain Store was located at 143 Main Street. The signs in the windows announce the availability of tickets to the envelope employees' excursion to Nantasket Beach and Plymouth Rock.

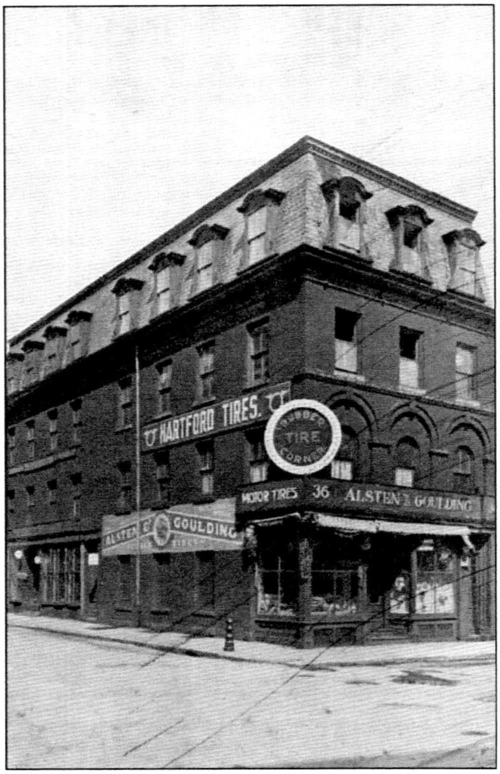

The Alsten and Goulding Company was located at 36 Foster Street. It was a wholesaler and retailer of rubber tires for automobiles, carriages, and bicycles. The site became known as "the rubber tire corner."

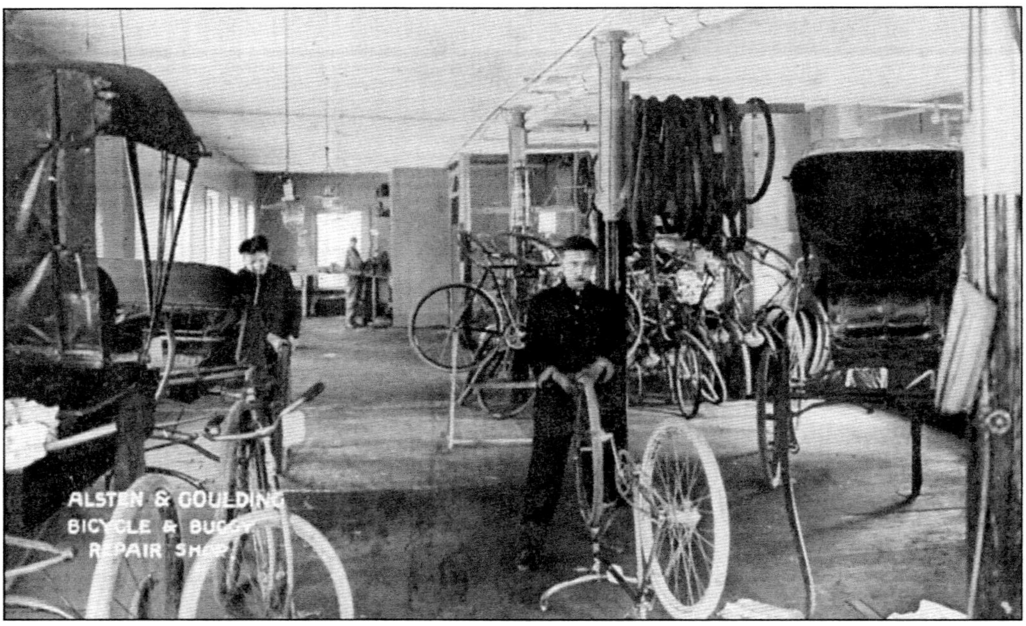

The Alsten and Goulding Bicycle and Buggy Repair Shop is shown here. A 1911 advertisement says that, "it is the largest vulcanizing plant in central New England."

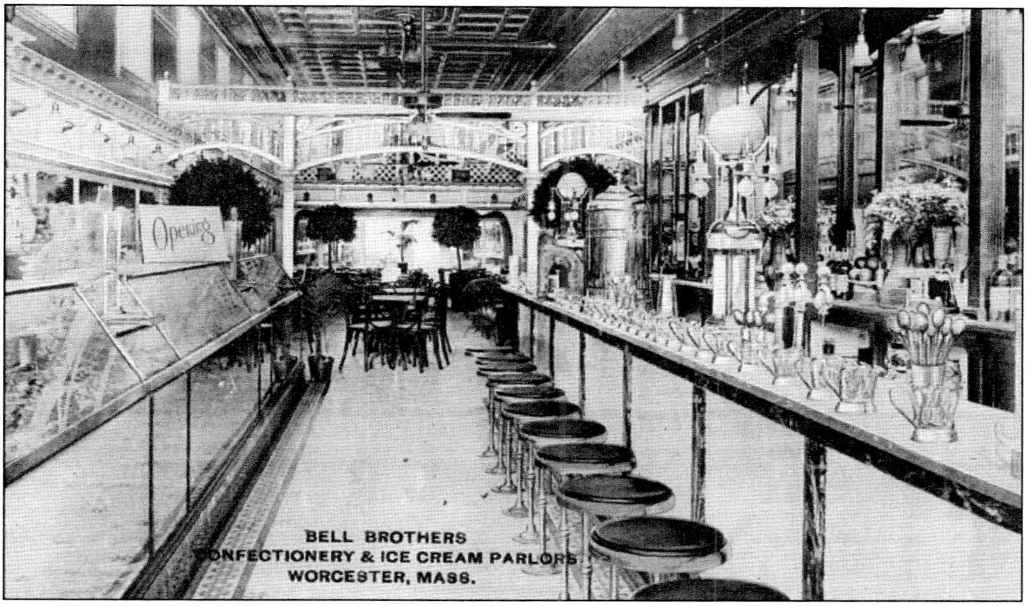

Bell Brothers Confectionery and Ice Cream Parlor opened at 152 Front Street before 1910. The Bell brothers also owned a store at 558 Main Street. The store at 152 Front Street was later occupied by the Union Loan Company, a pawn shop owned by the author's father prior to its demolition, which made way for the Worcester Center Galleria.

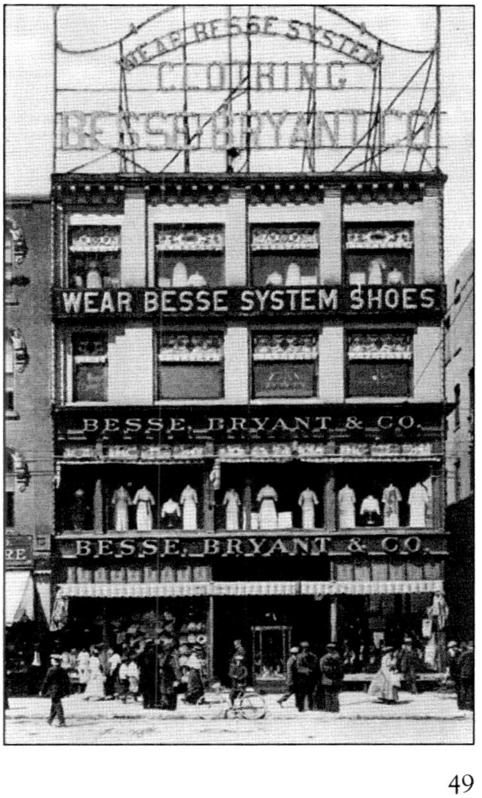

The Besse-Bryant Company was located at 24 Front Street. This store was one of 27 stores in the Besse System. The Besse System celebrated its 50th anniversary in 1927. The stores of the Besse System had the purchasing power of a chain store, but each one was operated as an individual store whose manager lived in the community in which it was located.

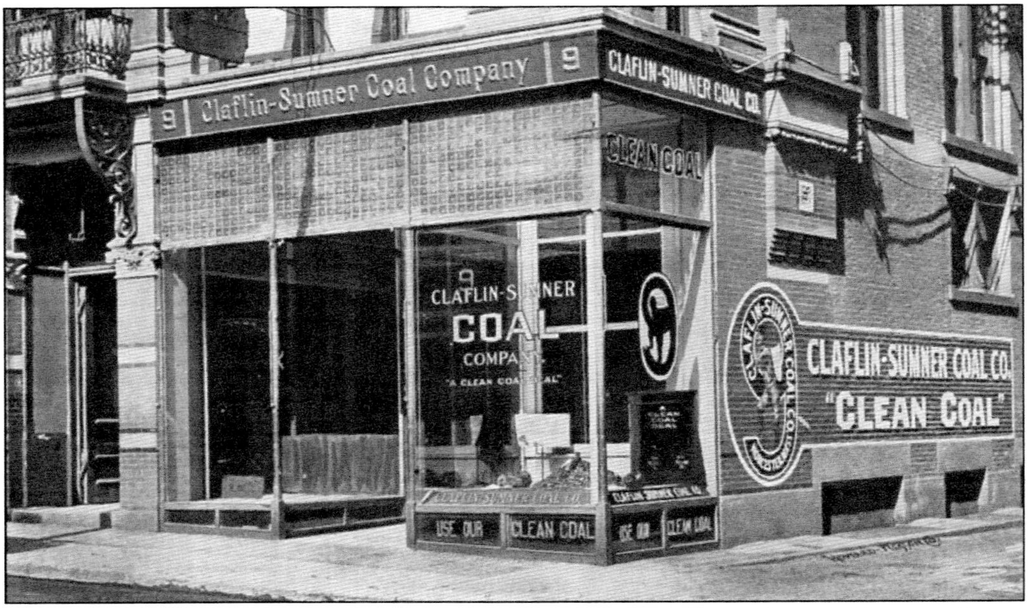

The general offices of Claflin-Sumner Coal Company were located at 9 Pleasant Street. Wholesalers and retailers of anthracite and bituminous coal, the company maintained yards on Southbridge and Shrewsbury Streets.

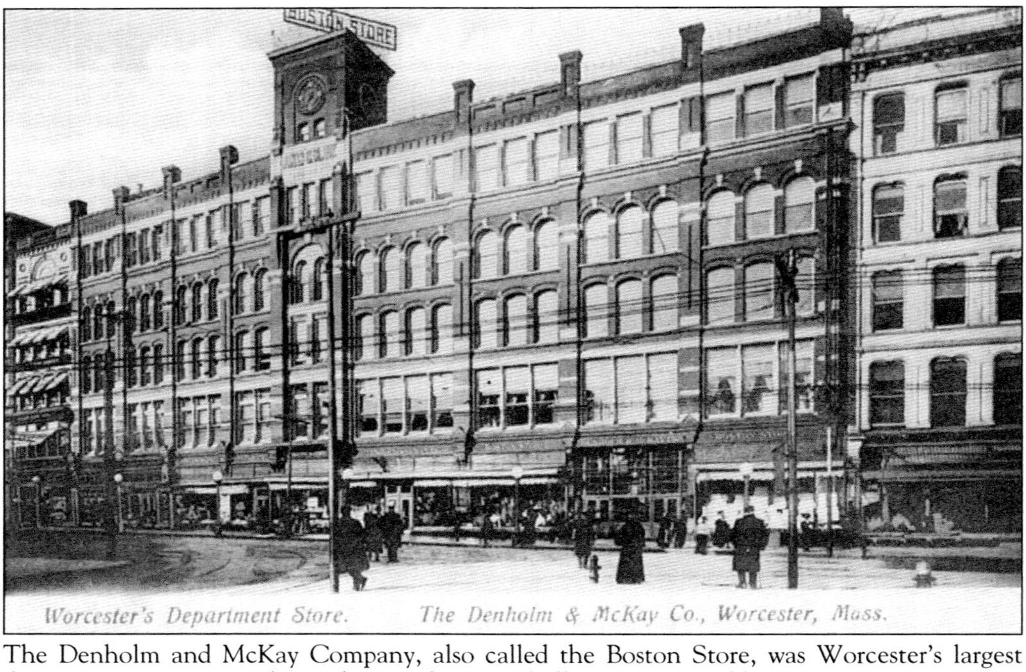

The Denholm and McKay Company, also called the Boston Store, was Worcester's largest department store. It was located across from city hall, opposite Franklin Street.

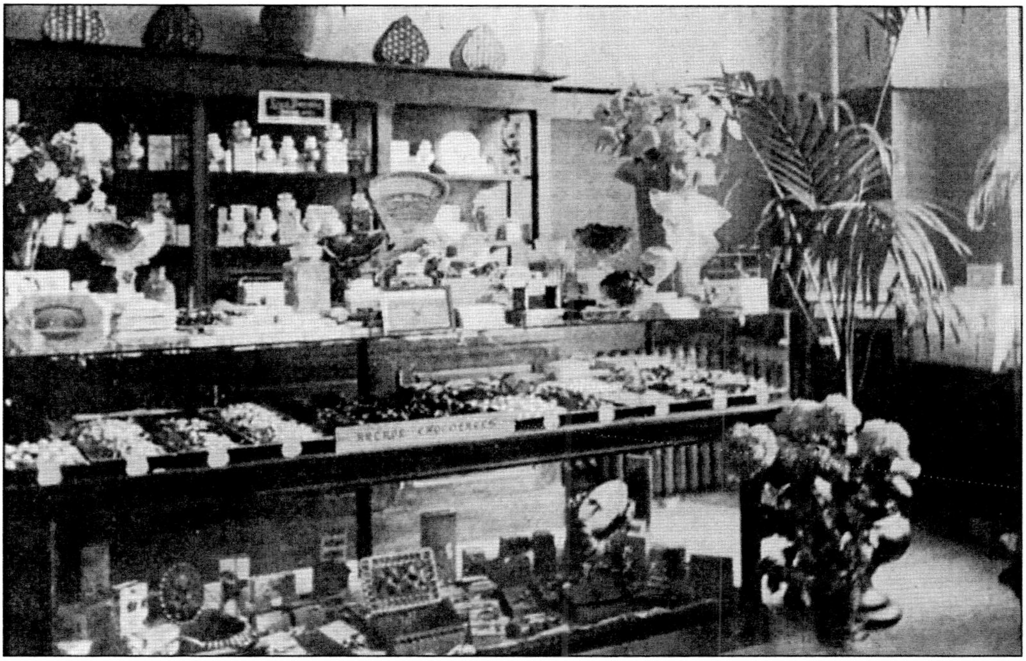

The new Slater Building contained an arcade of stores. This is the Beatrice Gloucester Candy Shop, located in the arcade. It carried everything in the line of confectioneries.

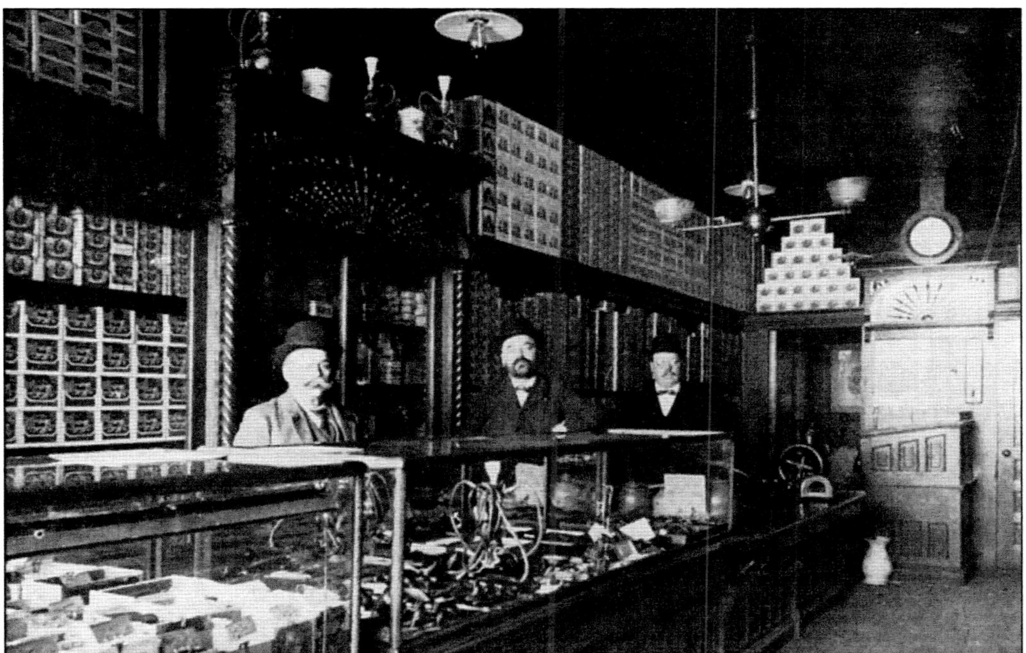

Jacob Holden and Antipas F. Earle celebrated ten years, from March 15, 1888, to March 15, 1898, in the cigar and tobacco business. Their shop was located at 434 1/2 Main Street.

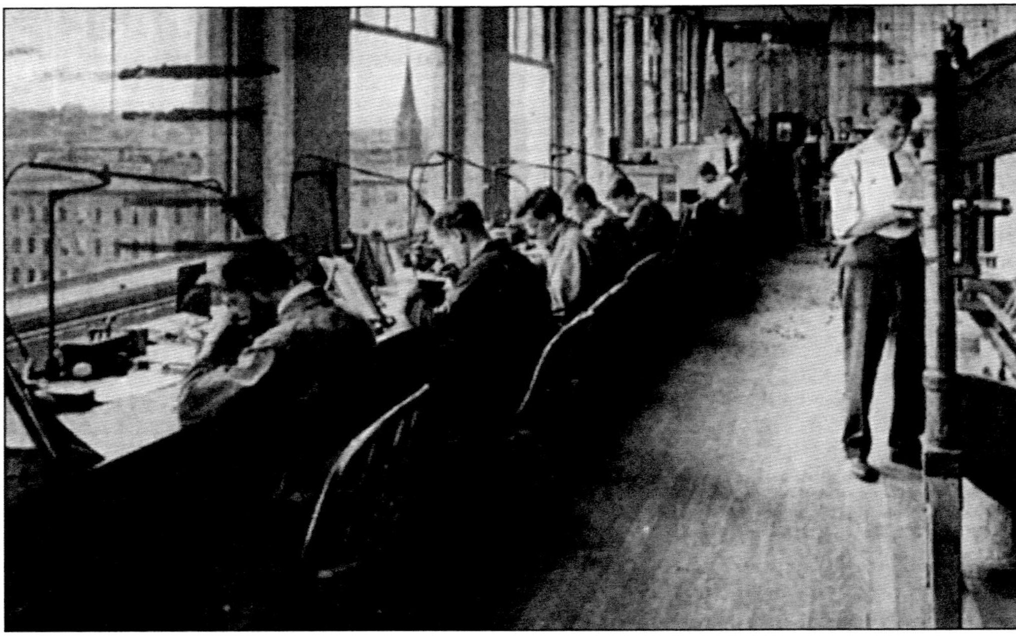

The halftone engraving room of the Howard-Wesson Company was located on the fifth floor of the Day Building on Main Street in 1910. In 1921 it was located in the Graphic Arts Building located on the corner of Foster and Commercial Streets. The company printed catalogues, magazines, letterheads, cards, and announcements using the halftone process.

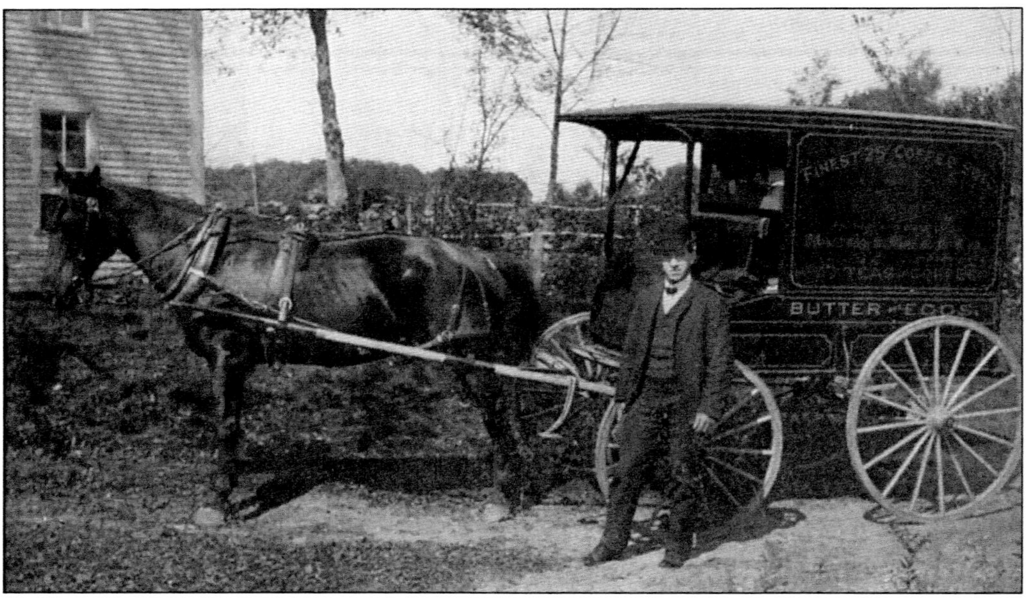

A.E. Hurd stands beside his horse and wagon. A resident of Charlotte Street, he sold his wares of teas, coffees, spices and extracts, butter, eggs, canned goods, and small groceries in the area around south Main Street.

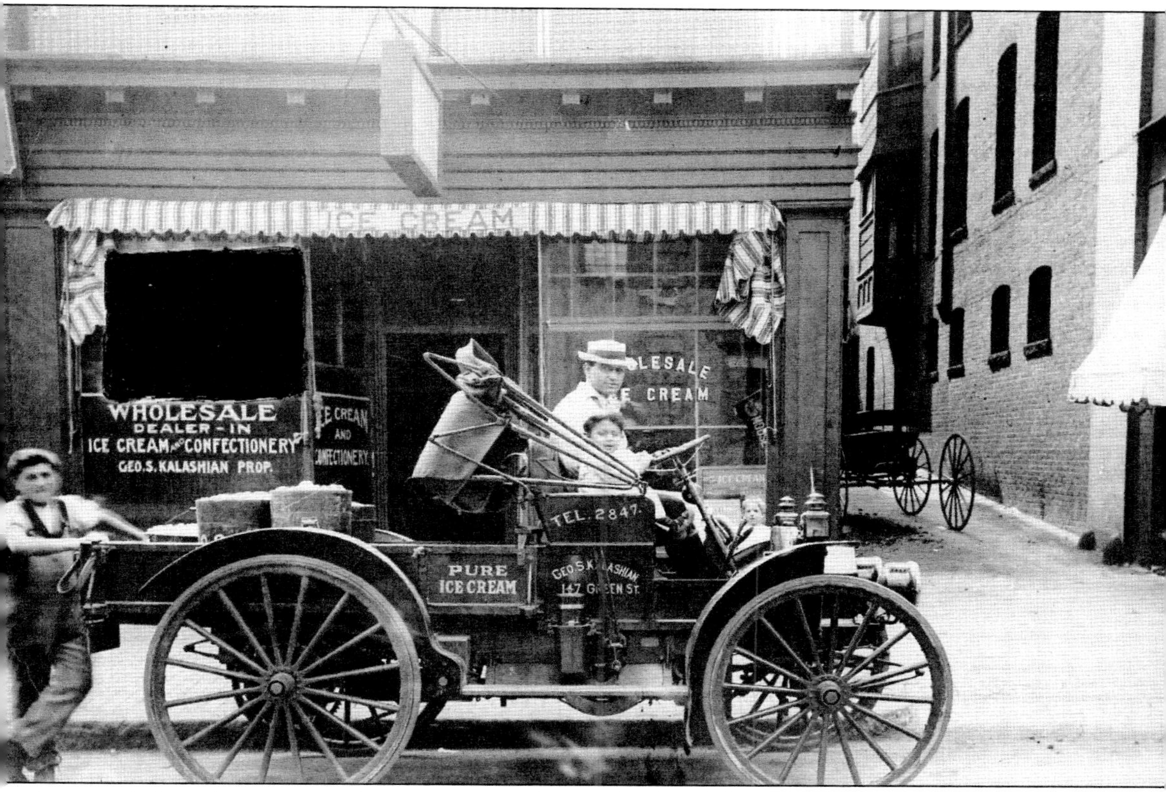

George S. Kalashian poses in his delivery truck outside of his 147 Green Street Ice Cream and Confectionery Store, which manufactured velvet ice cream. A 1910 advertisement states, "Never hesitate to order by phone. No order too small for our attention; none too large for our facilities."

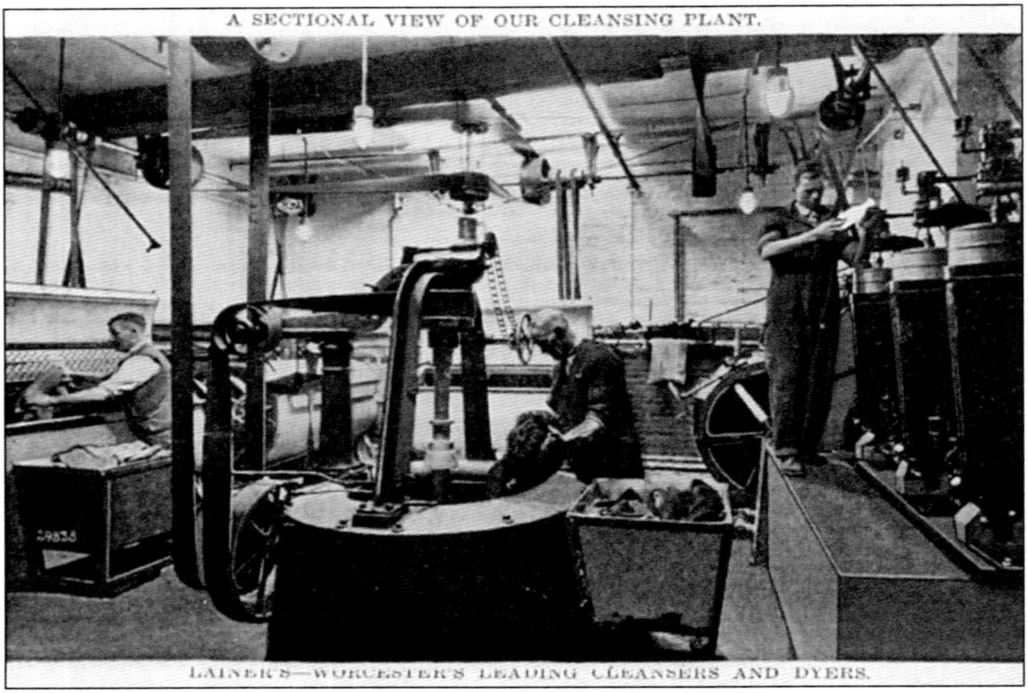

The cleansing plant of Lainer's, Worcester's largest cleaners and dyers, is shown here. Offices were located at 73 Green Street, and the factory was located on Plymouth Street.

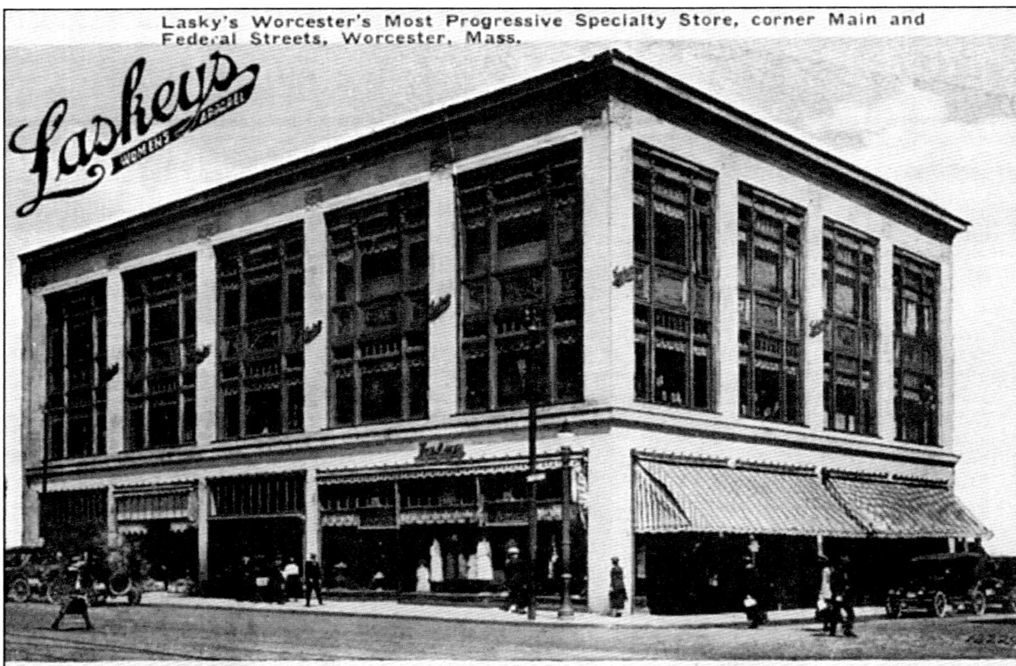

Laskey's was located on the corner of Federal and Main Streets. It was a retailer in women's apparel. In 1928 this location became a Filene's store.

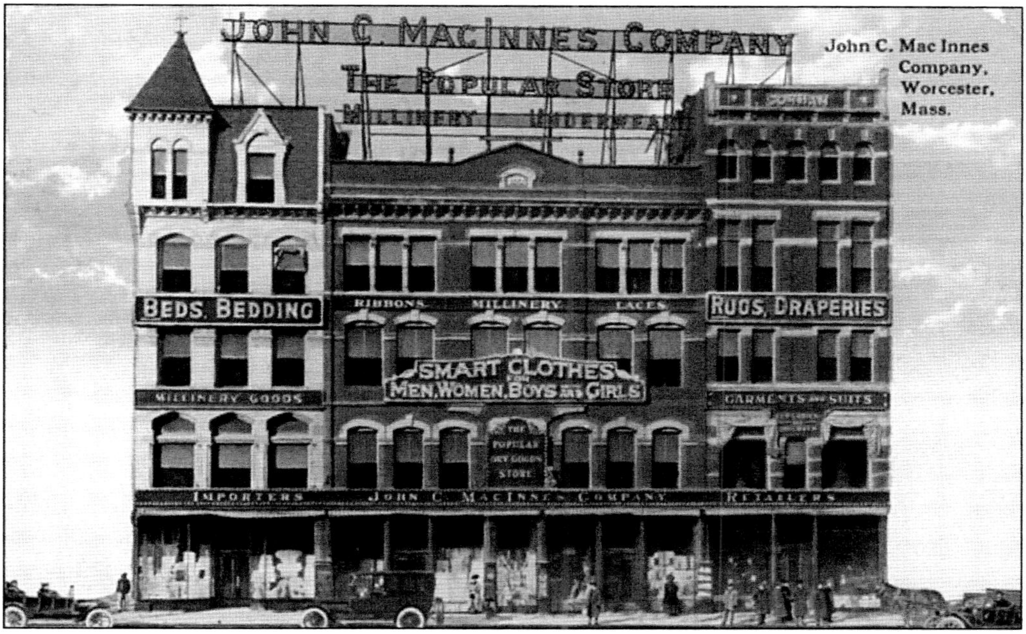

The John C. MacInnes Company was located at 454 Main Street across from city hall. It was a wholesale and retail dealer in dry goods, silks, draperies, cloaks, etc. The business was founded in 1873. By 1898 it had grown to encompass all four floors of three adjacent buildings.

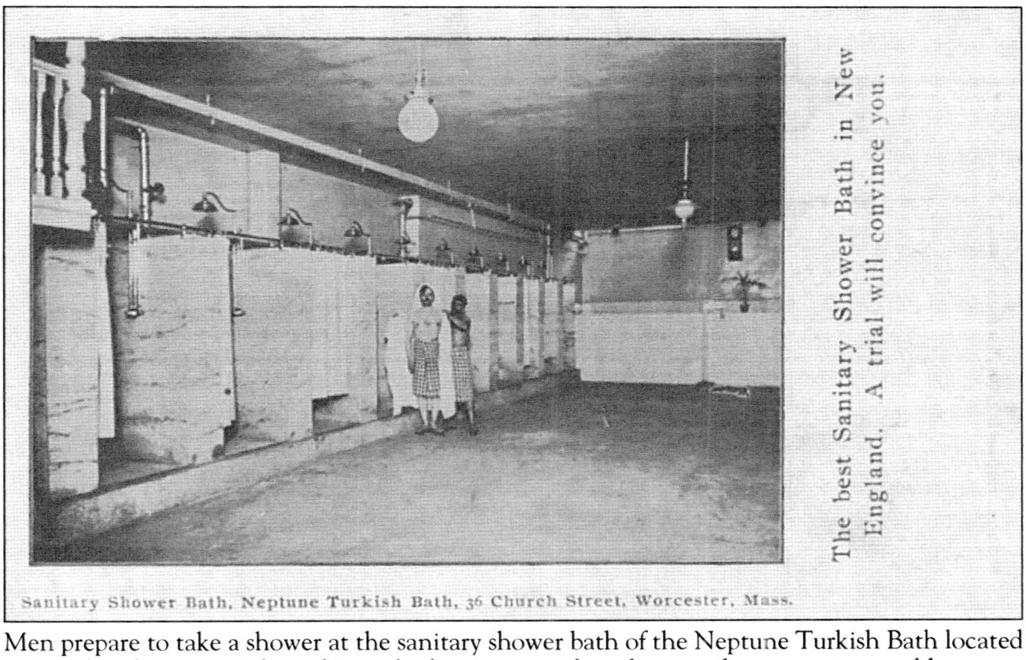

Men prepare to take a shower at the sanitary shower bath of the Neptune Turkish Bath located at 36 Church Street. After taking a bath you were advised to use the swimming pool by a sign which read, "to avoid catching a cold you must take a good swim in the pool after the bath."

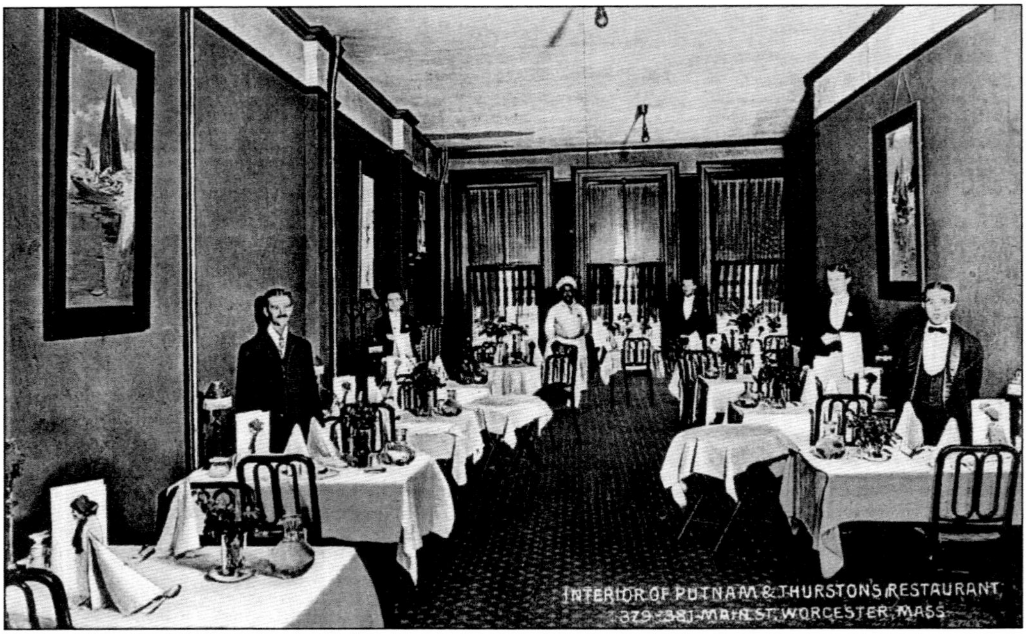

The interior of the Putnam and Thurston's Restaurant, shown here, was located at 381 Main Street in 1910. The restaurant later moved to 27 Mechanic Street. Founded in 1858, the restaurant was operated by Edward J. Putnam and Frank E. Thurston in the late 1800s.

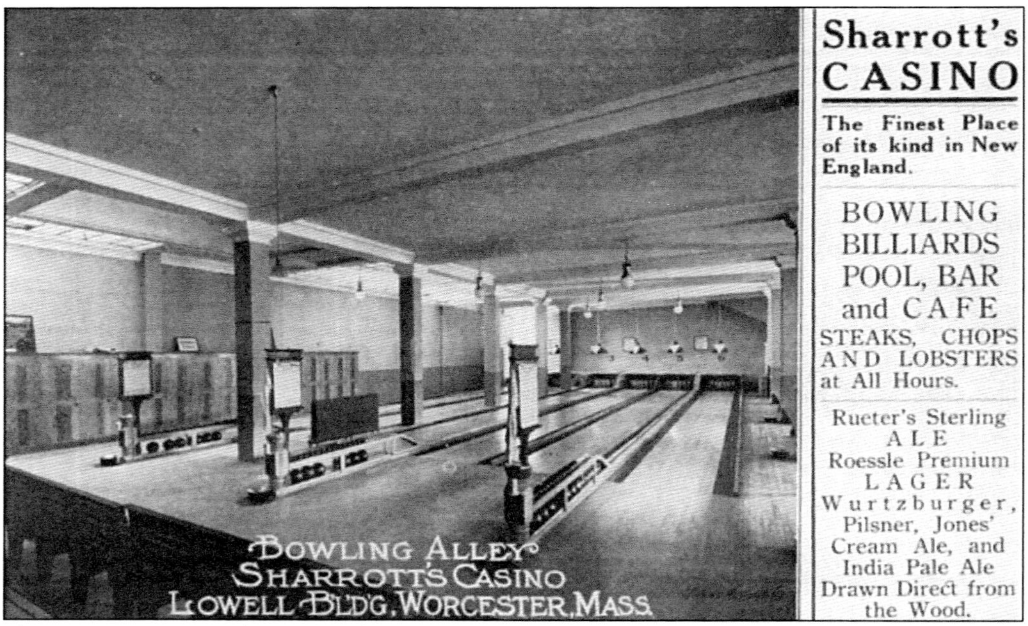

Sharrott's Casino was located in the Lowell Building at the corner of Norwich Street and Foster Street. The casino was operated by Frank A. Sanderson.

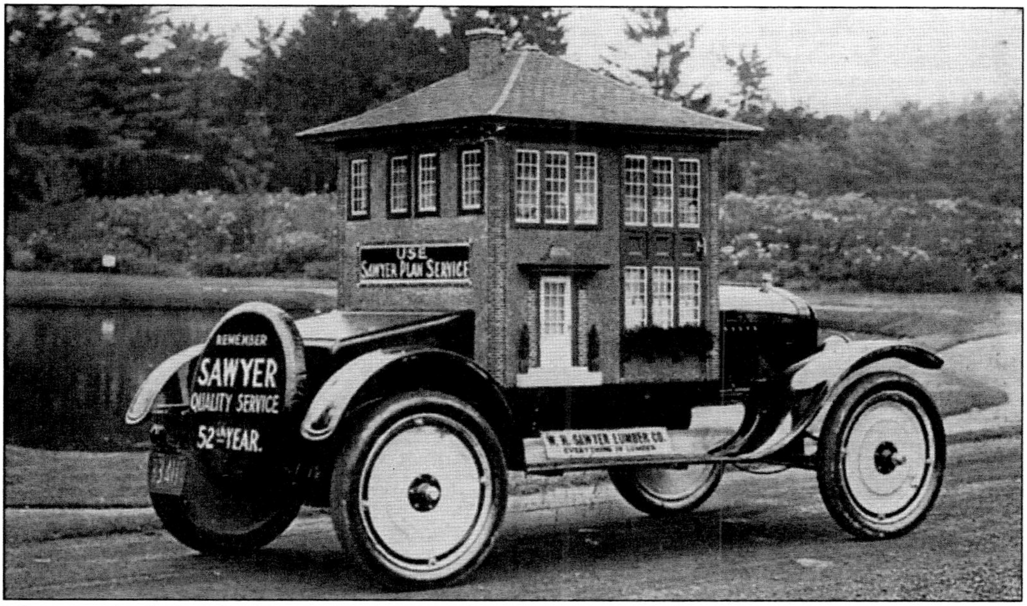

This car, built for the W.H. Sawyer Lumber Company in the 1920s, was used to advertise the company in many parades. The office and lumberyards of the company were located at 66 Lincoln Street near Lincoln Square. William H. Sawyer served the city as alderman, as a member of the parks commission, and as chairman of the commission that directed the construction of the new city hall.

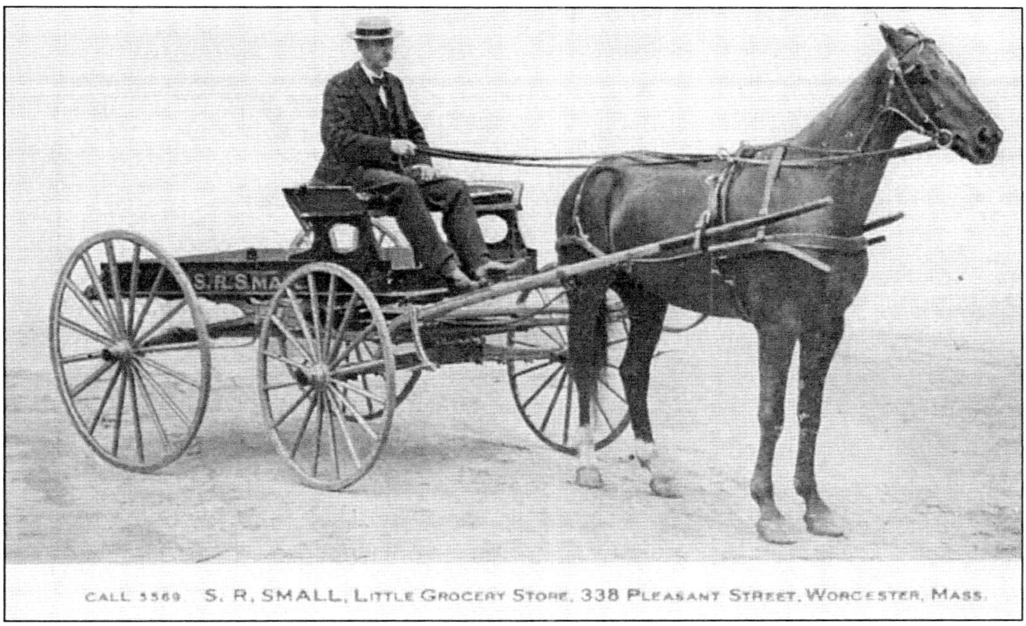

Samuel R. Small, operator of the "little grocery store" at 338 Pleasant Street, poses on his buck board. The store offered coffee, butter, flour, bundle wood, coke, charcoal, coal in bags, lard, canned goods, and fresh bread and milk for sale.

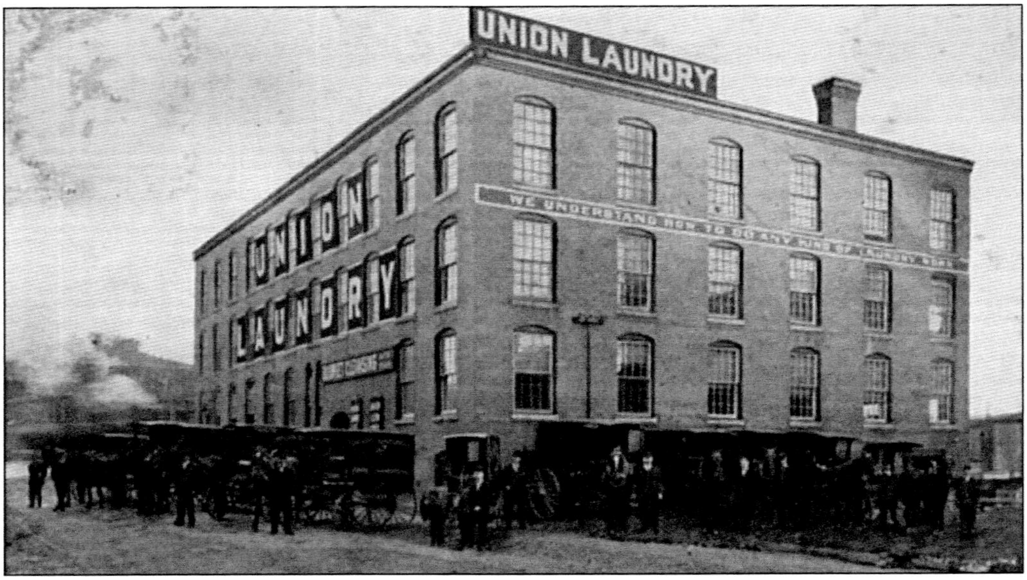

Delivery men pose with their wagons at Union Laundry c. 1910. The company, which kept 16 wagons and 21 horses employed in the collection and distribution of laundry, was located at the corner of Union and Exchange Streets. Founded in 1886 by David A. Scott, the company grew very rapidly. Mr. Scott originated the wet wash business in this country.

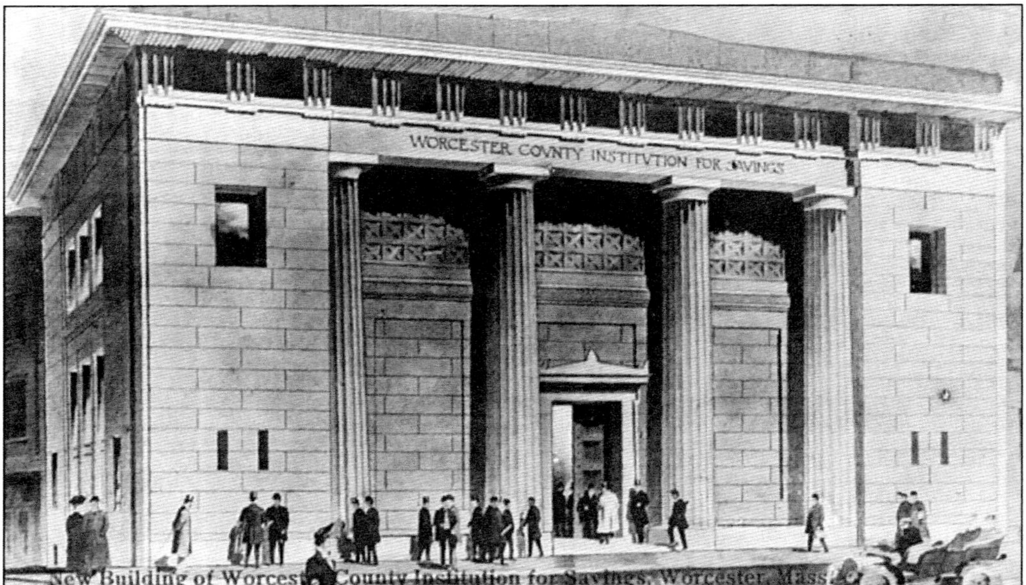

Worcester County Institution for Savings, the 11th savings bank chartered in the state, opened for business in its new quarters at the corner of Main and Foster Streets on October 29, 1906. The vault, three stories in height, was the largest bank vault in the city. The street-level floor was surrounded by 16 inches of cement and 3 inches of chilled steel. Equipped with various kinds of burglar-proof and alarm contrivances, the vault held the cash, securities, and valuable papers.

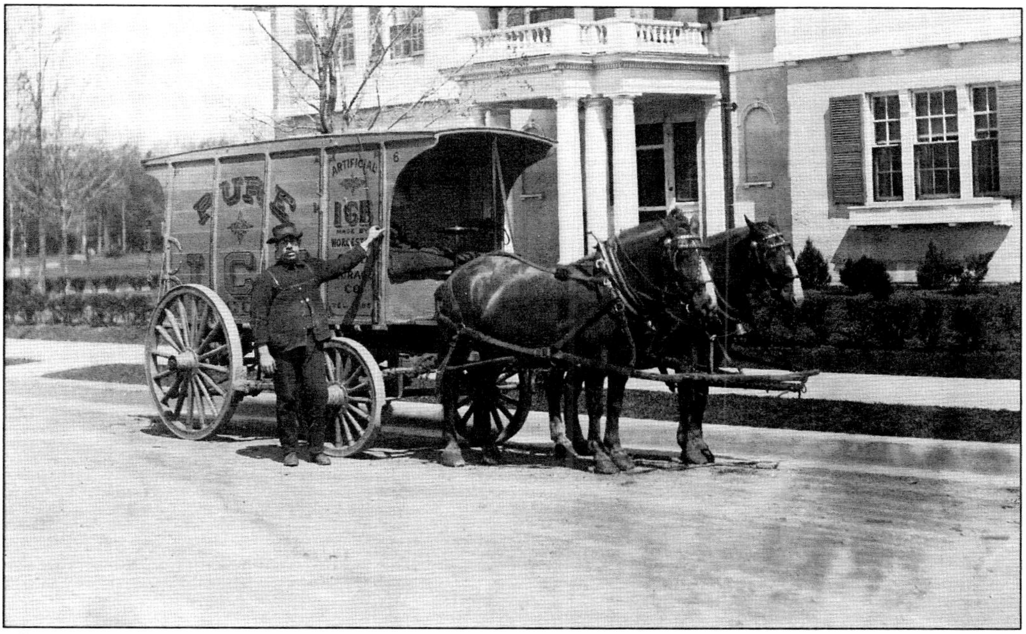

The ice man, with his wagon and team of horses, poses for this picture in front of a Main Street home. The owner of the wagon, Worcester Cold Storage Company, manufactured pure, artificially made ice from water furnished by their own, especially constructed, artesian well.

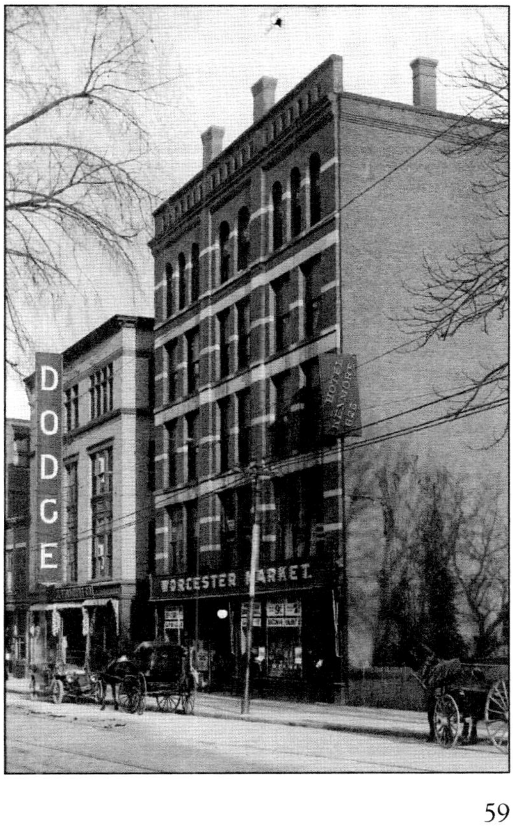

Shoppers are parked outside the Worcester Market at 621 Main Street near Madison Street. The rooms of the Hotel Kenmore were located above the market. The Dodge Furniture Store was located at 615 Main Street.

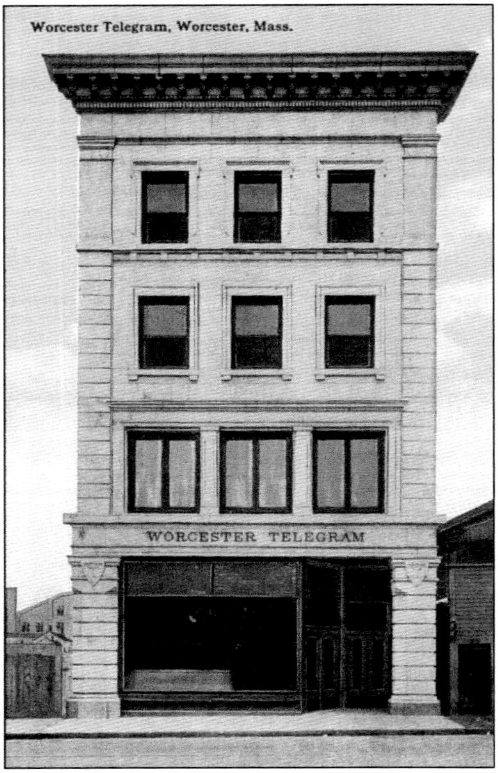

The new Worcester Telegram Building was built on Park (Franklin) Street c. 1910. The *Worcester Sunday Telegram*, a Republican newspaper, was started in 1884 by Austin P. Christy. In 1886 the first *Worcester Daily Telegram* was published.

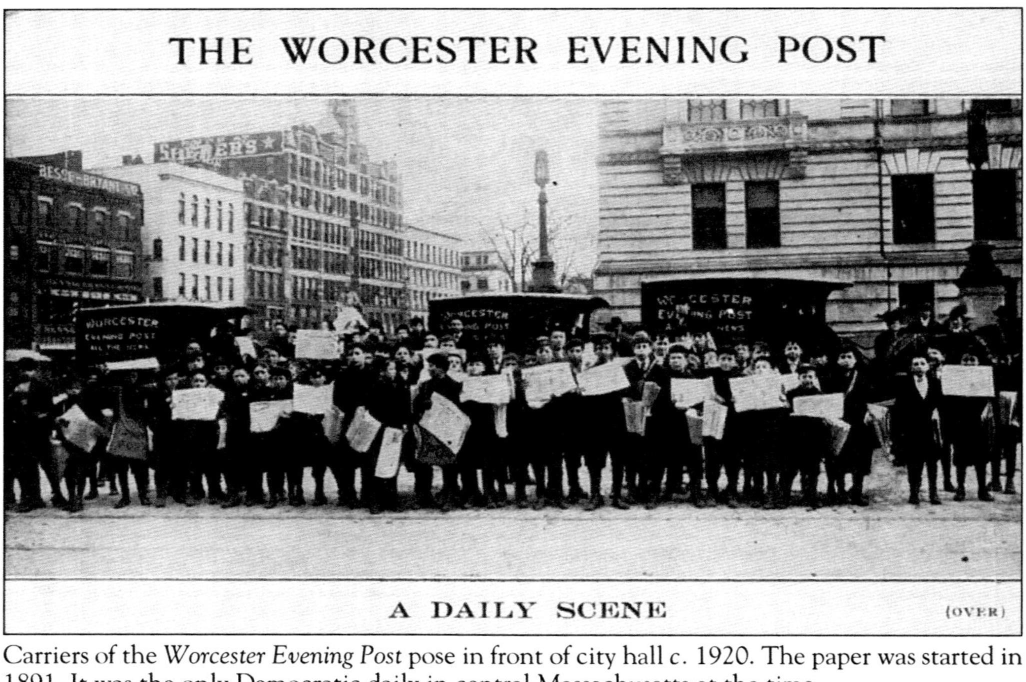

Carriers of the *Worcester Evening Post* pose in front of city hall c. 1920. The paper was started in 1891. It was the only Democratic daily in central Massachusetts at the time.

Five

BUILDINGS

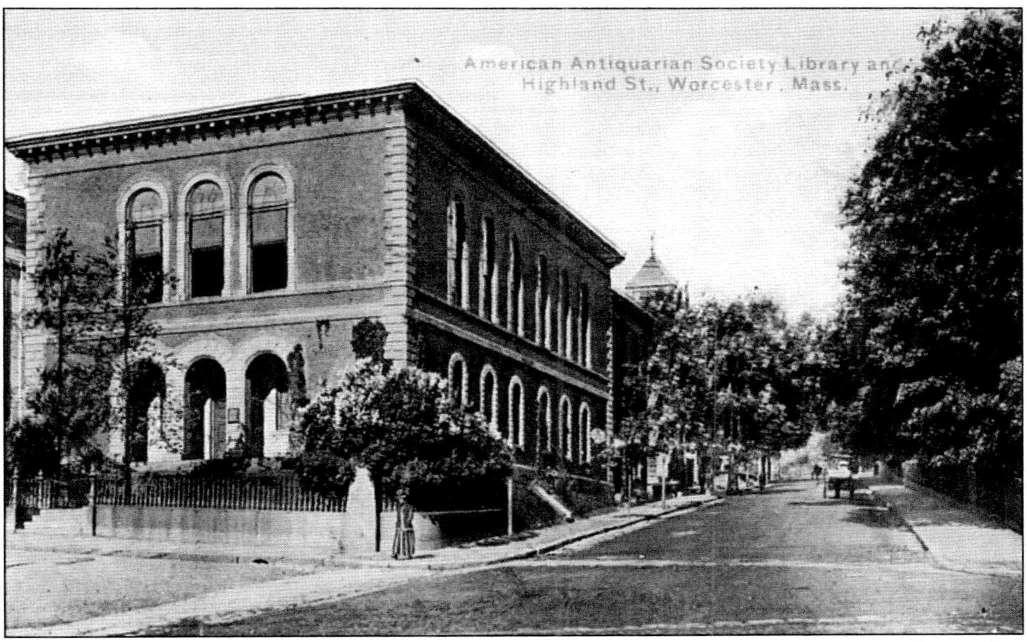

The American Antiquarian Society was founded by Isaiah Thomas in 1812. It was located at the corner of Highland Street and Court House Hill until the new building was constructed at the corner of Park Avenue and Salisbury Streets.

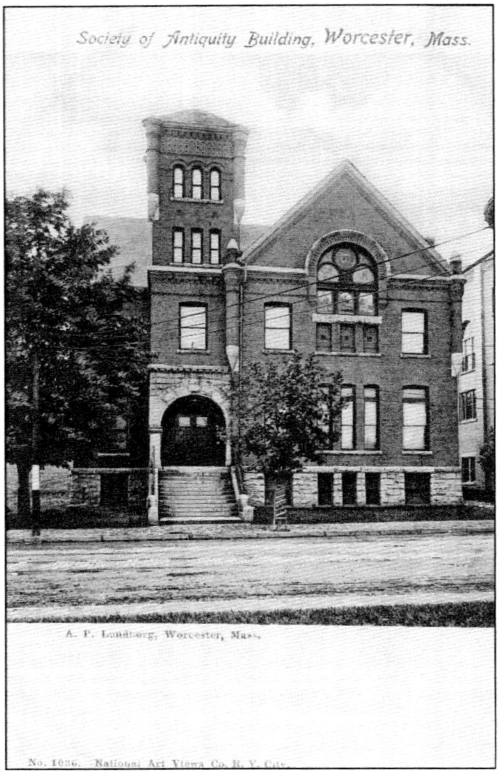

The Worcester Society of Antiquity was organized in 1875. In 1919 it changed its name to the Worcester Historical Society. Its purpose is "to foster in its members a love and admiration for antique research and archaeological science, and to rescue from oblivion such historical matter as would otherwise be lost."

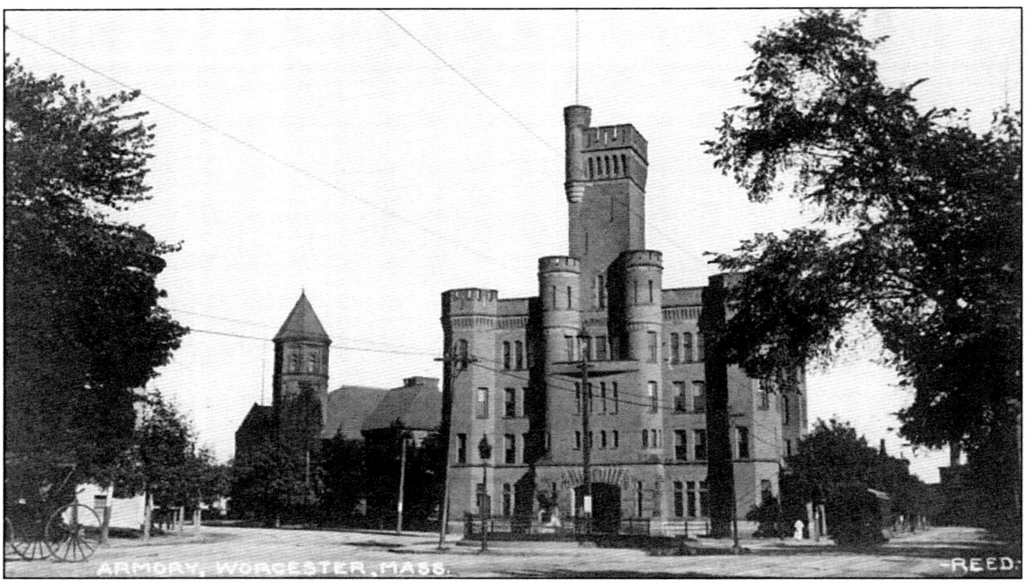

The Worcester Armory, located at Grove and Salisbury Streets, was erected in 1889 and dedicated on January 30, 1891. Prior to World War I, the armory was occupied by Companies A, C, and H, Second Infantry; Company G, Ninth Infantry; Battery B, First Field Artillery; and all of the Massachusetts Militia or National Guard.

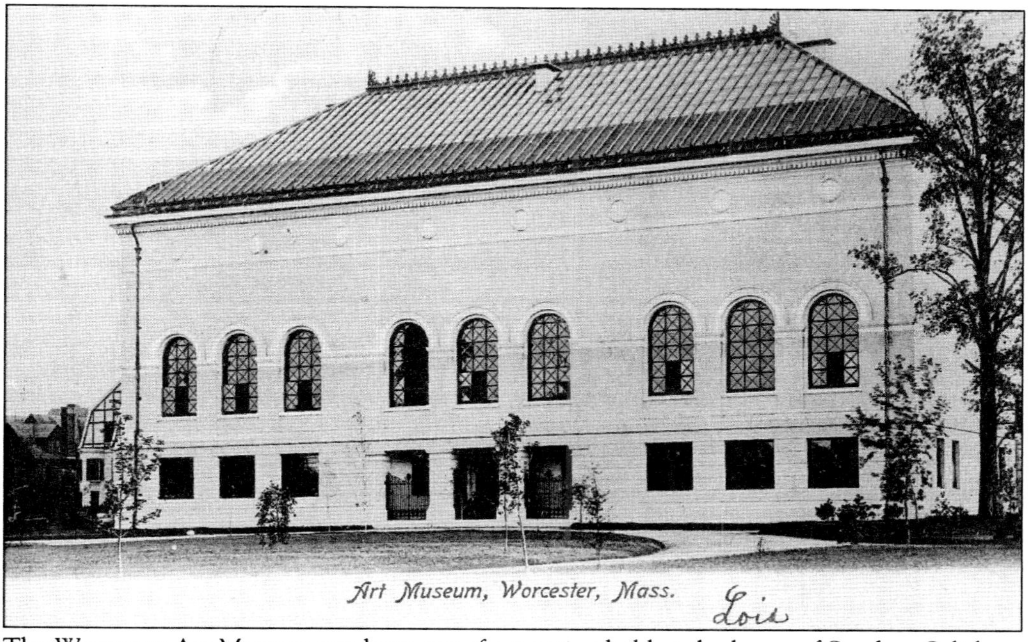

The Worcester Art Museum was born out of a meeting held at the home of Stephen Salisbury on February 25, 1896. Mr. Salisbury donated an acre of land and a fund of $100,000—half for construction of a building and the rest to be an endowment fund. The new museum on Salisbury Street was opened on May 10, 1898.

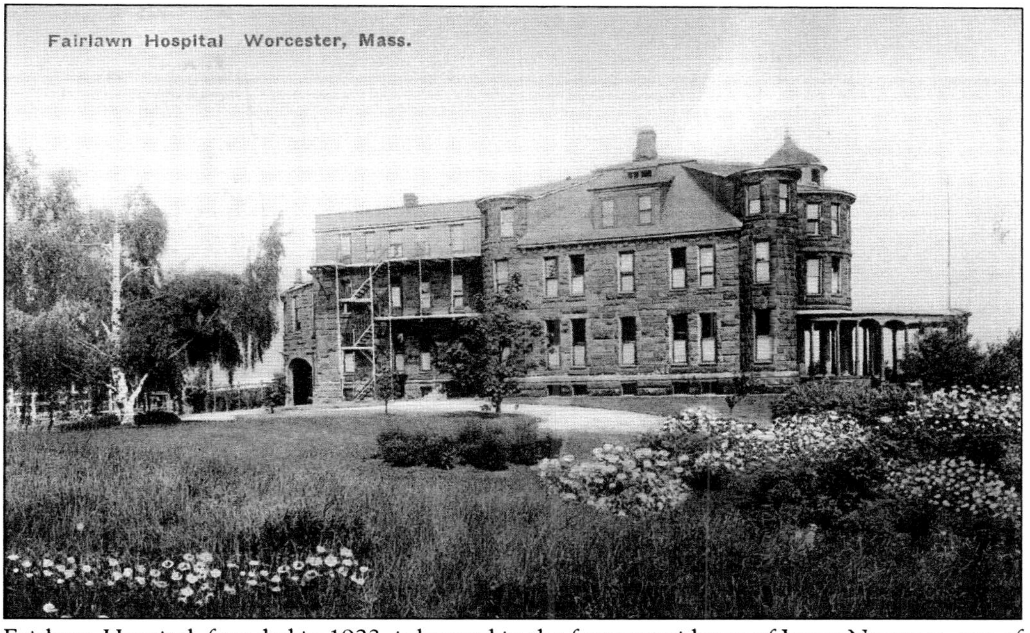

Fairlawn Hospital, founded in 1922, is located in the former residence of James Norcross, one of the founders of Norcross Brothers Company, Builders. Hospital wings have been added to the residence. James A. Norcross designed and built his residence in 1893.

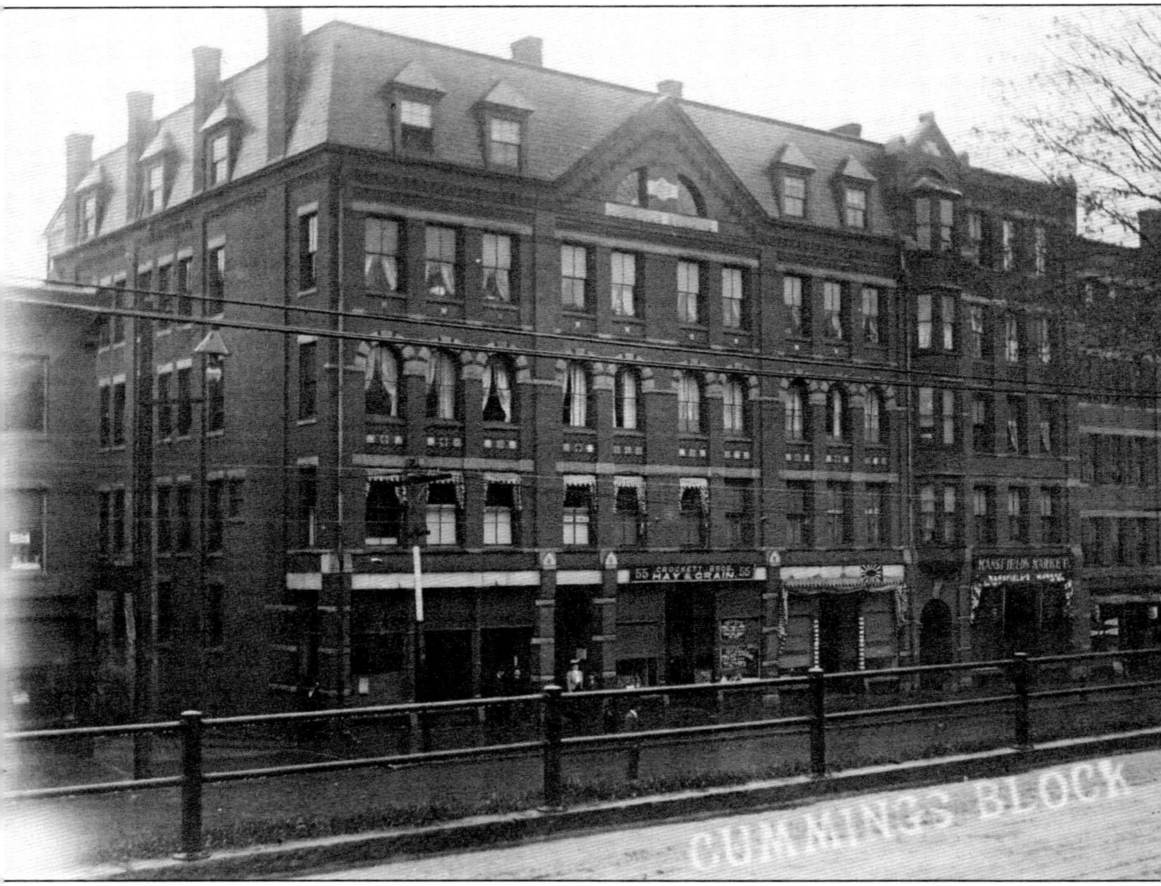

The Cummings Block, located at 53, 55, and 57 Main Street opposite Court House Hill in 1911, housed Station A of the United States Post Office. The upper floors of the building were apartments.

The Graphic Arts Building is located on the corner of Foster and Commercial Streets. It was the first of its kind to be erected in the business district of the city. The building was constructed entirely of reinforced concrete and glass. It was ready for occupancy at the beginning of 1913.

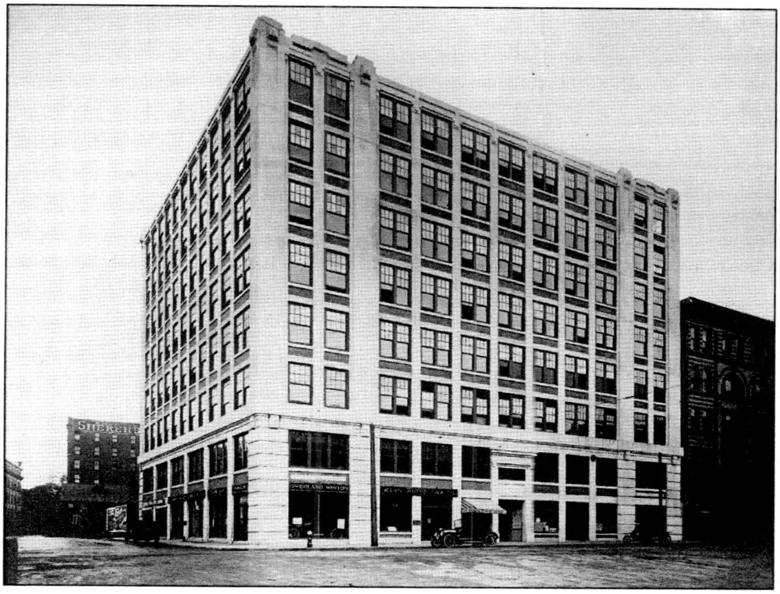

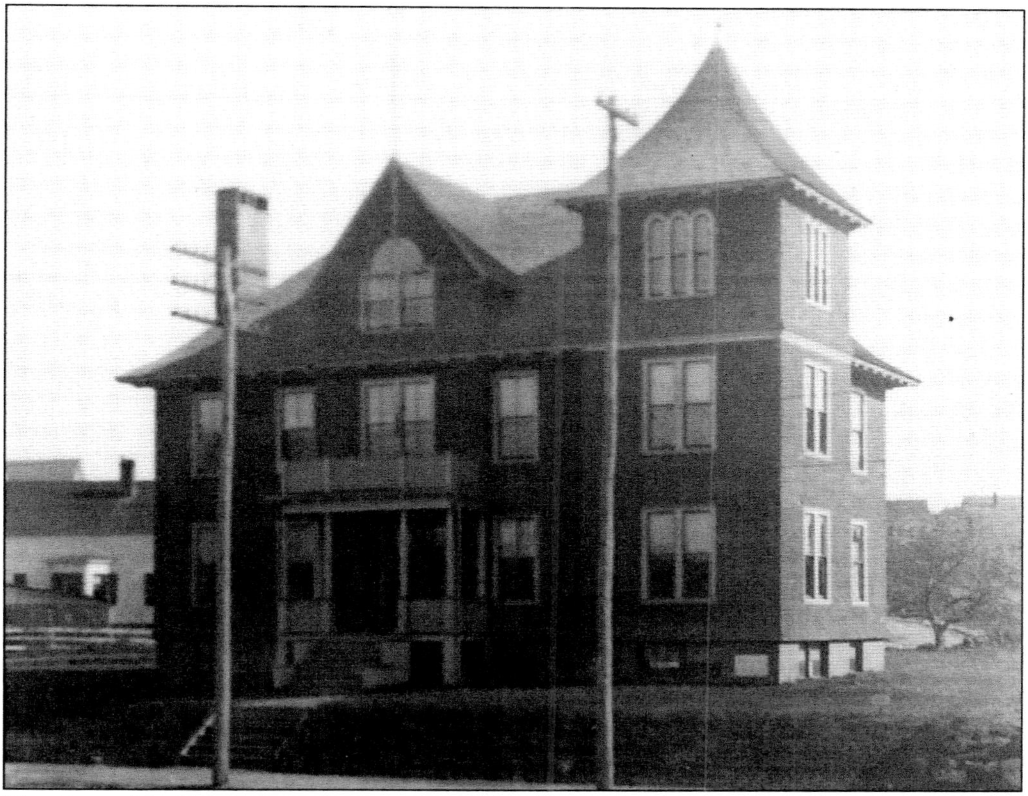

The Greendale Village Improvement Society was located at 480 West Boylston Street on the corner of Brooks Avenue. Its charter was approved by the Massachusetts State Legislature on April 10, 1897. The society was concerned with the general welfare of the citizens of Greendale. It planted trees, collected rubbish, plowed snow, and provided fire protection.

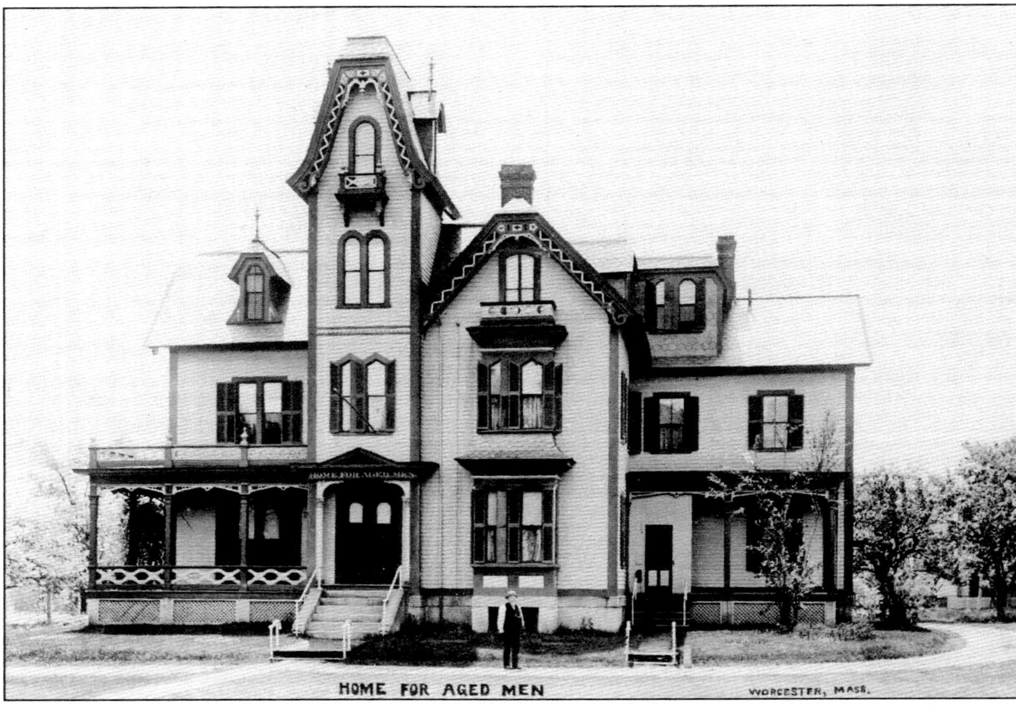

The Home for Aged Men was located at 1199 Main Street in an estate that was donated by Isaac Curtis. It was incorporated in 1874. In November 1891, the home was opened for residents.

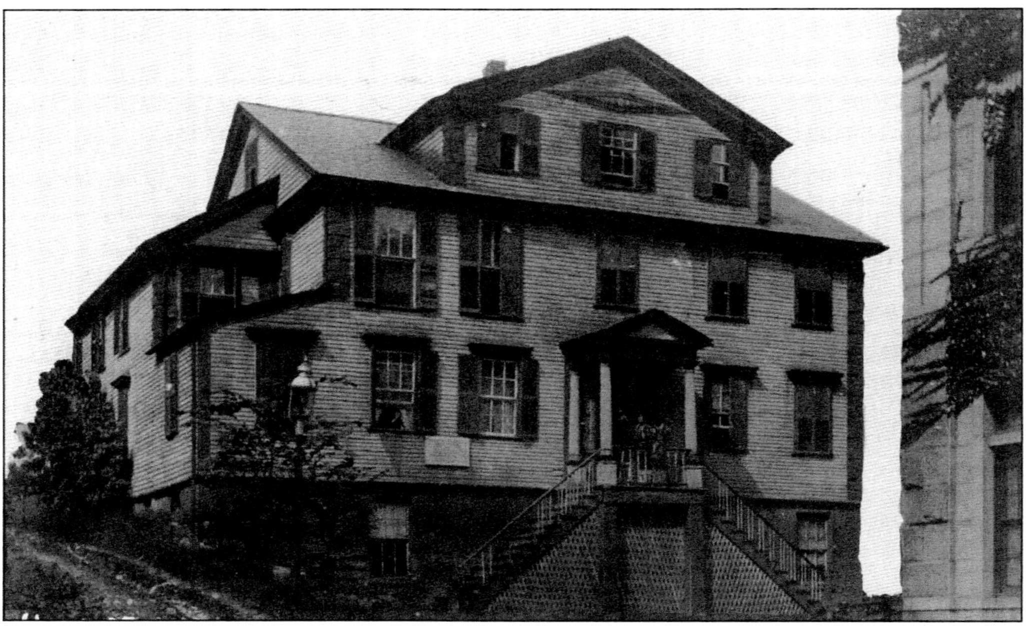

Isaiah Thomas began living in the house in 1775. It was located behind the courthouse near Lincoln Square. He was a printer, publisher, bookseller, and postmaster of Worcester. He published the *Massachusetts Spy*.

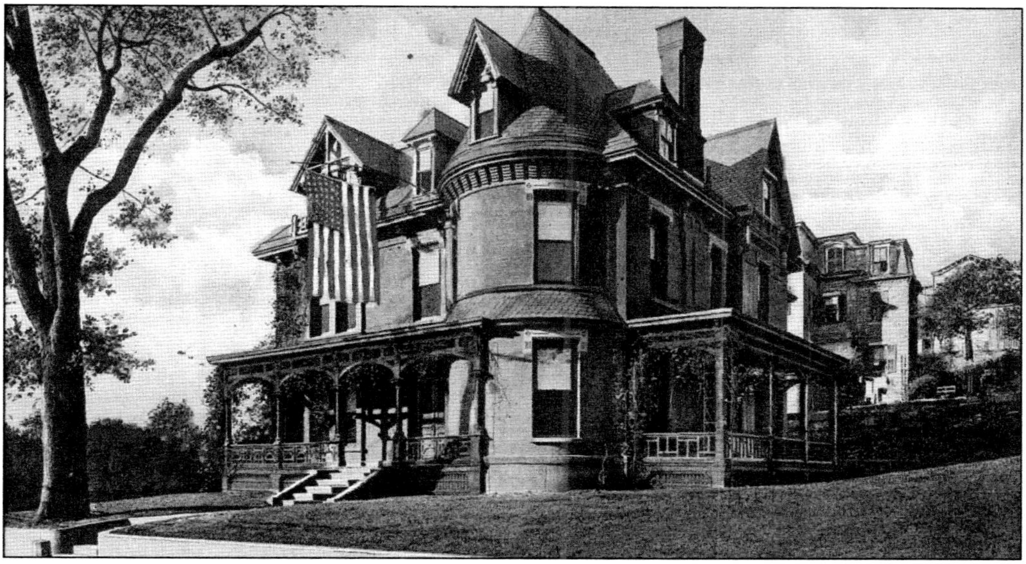

The Knights of Pythias Building was located at 114 Main Street at the end of Court House Hill. It was the former home of Francis H. Dewey, president of the Worcester Consolidated Street Railway Company The Worcester Knights of Pythias Charitable and Educational Association was organized June 30, 1914. On August 13, 1914, they took over the property at 114 Main Street. The three-story building had halls on the second and third floors. The ladies parlor and directors room was on the second floor, and the billiard, card, and reading rooms were on the street floor.

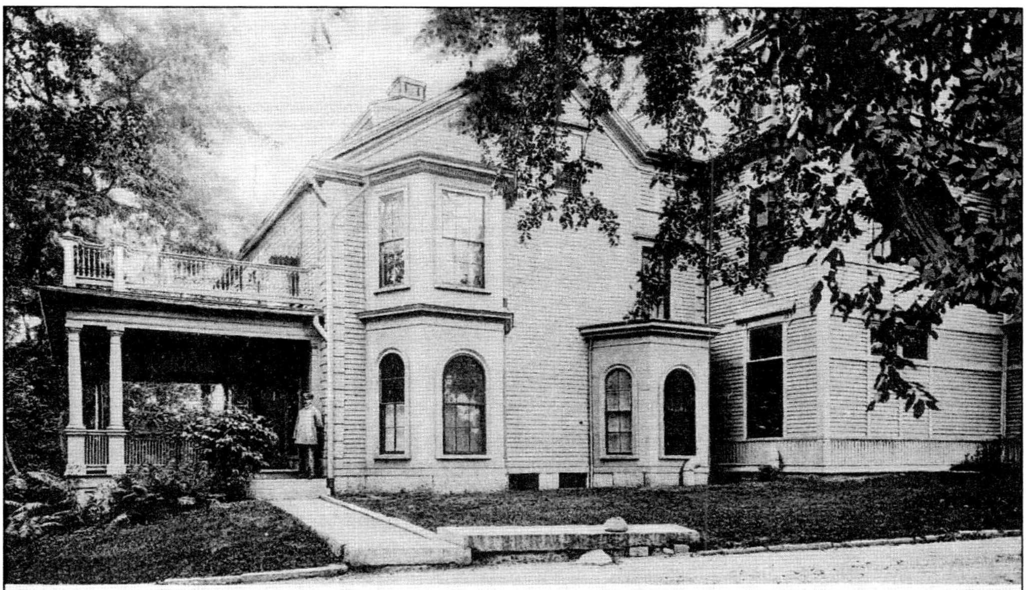

The mansion house at Green Hill Park, *c.* 1915, was rented by the park's commissioners for social occasions. A 1915 report indicated that between October 1914 and March 1915, the mansion was used eighty-one evenings for parties, which were attended by a total of 2,682 people.

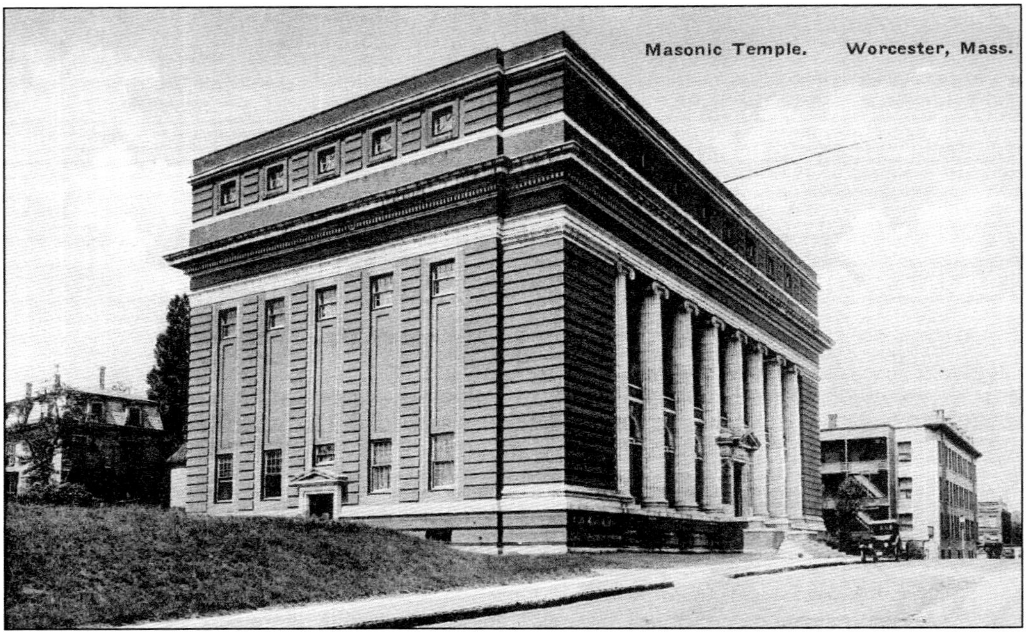

The Masonic Temple located on Mower (Ionic) Avenue between Main and Beacon Streets was dedicated on September 3, 1914. Starting in 1867 the Worcester Masonic Charity and Educational Association had met at the old Post Office Building on Pearl Street. In 1914 the association was composed of 33 members, consisting of 3 representatives from each of the 11 Masonic bodies of Worcester.

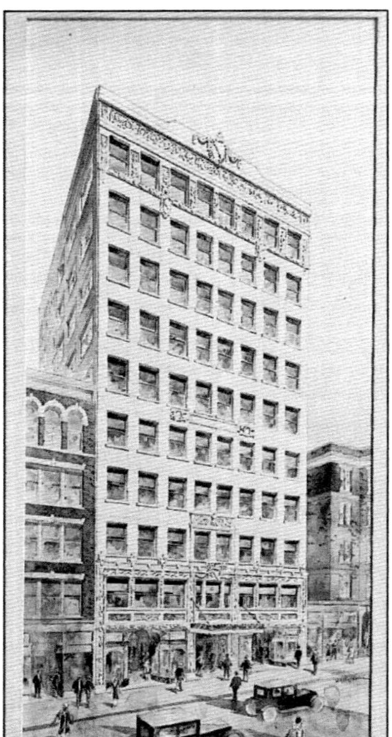

The Hotel Borden was torn down to make way for the construction of the Medical Arts Building at 36 Pleasant Street. The building was completed about 1925. As the name implies, floors two through ten of the building contained physician's offices. A pharmacy occupied the first floor.

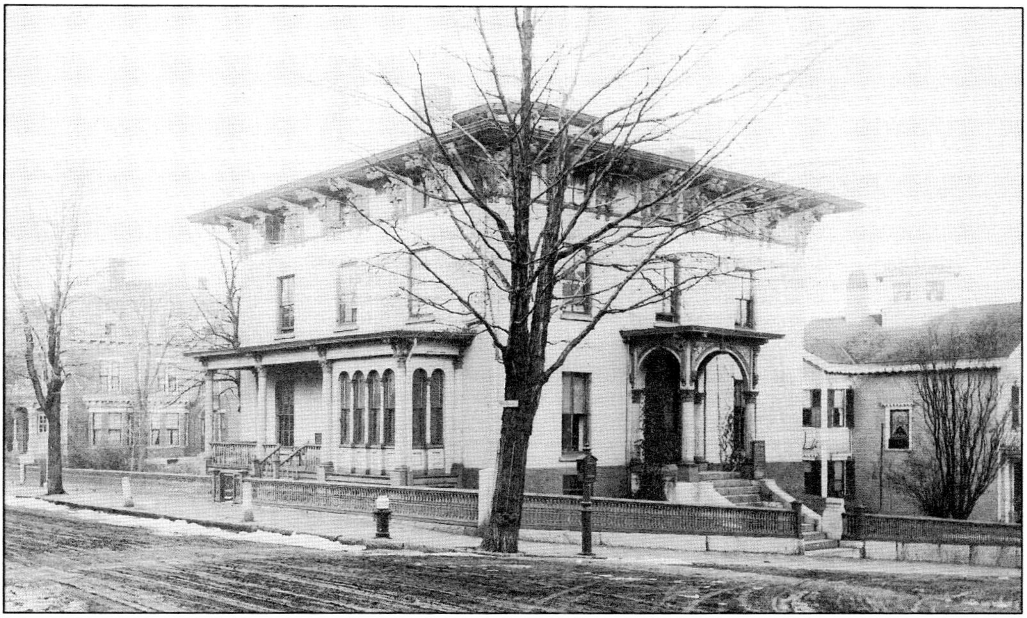

The building of the Worcester National History Society at 12 State Street was a bequest from the estate of the late Edward Conant in 1891. The object of the society is to instill a love of natural history in the minds of Worcester's youth.

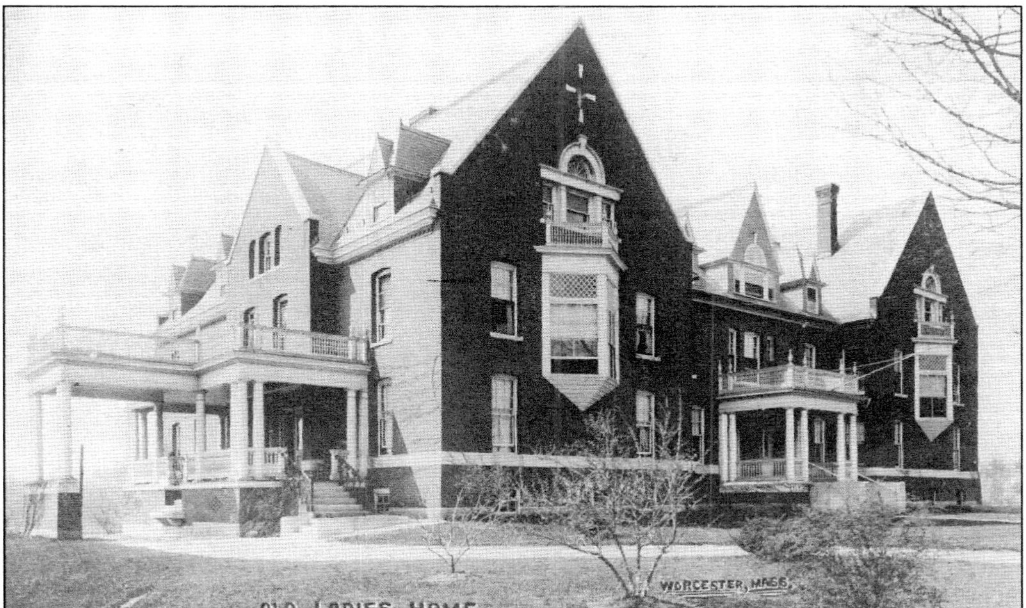

The Home for Aged Women was founded by Ichabod Washburn, a prominent manufacturer and philanthropist. He left a substantial portion of his estate toward its endowment. The home pictured here at 1183 Main Street was occupied on May 21, 1896.

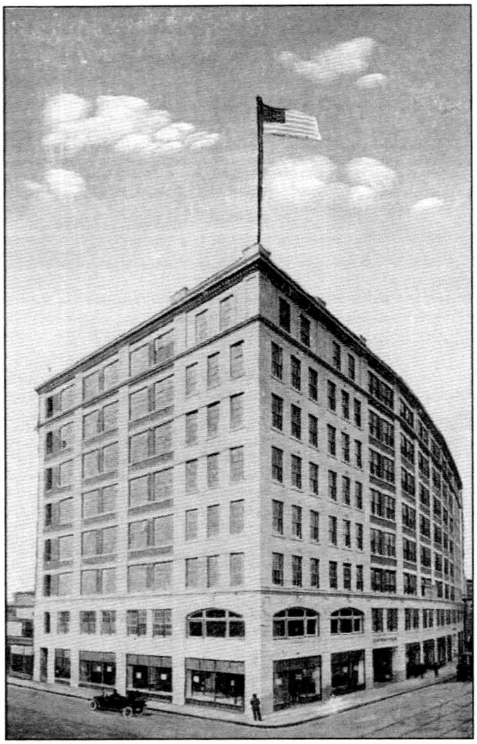

The Osgood Bradley Building is located at the corner of Grafton and Franklin Streets. The building was constructed in 1916. The site is that of the old Bradley Car Works. The structure is eight stories high. A siding from the Boston and Albany Railroad, permanently erected in concrete, runs directly into the property at the third-floor level.

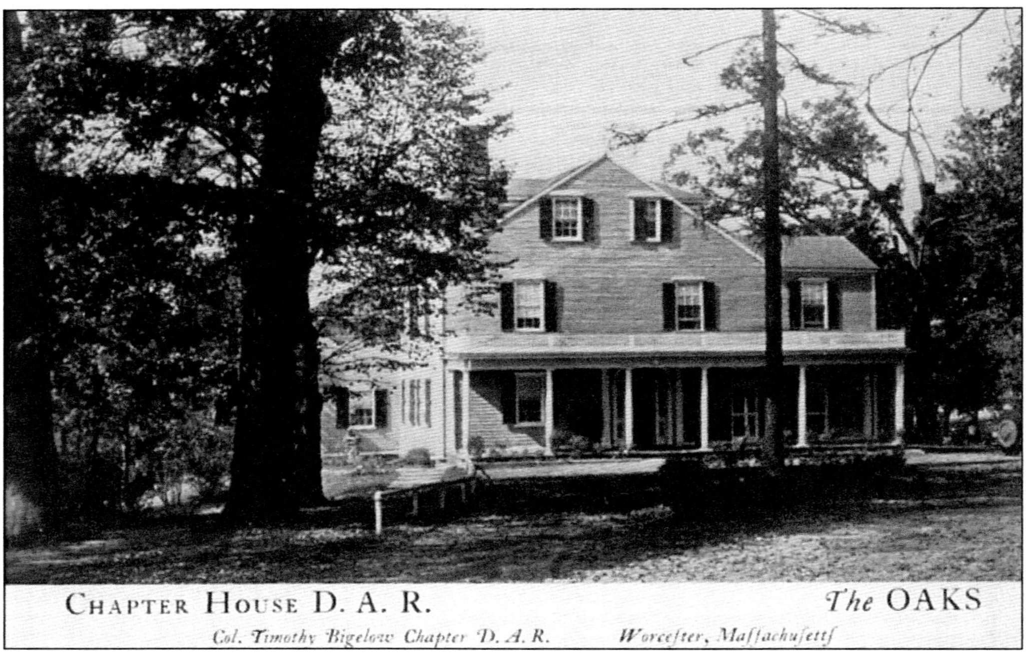

The Timothy Paine House is located at 140 Lincoln Street. The house, known as The Oaks, was built by Tory Judge Timothy Paine prior to the Revolutionary War. It was owned by the Paine family until 1914, when it was sold to the Daughters of the American Revolution.

The Odd Fellows Building at 674 Main Street was dedicated on November 8, 1906. The building was arranged with various lodge rooms, anterooms, and large halls—all for the use of the city's Odd Fellows.

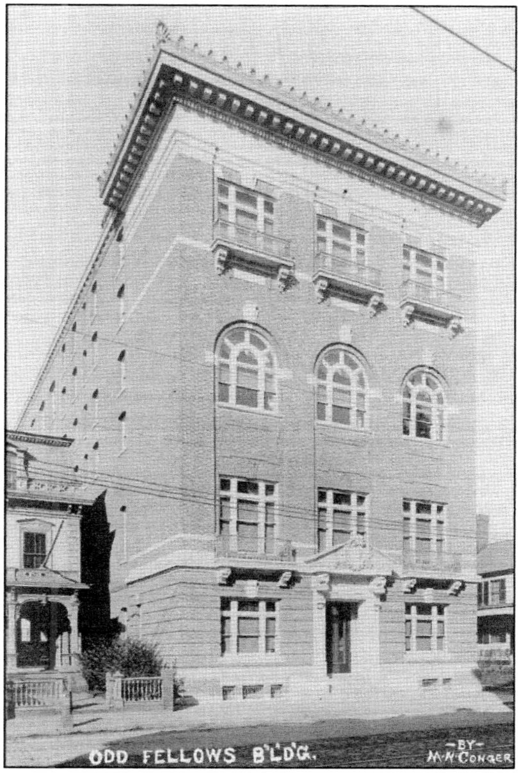

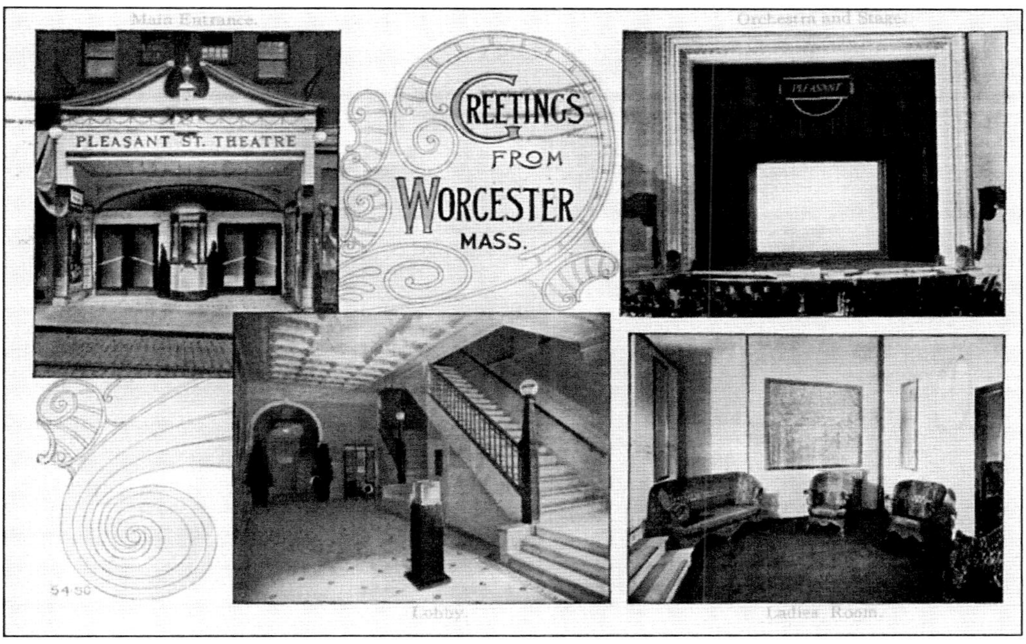

Lynch's Pleasant Street Theater is located at 17 Pleasant Street. Shown here are the main entrance, orchestra and stage, lobby, and ladies' room. When built in 1890, the theater was known as Lothrop's Opera House.

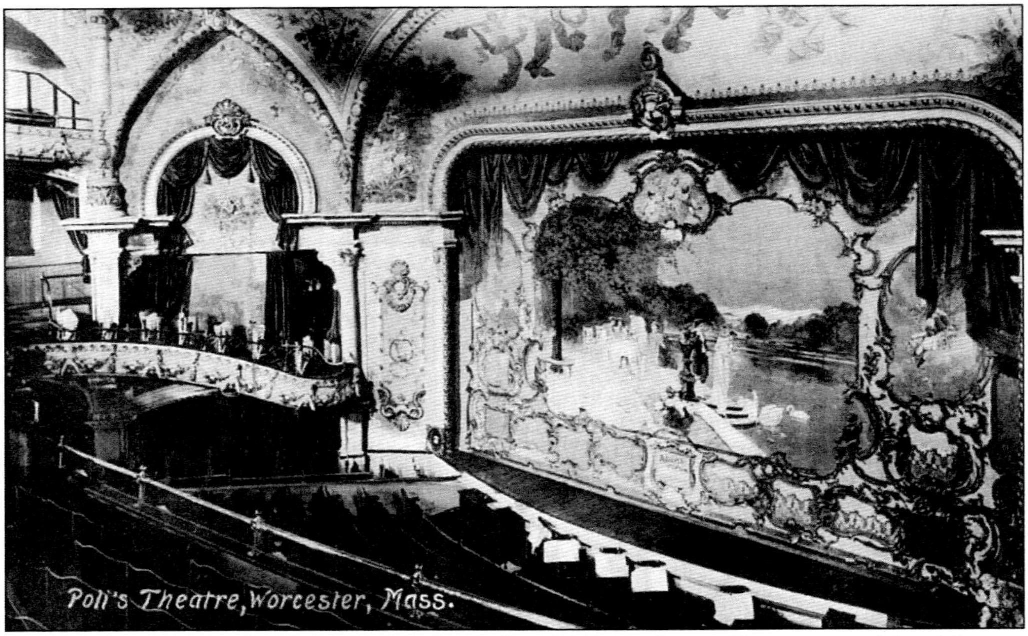

Here is the interior of Poli's Theater, located at 28 Front Street. It was owned by Sylvester Z. Poli, who owned a similar theater in Springfield, Massachusetts. Poli later owned the Elm Street Poli Theater and the Franklin Square Theater. The theaters were sometimes used by stock companies, sometimes as vaudeville houses, and sometimes for motion pictures.

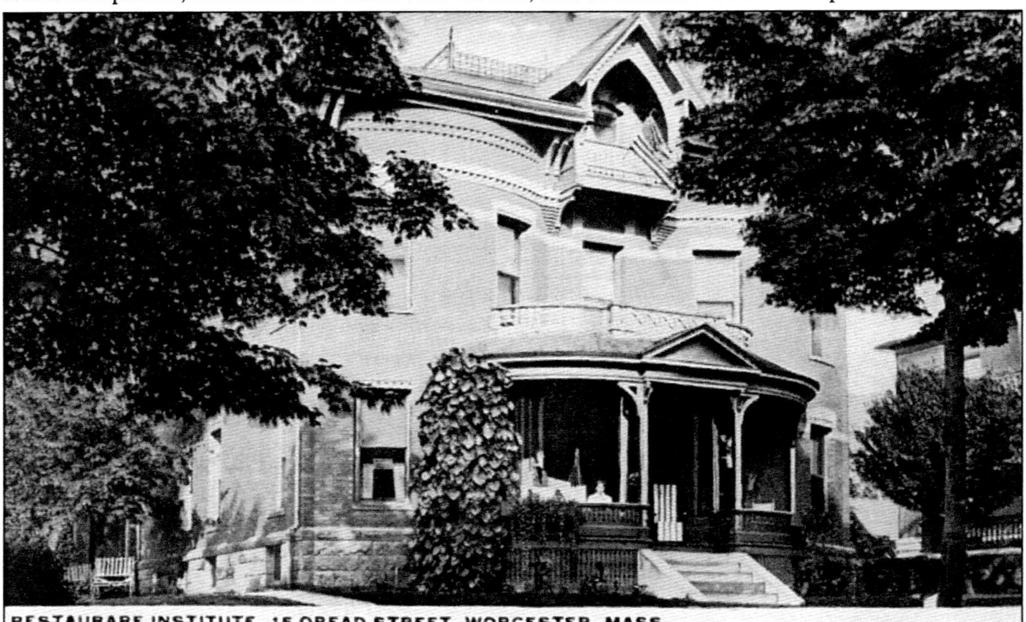

RESTAURARE INSTITUTE, 15 OREAD STREET, WORCESTER, MASS.

The Restaurare Institute was located at 15 Oread Street *c.* 1916. It lead the world in the treatment of alcoholism and drug diseases. Alcoholics were sobered in 30 minutes, their craving destroyed instantly without sickness. The institute was operated by physicians J.H. and E.B. Brownell.

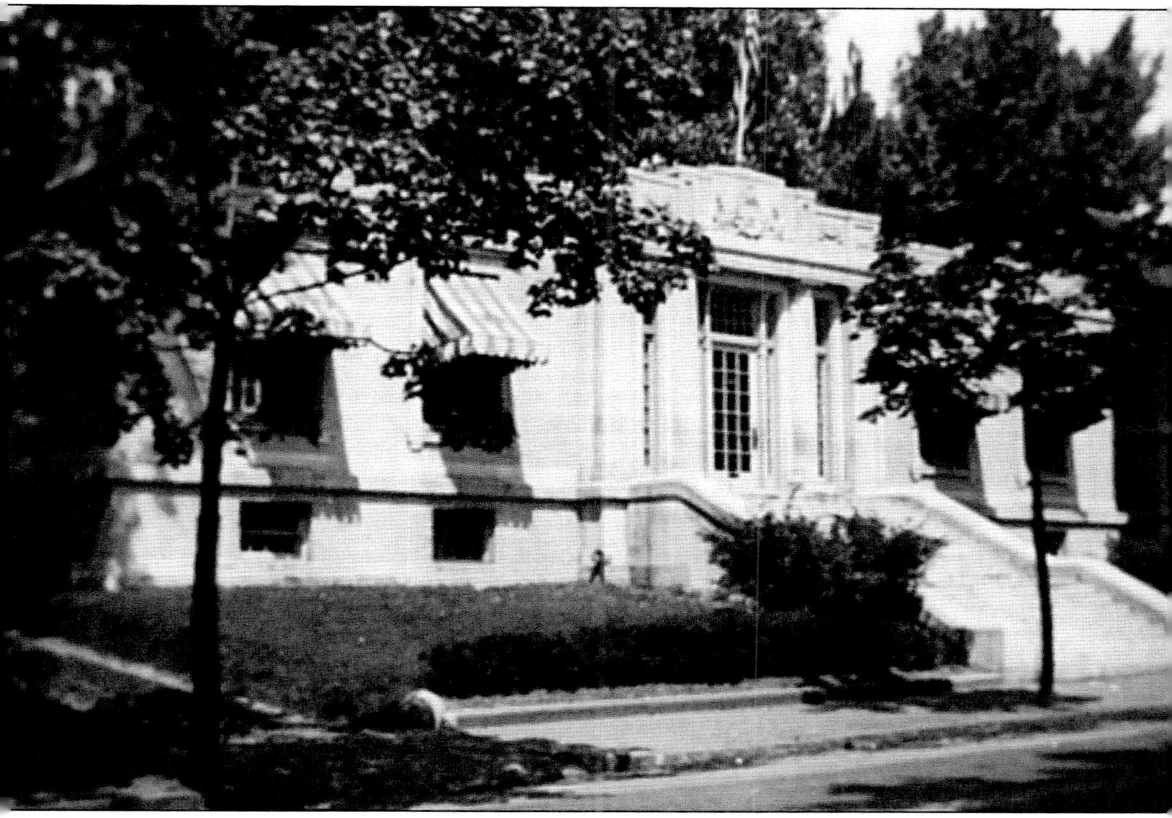

Shown here is the South Worcester Branch Library. Samuel S. Green, after 38 years as the city's head librarian, resigned in 1909. The opening of branch libraries had been suggested by him in the past. Ex-Mayor James Logan was responsible for securing a gift of $75,000 from Andrew Carnegie to build three such branch libraries. Three cornerstones were laid on March 27, 1913—one at Greendale, one at Quinsigamond, and one at South Worcester. The libraries were opened in February 1914.

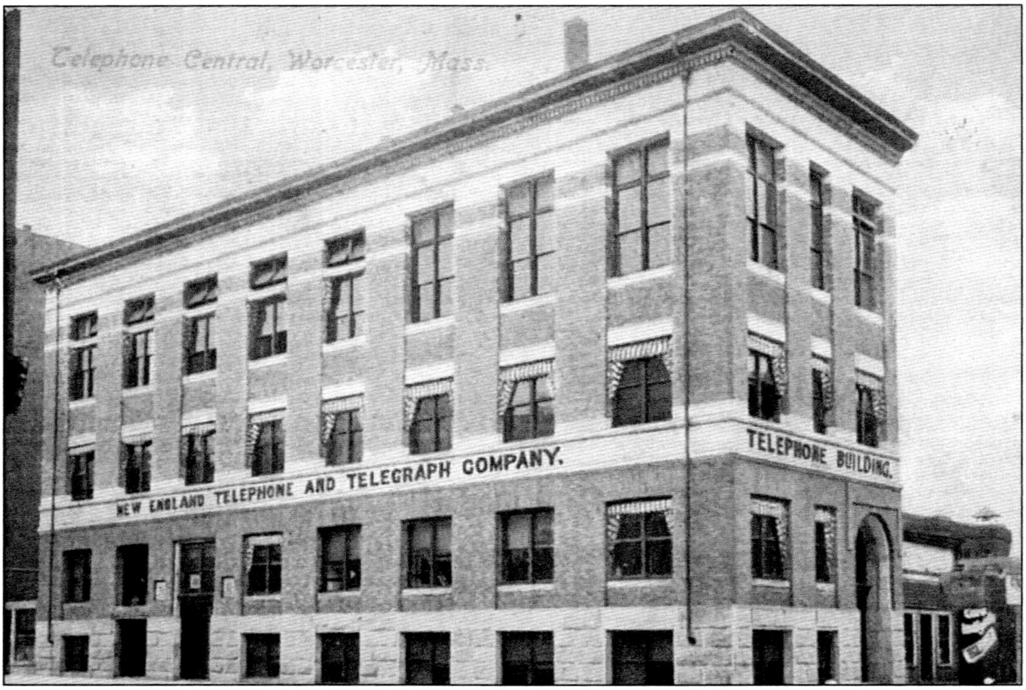

The exchange of the New England Telephone Company was located on the corner of Mechanic and Norwich Streets. The telephone company moved into the building on June 20, 1896. At that time there were 1,376 subscribers; in 1906 there were 9,289; and in 1914 there were 15,000.

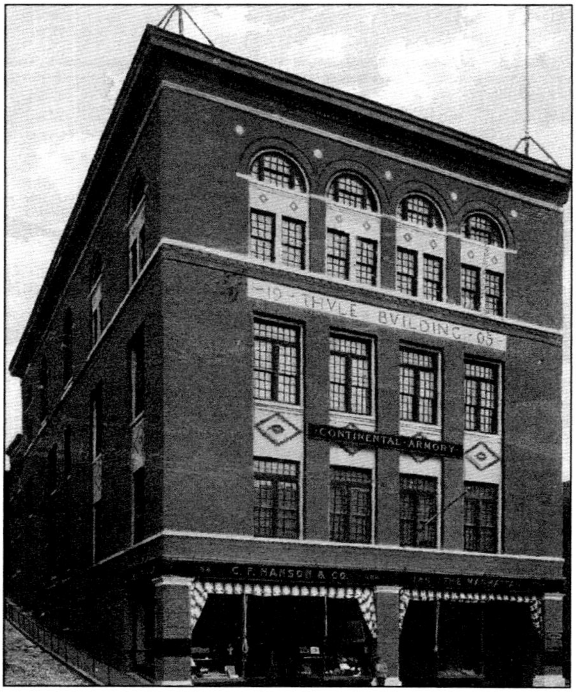

Located at 184 Main Street at the corner of George Street is the Thule Music Hall Association Building. It was erected in 1905 by the Swedish citizens of the city and contained the Thule, Svea, and Continental Halls—the finest of their kind for lodges, concerts, balls, fairs, and banquets.

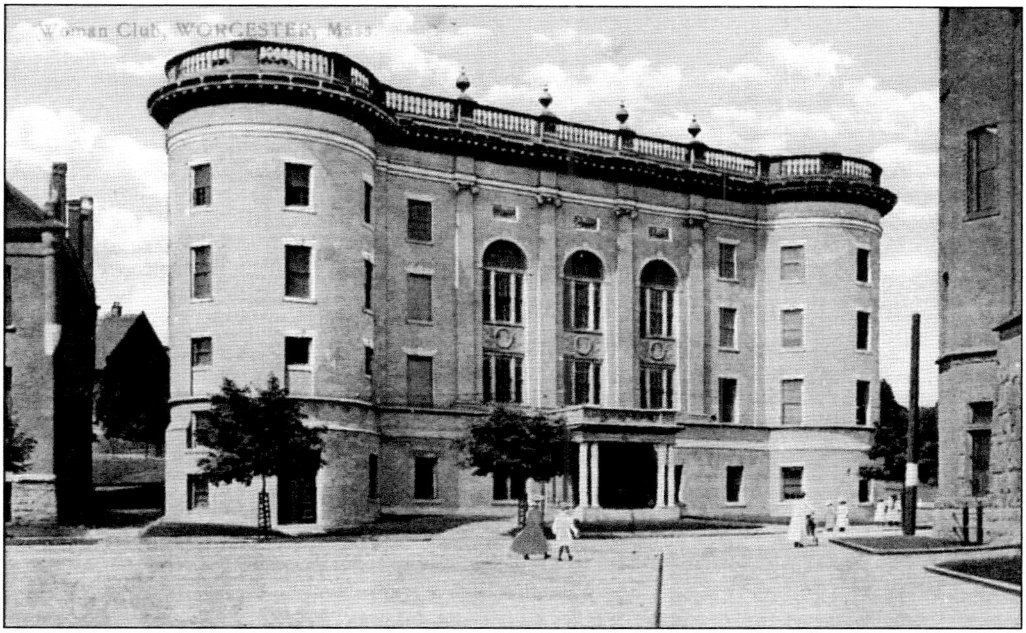

The Woman's Club Building is located on the corner of Salisbury and Tuckerman Streets. The club was the most exclusive women's organization in the city. It was organized in December 1880.

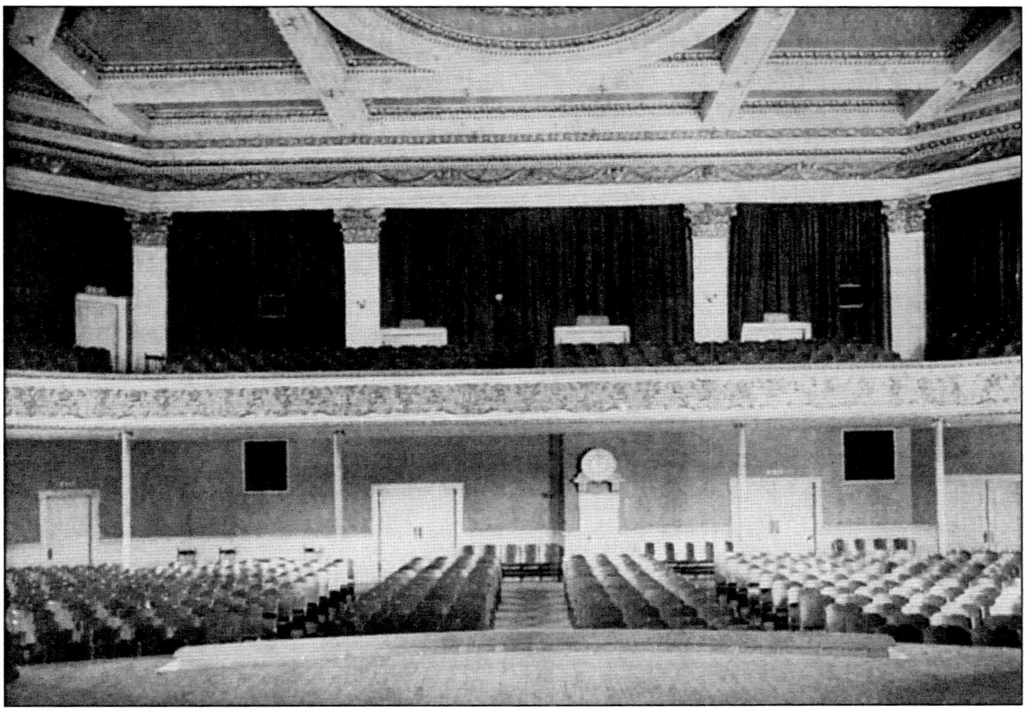

Tuckerman Hall is located in the Woman Club's Building. The building was constructed c. 1902 on land given to the club by Stephen Salisbury.

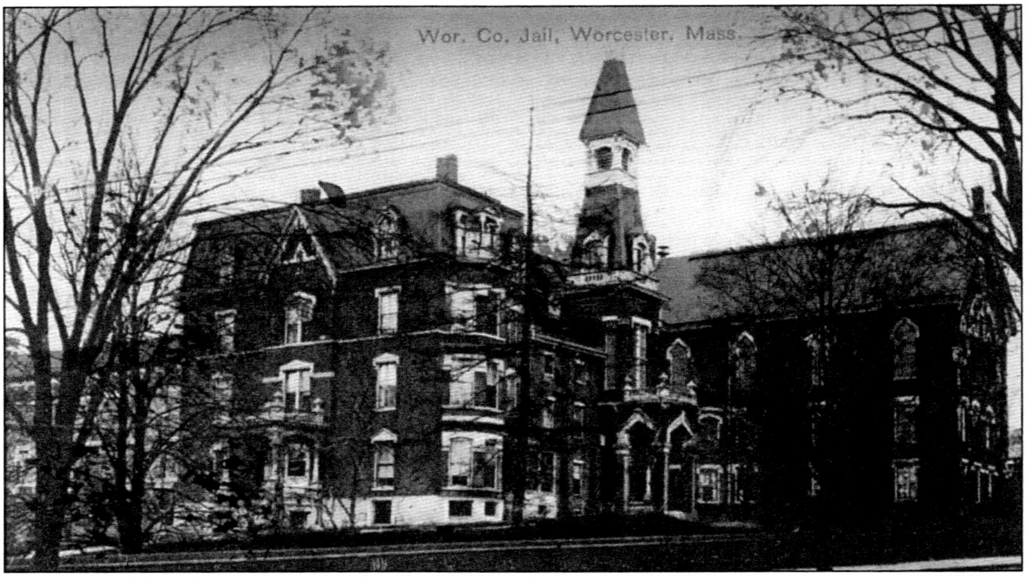

The Worcester County Jail was located on Summer Street. The first County House of Correction was erected in 1819. In 1832 40 cells were installed. In 1873 the building was completely renovated. It was relocated in the 1960s to Boylston to make way for a new post office.

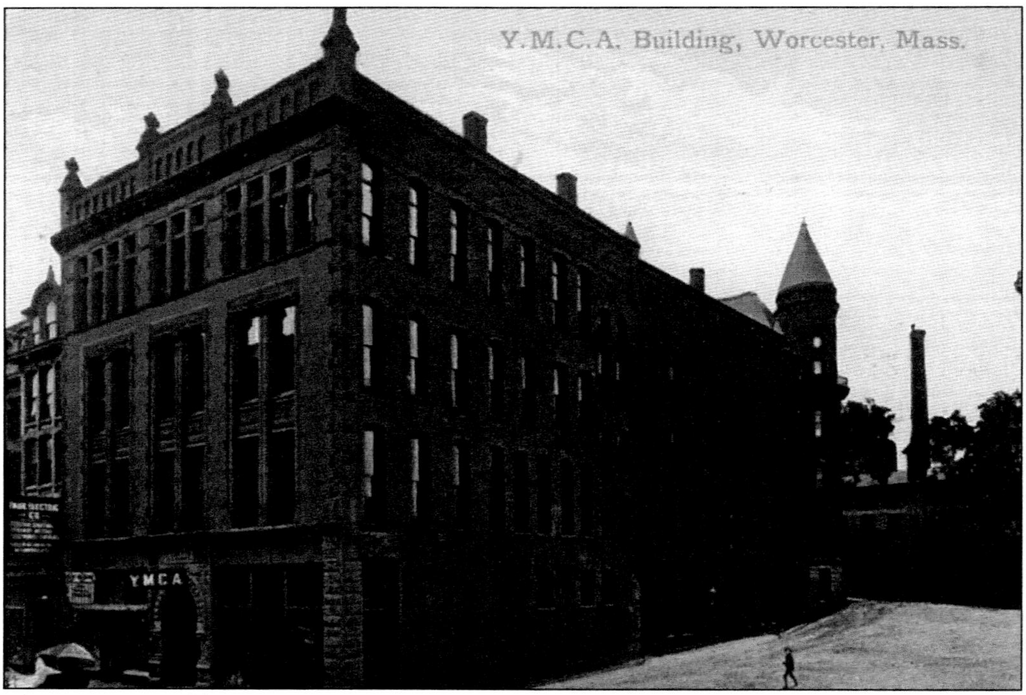

The YMCA Building, located at 10 Elm Street, extended the entire block with a second entrance on Pearl Street. Constructed in 1887, it contained one of the finest gymnasiums in the country. The building was 154 feet long, 58 feet at its widest point, and cost $150,000 to complete and furnish.

Six

Religion

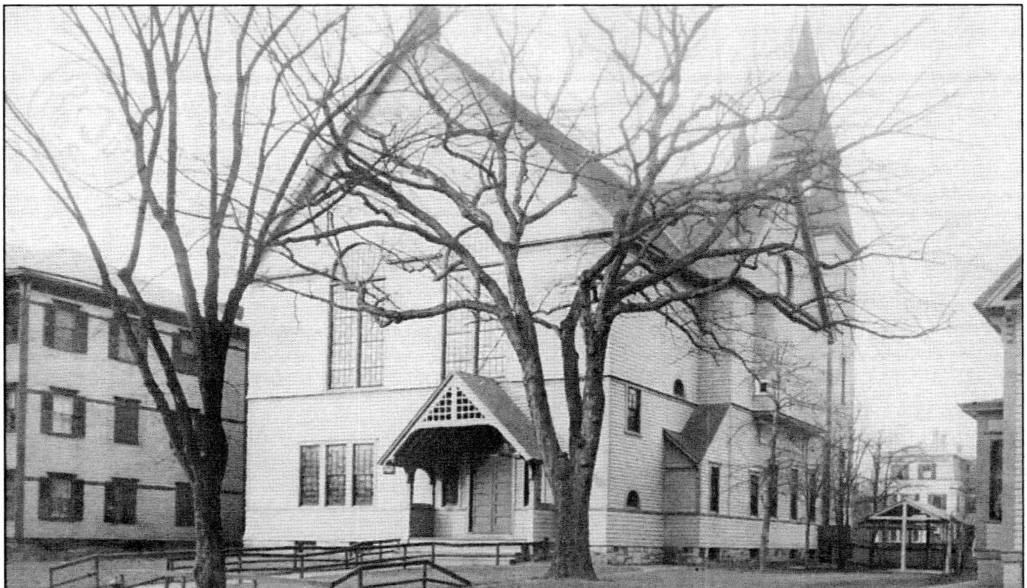

The Dewey Street Baptist Church, pictured here *c.* 1910, was located at 305 Park Avenue. The church was founded in 1872 in a chapel that was built on Dewey Street. The new meetinghouse on Park Avenue was first used for services on Thanksgiving Day in 1886.

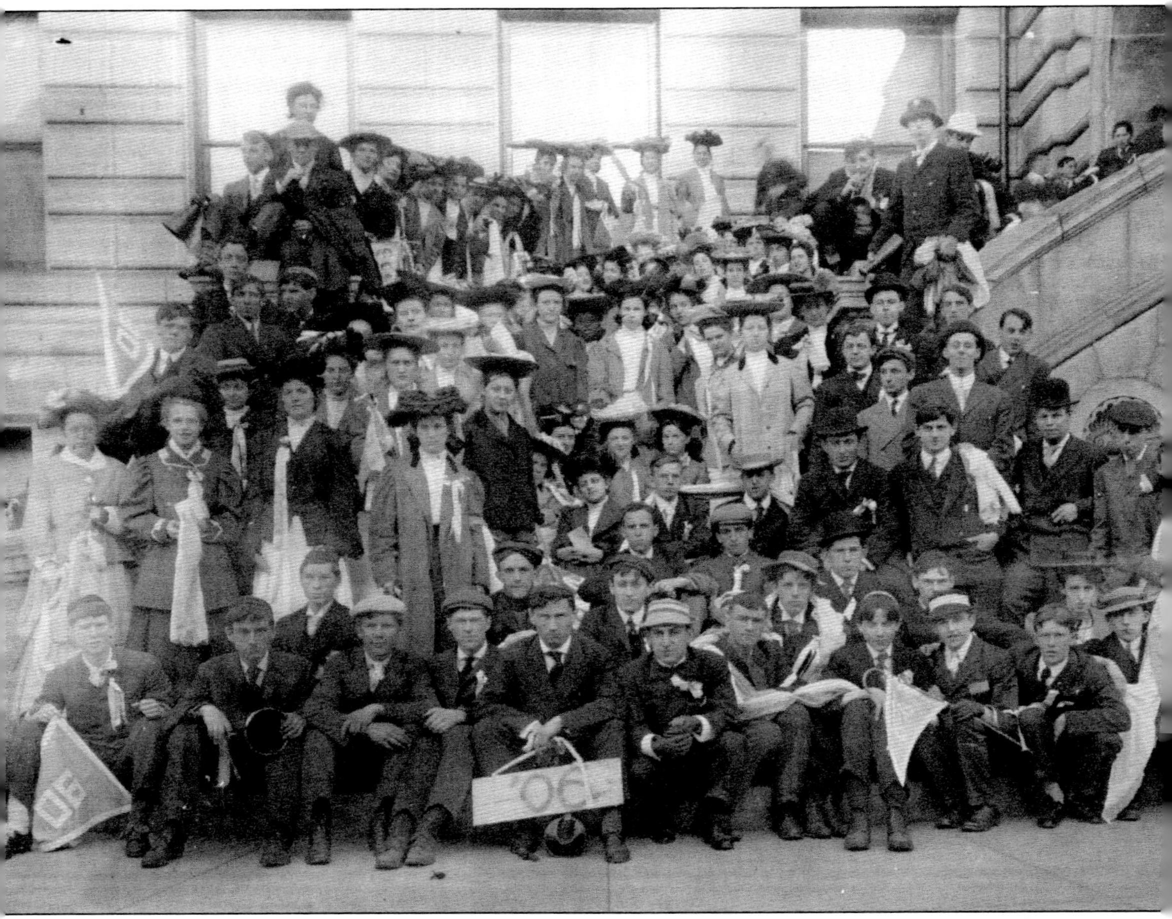

The Massachusetts Christian Endeavor Union held its 1906 convention from October 25–28. Conventionaires posed on the steps of city hall for this picture. The First Baptist Church was the headquarters for the convention. The Young People's Society of Christian Endeavor was founded February 2, 1881. It is nonsectarian, but confined chiefly to the Congregational, Baptist, and other Protestant churches.

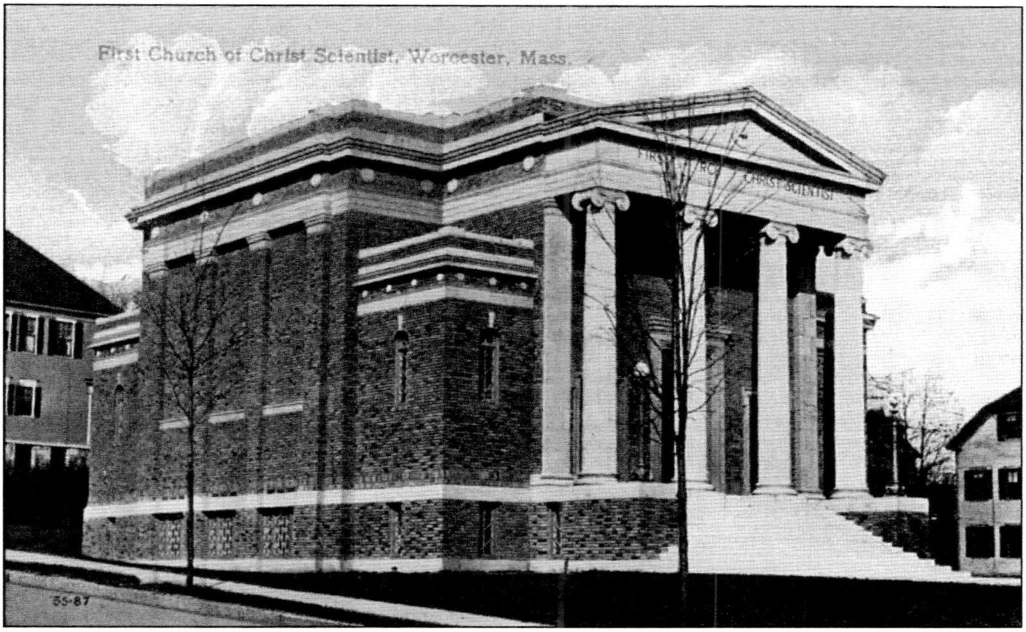

The First Church of Christ Scientist held its city meetings at the Woman's Club until 1913. The building shown here on Main Street, near Oberlin Street, was opened in 1913.

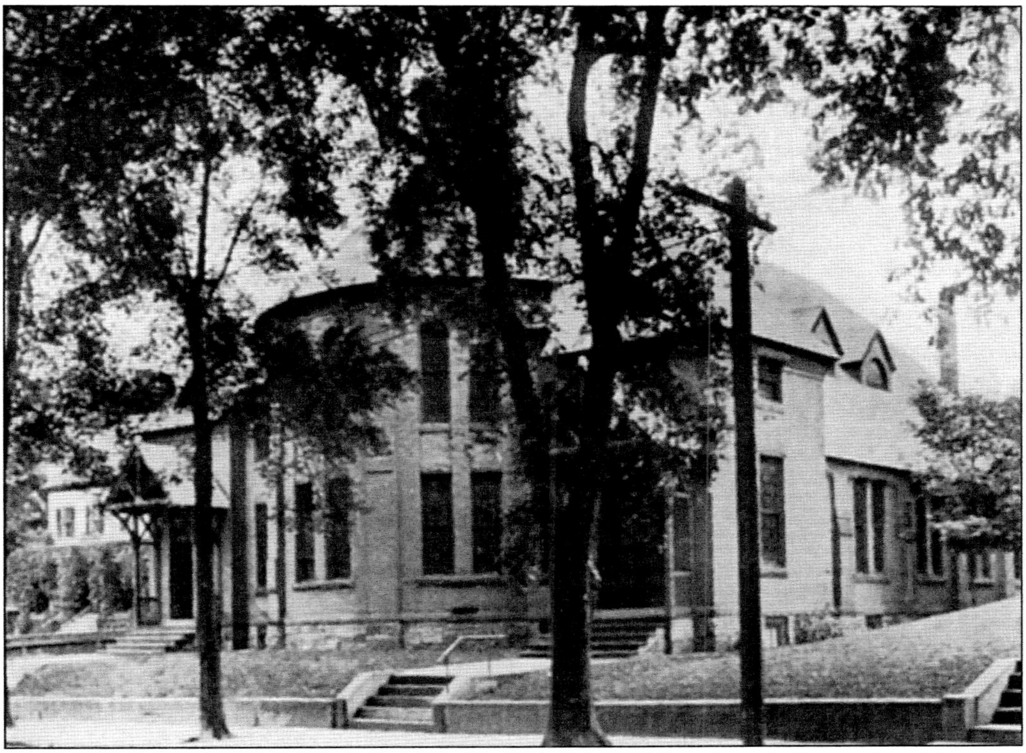
The First Church of Christ Disciples was founded in 1860. This church, located on 829 Main Street at the corner of Benefit Street, was dedicated on September 12, 1886.

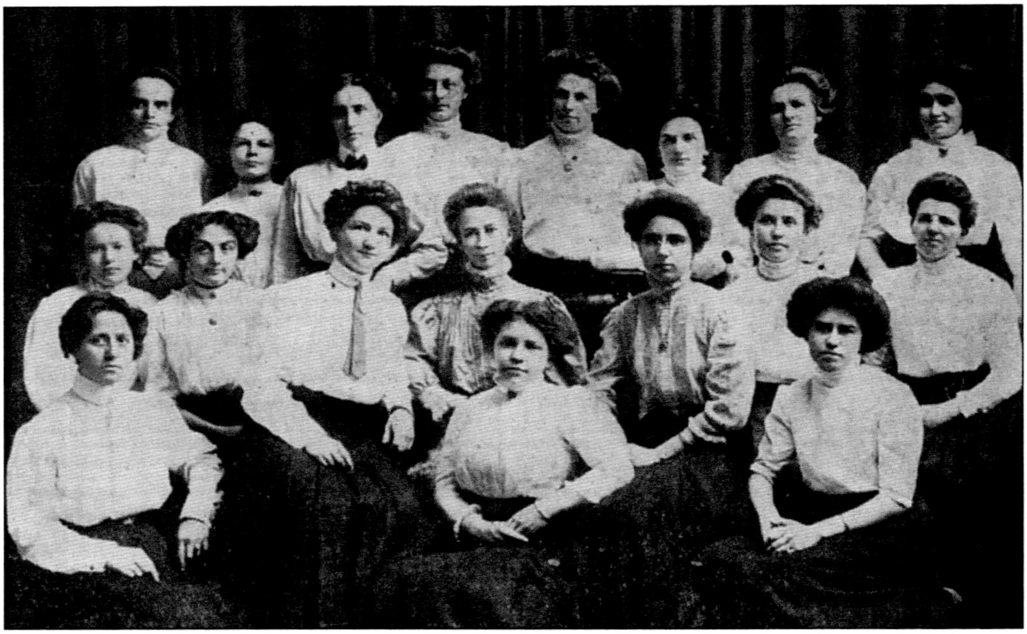

The Inasmuch Club of the Highland Street Church of Christ was organized on September 22, 1908. The work of the club was to help the church, aid the needy, and to look after sick people and shut-ins.

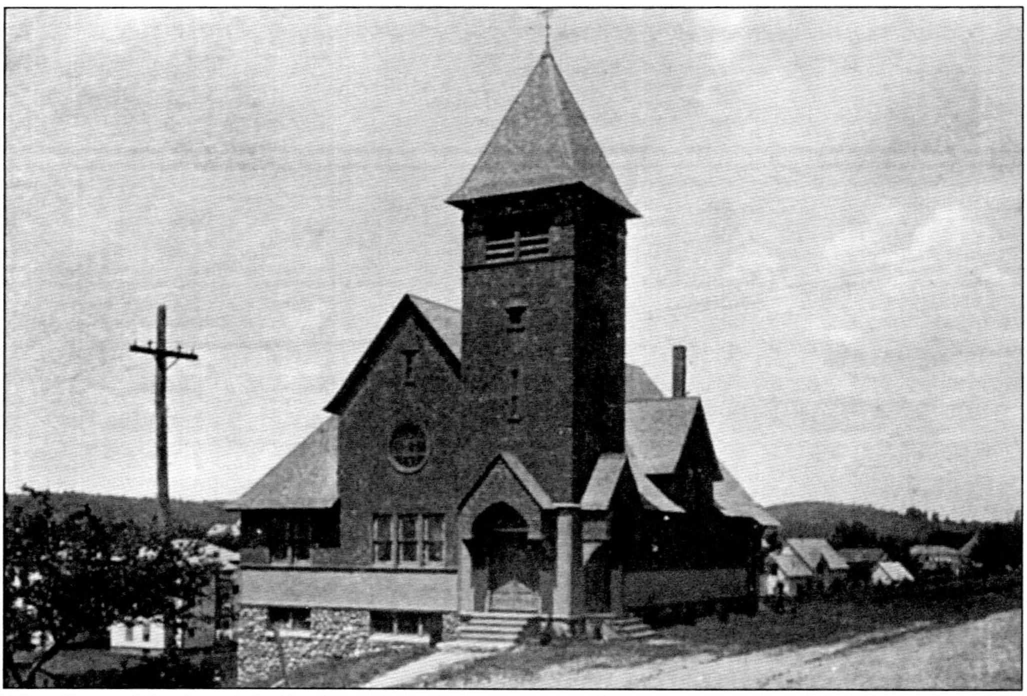

The Greendale People's (Independent Congregational) Church, pictured here in Greendale c. 1910, was founded in 1895. Its actual location was on Francis Street at the corner of Bradley Avenue.

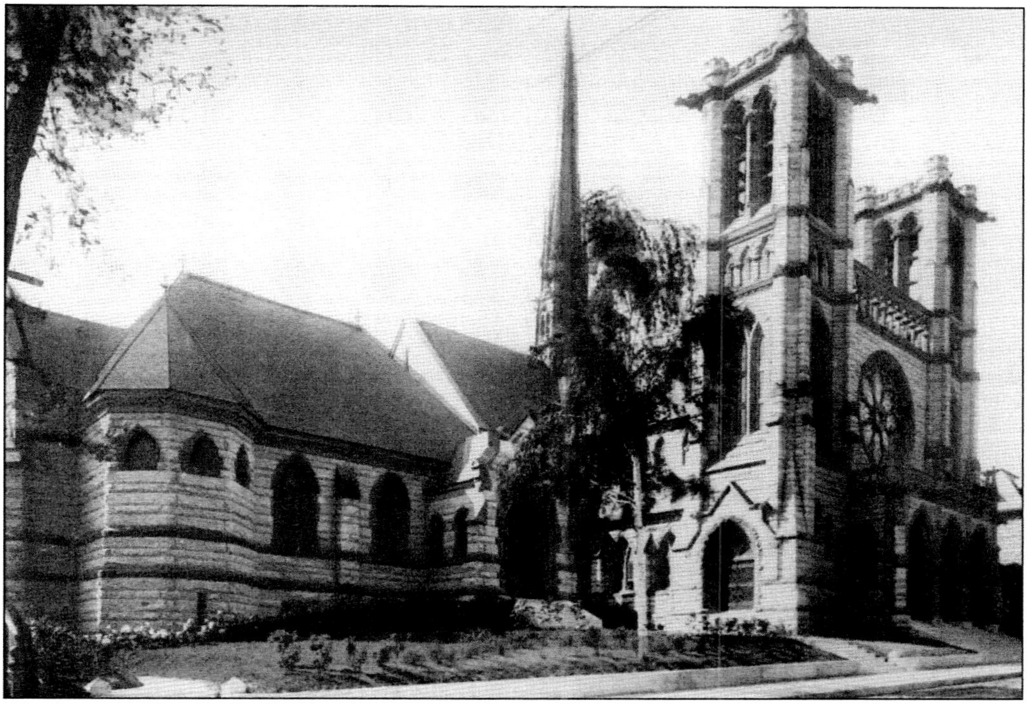

The Union Church, located on Chestnut Street opposite Pearl Street, was founded in 1836. This church was constructed by the Webb Granite and Construction Company of Worcester in 1898. A popular fair called "The Marketplace" was held by the Woman's Association of the Church in 1910.

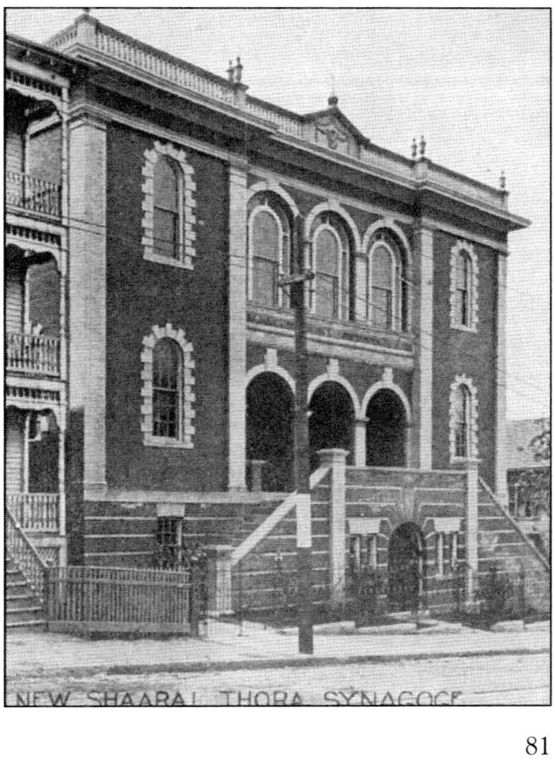

The Shaarai Torah Synagogue is located on 32 Providence Street. The congregation was established in 1904 and the synagogue was built in 1906. The cornerstone was laid on April 29, 1906. Mayor John T. Duggan and Congressman Rockwood Hoar were among the speakers at the ceremony.

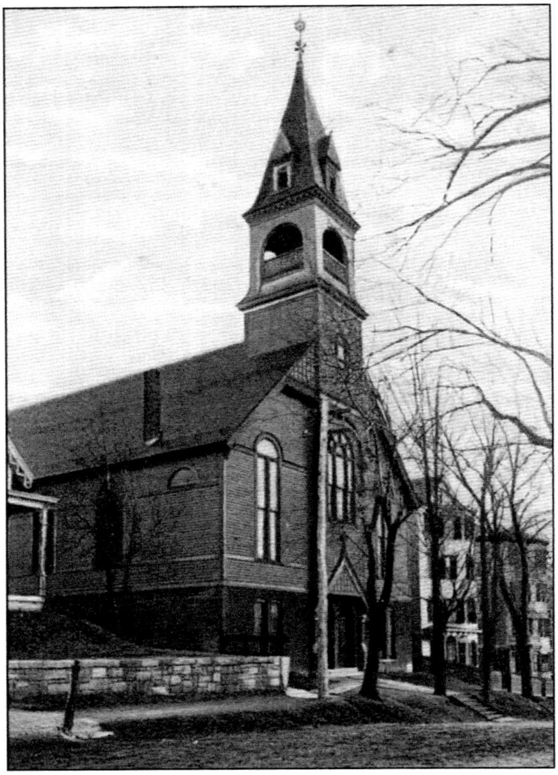

The Swedish Evangelical Lutheran Gethsemane Church, shown here c. 1906, was located on Mulberry Street near Prospect Street. Incorporated in 1881, it was known as the First Lutheran Church. In 1911 the congregation moved to a new church at Belmont and Orchard Streets.

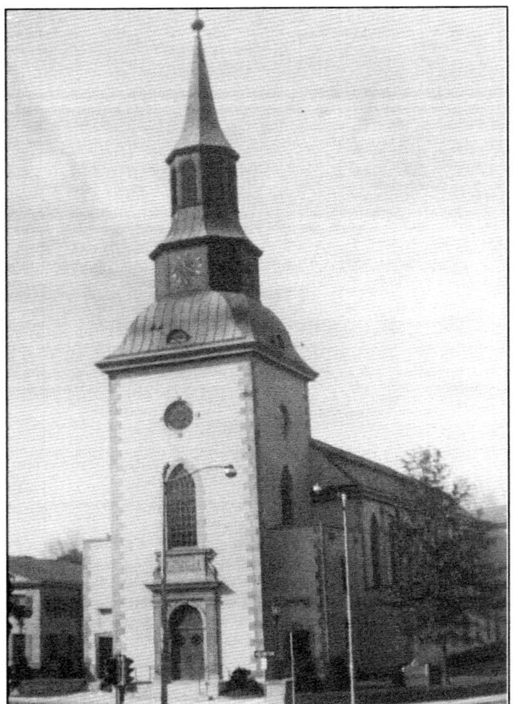

The Trinity Evangelical Lutheran Church was built at the corner of Lancaster and Salisbury Streets in 1952. Three Lutheran parishes were consolidated. They were the Swedish Evangelical Lutheran Gethsemane Church, the Swedish Finnish Evangelical Lutheran Church, and the Calvary Lutheran Church.

The Trinity Methodist Episcopal Church was located on the corner of Chandler and Main Streets. It was the successor to the first Methodist church in the city. The church building was constructed in 1871 and could probably seat more worshippers than any other Protestant church in the city. It was torn down in 1929 to make way for the widening of Chandler Street.

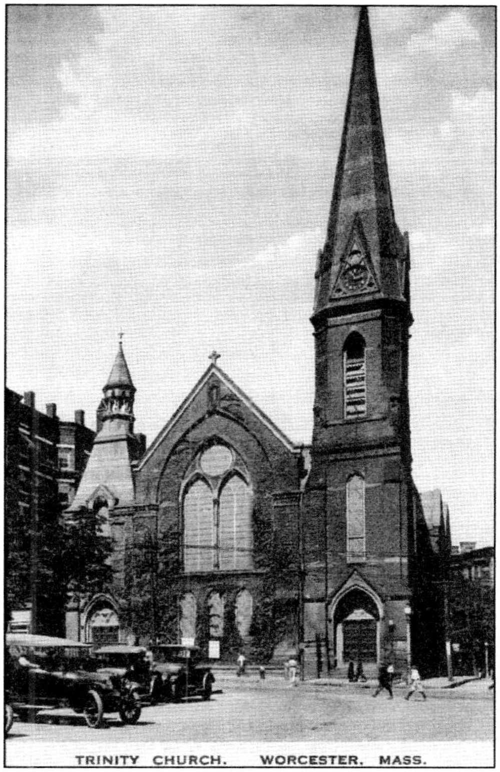

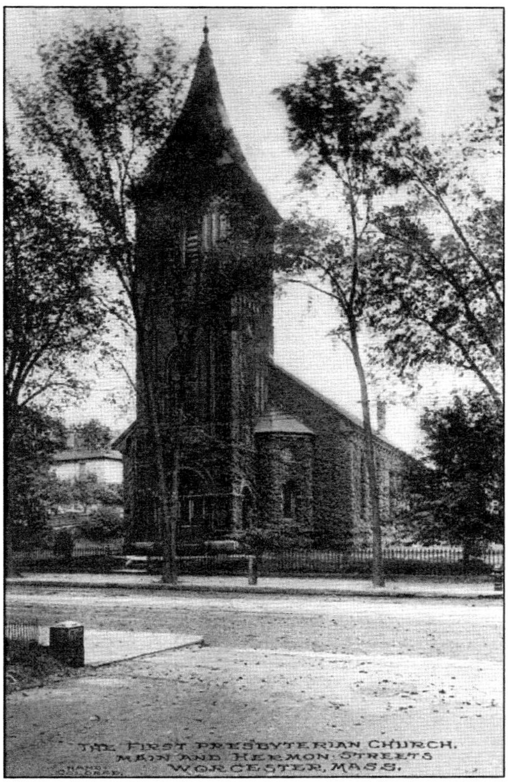

The First Presbyterian Church, located on the corner of Main and Hermon Streets, pictured here c. 191C, was founded in 1886. Its present location was formerly occupied by the Main Street Baptist Church.

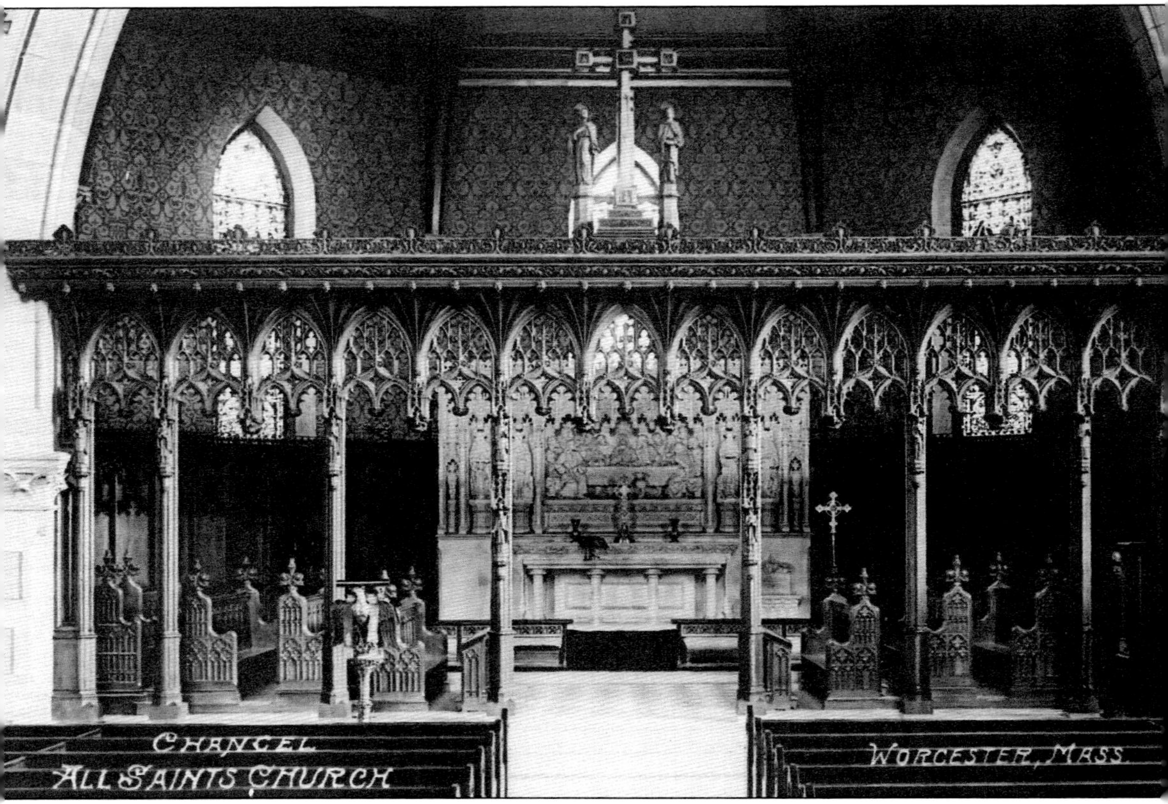

This is the Chancel of the All Saints Church. The church, located on the corner of Pleasant and Irving Streets, was dedicated in 1877. It was built using Longmeadow Brownstone. Both the church and its chapel contain organs.

St. John's Church, originally called Christ's Church, is located on Temple Street. It was the first Catholic church in central or western Massachusetts, and is the mother parish of two dioceses: Springfield and Worcester. This church was constructed in 1845.

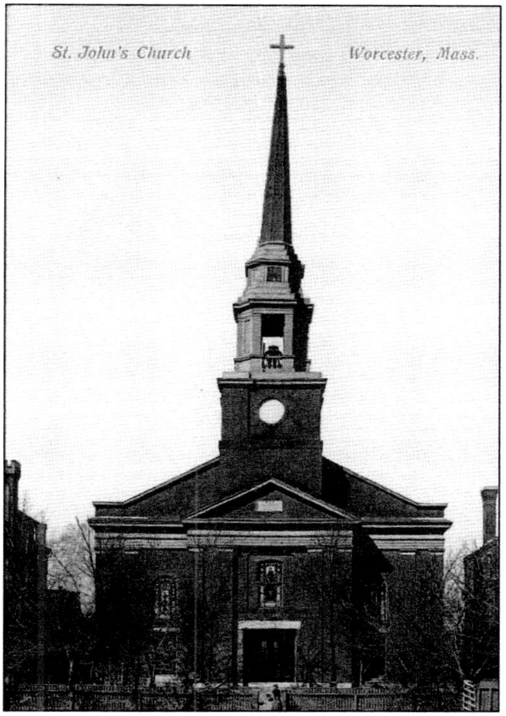

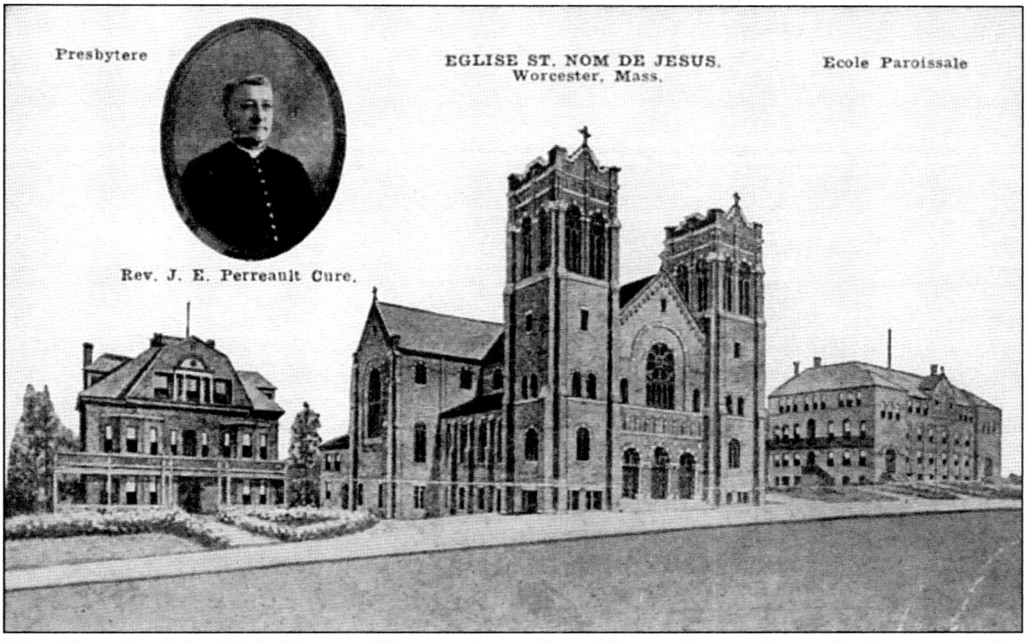

The Church of the Holy Name of Jesus is located on Illinois Street. It was built to serve the French Roman Catholics in the southern part of the city. Work on the church began in 1895 when a basement place of worship was built, and the church was occupied in 1896. Work on the church continued in stages until it was dedicated on December 24, 1916. The rectory was built in 1896 and the parish school in 1898.

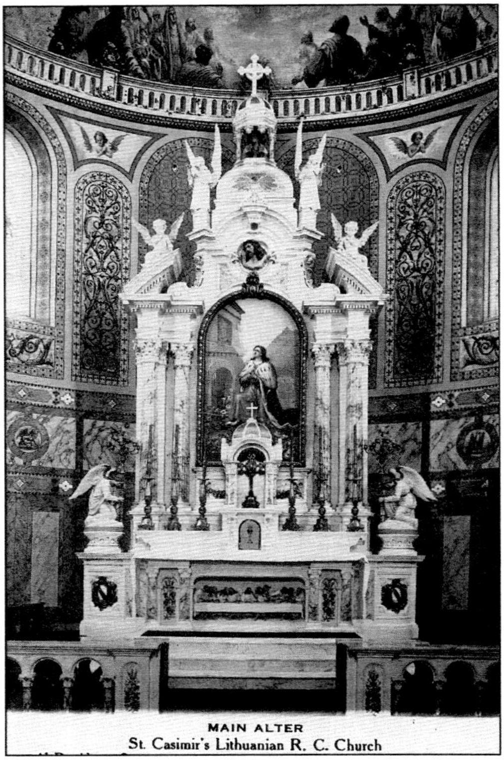

This is the main altar of St. Casimer's Lithuanian Roman Catholic Church—the first Lithuanian church in the city. The cornerstone of the church, located on the corner of Providence and Waverly Streets, was blessed on May 31, 1903, and six months later the first services were held in the basement. The church was blessed on October 12, 1916.

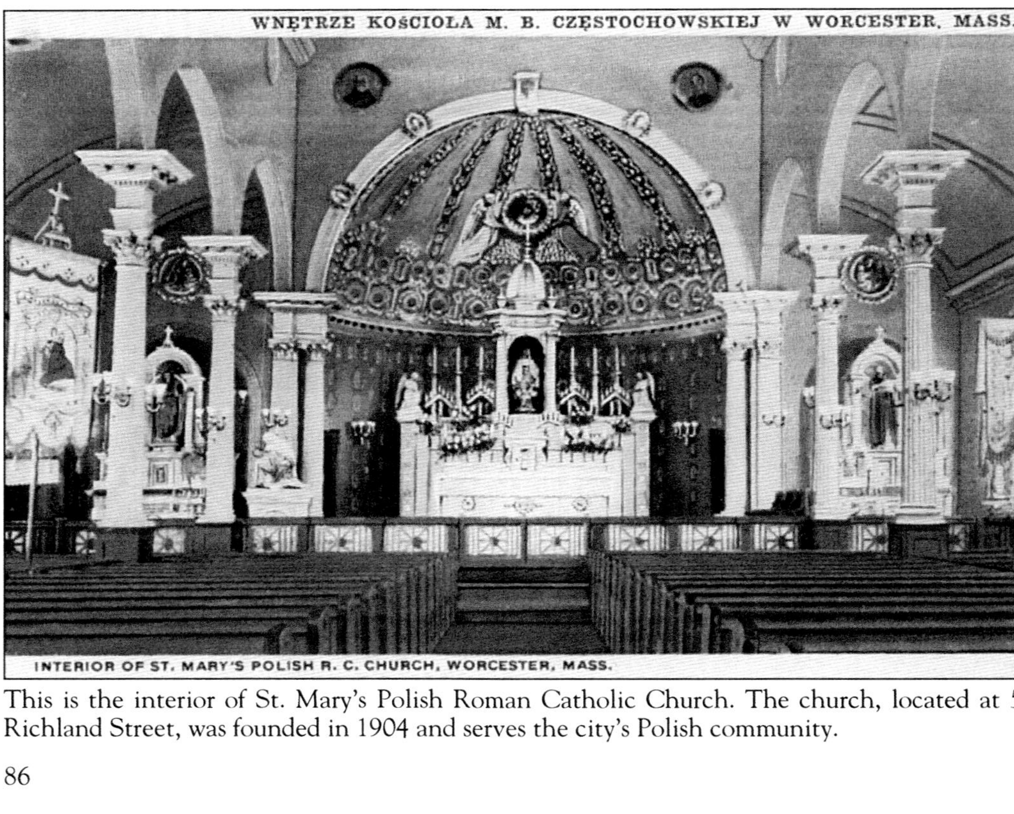

This is the interior of St. Mary's Polish Roman Catholic Church. The church, located at 5 Richland Street, was founded in 1904 and serves the city's Polish community.

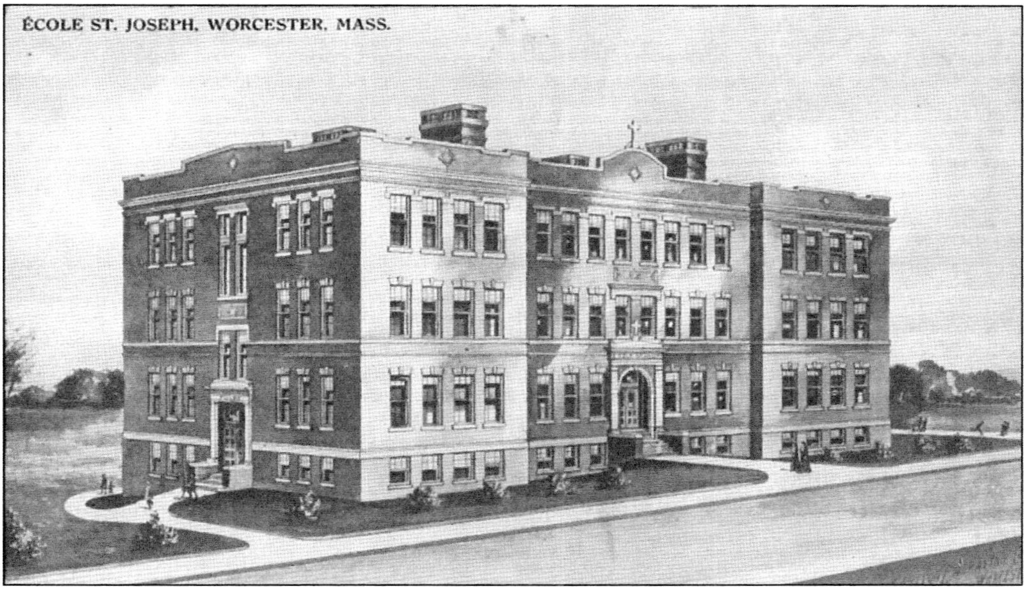

St. Joseph's Grammar School was located at 81 Plantation Street. It was one of the many schools in the Catholic parochial school system. The first parochial school was in the first Catholic parish. It was named St. John's School for Girls and was opened in 1872. In the 1950s the system contained 52 elementary and 16 secondary schools.

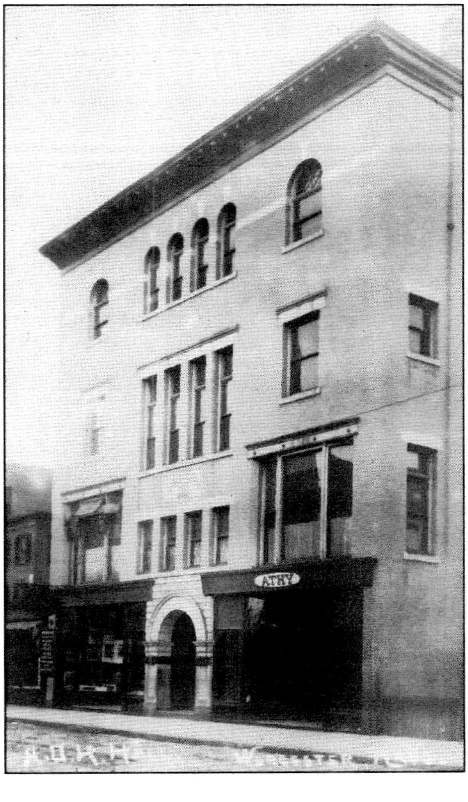

The AOH Hall was located at 26 Trumbull Street. The Ancient Order of Hibernians, a Catholic-Irish Society, was established in 1863 to assist Irish Immigrants. Located at street level is the Athy Funeral Home.

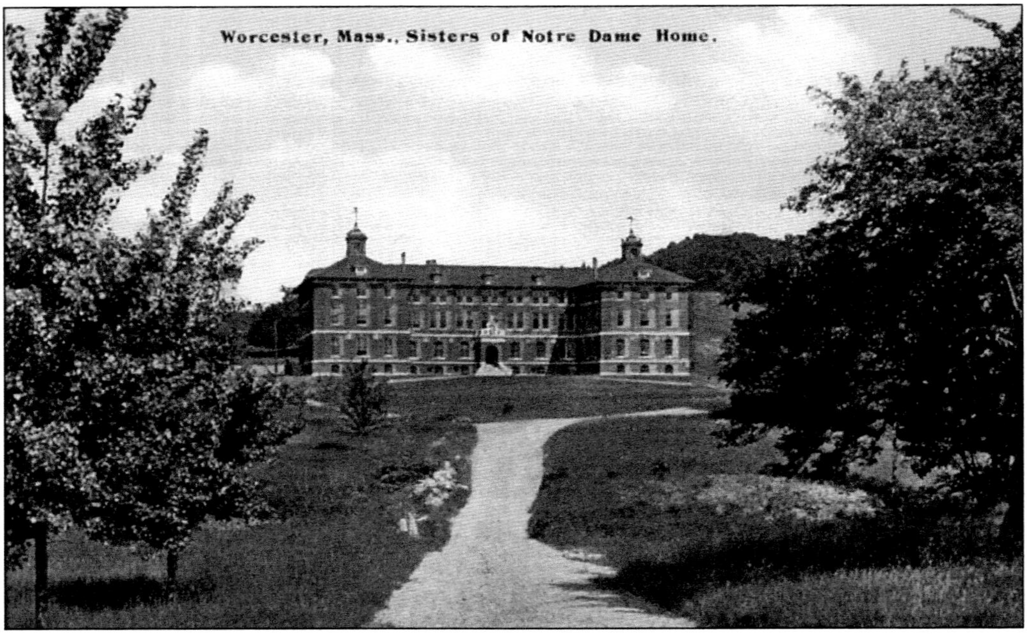

The Sisters of Notre Dame De Namur maintain a residence and convent at 555 Plantation Street, which overlooks the north end of Lake Quinsigamond. It was constructed in 1900 by McDermott Brothers, general building contractors.

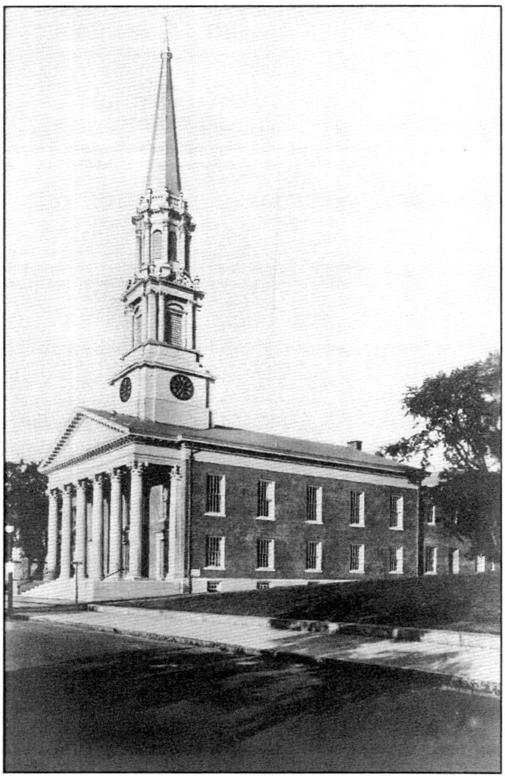

The First Unitarian Church located at 90 Main Street on Courthouse Hill was founded in 1785. The church was severely damaged by the hurricane in 1938. This picture was taken after the church was rebuilt.

The Second Advent Christian Church, located at the corner of Chandler and Piedmont Streets, was founded in 1842. The Second Advent movement in the city was made in anticipation of the predicted end of the world on February 15, 1843. After the fatal day had passed, a formal organization of the Adventists took place.

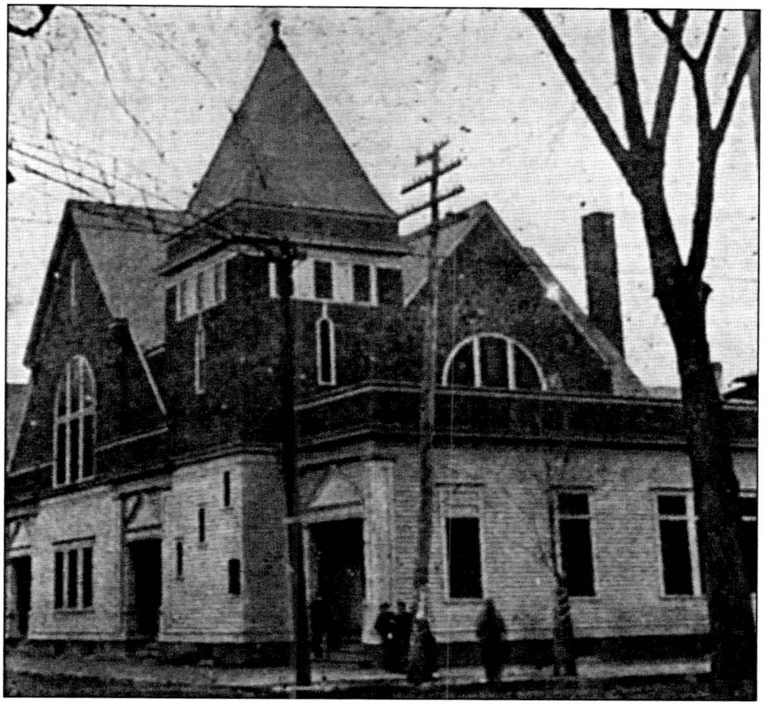

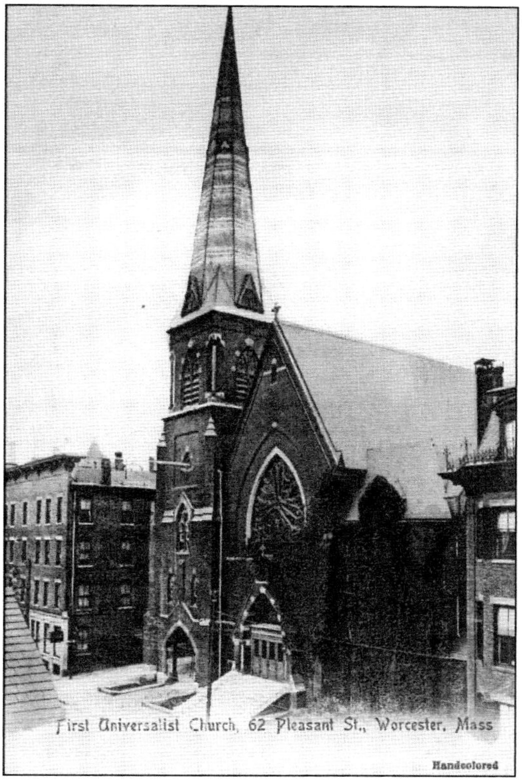

The First Universalist Church, located at 62 Pleasant Street, was founded in 1841. The first house of worship was located at the corner of Main and Foster Streets until the new church on Pleasant was occupied in 1871.

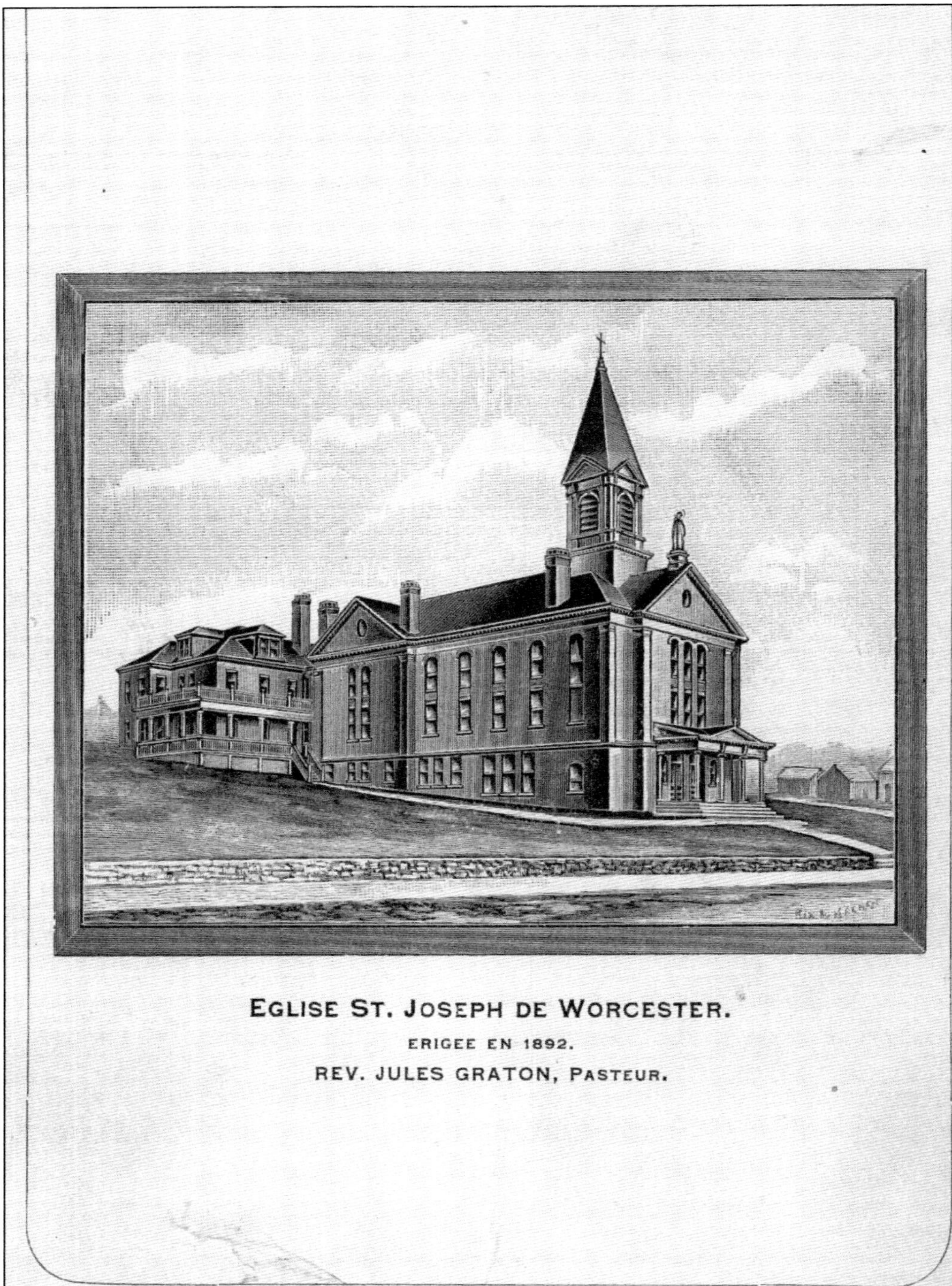

St. Joseph's Church, erected in 1892, was built to serve French-Canadian Catholics in the city. In 1930, after moving to its new church on Hamilton Street, the congregation sold the church building to St. George's Syrian Orthodox Church. St. George's was organized in 1905 and was first located at 100 Wall Street. It relocated to 32 Wall Street in 1930.

Seven

SCHOOLS

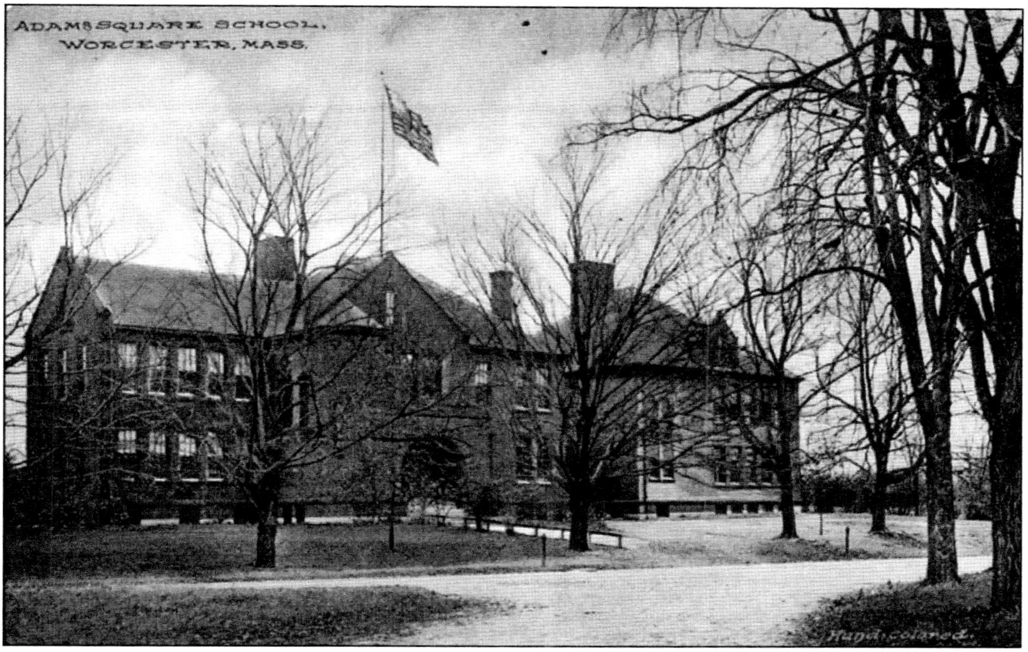

The Adams Square School was one of seven schools built during the term of Mayor Samuel Winslow (1886–90). It was located on Burncoat Street opposite Millbrook Street. It served grades one to eight in 1915. There were 9 teachers and 312 pupils in the school.

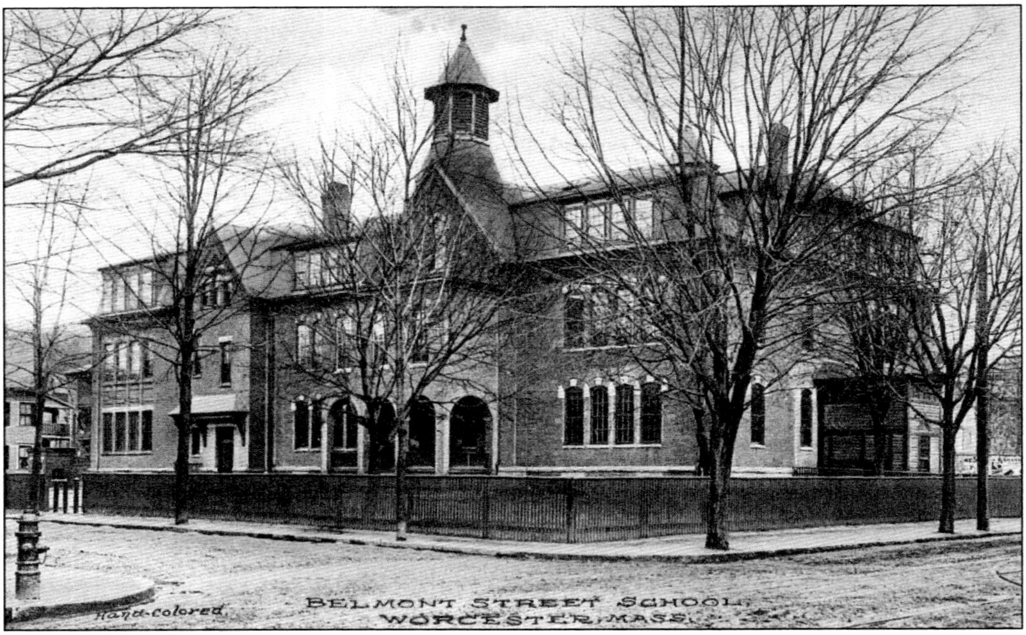

The Belmont Street School, located on Belmont Street at the corner of Clayton Street, served grades one to eight in 1915. There were 19 teachers and 665 pupils.

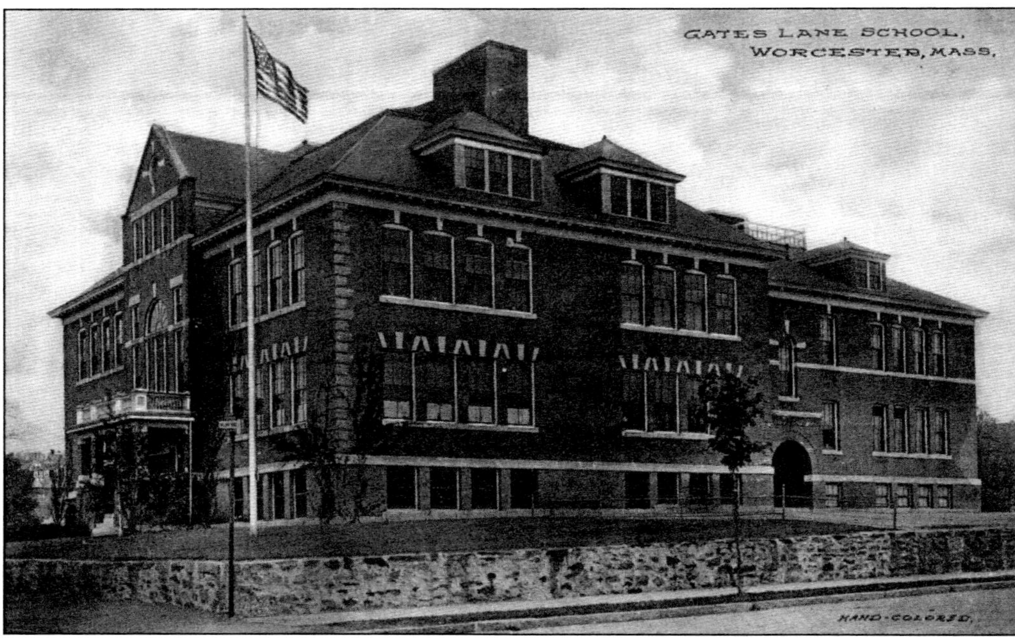

Gates Lane was named after Simon Gates, an early settler in the city. The Gates Lane School, located at Gates Lane and Main Street near Webster Square, served grades kindergarten through eight in 1915. There were 15 teachers and 529 pupils.

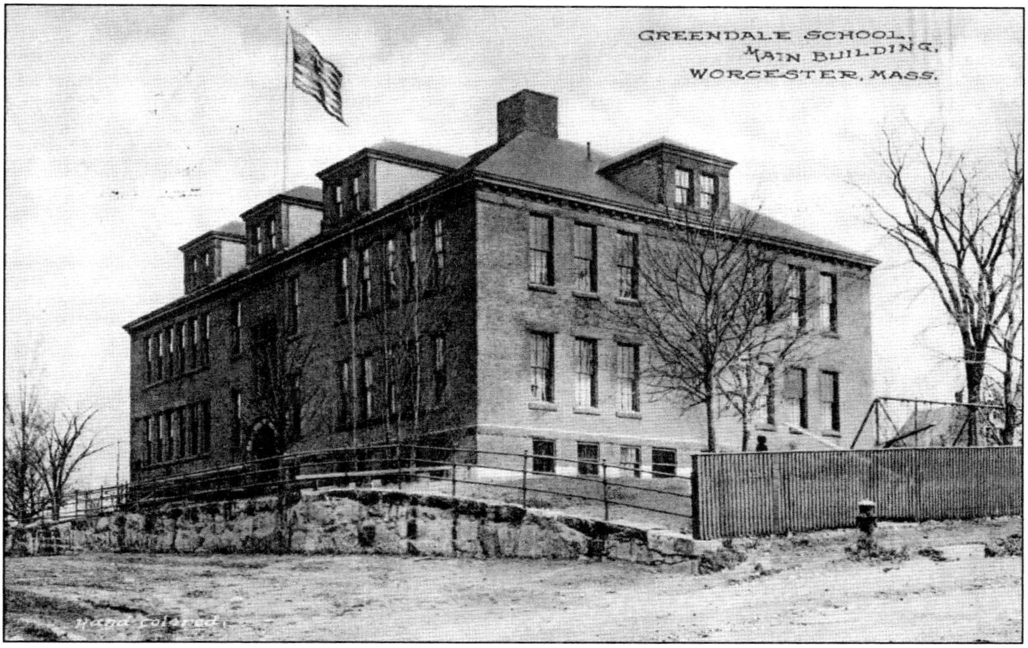

The Greendale School, located on Leeds Street at the corner of Fairhaven Road, served grades kindergarten to eight. In 1915 there were 12 teachers and 403 pupils.

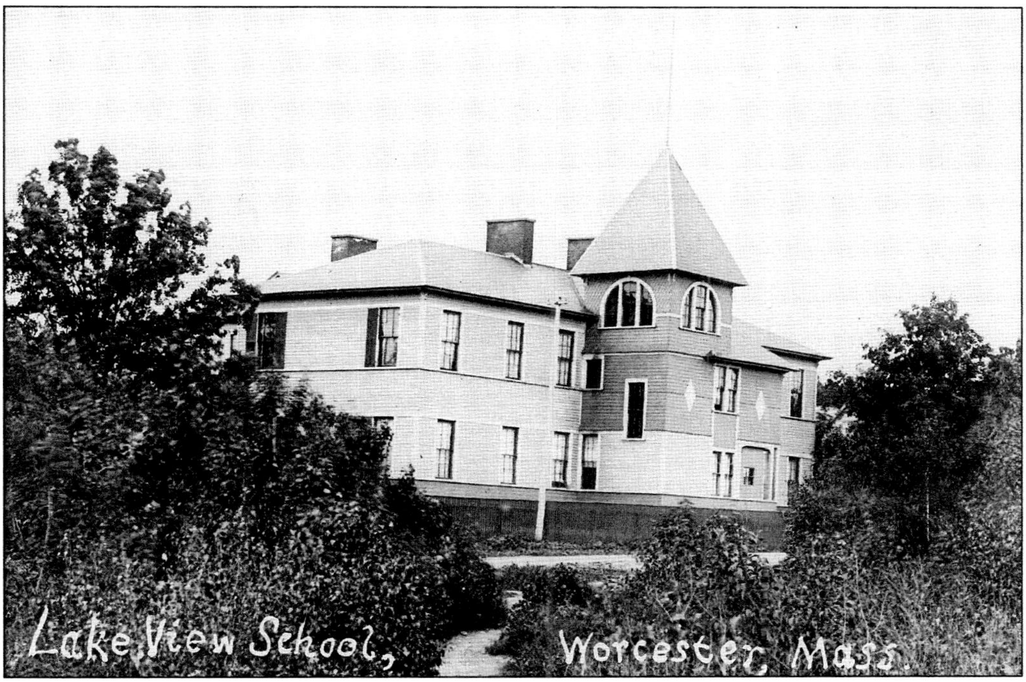

Lake View was a settlement west of Lake Quinsigamond and south of Belmont Street. A railroad station, schoolhouse, church, post office, and stores were all located there. The Lake View School was located on Lakeview Street. It served grades kindergarten to eight. In 1915 there were 7 teachers and 241 pupils.

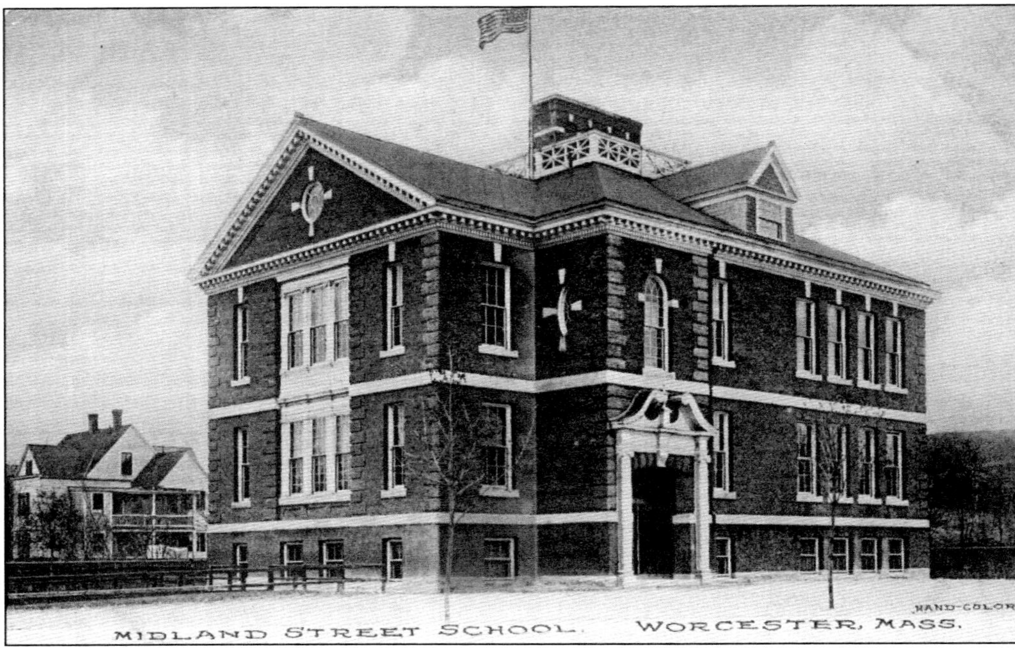

The Midland Street School is one of the many schoolhouses built during the 1896–98 period. These schoolhouses provided accommodations for 2,800 pupils. Located on the corner of Midland and Huntley Streets near Newton Square, it served grades kindergarten to seven in 1915. There were 10 teachers and 331 pupils.

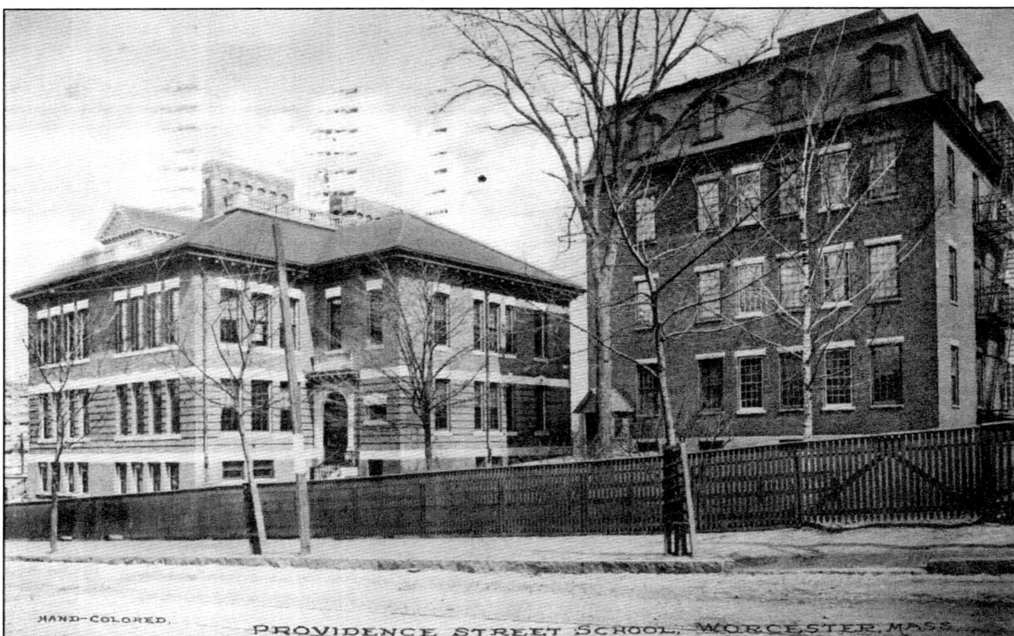

The first Providence Street School building was completed in 1865 at a cost of $10,743. Located on Providence Street at the corner of Grafton Street, it served grades kindergarten to seven in 1915. There were 21 teachers and 675 pupils.

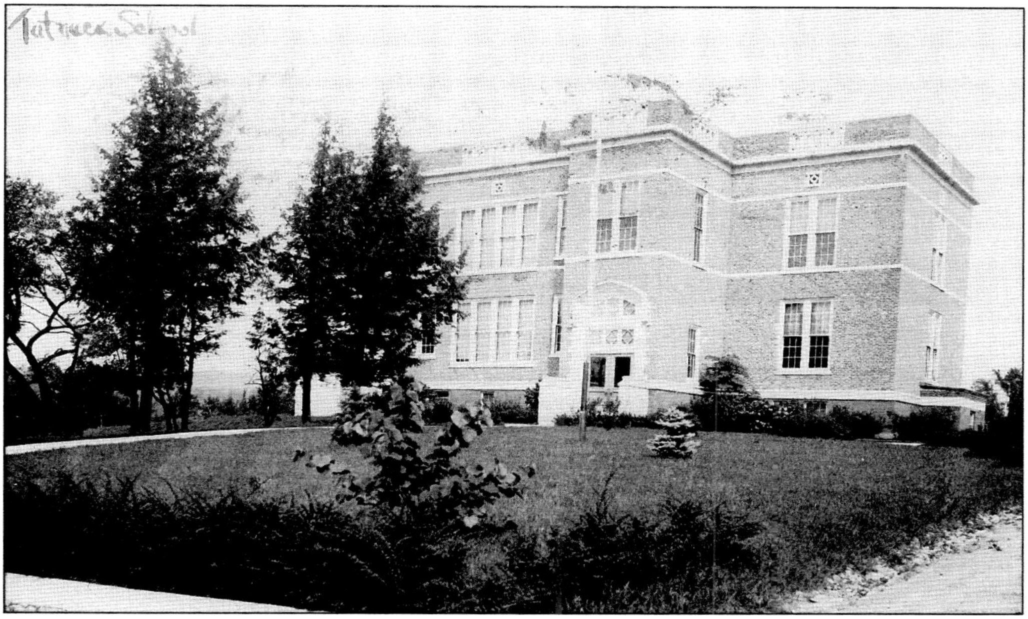

The First Tatnuck School was built around 1860 and housed 56 pupils. As the city's population pushed westward, the Tatnuck School seen in this photo was constructed. Located on Pleasant Street opposite Willard Avenue, it served grades kindergarten to eight in 1915. There were 8 teachers and 247 pupils.

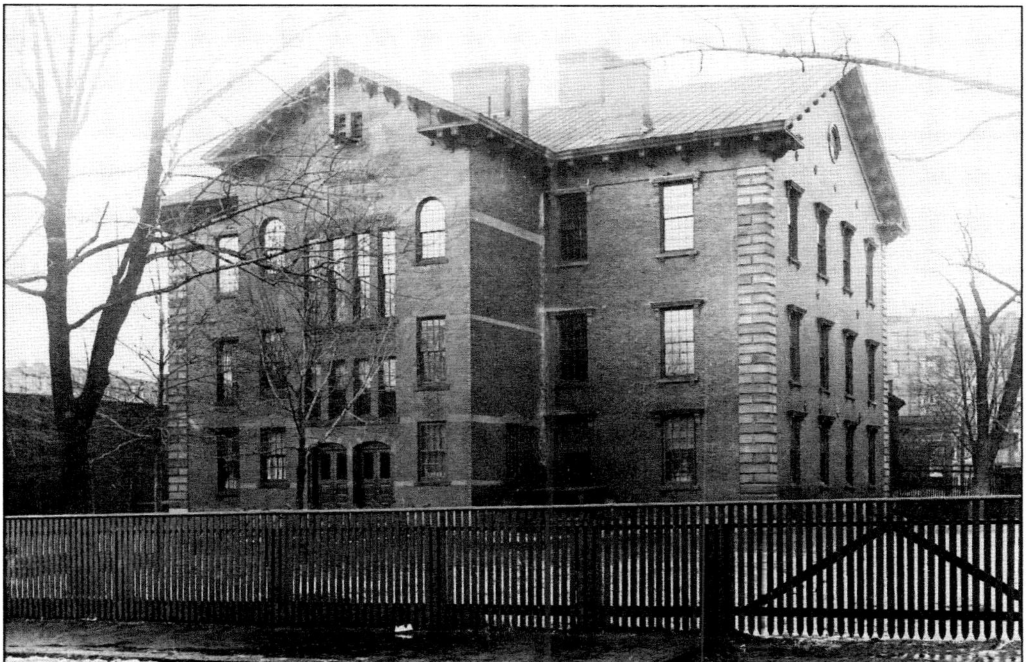

The Thomas Street School was built around 1851, during the term of Peter C. Bacon, the city's third mayor. Located on the corner of Thomas and Summer Streets, it served grades kindergarten to eight in 1915. There were 13 teachers and 434 pupils.

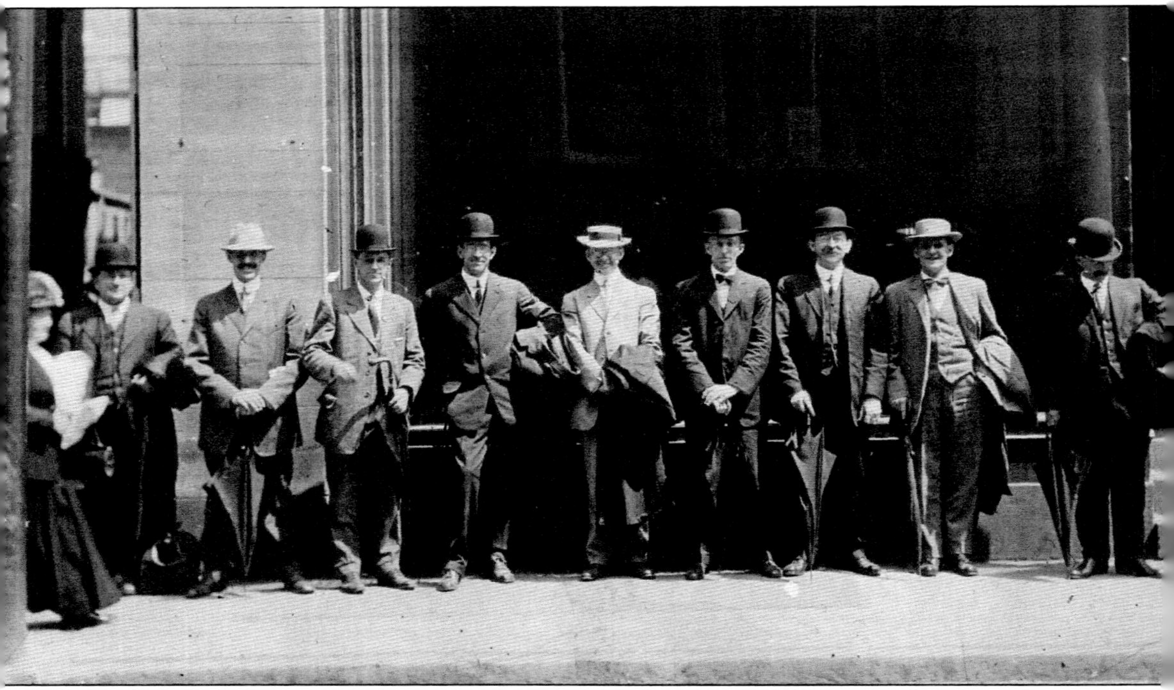

Pictured here are the manual arts teachers of the public schools. The poster in the window is dated May 16, which means this picture was probably taken during spring vacation in April, as they seem prepared for April's showers and cool weather. The picture was mailed on June 22, 1911, by Arthur A. Pelton, a manual training teacher, to Daniel Dyer. From left to right are three unidentified teachers, Ball (of the Manual Training School), Traill (Millbury Street School), Donaldson, Atkins (Dix Street School), Bean (director of the Manual Training School), an unidentified teacher, and Dyer (Belmont Street School).

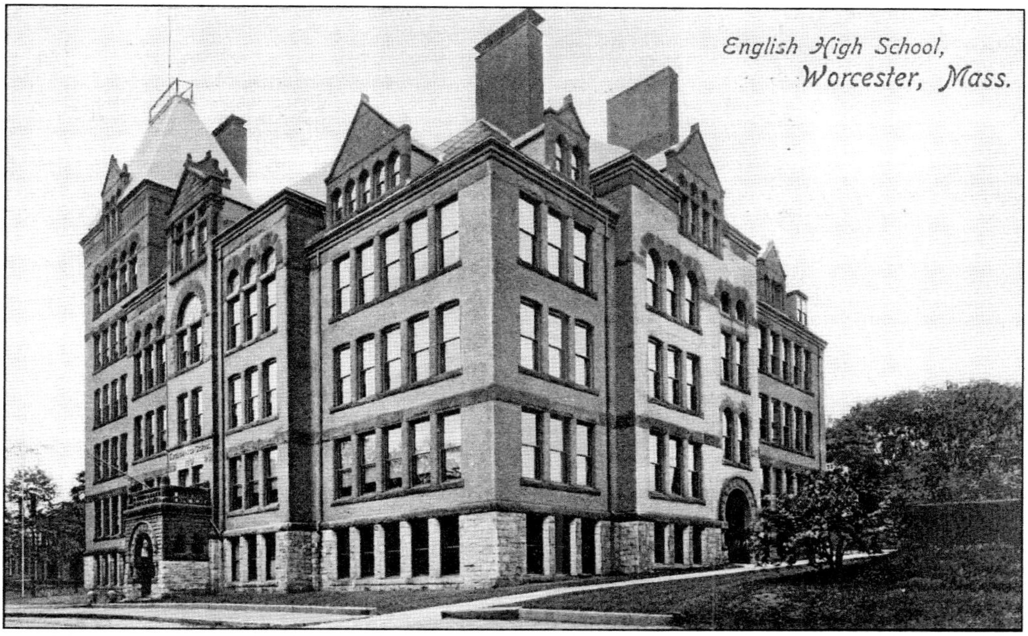

English High School was located at the corner of Irving and Chatham Streets. When the curriculum of the high schools was changed at the end of the 1914 school year, the name of the school was changed to Classical, and the name of the school formerly known as Classical was changed to Commerce.

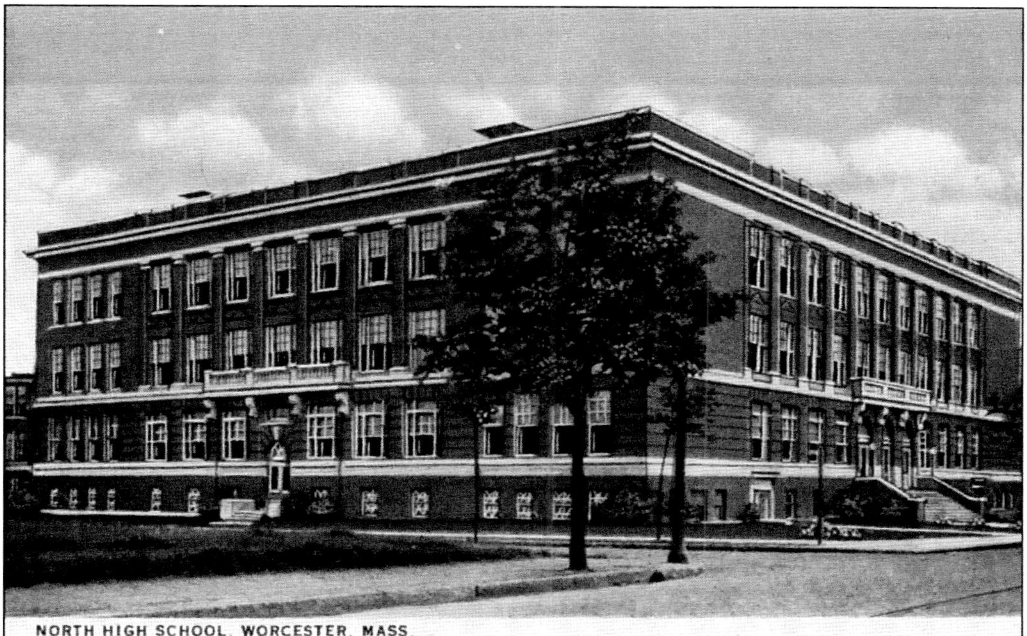

North High School was located on the corner of Salisbury and Lancaster Streets opposite the Worcester Art Museum. Occupied in 1915, it was the city's fourth high school.

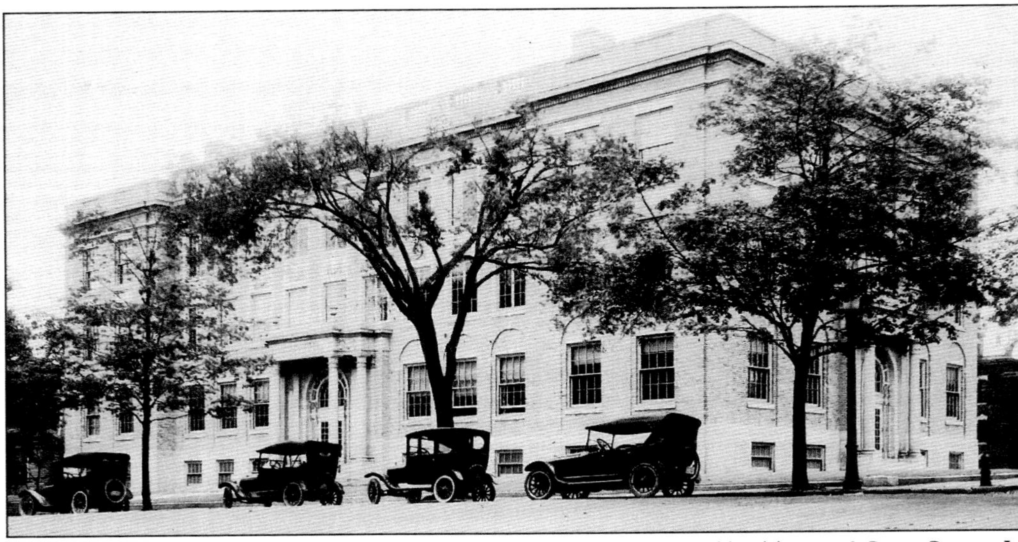

On September 20, 1911, Girl's Trade School was opened in a leased building at 2 State Street. In less than three years the building was over-crowded. The city purchased land for a new building near the corner of Chatham and High Streets. David H. Fanning, president of Royal Worcester Corset Company, presented the sum of $100,000 to the city for use towards the erection of a new building. That new building was named the David Hale Fanning Trade School for Girls and was dedicated on December 20, 1921.

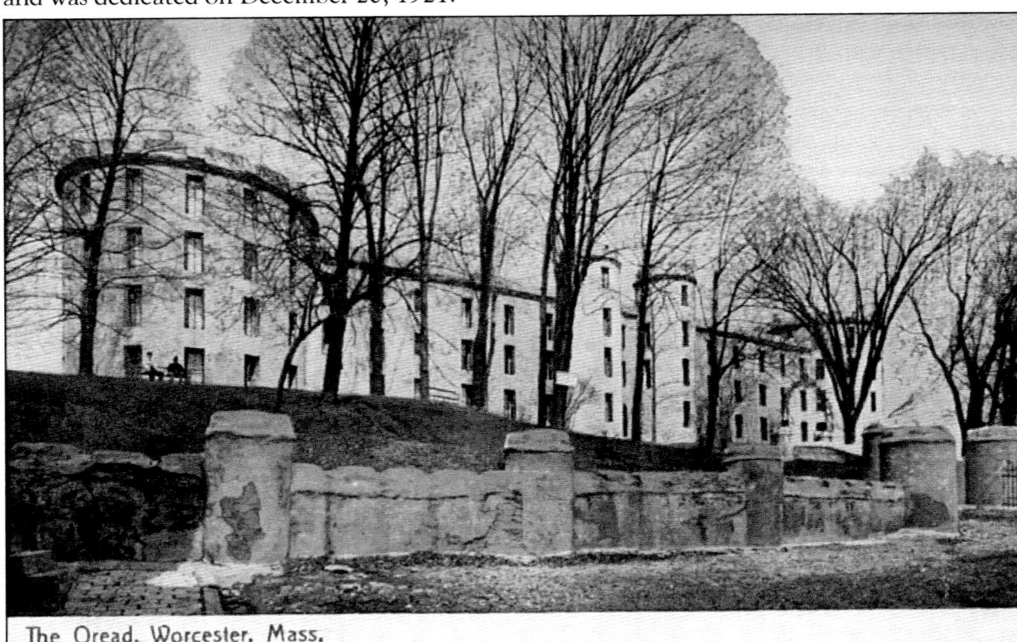

The Oread was located on Goat's Hill at the end of Castle Street off of 800 Main Street. Eli Thayer, educated in Worcester at the Manuel Labor School and a graduate of Brown University, returned to Worcester to act as principal of Worcester Academy. While there, he was convinced that women should be given the advantages of pre-college, higher education. In 1851 he established the Oread School for Women.

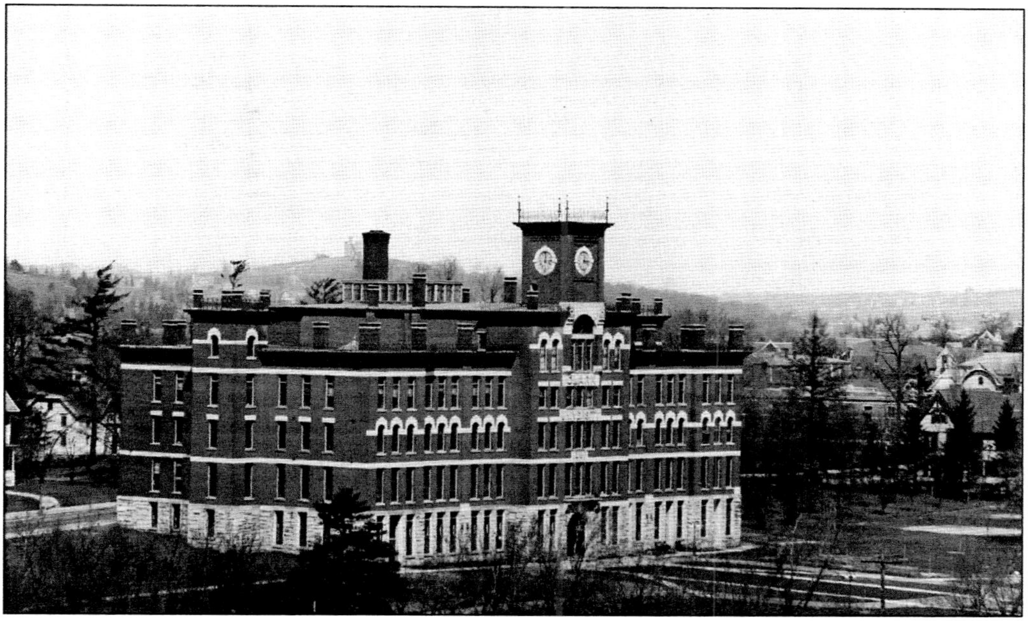

Clark University was founded by Jonas Clark. He chose Worcester because of its central location among the colleges of the East. The charter of the university was granted by the legislature of Massachusetts in 1887.

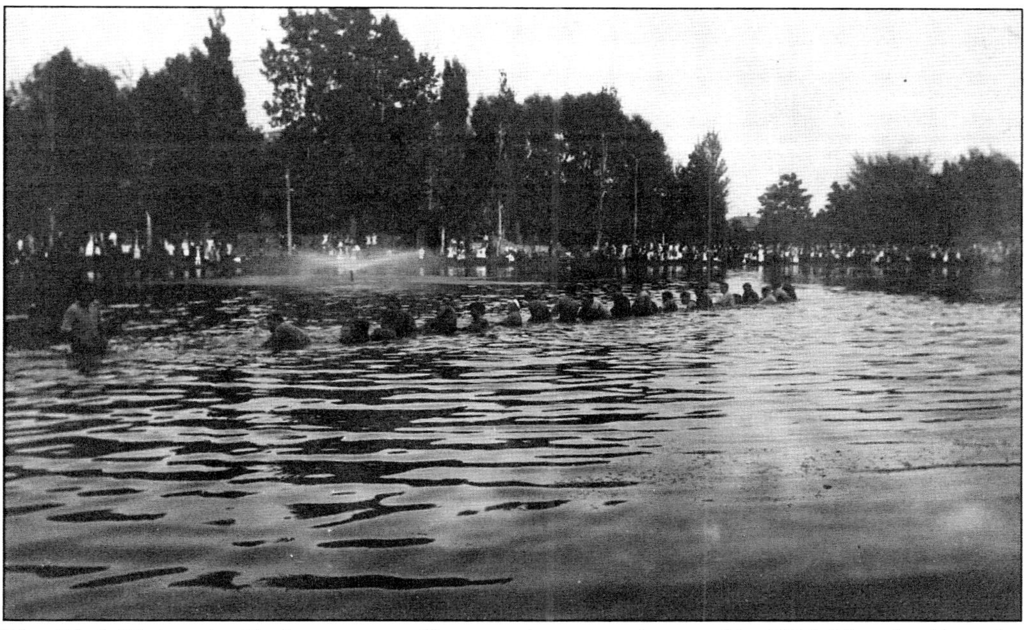

The Clark University Freshmen were all wet at the university pond in 1914. They had lost the annual rope pull to the juniors. The message on the back of the picture says, "This is a picture of our annual rope pull. The juniors stand on one side of the pond and the freshmen stand on the other side, and the tug of war ensues. This year we, the juniors were fortunate enough to pull the freshmen through."

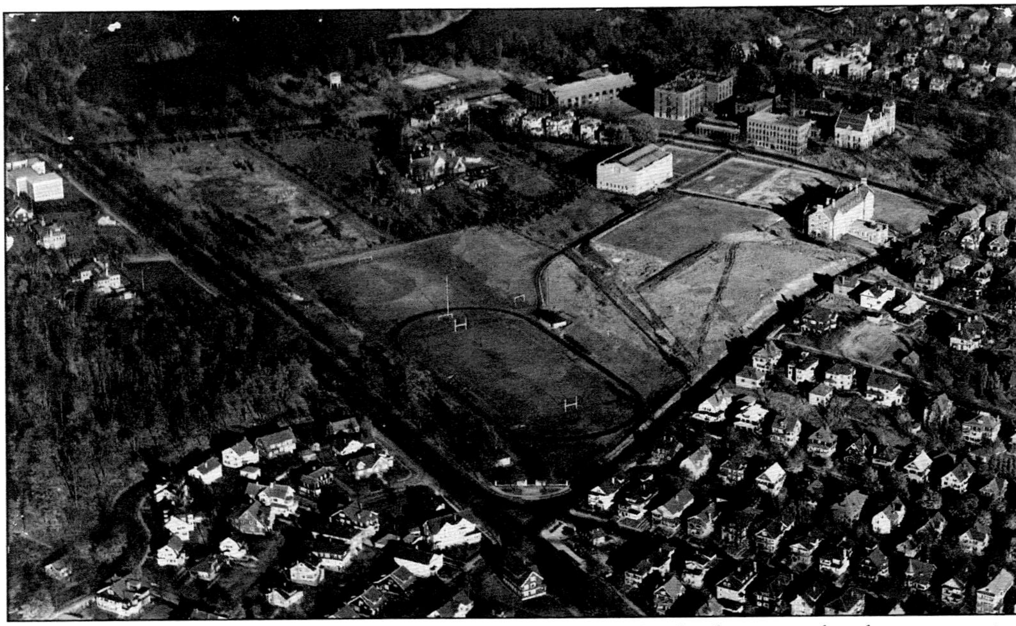

An aerial view shows the Worcester Polytechnic Institute. In the foreground is the intersection of Park Avenue and Institute Road. The campus of the school is in the upper right and the athletic field is in the center of the picture.

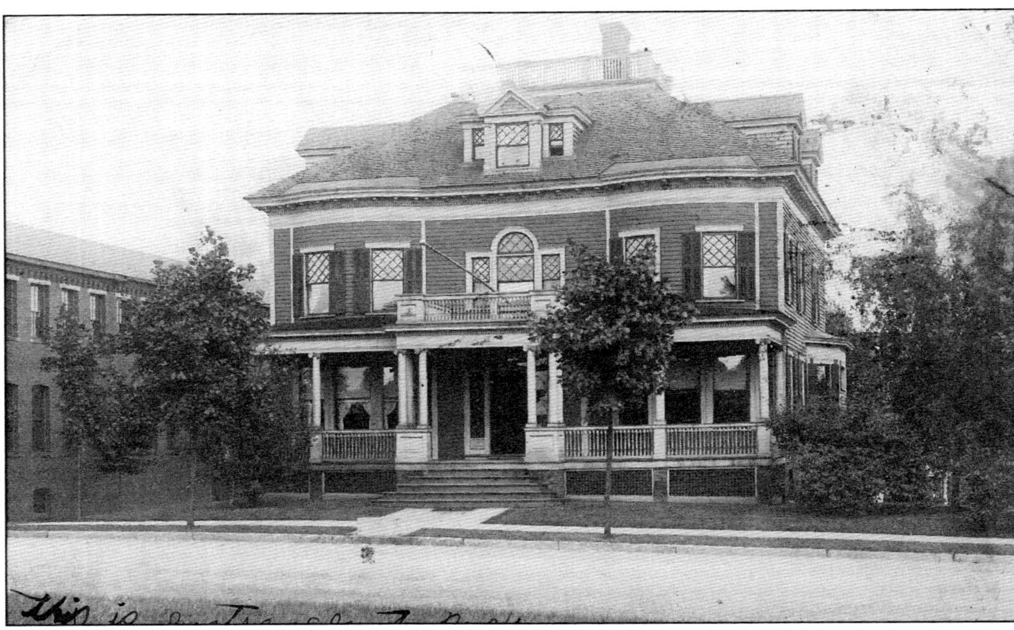

This is 6 Humbolt Avenue, the chapter house of Sigma Alpha Epsilon Fraternity at Worcester Polytechnic Institute, *c.* 1920. There were six other fraternities with chapter houses—Phi Gama Delta, Delta Tau, Alpha Tau Omega, Theta Chi, Lamda Chi Alpha, and Phi Sigma Kappa.

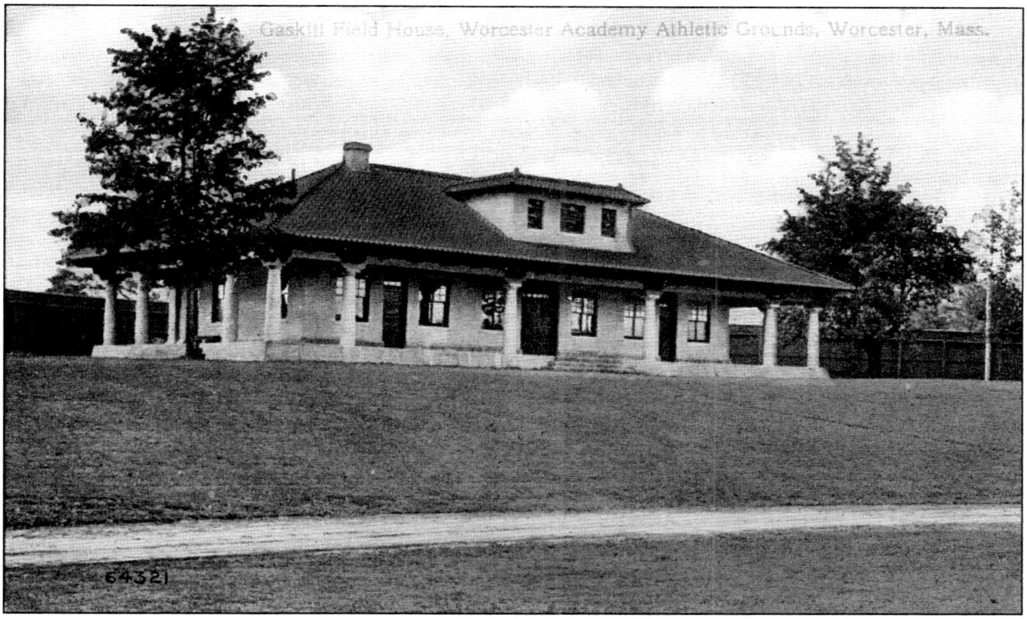

Gaskill Field is Worcester Academy's athletic grounds. The field house and grounds, located on Providence Street, were constructed and finished in 1910. The field was named in honor of Judge Francis A. Gaskill, the third president of the board of trustees. It contains two baseball fields, the football field, a quarter-mile track, three tennis courts, and the field house.

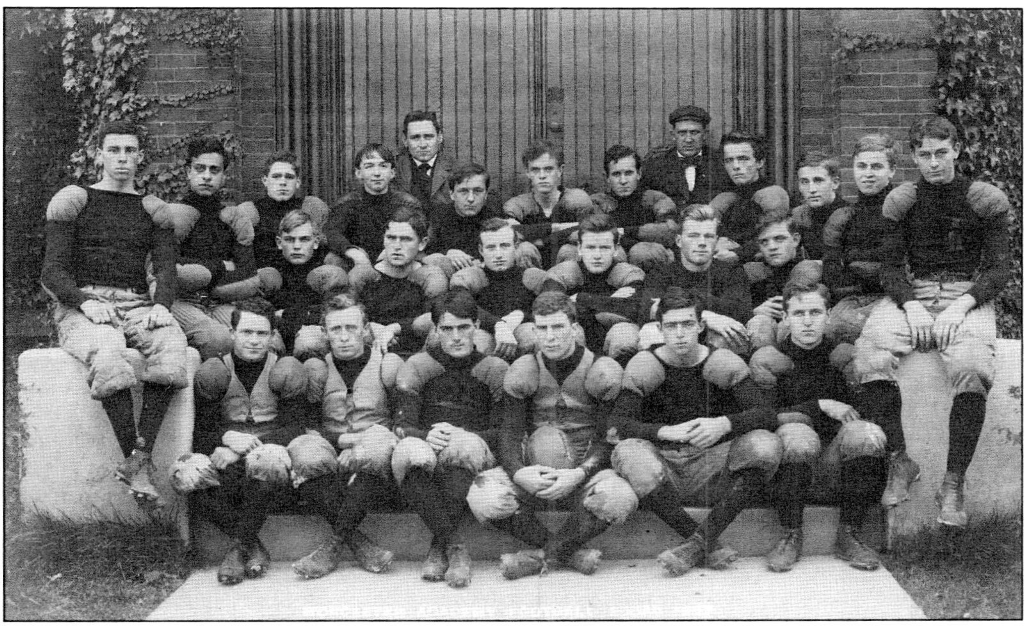

The freshmen of this 1907 Worcester Academy Football Squad would play their final season in a brand-new field. They played against the following teams in 1910: Morris Heights School, Springfield Training, Dartmouth freshmen, Wesleyan Academy, Cushing Academy, Harvard Freshmen, and Williston Academy. Their record was two wins, three losses, and two ties.

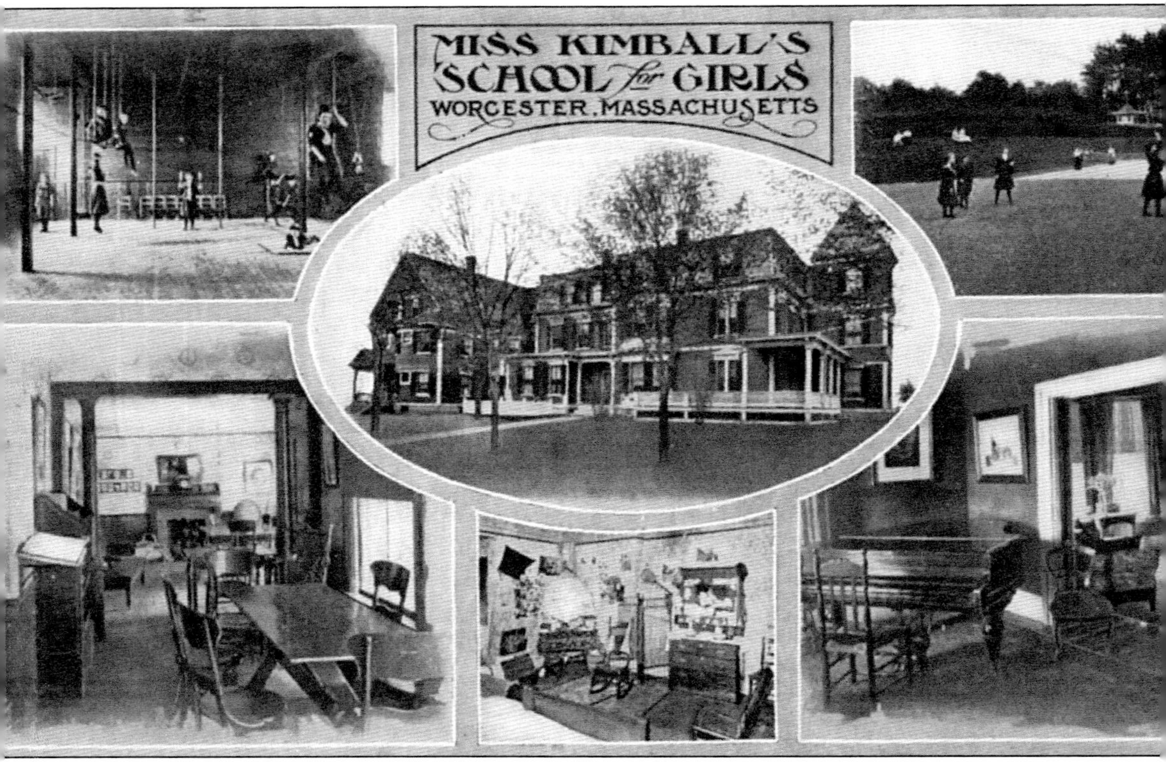

Miss Kimball's School for Girls was located on the corner of May and Woodland Streets. It offered college-preparatory courses and special courses for young ladies and girls. Superior advantages were had in music, art, languages, physical fitness, and voice culture.

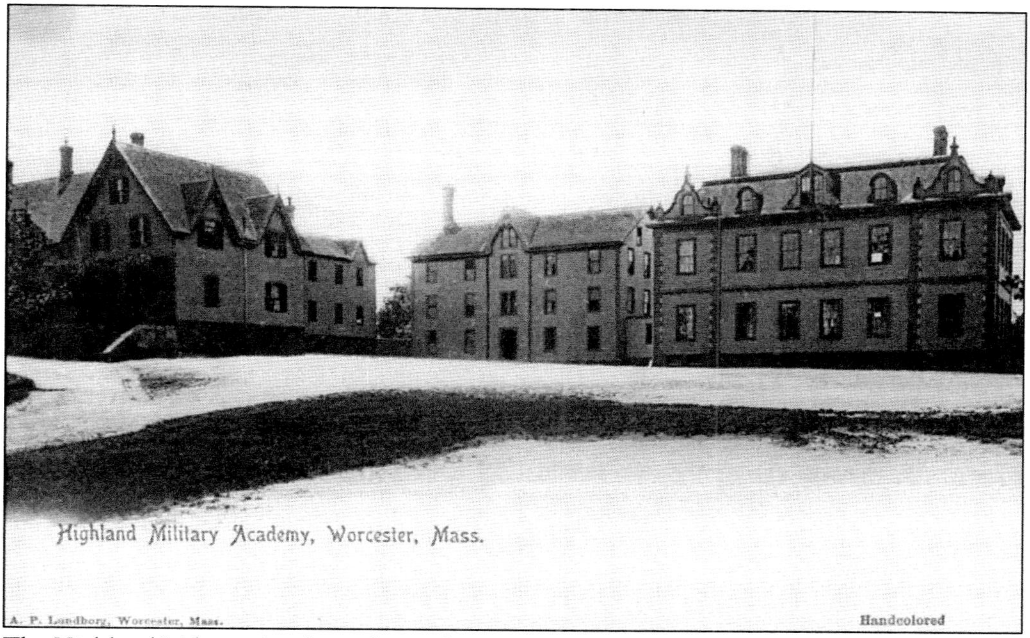

The Highland Military Academy, located on Salisbury Street, was founded by Caleb B. Metcalf in 1856. He was a teacher in Worcester's public schools for many years. This school was a boarding school and a large number of its pupils came from a distance. The school continued until 1912, when the property was sold for residential purposes.

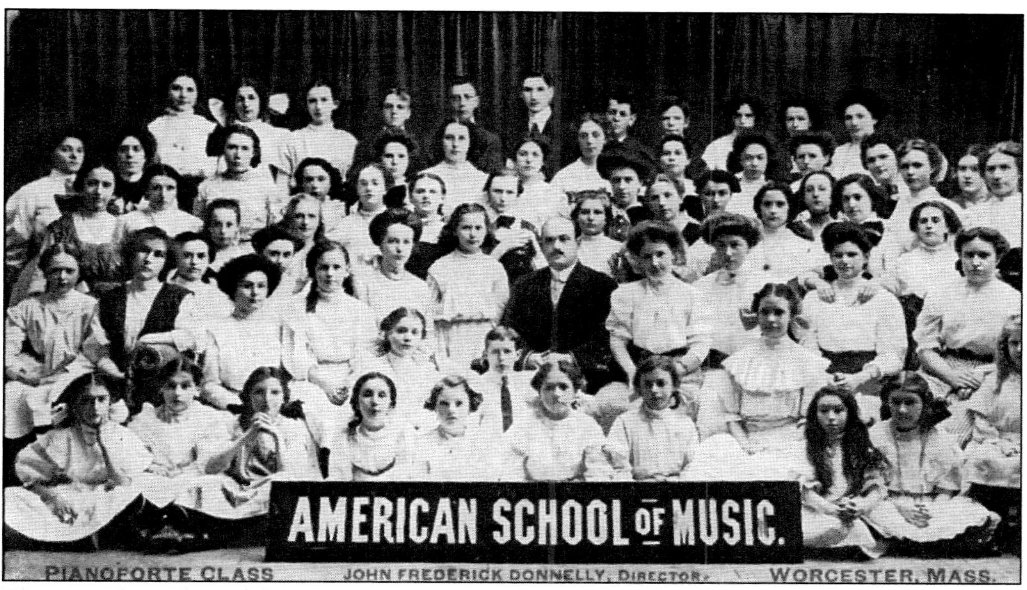

The pianoforte class of the American School of Music poses for this picture with Director John F. Donnelly. In 1912 Mr. Donnelly was a music teacher with offices in the Taylor Building at 476 Main Street.

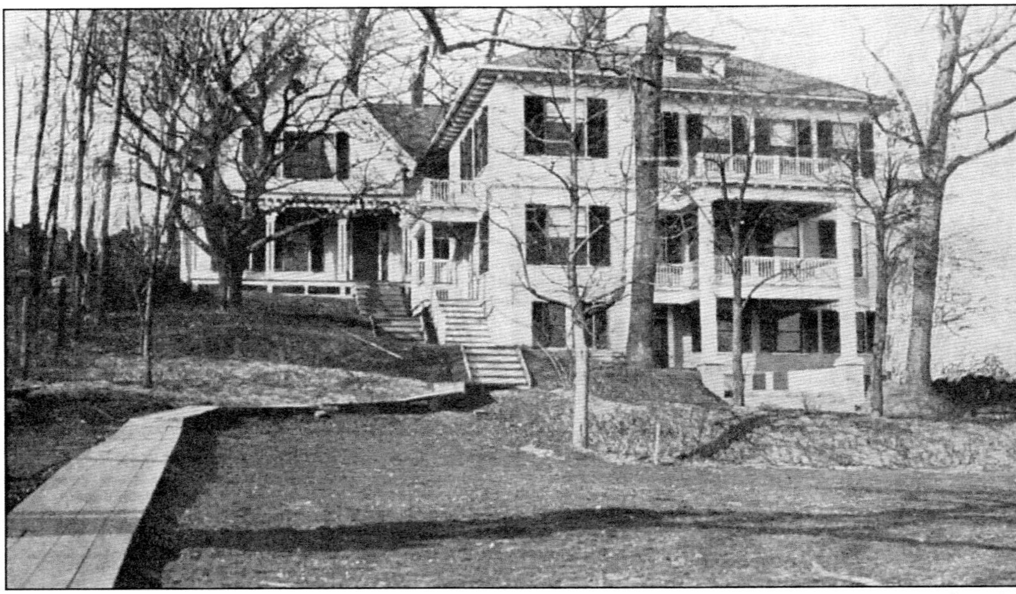

The Domestic Training Institute, shown here *c.* 1910, was located at 158 Institute Road at the home of Mrs. Frank M. Wethered. She was a former teacher at the School of Domestic Science, which was located at the Oread Castle. When owner Henry D. Perky passed away, several of the students approached Mrs. Wethered to continue their studies. She agreed to help and the Worcester Domestic Science School was born. The school occupied several buildings on Institute Road and Dean Street.

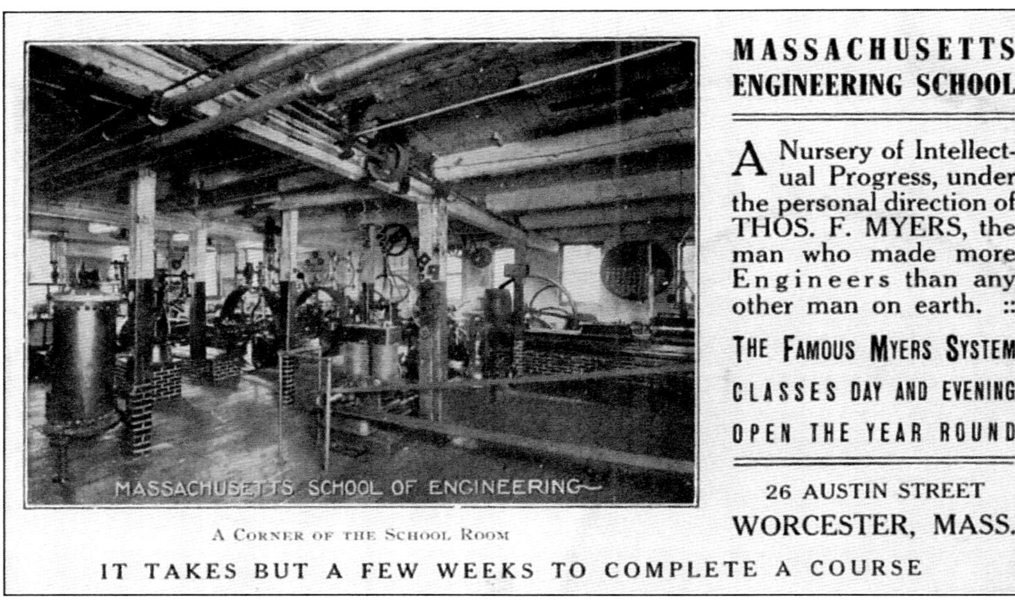

The Massachusetts School of Engineering was established in 1905. Thomas F. Meyers was the director of the school. He also established schools of engineering in Boston and Springfield. Students were trained for positions as stationary fireman and engineers. The school was often called upon to inspect the large steam and electric plants in the factories and mills of the city.

Eight

EVENTS

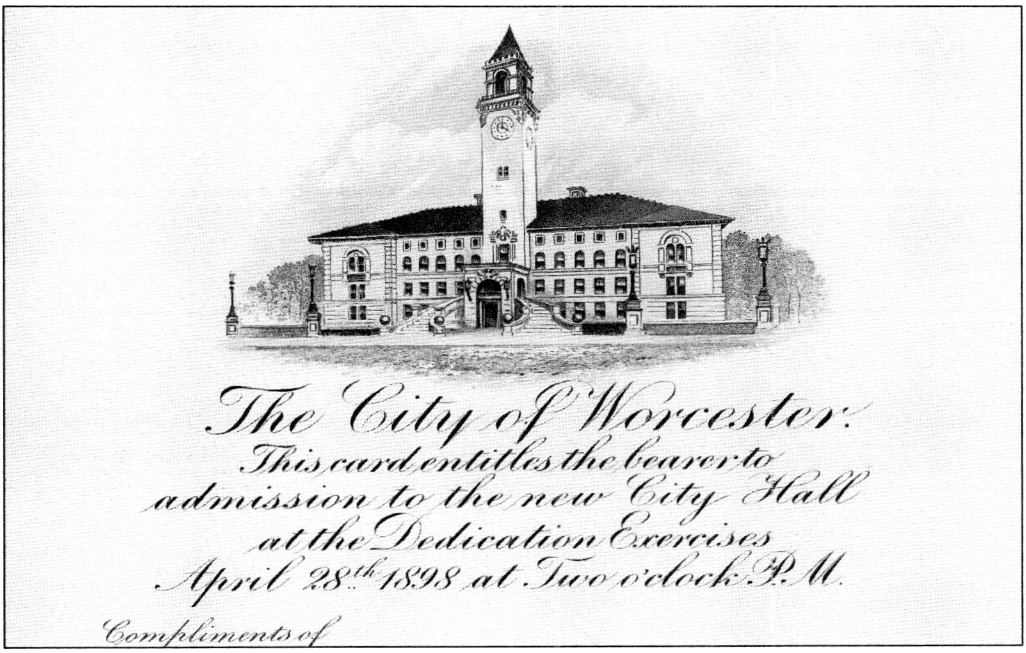

On April 23, 1894, the General Court passed an act to allow the city to borrow over its debt limit for the purpose of building a new city hall. On April 23, 1896, the contract for the construction of the building was awarded to Norcross Brothers. The cornerstone was laid on September 12, 1897, and the new city hall was dedicated on April 28, 1898. Although $650,000 was appropriated for the task, the final cost of the building and its furnishings was $23,031.23 less than that amount.

The White City

On Lake Quinsigamond,
WORCESTER, MASS.
Will Open May 20, 1905

DESCRIPTIVE CIRCULARS for the best place for small or large excursions in New England.

ATTRACTIONS.

Restaurant—To be run by an experienced hotel man.
Base Ball Grounds and Athletic Field—Free to patrons of the Park.
Boat House—With the best line of boats and canoes in New England.
Chutes—Longest east of Coney Island.
Scenic Railway—Most picturesque and exciting in the country.
Old Mill—¾ of a mile underground in subterranean courses,
Circle Swing—An air-ship over land and lake.
Bumps—A sure cure for the mumps.
Ball Room—The largest and finest in New England.
Laughing Gallery—Showing you under all possibilities.
Sea-on-Land—Where the "landlubber" gets a real taste of a sea trip while still on land.
Carousel—With jumping horses, mirrors and lights.
Automatic Vaudeville—Introducing all the latest mechanical wonders.
Observation Wheel—Fun for everybody.
"The Pike"—'Nough said.

AND

The Finest Grove and Scenery in the World.

All Electric Lines Direct to the Park.
Boston & Worcester St. Ry. Direct to Gates.

WRITE TO

F. H. BIGELOW, - - WHITE CITY, WORCESTER

In spite of workers threatening to strike, the white city was expected to open for the season on May 20, 1905. Although actually located on the Shrewsbury side of Lake Quinsigamond, all references to the park indicated it was in Worcester. The Worcester Consolidated Street Railway played a large roll in the financing of the park.

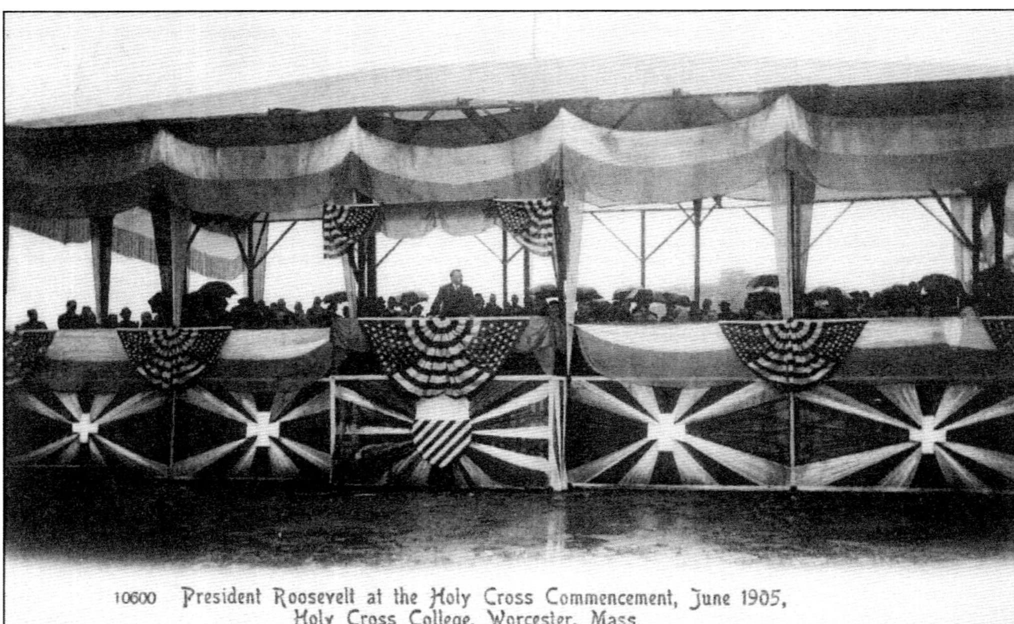

President Theodore Roosevelt visited Worcester for the second time on June 21, 1905. He arrived at Union Station at 9:28 a.m. to the cheers of thousands. He proceeded to the commencement exercises at Clark College. After Clark's exercises he went to the graduation at Holy Cross College. He left Union Station at 2:30 p.m. for Washington.

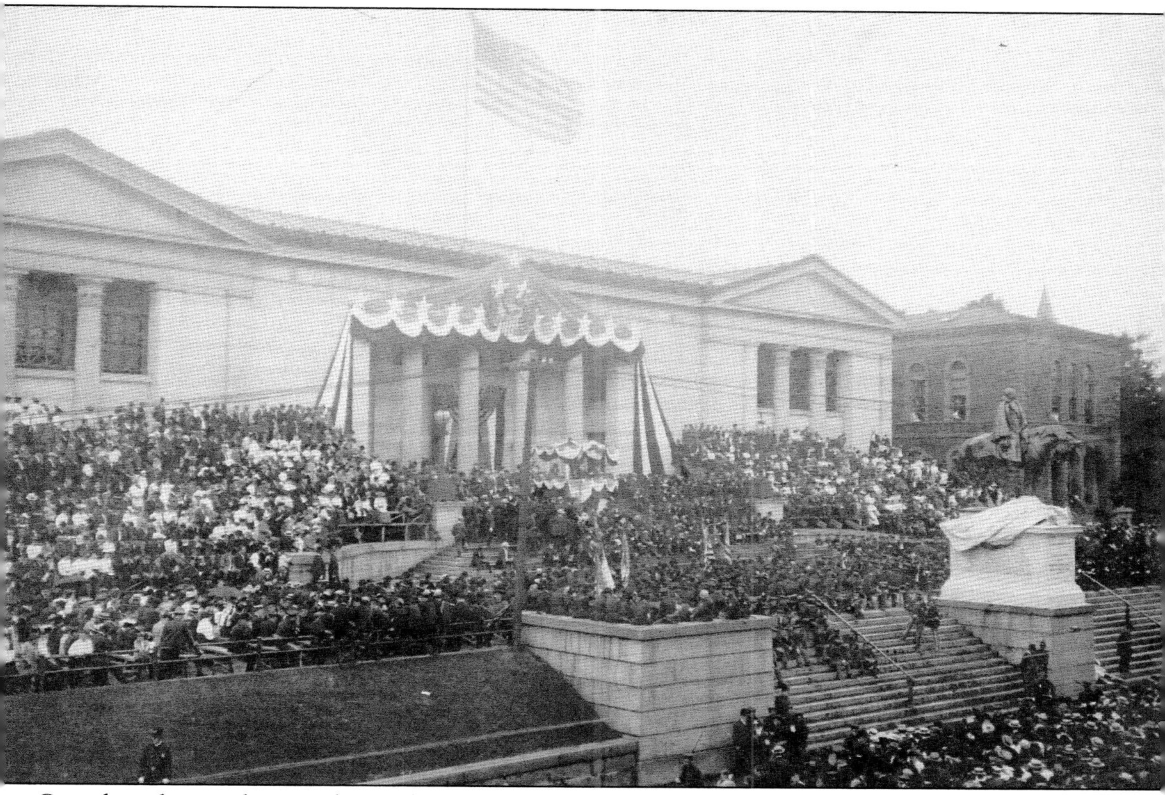

Crowds gather at the courthouse for the unveiling of the equestrian statue of Major-General Charles Devens on July 4, 1906. General Devens, a lawyer with a degree from Harvard, served as city solicitor for three years prior to entering the military to lead troops in the Civil War. After the war he was named a judge in the Supreme Court of Massachusetts. He also served as attorney general of the United States during the administration of President Hayes. General Devens died on January 7, 1891, at the age of 71, after a brief illness.

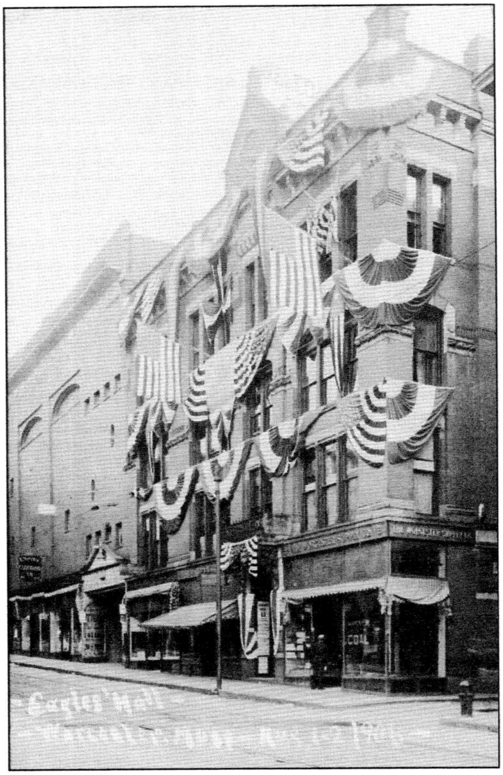

Eagle's Hall on 11 Pleasant Street was decorated with flags and buntings in celebration of the 1906 state convention of the Massachusetts Association of the Fraternal Order of Eagles that took place on August 1–2. Delegates from 40 of the 52 aeries of the state participated in a parade that was reviewed by Governor Curtis Guild.

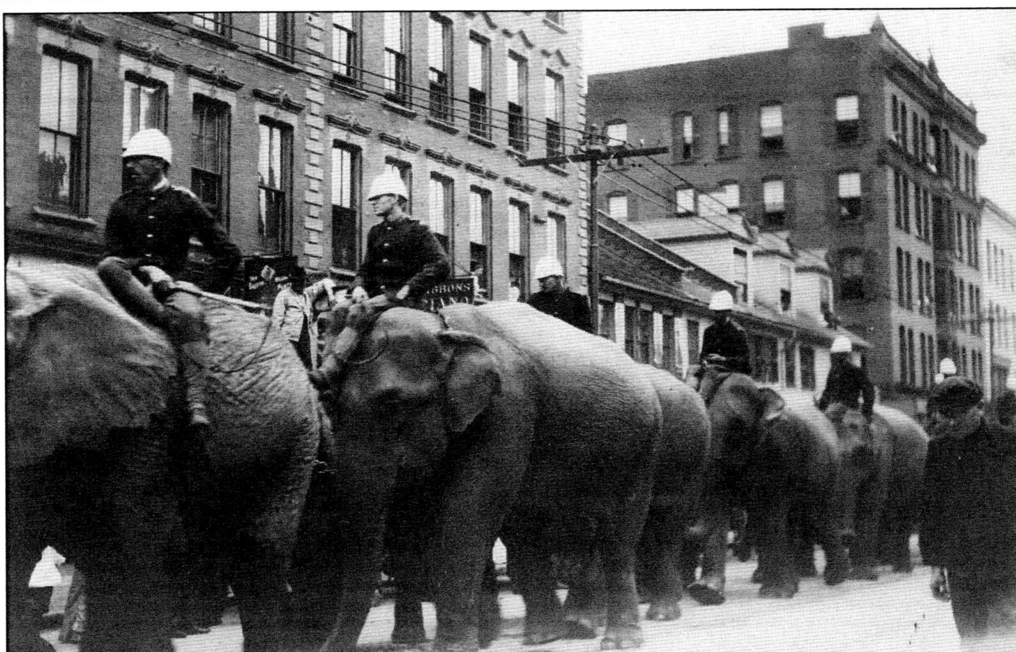

The circus came to town in 1906. The parade of elephants passes Gibbons Piano at 145 Main Street and Ballou's Paint Store at 143 Main Street on its way to Lincoln Square.

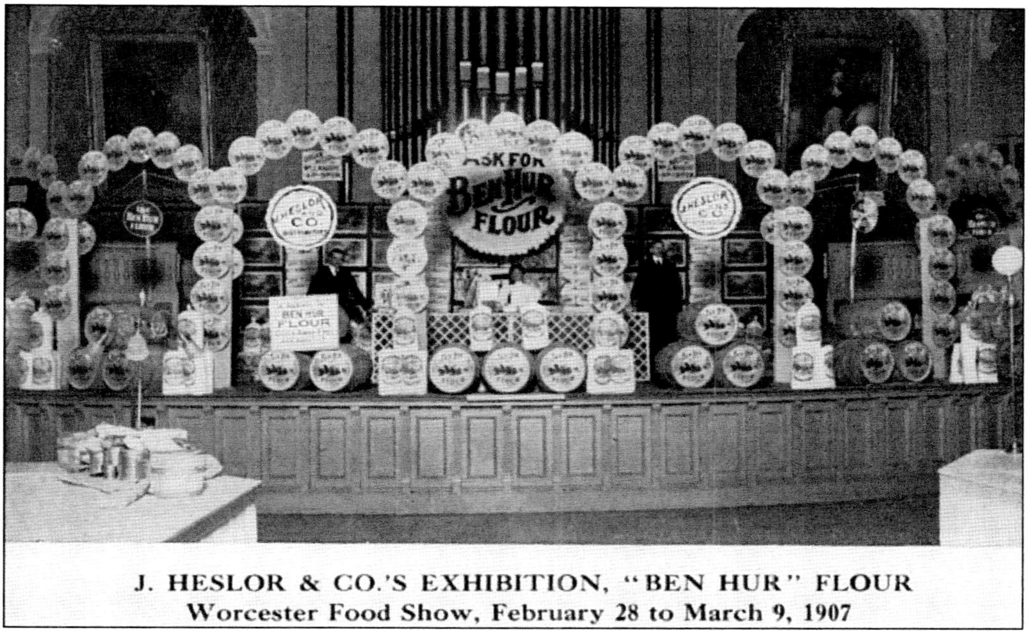

The Worcester Food Show was held at Mechanics Hall from February 28 to March 9, 1907. A great showing of splendid exhibits, pretty young women daintily dressed in white and colors, sweet music, the aroma from a variety of foods, and attractive booths were the magnets drawing crowds to the food fair.

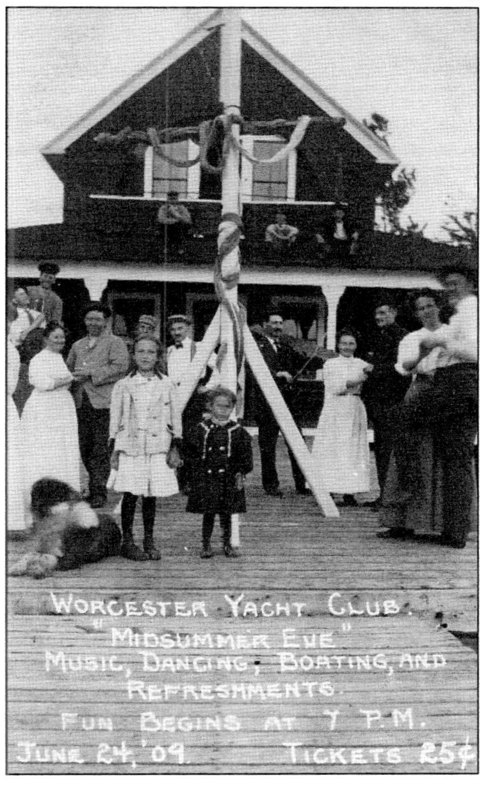

Members of the Worcester Yacht Club pose in front of their clubhouse on Indian Lake. The club was an organization of those who owned boats and canoes on Indian Lake.

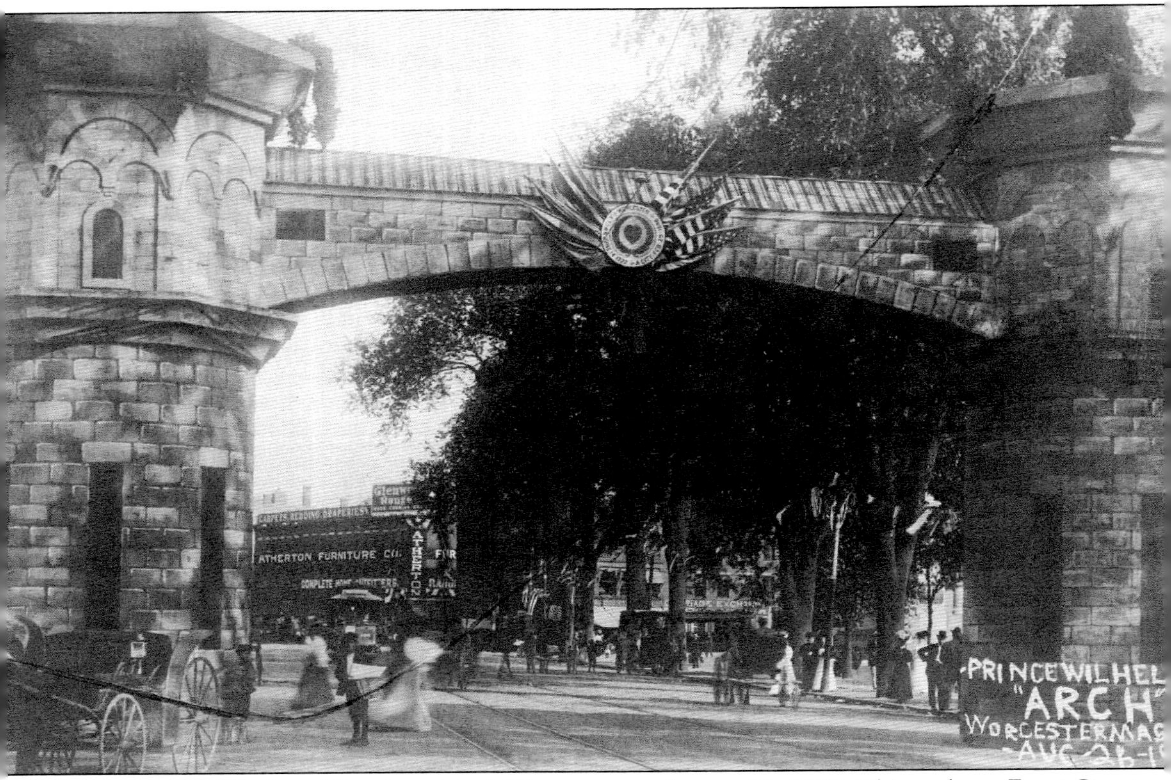

Prince Wilhelm of Sweden visited Worcester on August 26, 1907. This arch on Front Street was constructed in his honor. Thousands of Swedish immigrants and their children gathered to greet him. After accepting a key to the city from Mayor John T. Duggan, the prince proceeded to Mechanics Hall to give an address expressing his thanks to the city for its hospitality.

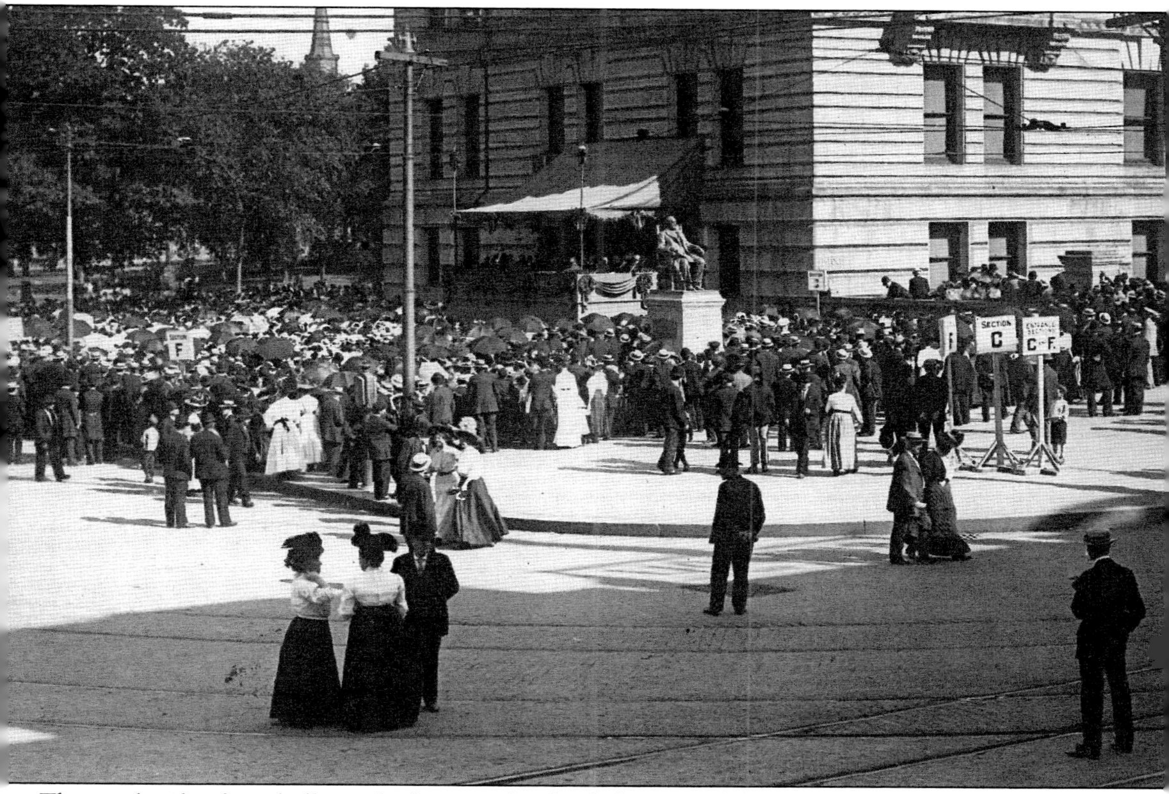

The north side of city hall was the location for the dedication of the George Frisbie Hoar statue on June 26, 1908. The late senator was memorialized by the city after his death on September 30, 1904, with services at Mechanics Hall on Patriots Day, April 19, 1905. He was a resident of the city for more than 50 years.

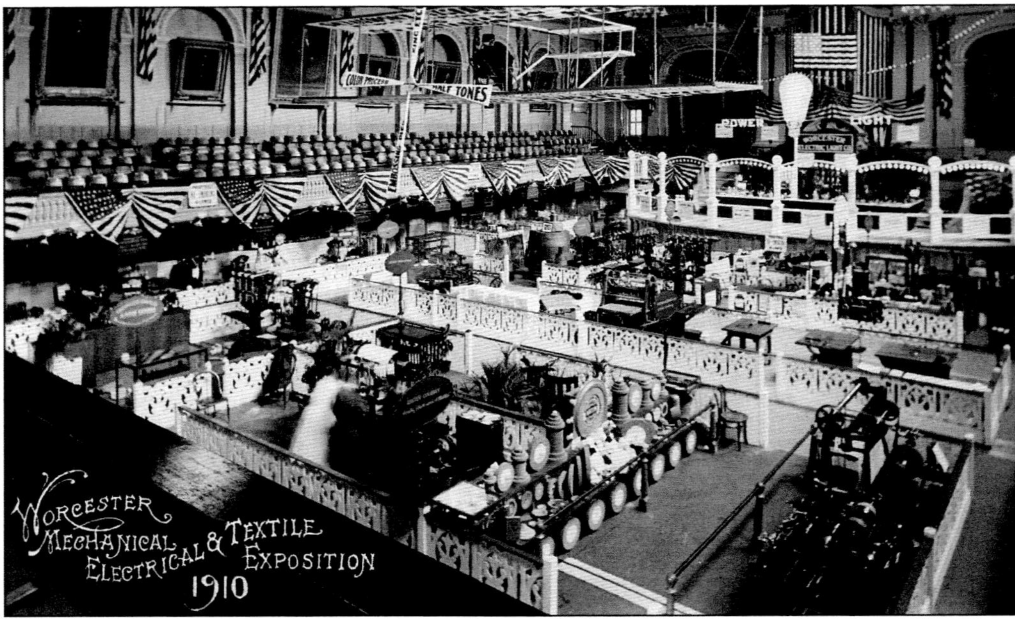

The Worcester Mechanical, Electrical, and Textile Exposition was held at Mechanics Hall from February 2–5, 1910. This is a view looking from the rear balcony towards the stage. One of the displays was a house of electricity in which only electrical devices were used for various things, from toasting bread to ironing clothes.

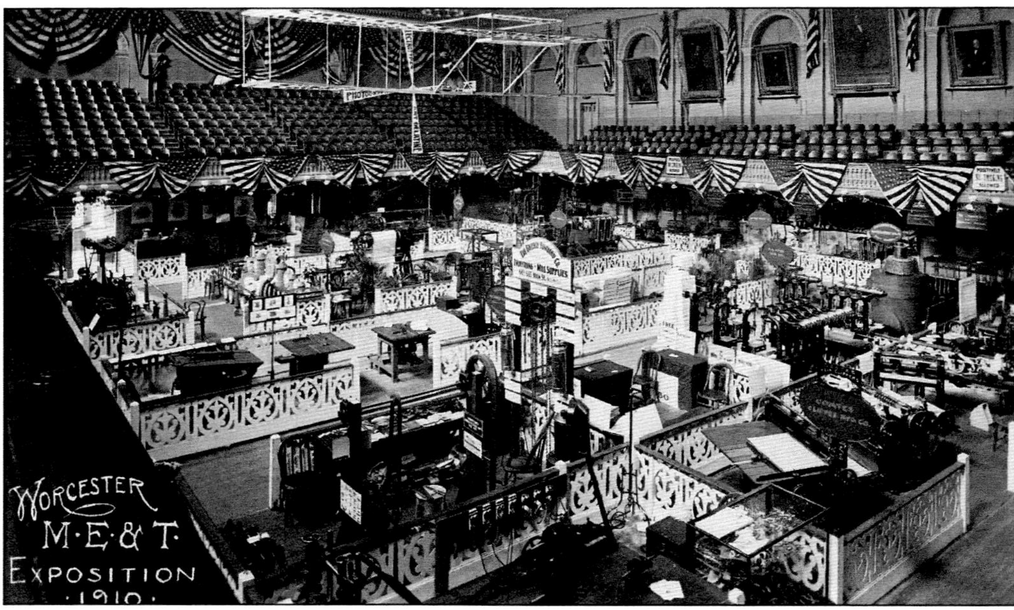

This is a view of the 1910 exposition looking from the balcony near the stage towards the rear. The exposition had 70 interesting and educational exhibits, some of which included chickens hatched by electricity, a demonstration of how envelopes were made, a new system of water pumping, an elastic stocking loom, and a Turkish towel loom.

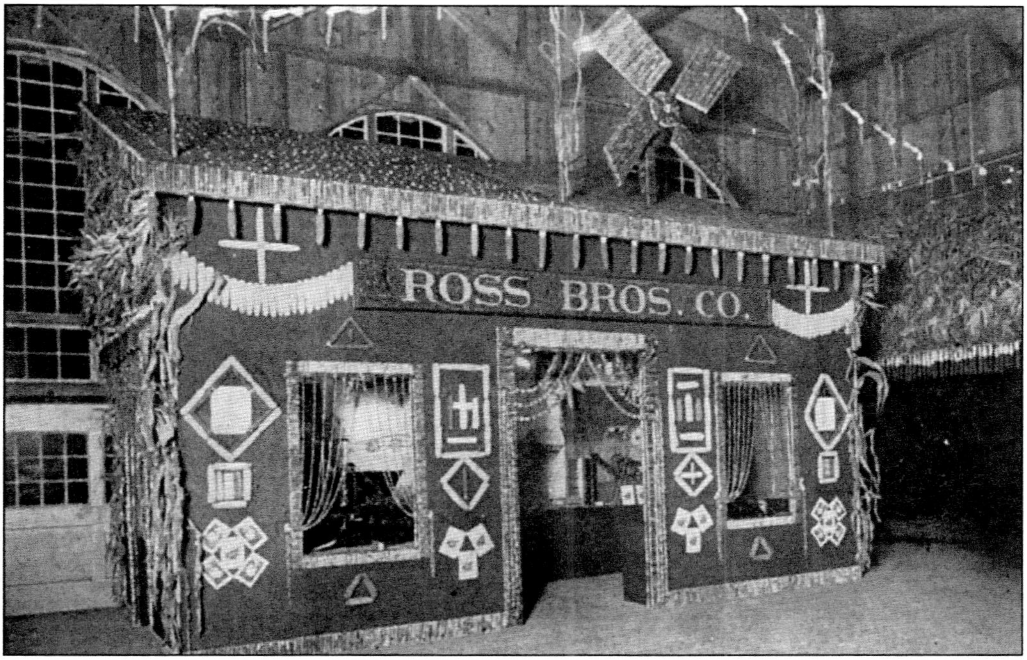

The New England Corn Show was held at the fair grounds in Greendale from November 7–12, 1910. It was the first of its kind in New England. One of the displays, the bungalow of corn shown here, was shingled with ears of corn. On the roof was a Dutch windmill operation constructed using corn stalks. Draperies, found in each window, were made of corn kernels.

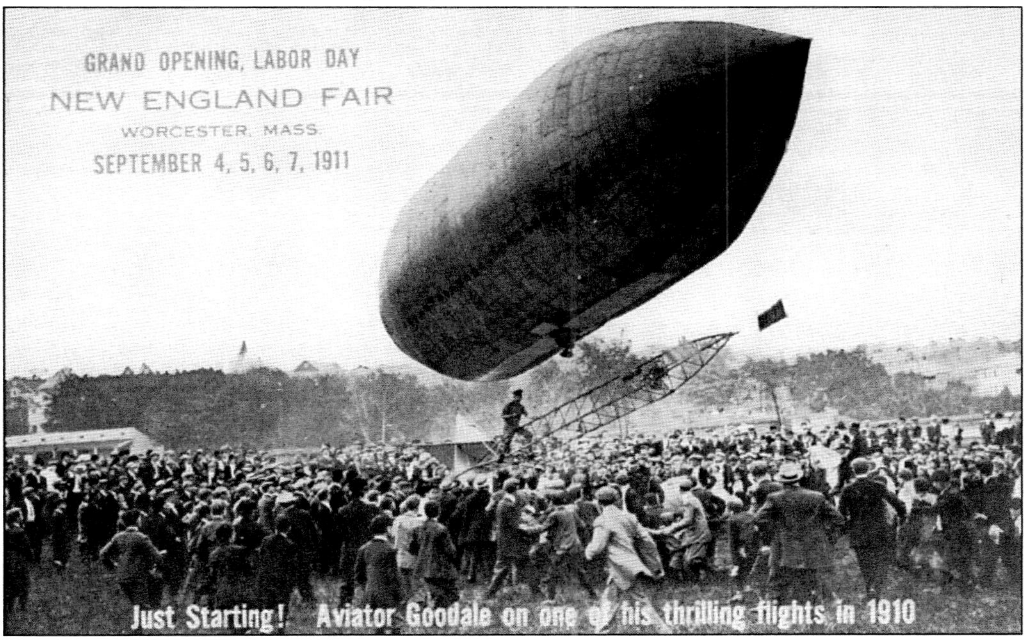

The events of the 1910 New England Fair were highlighted by aviator Frank W. Goodale and his airship. Mr. Goodale, only 21 years old, was expected to fly the airship to city hall, circle the clock tower, and sail back to the fair grounds.

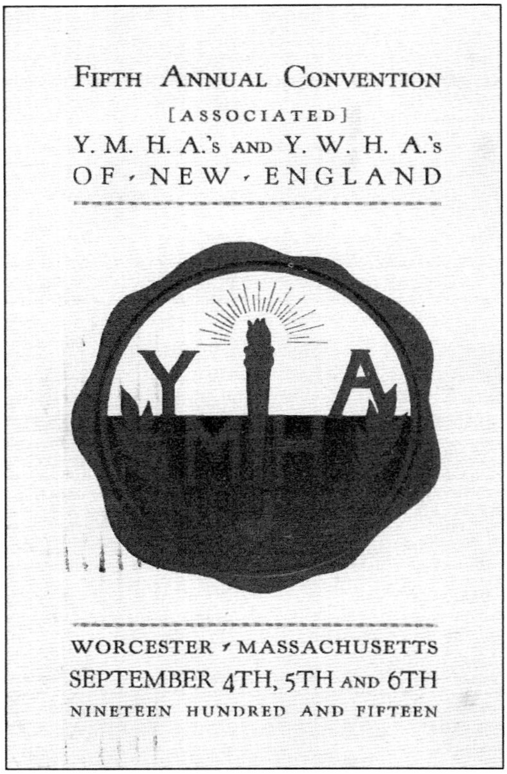
FIFTH ANNUAL CONVENTION
[ASSOCIATED]
Y. M. H. A.'s AND Y. W. H. A.'s
OF · NEW · ENGLAND

WORCESTER · MASSACHUSETTS
SEPTEMBER 4TH, 5TH AND 6TH
NINETEEN HUNDRED AND FIFTEEN

The Convention of the Young Men's Hebrew Associations and the Young Women's Hebrew Associations of New England took place at the Bancroft Hotel. Large meetings also took place at Mechanics Hall. There was a field day that Monday at Boulevard Park.

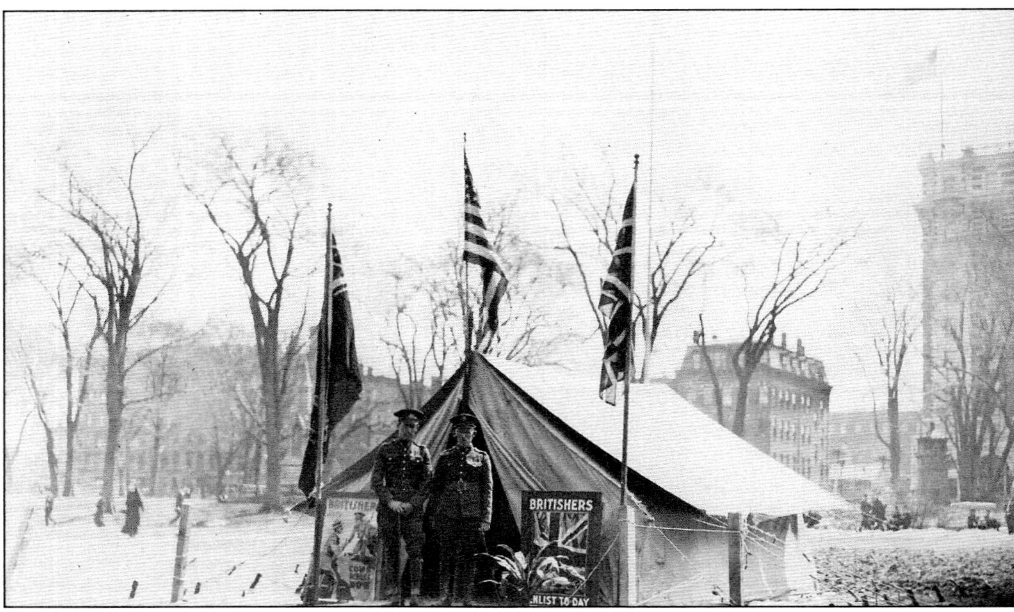

These British soldiers, set up on the common *c.* 1916, were recruiting British citizens in the United States to join the war effort. Great Britain called up five million men to fight in the war during 1916 and 1917. The messages on the posters say, "Britishers Come Across Now," and, "Britishers Enlist Today."

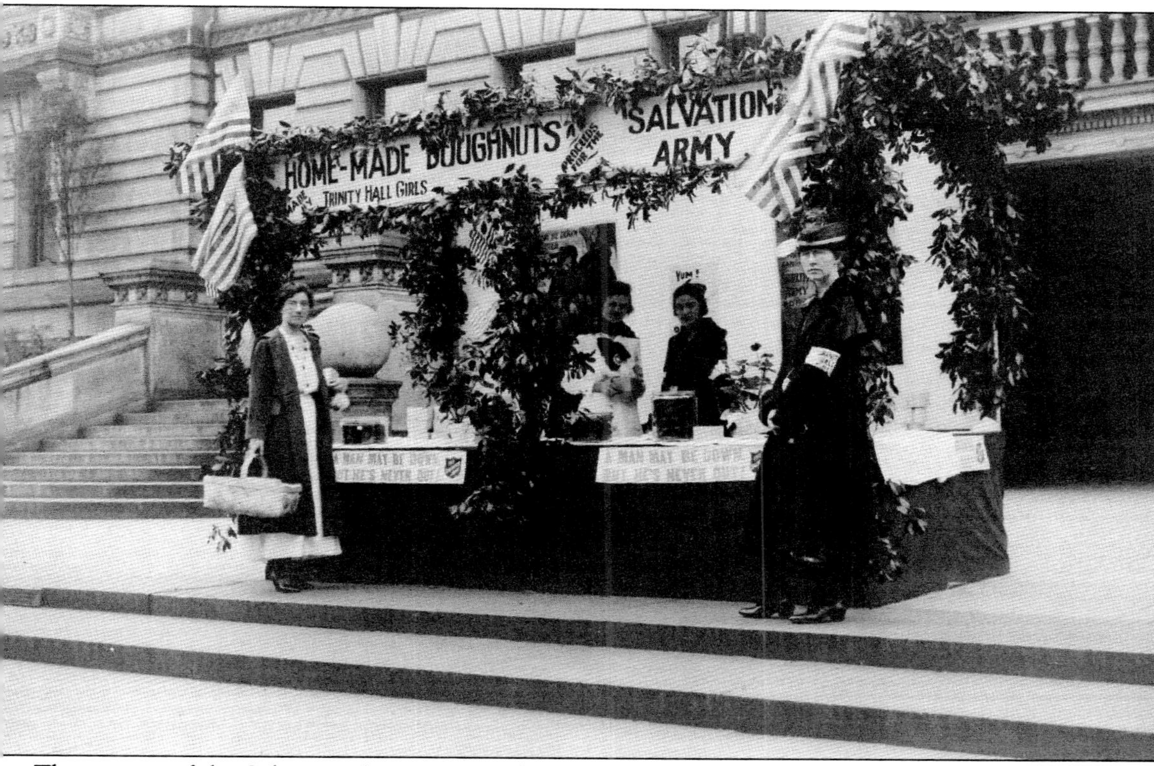

The women of the Salvation Army "manned" this booth in front of city hall during the week of May 19–25, 1919. The National Salvation Army Fund Raising Drive began on May 19, 1919. Saturday, May 25, 1919, was declared "Donut Day." The women's committee handed out imitation donuts as tags to each person who donated to the army's home service fund. Real donuts were also sold.

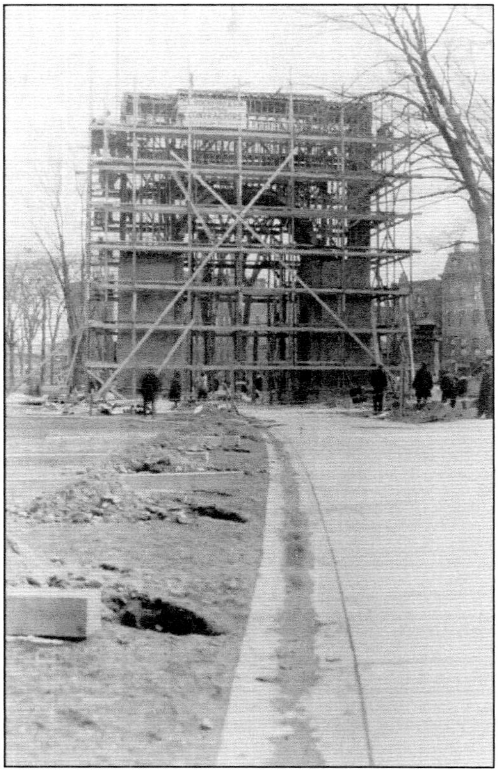

The Victory Arch on the common was constructed by L. Rochford and Son General Contractors. Plaster was the material used for the job. The total height was 52 feet and the width was 40 feet. The opening of the arch was 20 feet wide and 32 feet high.

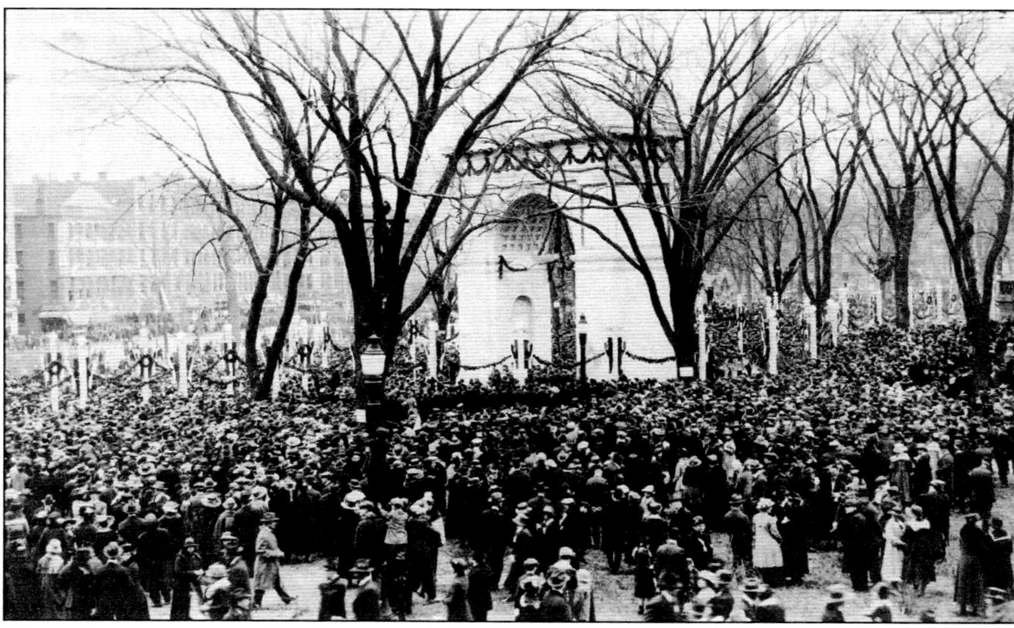

This arch was constructed on the common in April of 1919. It was built to honor all of Worcester's boys who enlisted in either the army or the navy for service in the war. The returning soldiers passed under the arch on May 1, 1919, during a big welcome-home parade.

Nine

DISASTERS

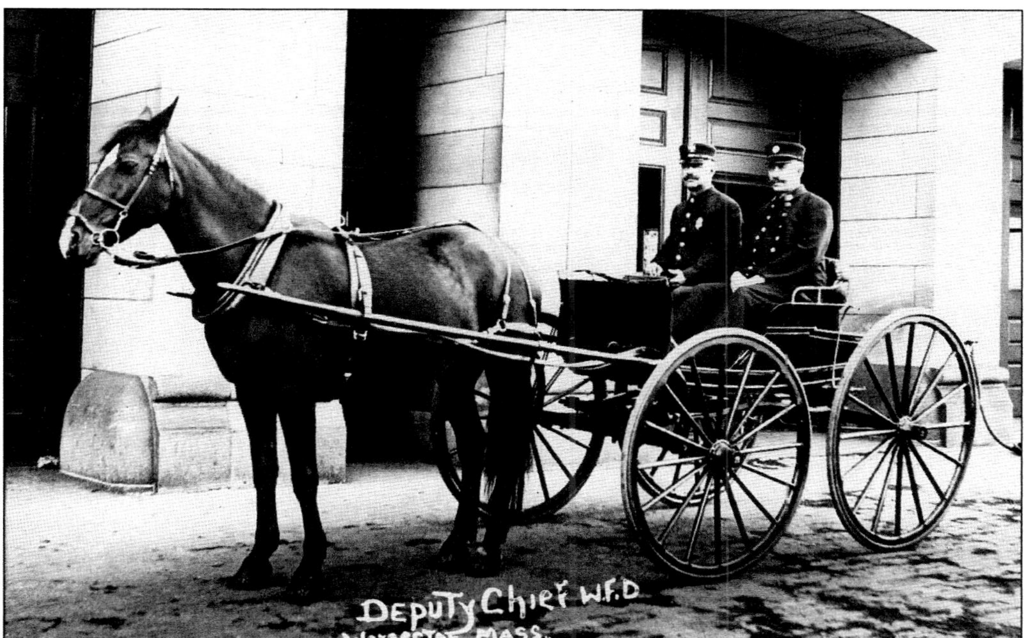

The deputy-chief engineer sits with his driver in front of the Fire Department Headquarters Building on the corner of Mercantile and Foster Streets, c. 1910. In 1911 the chief engineer was George S. Coleman and the deputy-chief engineer was Wesley N. Avery.

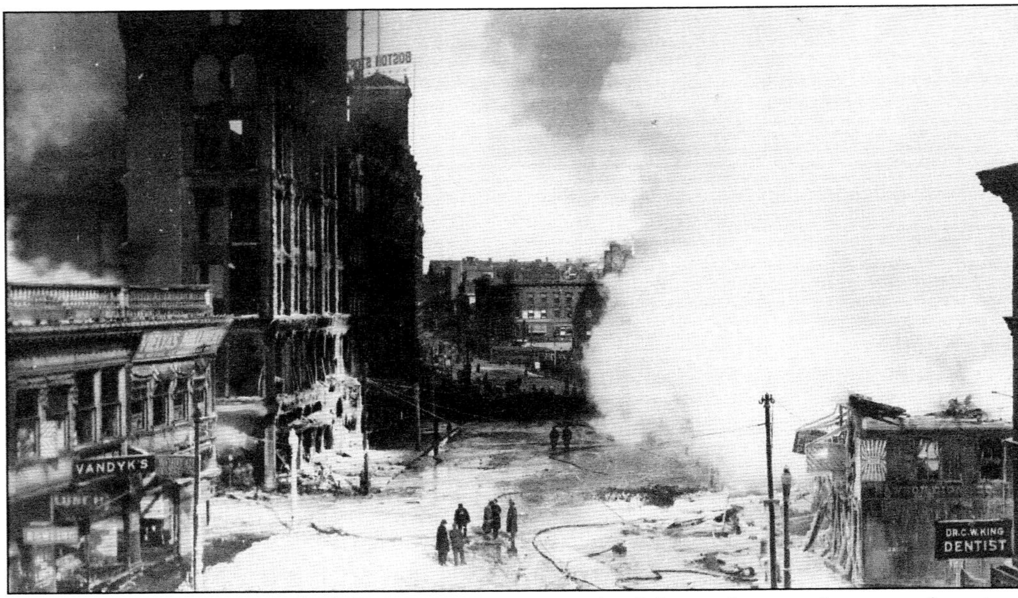

The Knowles Building on the left was in ruins as a result of the city's worst fire up to that time. It occurred at 3:00 a.m. on January 19, 1921. A night watchman for the adjacent S. Marcus Store discovered the fire around the elevator well on the first floor. Fortunately the wind was blowing from the northwest. Had the wind been blowing from the south, it was doubtful that the fire could have been prevented from going all the way through to Court House Hill.

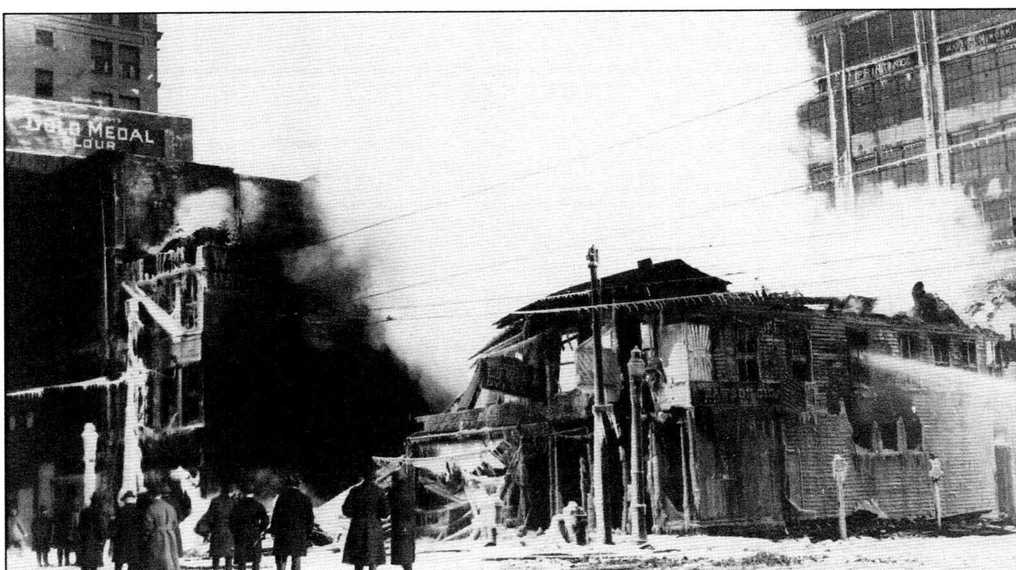

Flames from the Knowles Building jumped across Main Street to the east side and destroyed the W.H. Sawyer block, partially destroyed the Willard Hardware block, the Monahans Sporting Goods Store, and the Williams Book Store. Fifteen small fires were set by sparks from the large fire.

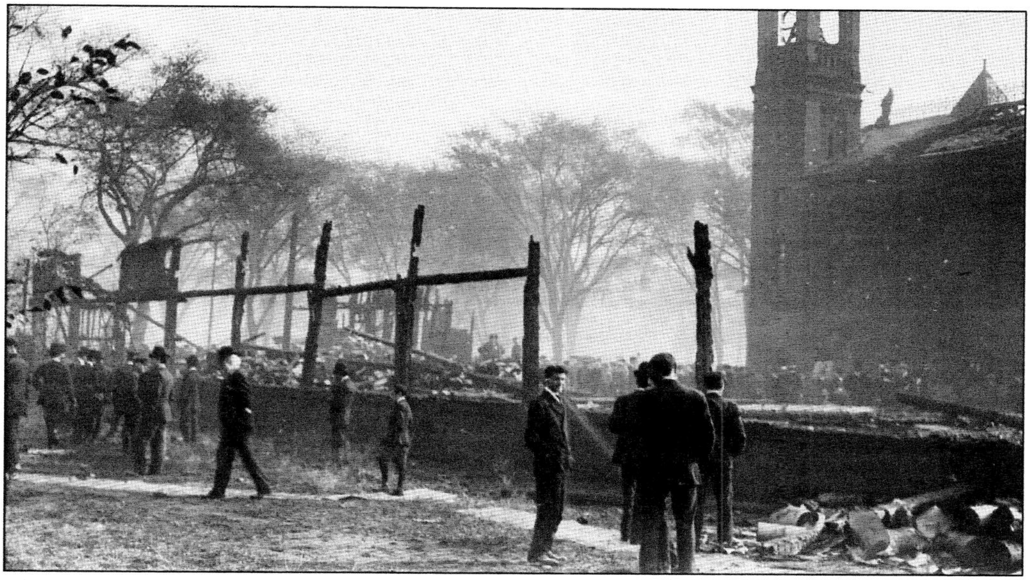

This was the scene on Park (Franklin) Street, across from city hall, after a fire that started in Samuel Starkworth's Wallpaper Store at 10:30 p.m., October 14, 1908. An entire city block was razed, including Notre Dame Church.

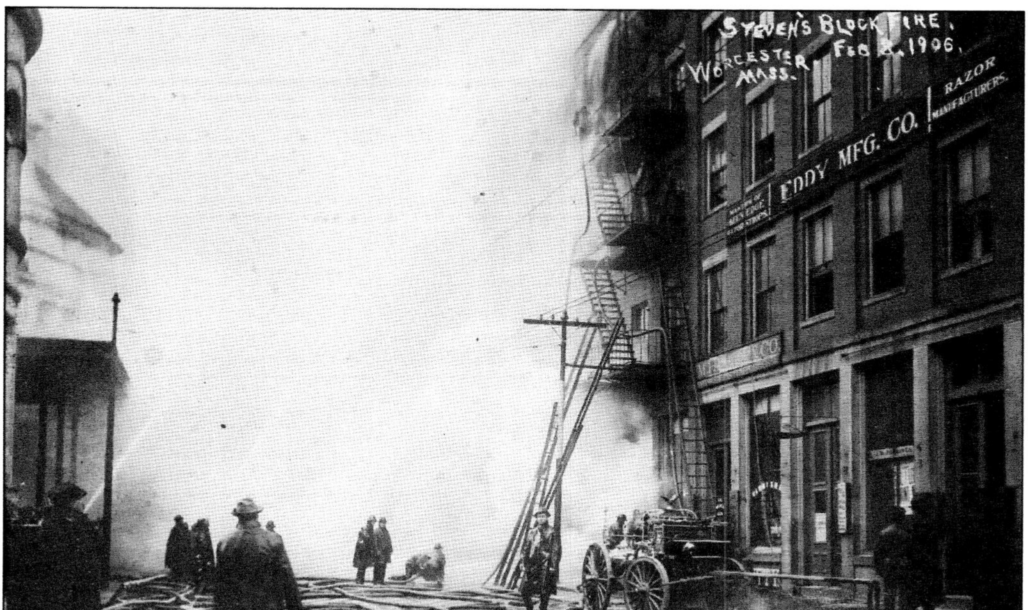

A major fire in the Steven's block, on Southbridge Street across from the post office, occurred on February 8, 1906. Ten firemen were injured while fighting the four-alarm fire. It was one of the hardest-fought fires in years.

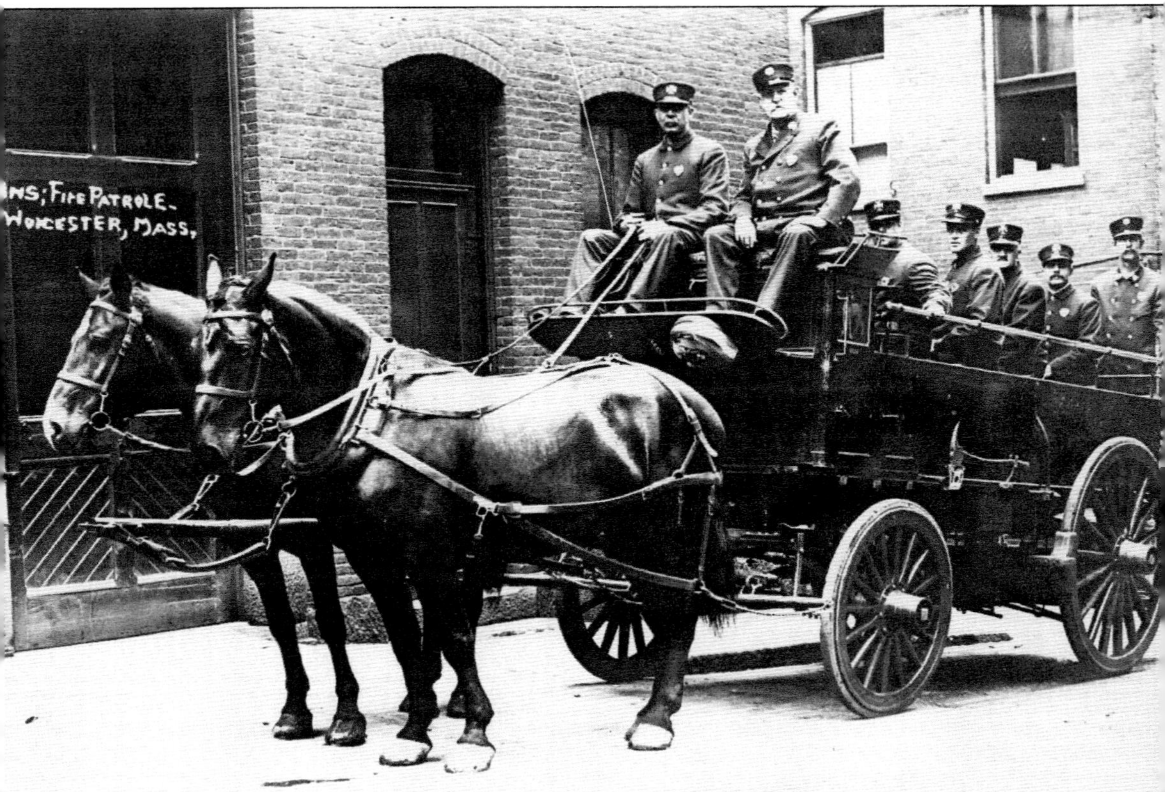

The Worcester Protective Department of Insurance Fire Patrol was stationed at Barton Place across from city hall. It was supported by the insurance companies doing business in Worcester for the protection of property from damage by fire and water. In 1911 the patrol consisted of nine members.

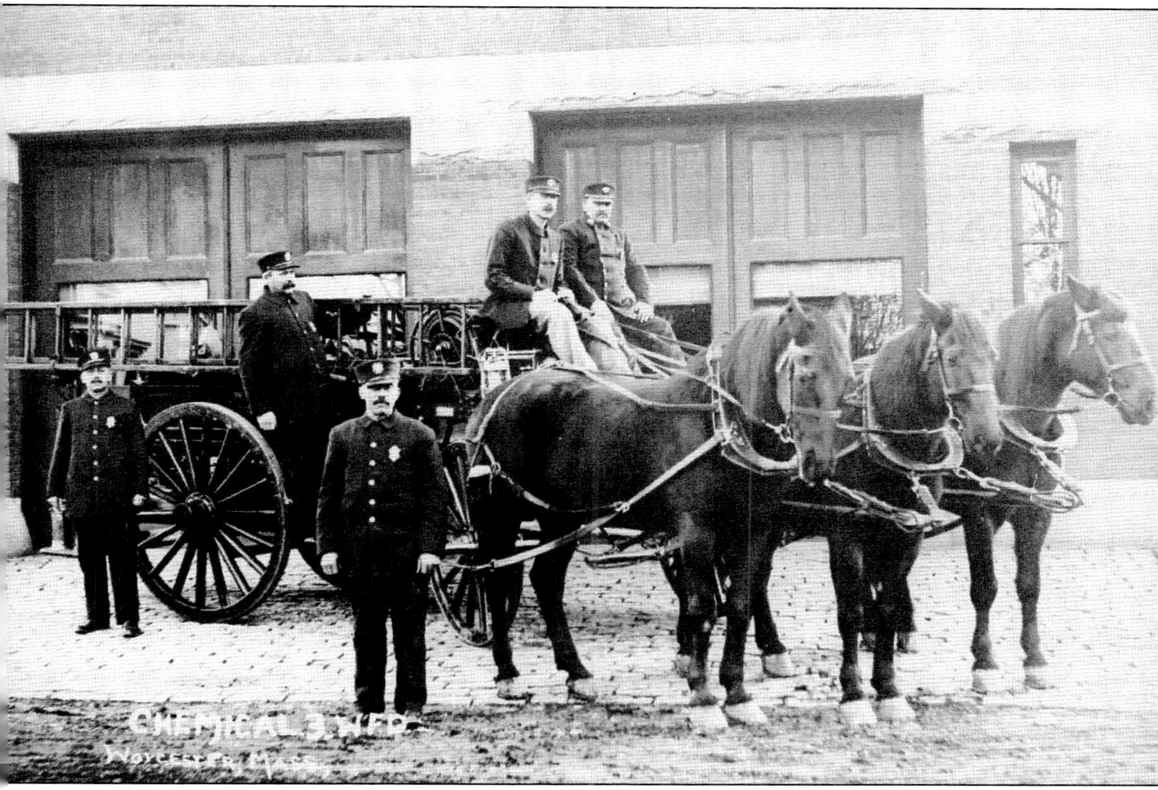

Three horses pull the men of Chemical Number Three. The city had three chemical companies in 1911. They were located at the stations on John Street, Foster Street, and Burncoat Street.

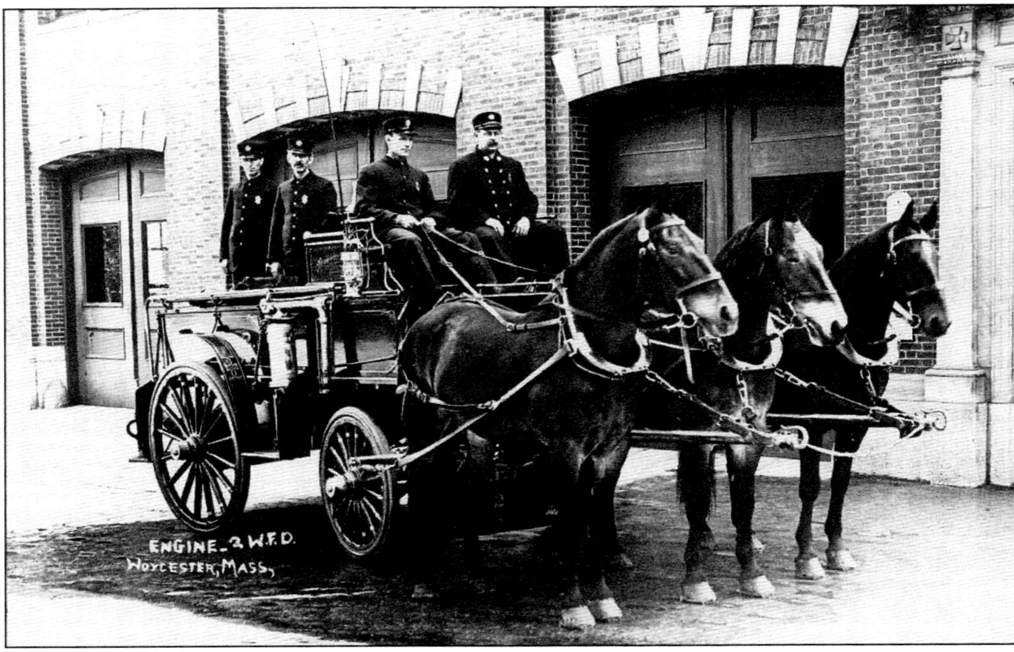

The men of Engine Number Two pose in front of their station house at 108 Beacon Street c. 1910. The city maintained seven engine companies in 1911. In addition to Beacon Street, the other companies were located at Mercantile Street, School Street, Pleasant Street, Webster Street, Bloomingdale Road, and Eastern Avenue.

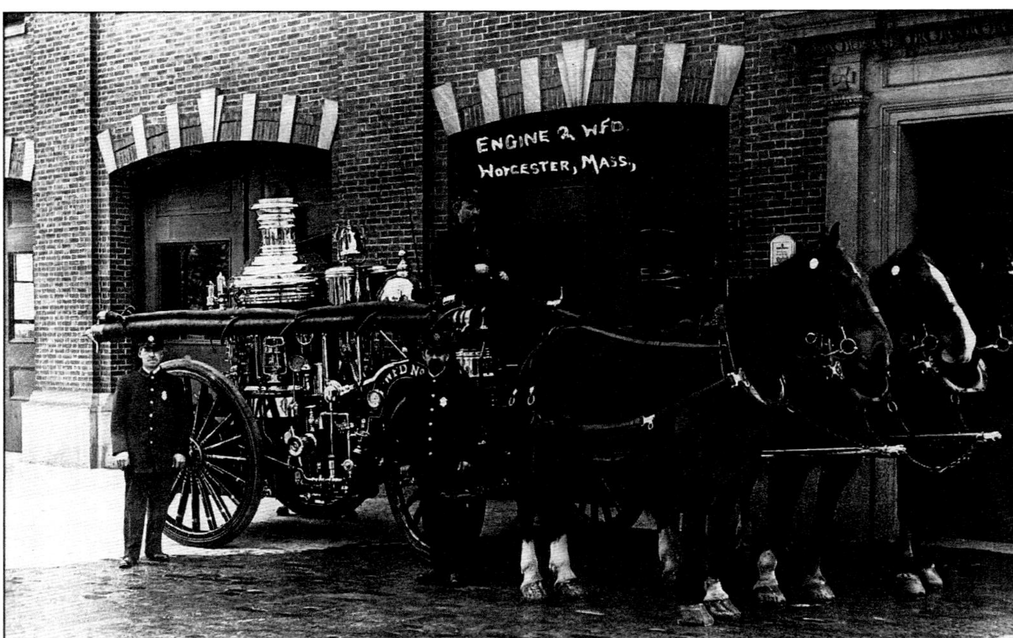

This is the steamer part of Engine Two. In 1911 engineers of steamers were paid $3.10 per day.

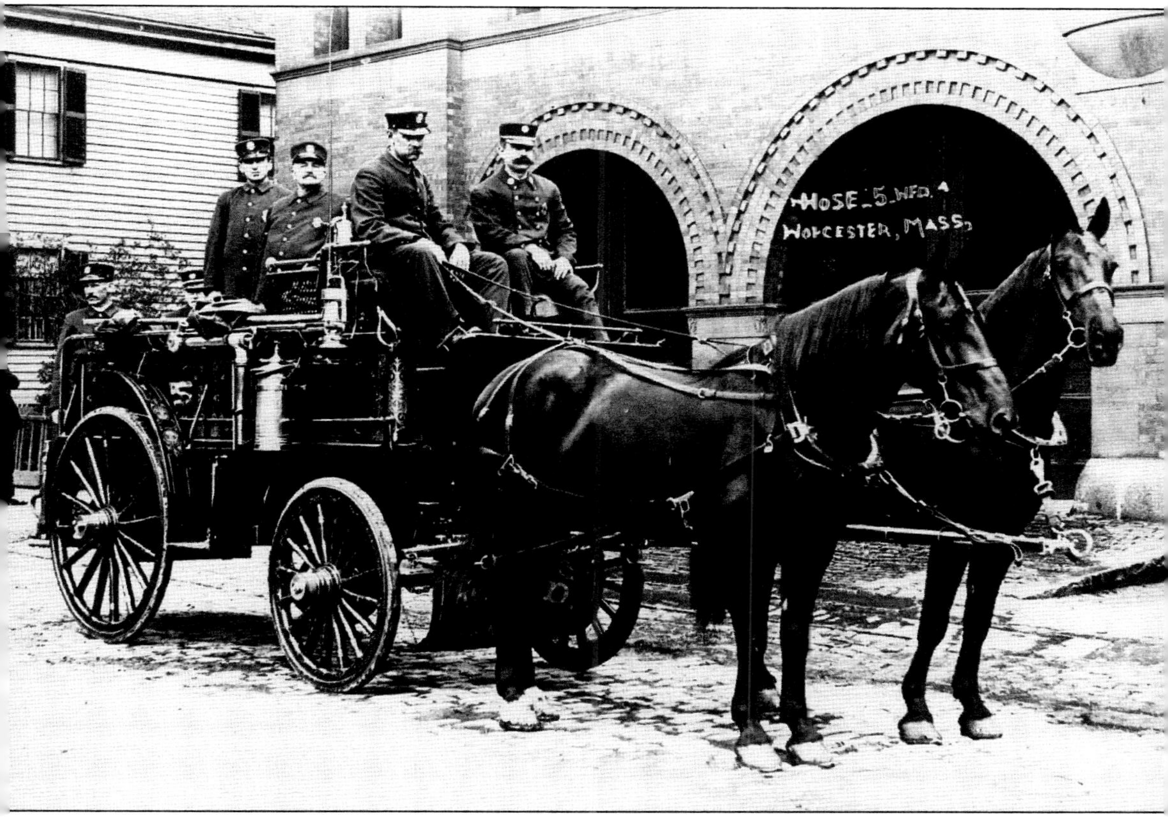

The men of Hose Company Number Five are shown here *c.* 1910. In 1911 Worcester had eleven hose companies. They were stationed at Prescott Street, Grafton Street, Cambridge Street, Foster Street, Portland Street, Millbury Street, Lamartine Street, Providence Street, Woodland Street, West Boylston Street, and Mercantile Street.

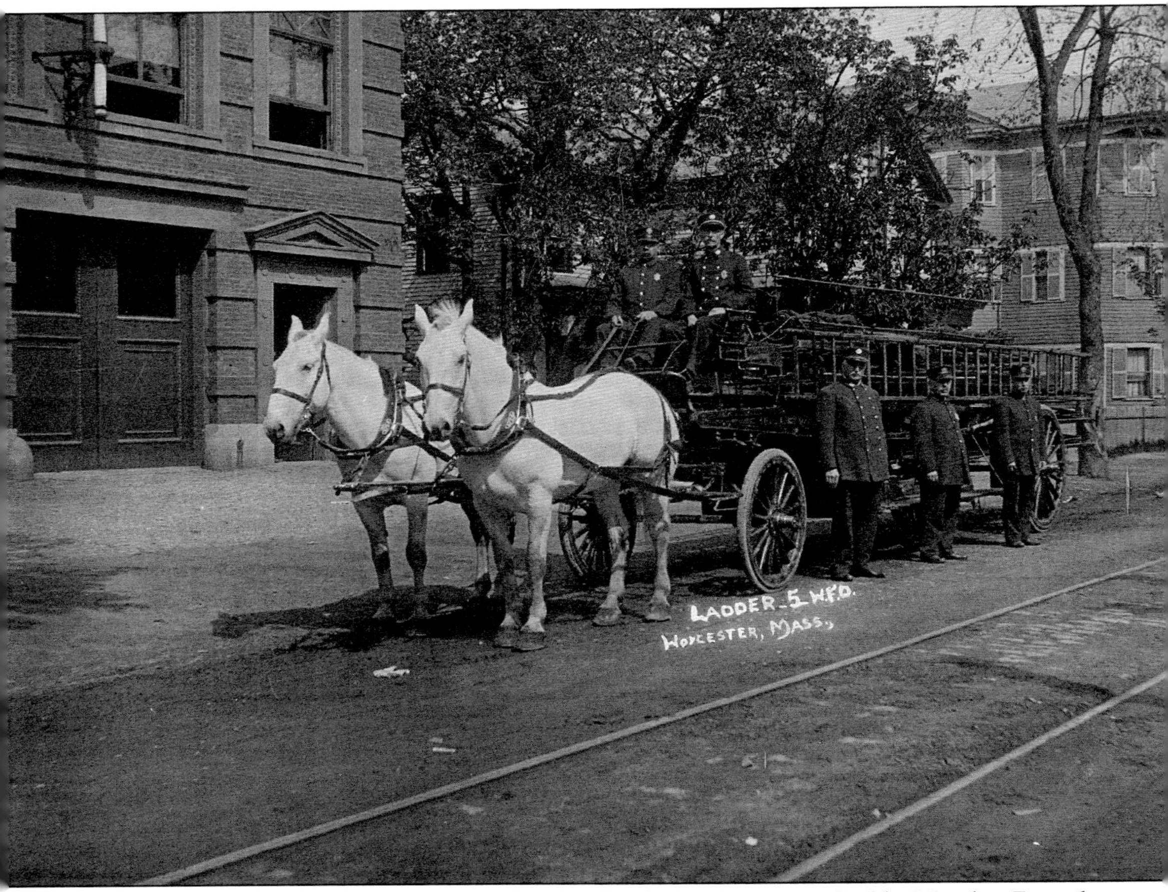

Six men were assigned to Ladder Company Number Five in 1911. Ladder Number Five, shown here, was located at the 100 Providence Street Fire Station. There were five other ladder companies in the city. They were located at the stations on Portland Street, Prescott Street, Mercantile Street, Webster Street, and West Boylston Street.

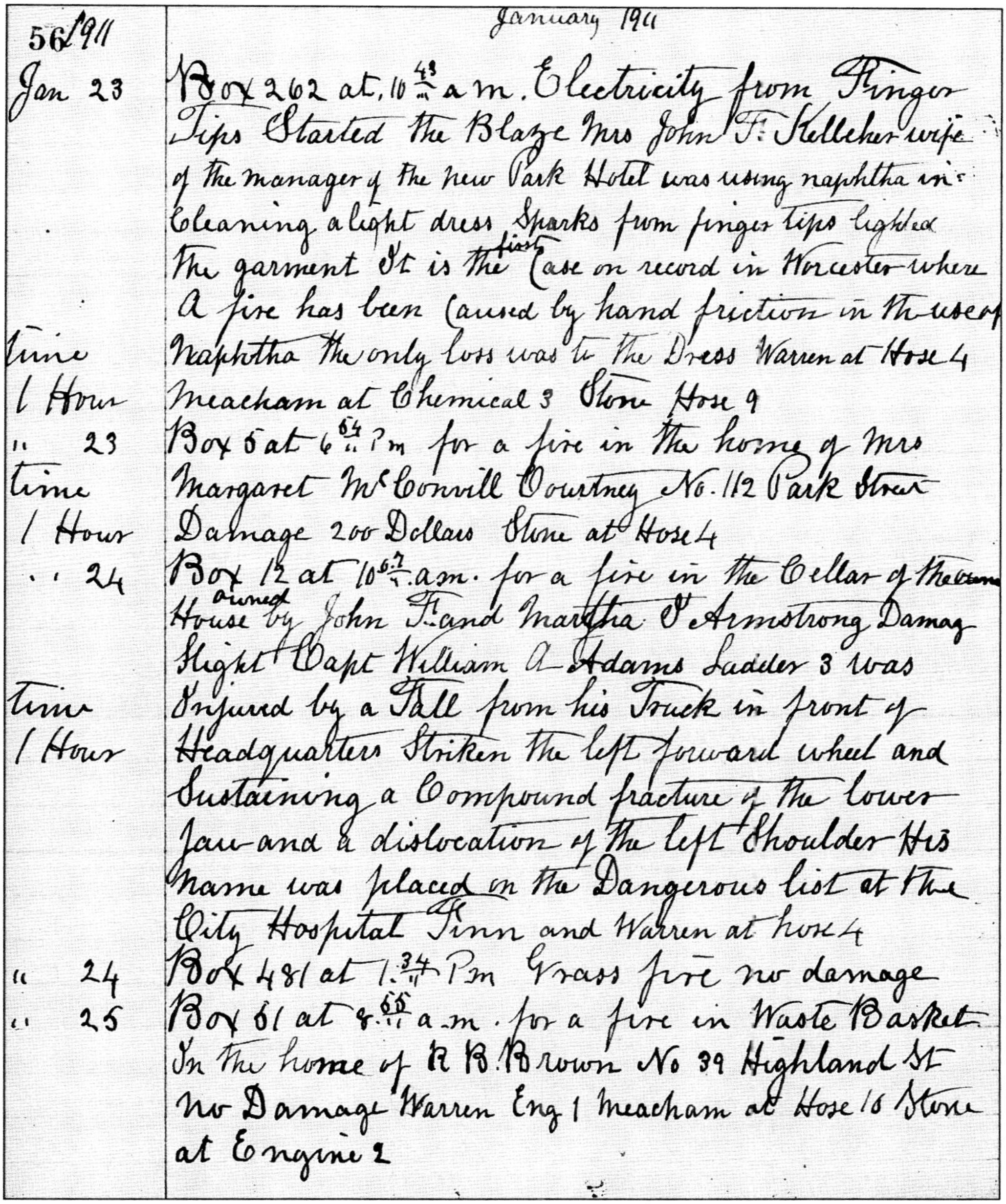

56 1911 January 1911

Jan 23 Box 262 at 10 43 a.m. Electricity from Finger Tips Started the Blaze Mrs John F. Kelleher wife of the manager of the new Park Hotel was using naphtha in Cleaning a light dress Sparks from finger tips lighted The garment It is the first Case on record in Worcester where A fire has been Caused by hand friction in the use of Naphtha the only loss was to the Dress Warren at Hose 4

time 1 Hour Meacham at Chemical 3 Stone Hose 9

" 23 Box 5 at 6 54 P.m for a fire in the home of Mrs Margaret McConvill Courtney No. 112 Park Street

time 1 Hour Damage 200 Dollars Stone at Hose 4

" 24 Box 12 at 10 57 a.m. for a fire in the Cellar of the House owned by John F. and Martha J. Armstrong Damage Slight Capt William A. Adams Ladder 3 was Injured by a Fall from his Truck in front of Headquarters Striken the left forward wheel and Sustaining a Compound fracture of the lower Jaw and a dislocation of the left Shoulder His name was placed on the Dangerous list at the City Hospital Finn and Warren at Hose 4

time 1 Hour

" 24 Box 481 at 1 34 P.m Grass fire no damage

" 25 Box 61 at 8 55 a.m. for a fire in Waste Basket In the home of R B. Brown No 39 Highland St no Damage Warren Eng 1 Meacham at Hose 16 Stone at Engine 2

Each fire station maintained a daily log of the alarms it responded to. This is a page from the daily log of Engine Number Four stationed on Pleasant Street, dated January 23–25, 1911. One of the entries for January 23 reads, "Box 262 at 10:43 a.m. Electricity from finger tips started the blaze. Mrs. John F. Kelliher, wife of the manager of the new Park Hotel, was using Naphtha in cleaning a light dress. Sparks from finger tips lighted the garment. It is the first case on record in Worcester where a fire has been caused by hand friction in the use of Naphtha. The only loss was to the dress."

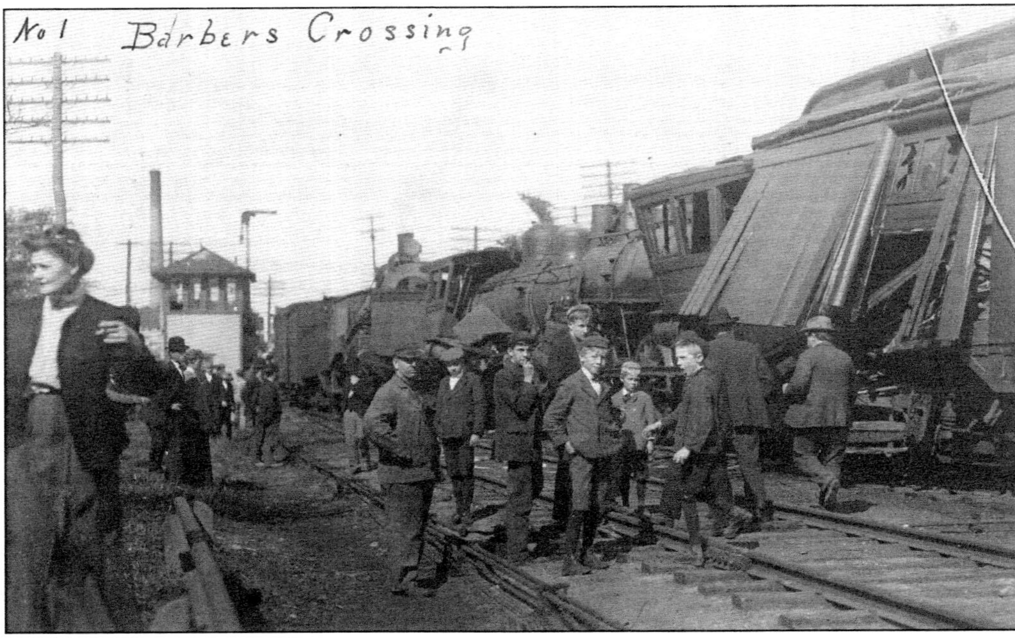

A crowd gathers at the train wreck that occurred at Barber's Crossing, in the Greendale section of the city, at noon on October 2, 1907.

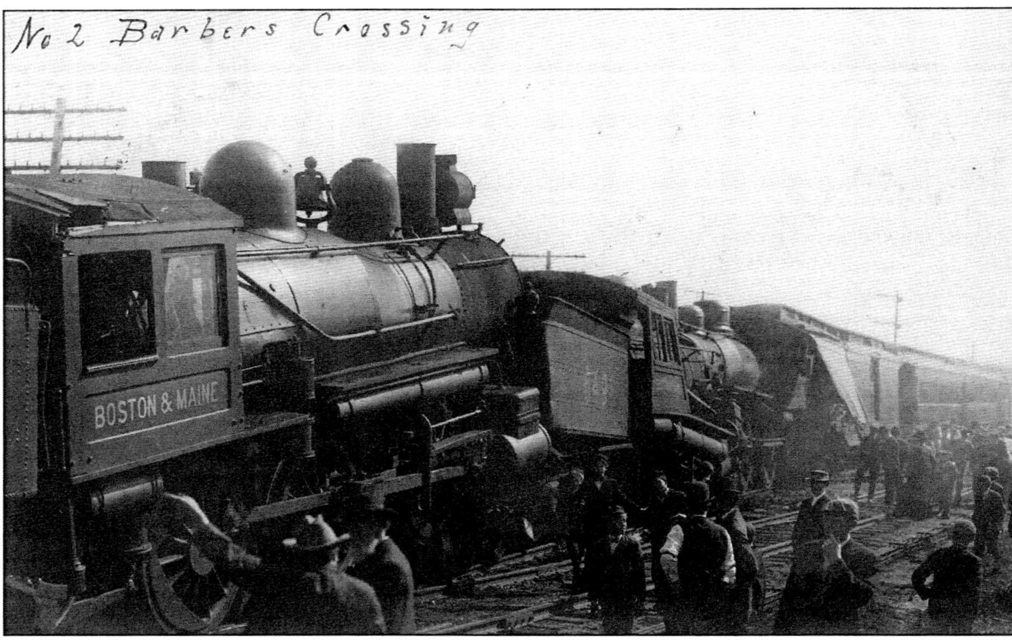

The wreck at Barber's Crossing was between a Boston and Maine freight train. The engineer of the passenger train failed to see the signal that told the passenger train to stop.

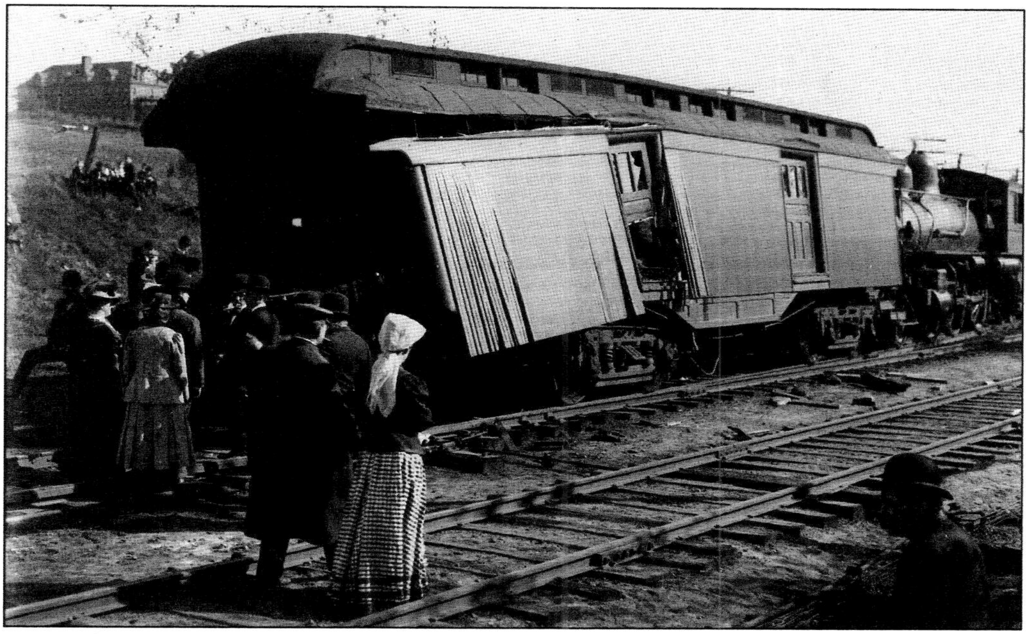

A crowd has gathered to view the wrecked cars from the Barber's Crossing wreck. Six people were injured in the wreck. The engines were reduced to scrap iron, and the freight and passenger cars became kindling wood.

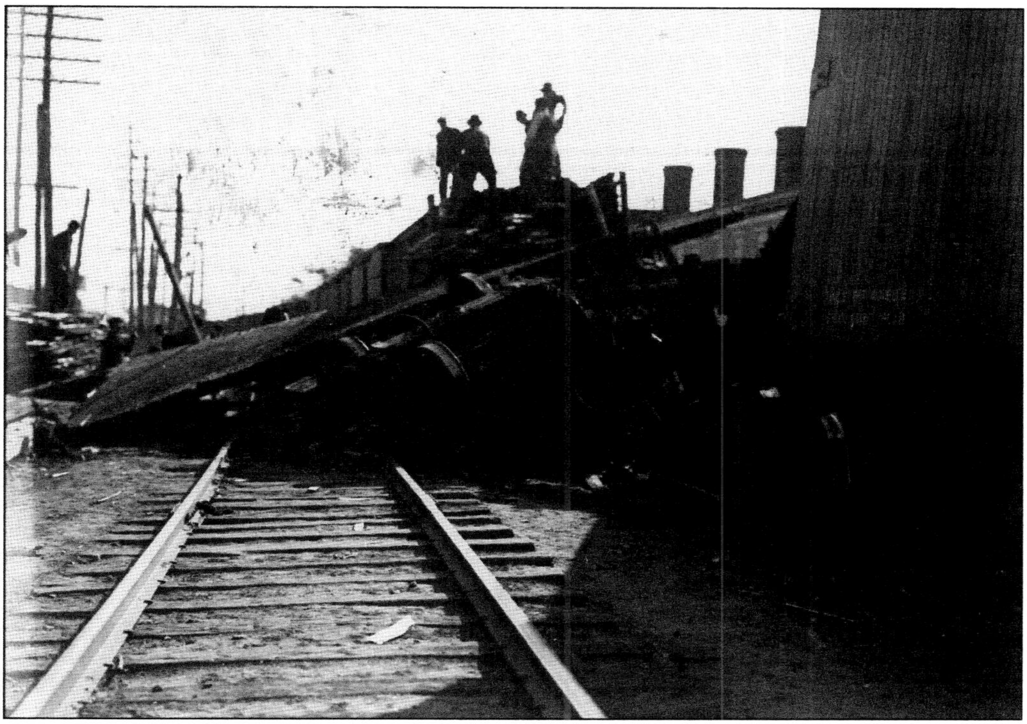

People stand on the wrecked cars at Barber's Crossing. Wreckage can be seen blocking the tracks. On the right you can see the chimneys of the Norton Company.

Selected Bibliography

Blanchard, F.S. and Company. *Dictionary of Worcester and Vicinity*. 1889.

Carlson, Stephen and Thomas Harding. *Worcester Trolleys Remembered*. Worcester: Worcester Regional Transit Authority, 1985.

City of Worcester. *Memorial Services of George Frisbie Hoar*. Worcester: Blanchard Press, 1907.

Diocese of Worcester. *Official Reference and Information Guide*. 1915.

Drew Allis Company. *Worcester Directories 1892–1930*.

Eastus, Charles W. and John F. McClymer. GA *Til Amerika: The Swedish Creation of an Ethnic Identity for Worcester, Massachusetts*. Worcester: Worcester Historical Museum, 1994.

Farnsworth and O'Flynn. *The Story of Worcester Massachusetts*. Worcester: Davis Press, 1934.

Feingold, Norma. *Shaarai Torah: Life Cycle of a Synagogue*. Worcester: Worcester Historical Museum, 1991.

Frost, Jack. *The Church in Worcester, New England*. Hawthorne Press, 1956.

Knowlton, Elliot B. and Sandra Gibson-Quigley. *Worcester's Best* (2nd Edition). Worcester: Preservation Worcester, 1996.

Mange, Paul. *Our Inns From 1718–1918*.

Nutt, Charles. *History of Worcester and its People*. New York: Lewis Historical Publishing Company, 1919.

Park Commissioners. *Annual Report 1914–15*. Worcester: Commonwealth Press, 1915.

Rice, Franklin P. *The Worcester of Eighteen Hundred and Ninety-Eight*. Worcester: Blanchard and Company, 1899.

Trinity Lutheran Church. *Trinity Lutheran Church*. Worcester: Commonwealth Press, 1952.

Sandrof, Ivan. *Your Worcester Street*. Franklin Publishing, 1948.

Spears, John P. *Old Landmarks and Historic Spots*. Worcester: Commonwealth Press, 1931.

Tulloch, Donald. *Worcester City of Prosperity 1914*. Worcester: Commonwealth Press.

WPI. *The Aftermath 1923*. Heffernan Press.

Worcester Telegram. *Worcester Telegram* (1905 to 1920 editions).

Worcester Bank and Trust Company. *Some Historical Houses of Worcester*. Walton Printing and Advertising Company, 1919.

Worcester Board of Trade. A *Tribute to the Colombian Year*. Worcester: F.S. Blanchard and Company, 1893.

Worcester Board of Trade. *Worcester* Magazine.

FOOTPRINTS IN TIME

A walk where New Hampshire began

I0806149

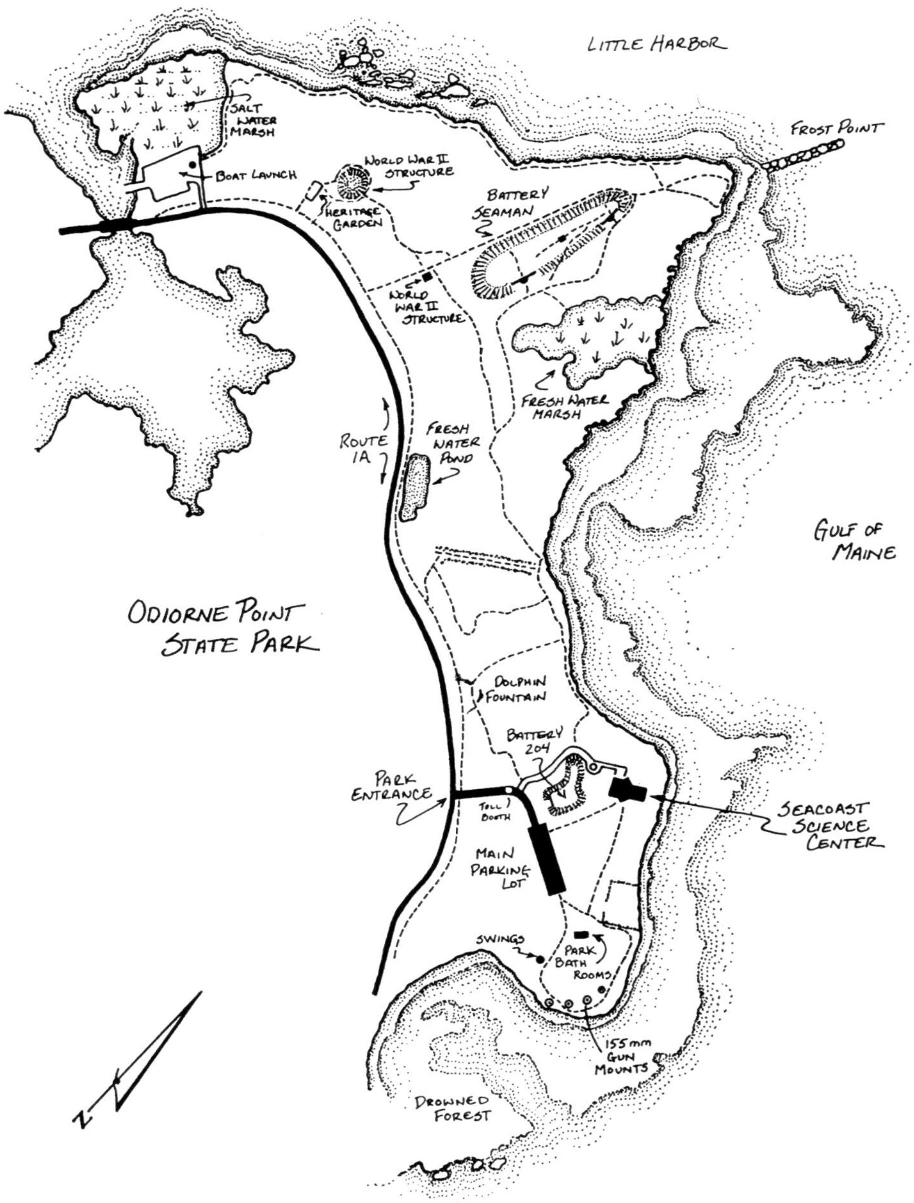
Little Harbor
Salt Water Marsh
Frost Point
World War II Structure
Boat Launch
Battery Seaman
Heritage Garden
World War II Structure
Fresh Water Marsh
Route 1A
Fresh Water Pond
Gulf of Maine
Odiorne Point State Park
Dolphin Fountain
Battery 204
Park Entrance
Toll Booth
Seacoast Science Center
Main Parking Lot
Swings
Park Bath Rooms
155mm Gun Mounts
Drowned Forest
N

FOOTPRINTS IN TIME

A walk where New Hampshire began

Compiled by Howard S. Crosby, Wendy W. Lull, and Richard T. MacIntyre

ISBN 978-0-7385-6398-5

Published by Arcadia Publishing
Charleston, South Carolina

Printed in the United States of America

Library of Congress Control Number: 2009924686

For all general information, please contact Arcadia Publishing:
Telephone 843-853-2070
Fax 843-853-0044
E-mail sales@arcadiapublishing.com
For customer service and orders:
Toll-Free 1-888-313-2665

Visit us on the Internet at www.arcadiapublishing.com

The Seacoast Science Center is open year round. Visitor hours vary seasonally; cal 603-436-8043 for current program schedules and hours. Odiorne Point State Park is als open throughout the year, hours vary seasonally. Park rest room facilities are open spring summer and fall. For Park information call 603-436-7406, or 603-436-1552.

Contents

Introduction

Seacoast Science Center

This book is the first illustrated walking guide of Odiorne Point State Park, a natural and cultural treasure of New England's seacoast. At last you can discover the fascinating stories of the land and the people who lived here whether you use the book as a guide to park trails, or read it at home.

The walking tour can be a one-to-two hour stroll, or a lifetime of exploration. (Combined, the history committee has spent over twenty-five years researching Odiorne's past and is constantly discovering new information!) Like the earliest Odiorne inhabitants, no matter which path you choose, you will find many reasons to return. Whether walking or relaxing at home, you are about to meet the courageous settlers who left all they knew for the promise of freedom in this place. You will hear the echoes of later families' aspirations and anger, successes and surrenders as they gave up their homes for their nation's defense.

Odiorne Point State Park has a landscape reflecting thousands of years of change. Your walk begins at the Seacoast Science Center and takes you past ice-age tree stumps, the ruins of once fine estates, and the remains of mighty military fortifications. You will walk along breathtaking sea-side vistas, through woodlands and meadows, past ponds and marshes. Afterwards, plan to spend some time with the Seacoast Science Center's exhibits to add to your understanding and enjoyment of the natural and cultural history of Odiorne Point.

This walk has been a popular guided tour since 1988, and is still conducted for park visitors and groups through the Seacoast Science Center. For information, call the Center at 603-436-8043. Enjoy your walk!

Welcome to the home of the Seacoast Science Center and a treasure of natural, social and military history.

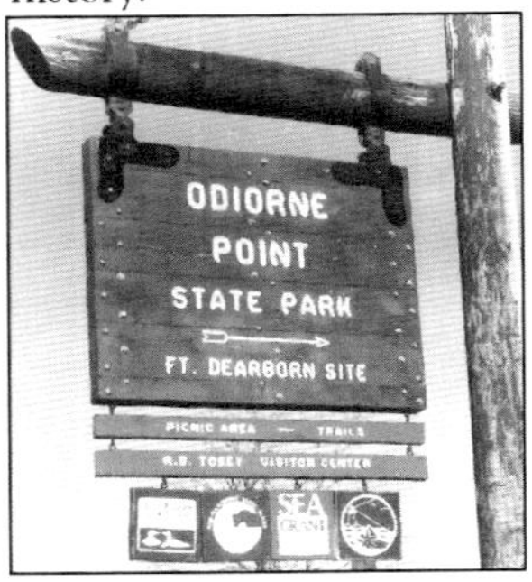

The Seacoast Science Center is managed by the Audubon Society of New Hampshire under contract with the State of New Hampshire, in affiliation with the Friends of Odiorne Point, Inc., and the University of New Hampshire Cooperative Extension/Sea Grant Program.

Completed in 1992, the Seacoast Science Center is the third structure at Odiorne Point used for environmental education since World War II.

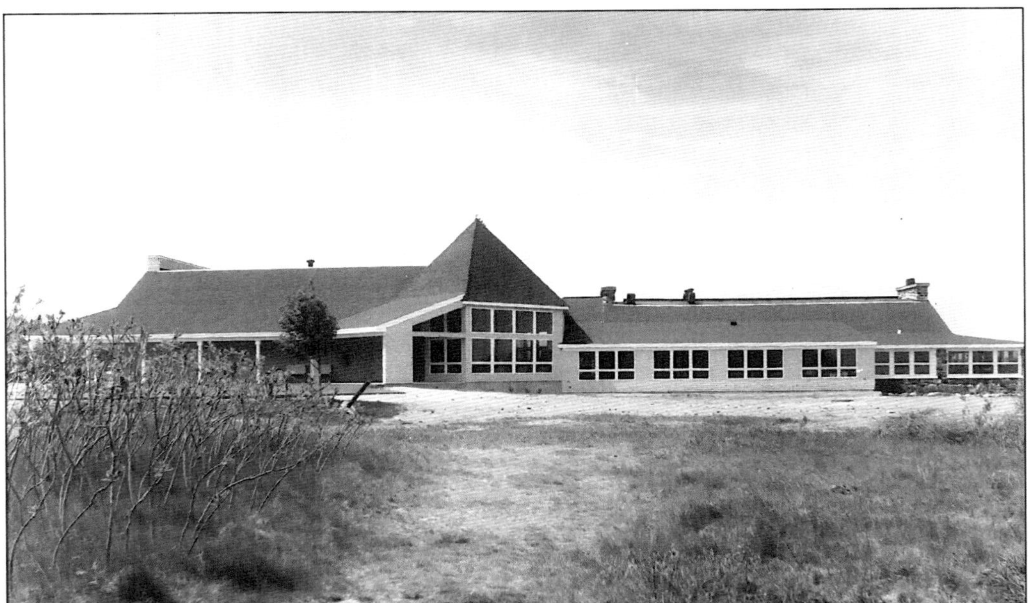

Safety and Conservation Guidelines: Tips to help improve your visit.

Help us retain the natural flavor of Odiorne Point State Park by following these important safety and conservation guidelines.

Around the Park:

1. Take only photographs, leave only footprints. Shells, sticks, flowers and plants are both habitat and food for the creatures that call Odiorne Point home. Hermit crabs live in empty snail shells; birds eat the grubs that burrow in dead sticks. Please honor our ban on collecting materials of all kinds. New Hampshire Parks are carry in/carry-out parks; please take your trash out of the Park and dispose of it properly.
2. When walking on the paved bicycle path, keep an eye and ear out for cyclists and roller-blade skaters.
3. Most of the plants and animals in the Park are not dangerous or poisonous, with the exception of poison ivy, which grows abundantly throughout the Park. There is a description and illustration of poison ivy on page 12 If you think you may have touched some during

your walk, scrub that part of you carefully with soap and water as soon as you finish your walk. Remember, wild animals tend to bite if provoked or if they feel threatened. For their protection and your own safety, please do not disturb our plants and animals.

4. Odiorne Point is generally a safe park, but it is also a big park. For your own safety, stay on the trails. Remember the gates close at sunset in summer, and earlier in the winter. Gate closing time is posted by the Park entrance.

On the Rocky Shore:

1. Assume slippery rocks! Coastal rocks are often wet from sea spray and can be very slippery. Even when they appear to be dry, take extra care for a sure footing.
2. Always wear sturdy, soft-soled shoes. The rocks may be smooth, but the barnacles are very sharp. Be careful when leaning against a barnacle-covered rock as it is easy to get a nasty scrape.
3. When exploring tide pools, remember to put rocks back bottom-side down where you found them because plants and animals live on rock bottoms and will die if exposed to air and sun too long. If you peek under the long seaweeds, please put these back also.

Seacoast Science Center to the Atlantic Shore Line

The first part of the Odiorne Point walking tour will take you from the Seacoast Science Center around the southern end of the state park. This section of trail winds past different sites, the stories of which are greatly separated in time. Here too you will have some of New Hampshire's best views of the Atlantic Ocean and the Isles of Shoals.

Your walk starts at the main entrance of the Science Center which encapsulates the summer home Robert Sugden built in 1920. Begin by walking straight ahead

As you exit the Science Center, look to your left for these two posts and proceed down the trail.

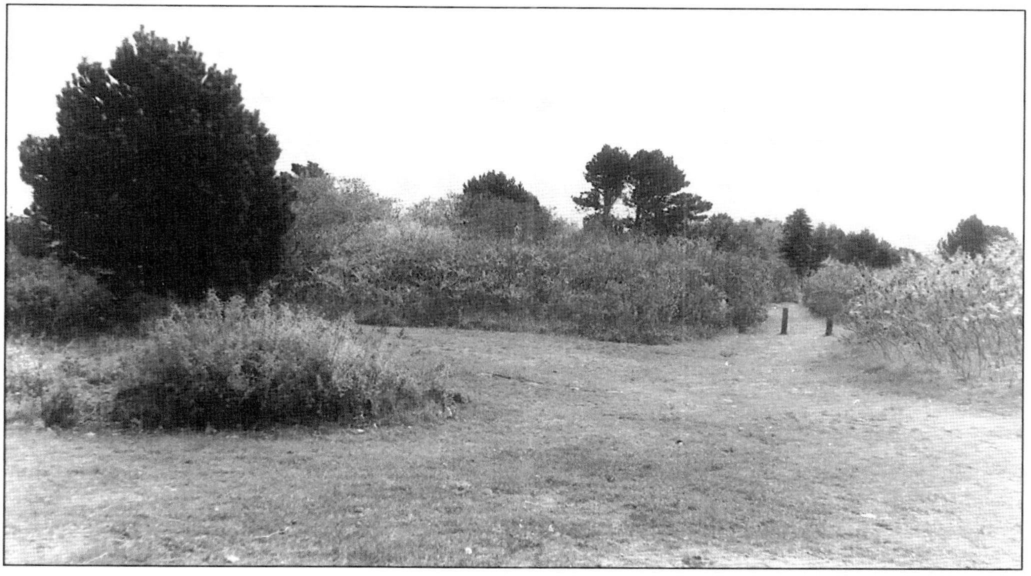

and slightly left so that the ocean is on your left. About 30 yards away you will see a set of posts marking a path cut through the omnipresent sumac bush. This is a non-poisonous variety called staghorn because of the pattern and velvety surface of its antler-like branches. Its dull red drupes (fruit) serve as food for many species of birds during the winter and also may be crushed and made into a delightful, tart drink. Sumac bark and leaves have a high concentration of tannic acid that is used for tanning leather.

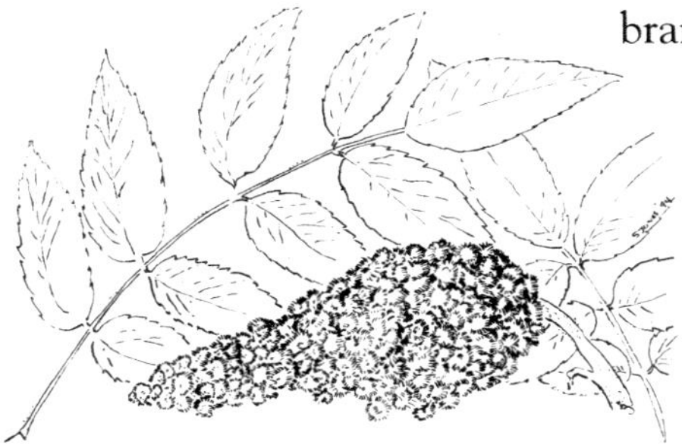

Staghorn sumac. Much of the area of what is now the Park was covered by the lawns of residential estates prior to World War II. This invasive staghorn sumac rapidly took hold when the lawns were no longer mowed during and following the war.

In addition to the sumac, another abundant plant here is poison ivy. From spring to early fall, walkers in the park with exposed skin should avoid the edges of the paths. Poison ivy may be recognized as a low, three-leaved plant the leaves of which are usually (but not always) shiny.

These paths also can become quite slippery when wet: walk carefully!

The path continues straight ahead for approximately 100 yards. At the end of this path, look left into a grassy area circumscribed by a stone wall.

This site marks the location of a home owned by Kathryn A. Stevens of Belmont, Massachusetts. Built in the 1920s on land purchased from Bertha Sugden, the summer home was one of the eleven homes which stood at Odiorne Point before World War II. A two-story house of seven or eight rooms, the Stevens' home had a glassed-in porch

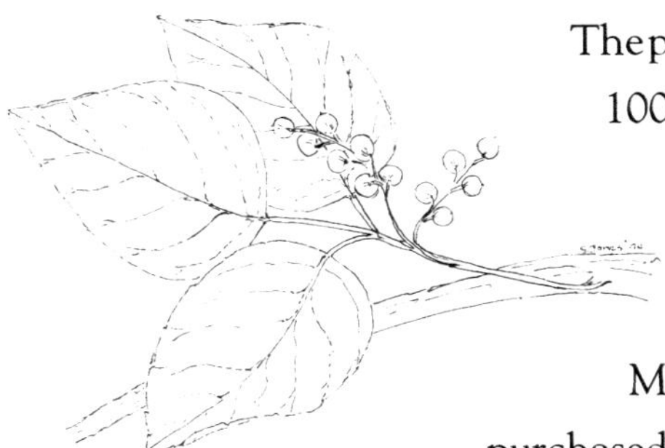

Along all of the trails in the Park, you should be on constant lookout forpoison ivy with its shiny green leaves in sets of three.

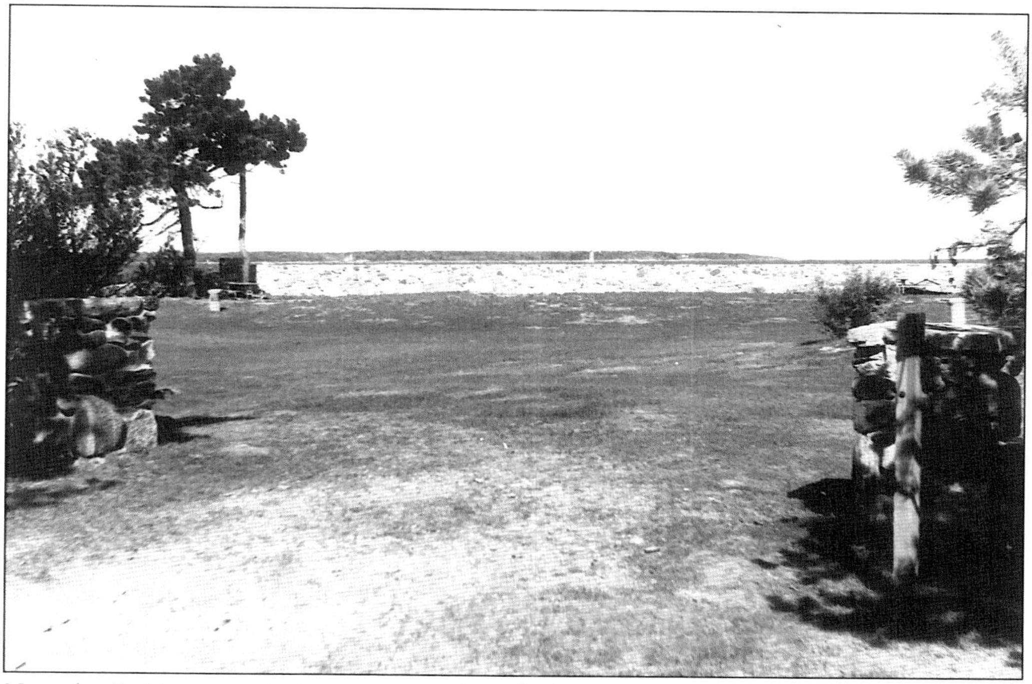

Now the Park's group picnic area, entry through these stone gate posts was to the Stevens' house.

across the ocean side which offered a grand view of the waters at the entrance to Portsmouth Harbor. It was razed by the federal government in 1942.

Odiorne Point is very much a place for the enjoyment of the community, but today this is the only part of the Park which may be reserved for private use. Except during winter months, any day might bring a group gathering, picnic, wedding, or family reunion. This beautiful area is very popular and must be booked well in advance.

Continue walking to the asphalt path and turn

left to proceed toward the open ocean. Historically, the area from north of the present Science Center to the cove on the southern rim of the Park was called Odiorne's Point, but local usage has applied the name to the entire peninsula. The asphalt path makes this entire area, including several picnic tables, accessible to those in wheelchairs and the handicapped.

This is the only known photograph of the Stevens' house taken from the vicinity of what is now the Seacoast Science Center.

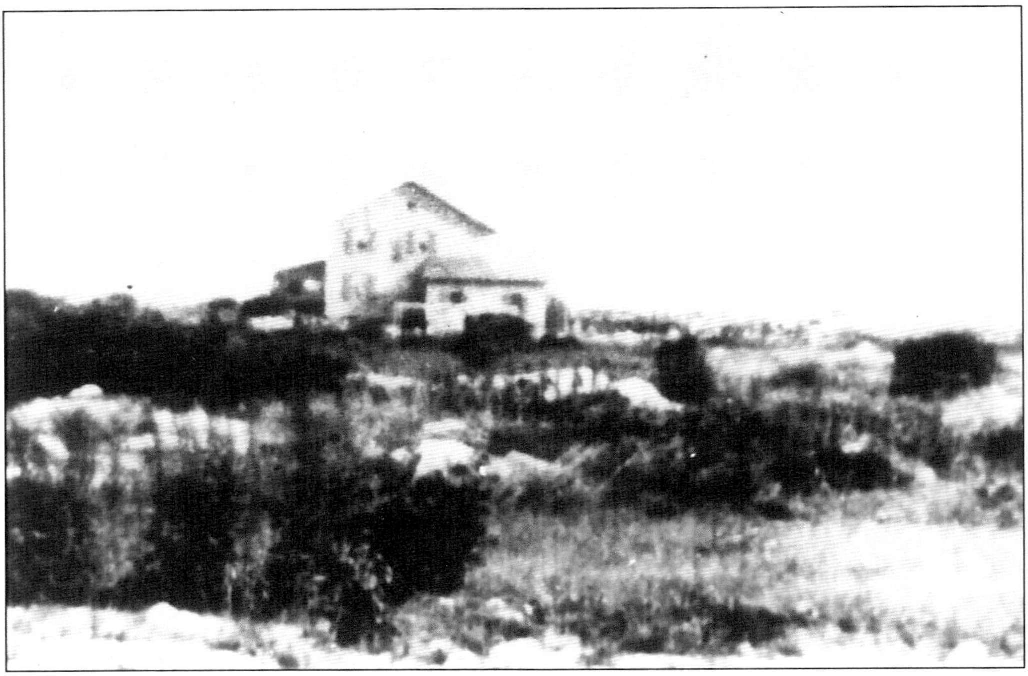

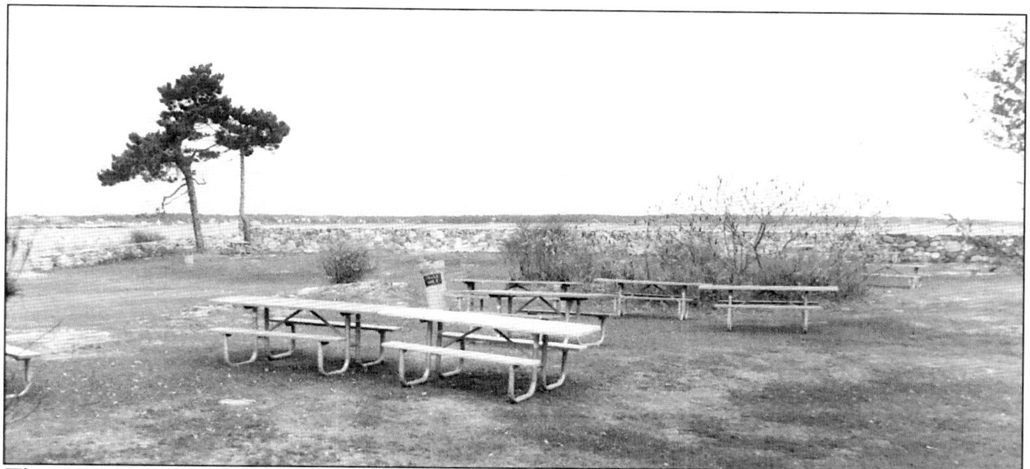

The Stevens property was completely surrounded by stone walls. The walls on the seaward side of the house were meant to keep the nor'easters from spraying salt water on the lawn. Over the years, nature has prevailed and the wall has required much repair. Significant repair was required after three "storms of the century" blasted over Odiorne Point in 1992. Note the steps for gaining access to the shore at the right end of the seaward wall.

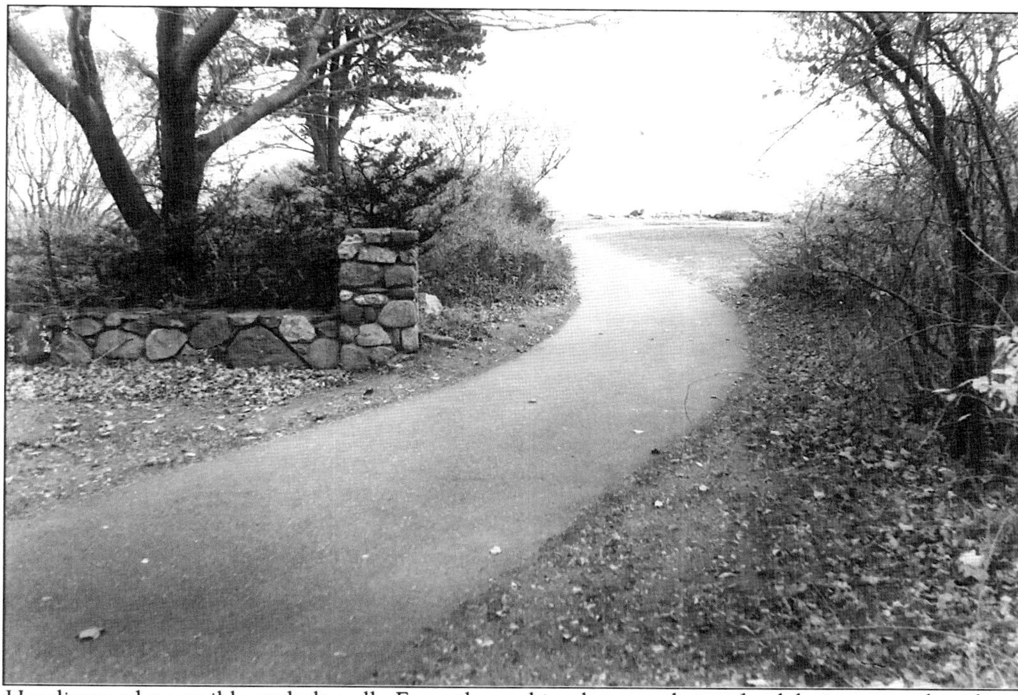

Handicapped accessible asphalt walk. From the parking lot, people in wheelchairs can make a loop of the south end of the park on the asphalt paths.

Atlantic Shore Line to the Gun Mounts

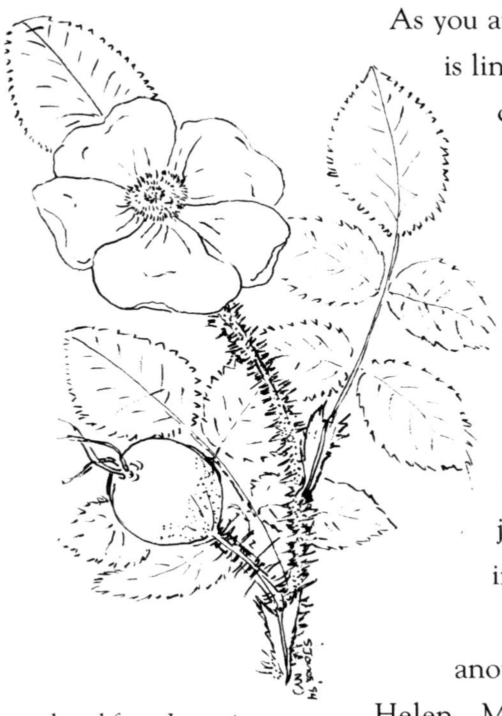

Introduced from Japan in the late 1800s, the salt-spray rose, Rosa rugosa, delights visitors with its perfumed flower and bright red fruit.

As you approach the rocky shore the paved path is lined on the left side by a profusion of rose called Rosa rugosa. This variety of rose was introduced from the Orient and thrives in the salt air along the shore line. The fragrance from this flower is an aromatic delight. After the flower petals fall away a small round fruit known as a "rose hip" is visible. The rose hip contains a very high concentration of vitamin C and is often made into a jam or tea enjoyed by health-minded individuals.

The area to your right is the site of another seaside summer home. In 1927, Helen McG. Graves of Contoocook, New Hampshire, purchased the land and together with her husband, Dr. Graves, built a gray, cedar shingled house here, which they named "Grarocks." Smoky blue shutters framed windows over the terrace at the rear of the house which overlooked a fabulous view of the

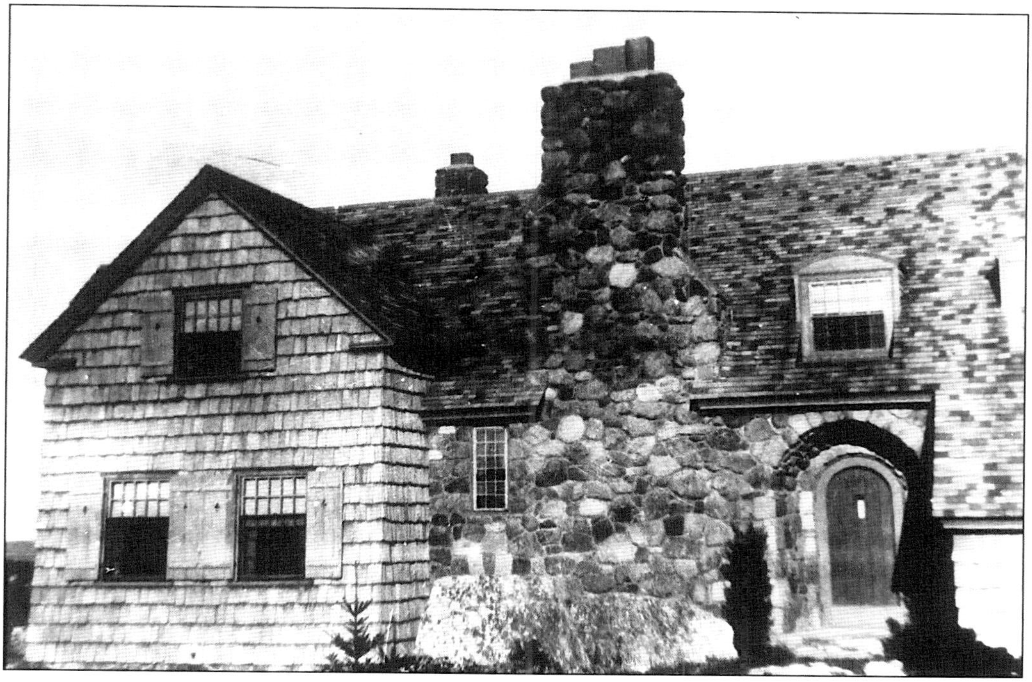

The front of the Graves' cedar shingled home, 'Grarocks', was approached by a long driveway from Route 1A.

Gulf of Maine. Guests were greeted at the front door facing inland, where masonry pillars flanked the drive. "Grarocks" had ten rooms altogether with a separate double garage containing a second floor apartment. The Graves' daughter, Robin, was married here at "Grarocks" in 1941. Sadly this home, like the Stevens', was razed in 1942. Beyond the next turn in the walk a gazebo was built to further enhance this magnificent summer home. It is interesting to note that these, like most other Odiorne Point properties, were owned by women. This was relatively unusual at the time and came about when shaky economic conditions threatened family property and wealth in the late

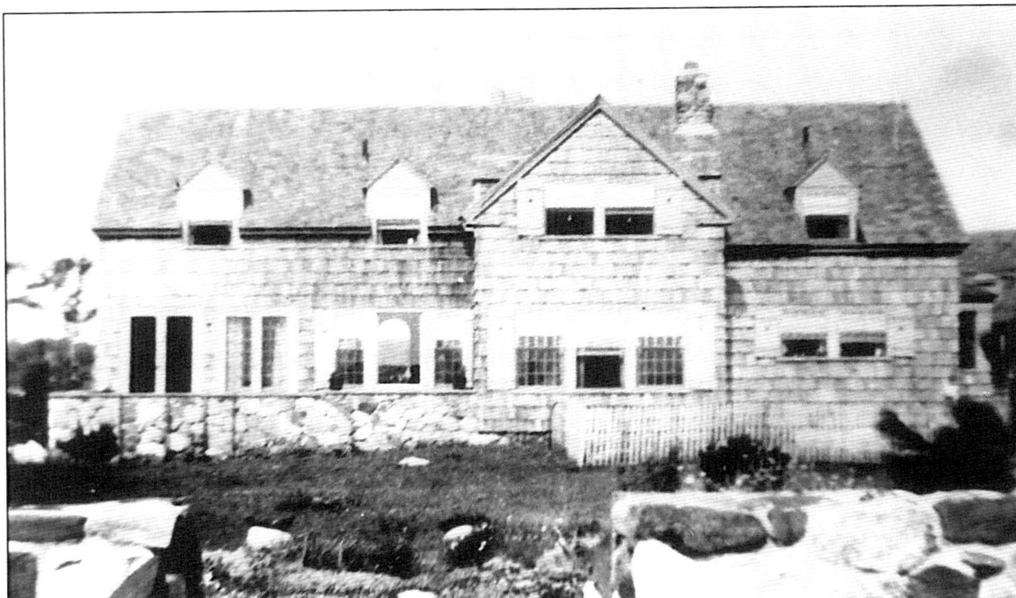

'Grarocks' had ten rooms and two bathrooms. The terrace at the rear of the house bordered on rocky shore.

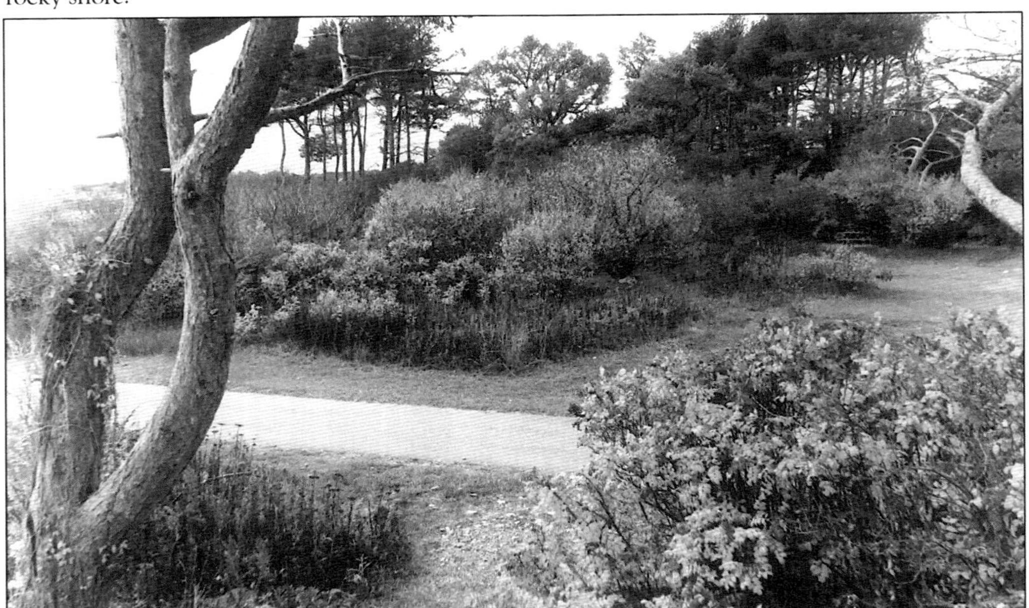

Area of the Graves' house today. Nothing remains of the house 'Grarocks' today in this view of where it stood. The house was leveled during World War II with the U.S. Army occupation of the land.

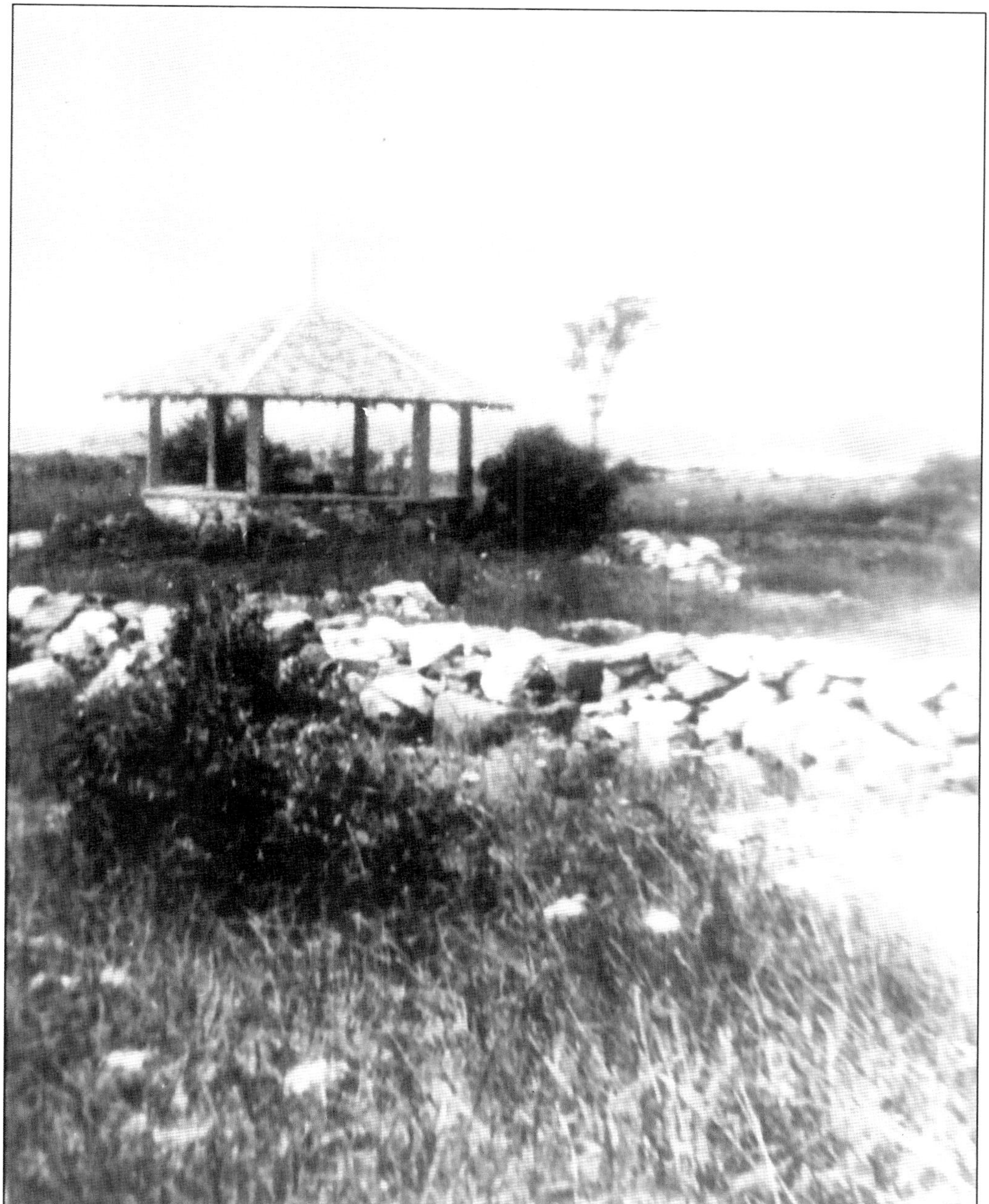

Graves' gazebo. On the outermost point of land, Dr. Graves built this summer house.

1920s and '30s as many men had their assets acquired in or transferred to their wives' names in an attempt to forestall seizure.

The islands you see from this point are the Isles of Shoals. The farthest island to the right (with the lighthouse) is White Island. This island was the childhood home of the famous poet Celia Thaxter: it became a part of Odiorne Point State Park in June 1992. As you look left from White Island, the next island you see is Star Island. On most days you will be able to make out a large white building on Star Island, the Oceanic Hotel, built in the 1800s and currently used for summer retreats by the Unitarian-Universalist and United Church of Christ Churches.

The next large island to your left is Appledore, the largest of the archipelago. In the 1800s Appledore

A rare glimpse of pre-war social life at Odiorne Point. Robin Graves' wedding reception at 'Grarocks', the summer of 1941.

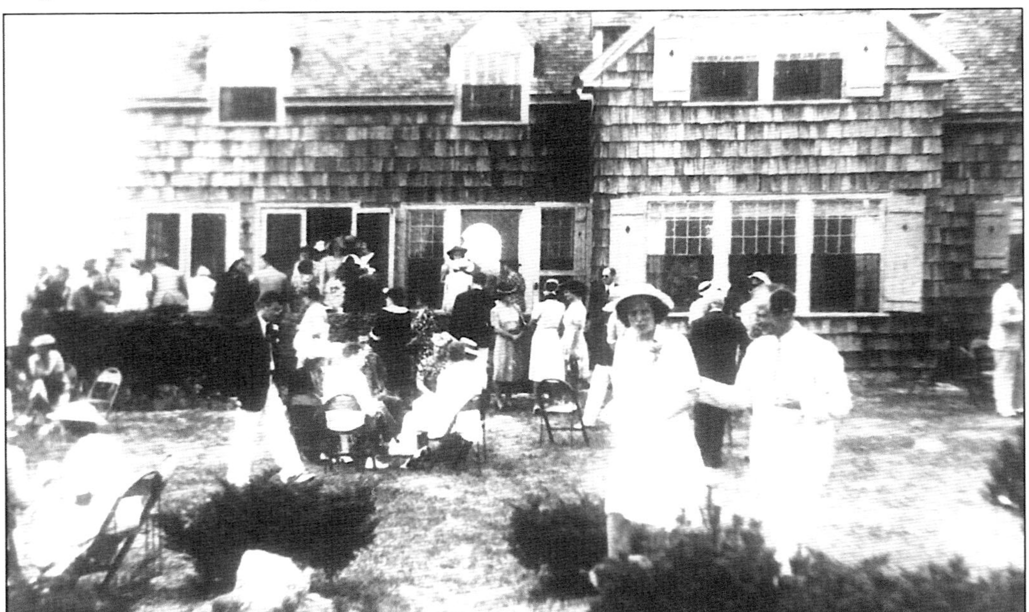

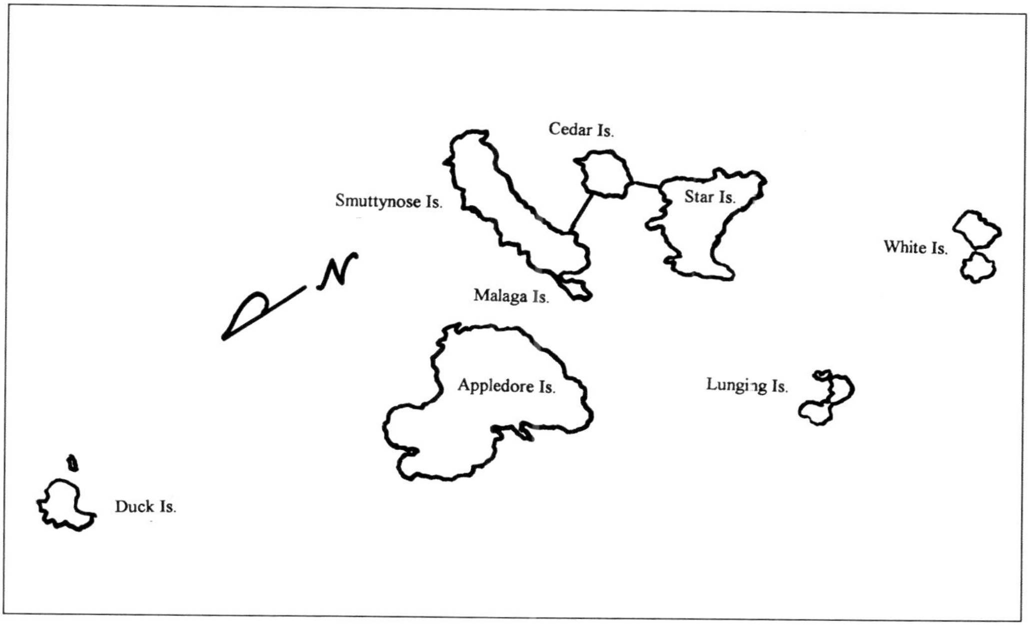

Sketch of the Isles of Shoals with perspective from the Panama mounts.

Island was the cultural center for summer visitors in New England. Celia Thaxter, by then a well-known poet, created a mecca for writers, artists and leaders of that era. Among others, she was hostess to fellow writers Walt Whitman, John G. Whittier and Nathaniel Hawthorne, to artist Childe Hassam and to New Hampshire native President Franklin Pierce. Appledore Island is now the location of the Shoals Marine Laboratory, an undergraduate marine science educational facility run jointly by Cornell University and the University of New Hampshire. A little to the left of Appledore, you may be able to see low-lying Duck Island. During World War II Duck Island was used by the military as a practice target. Today Duck is home to cormorants and gulls and is the southern-most breeding site for Harbor Seals.

Look further to your left along the horizon, and you might be able to see the faint gray lighthouse tower of Boon Island. This is the setting of Kenneth Roberts' 1956 historical novel "Boon Island" and the midwinter fight for survival of shipwrecked sailors.

At your extreme left, at the mouth of Portsmouth Harbor, is Whaleback Light. Built of granite in 1872, this light marks the harbor's entrance. Beyond Whaleback, in Maine, is Fort Foster, built for defense in 1896. It became part of the coastal system to defend the Portsmouth Naval Shipyard during World War II. Upriver you can see the bright white tower of Portsmouth Harbor Light in New Castle. This light is built on the foundation of the pre-revolutionary Fort William and Mary. Renamed Fort Constitution, the

Standing by the Graves' stone wall, a view towards the left finds the 59-foot Whaleback Lighthouse marking the entrance to Portsmouth Harbor.

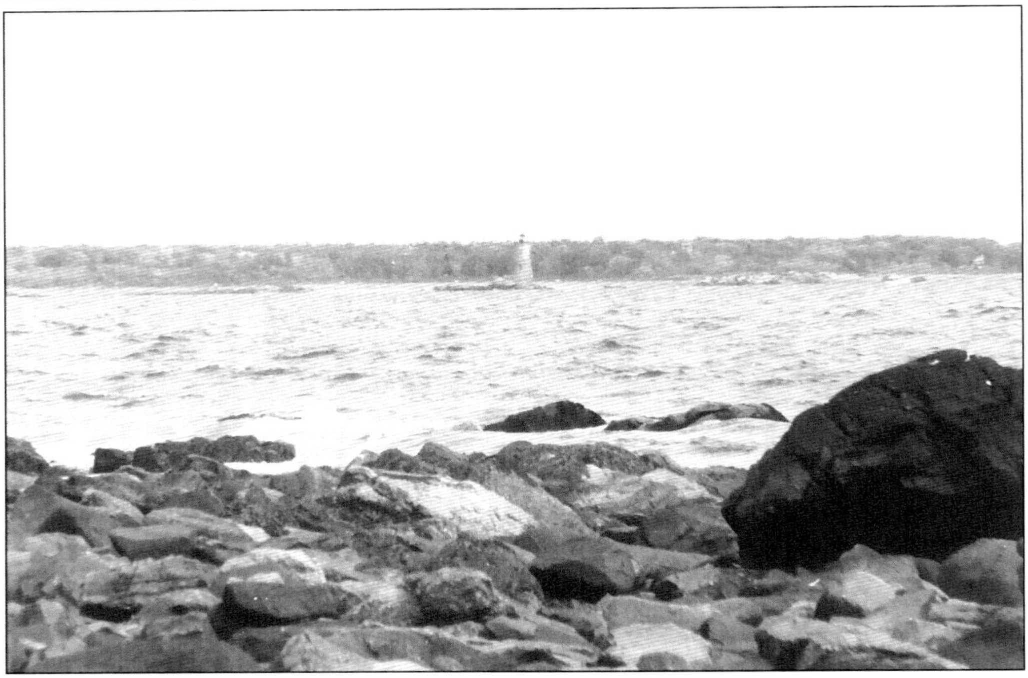

fort defended the harbor during the Revolutionary and Civil Wars, World Wars I and II, and is currently the site of a Coast Guard Station.

You might also see large ships entering or leaving the harbor. Often these ships will stand just off this point waiting for the right tide and the arrival of a pilot to take the ship up the Piscataqua River. The Piscataqua has very rapid tidal currents and eddies which require highly skilled navigation.

The open water you see is not the Atlantic Ocean: it is the Gulf of Maine. One of the most biologically productive bodies of water in the world, the Gulf is bounded on land by the Canadian provinces of Nova Scotia and New Brunswick, and the states of Maine, New Hampshire and Massachusetts. Its ocean boundaries are Georges and Browns Banks, underwater "hills" which keep the water of the Gulf circulating in this "sea within a sea." The Gulf waters have only one major connection to the North Atlantic Ocean waters, the channel between Georges and Browns Banks which are about 200 miles to the east of the Isles of Shoals. Because so many rivers empty into the Gulf, the waters are less salty than those of the Atlantic and have a counterclockwise circulation pattern. The physical boundaries of the Gulf cause some of the highest tides in the world, varying from 7 to 10 feet along Cape Cod to as high as 50 feet in Canada's Bay of Fundy.

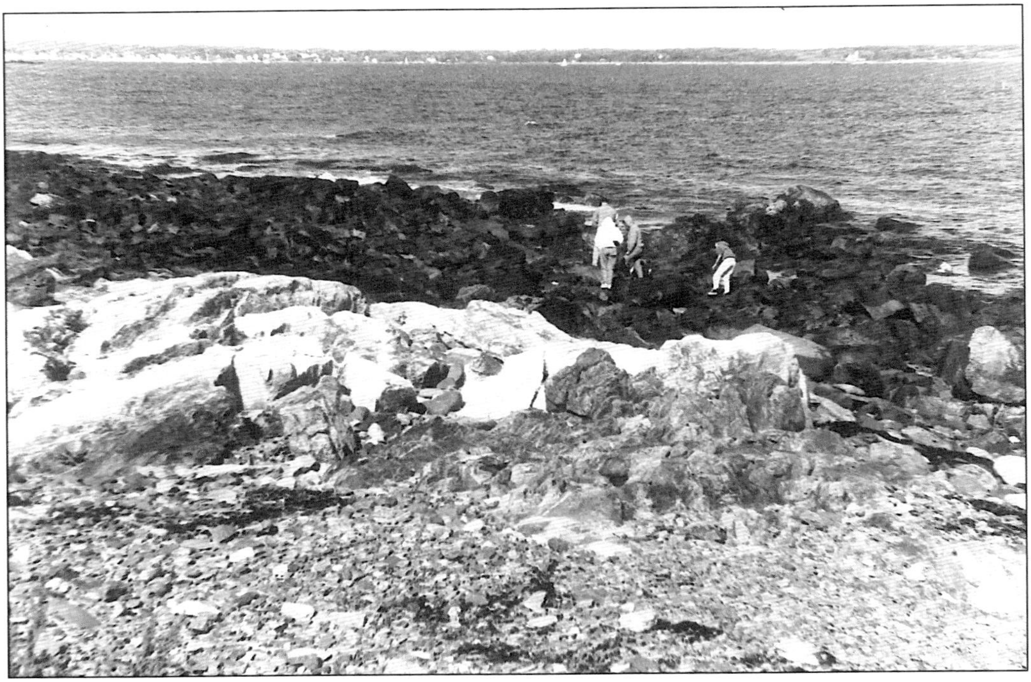

Odiorne Point's rocky shore provides some of the best tide pools from Massachusetts to Maine. Students and visitors flock here to unlock the mysteries of the tide pools.

As you continue along the rocky shore, you can see some fine examples of the geologic forces that formed this land.

As scientific methods improve and new information becomes available, our understanding of the earth's geological history is refined and rewritten. As late as the 1950s, it was thought that the continents had always been where they are: continents did not move. Today, geologists agree that continents are slowly, continuously moving. The northeastern United States, maritime Canada, and indeed the rocky shore in front of you, have played a major role in providing knowledge and an understanding of how the earth was formed.

Rocks are geologists' textbooks. Reading Odiorne's rocks you can see examples of the massive slabs of crustal rock (called plates) that churned up from the molten core of the earth and moved about its surface over hundreds of millions of years. In this process, known as plate tectonics, these plates repeatedly collide and tear away again, always changing shape and size. The northeastern United States is a jumbled result of at least three major collisions of these plates, which thrust up mountains that were at least as high as Mt. Everest or K-2 are today. The Appalachians, Taconics, Berkshires, Green Mountains and New Hampshire's White Mountains but have since been eroded over aeons to their present heights of between 4,000 and 6,000 feet.

In this small area, an experienced guide can unravel the geological wonders of Odiorne Point.

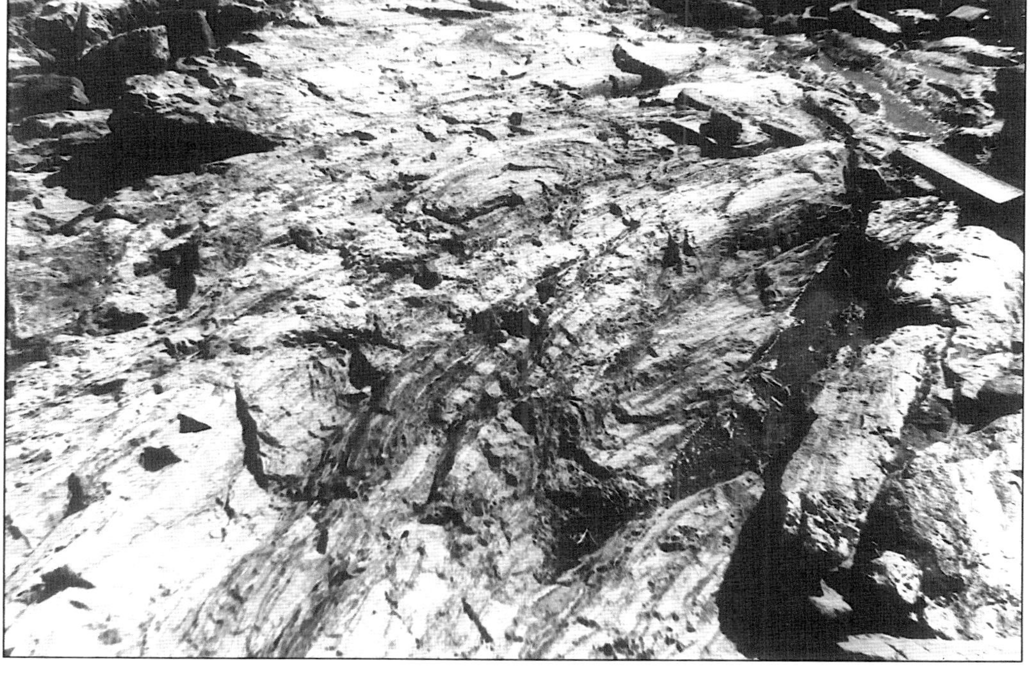

Geologists estimate that the last wrenching separation from North America occurred about 200 million years ago, tearing away parts of plate to form Greenland, Scotland, Scandinavia, and even Northwest Africa. After all this stretching, tearing, uplifting and glacial erosion, two types of rock are predominant: metamorphic schist and basalt (which was once volcanic magma). The presence of rock formations like those at Odiorne in Africa helps us track the movements of these giant plates throughout time. As you look out over this rocky shore, just imagine the power needed to break apart a giant plate of these rocks and move it thousands of miles away!

In addition to plate movement, glaciers were a potent force in determining the shape of the land upon which you walk today. Twenty thousand years ago,

Seen from the Panama mounts, this cove contains the roots of ancient trees together called 'The Drowned Forest'. The tower in the background was a visual observation post used to aim the guns at Odiorne Point. To the left of the tower is a tall siren, part of the emergency warning system of Seabrook nuclear power station.

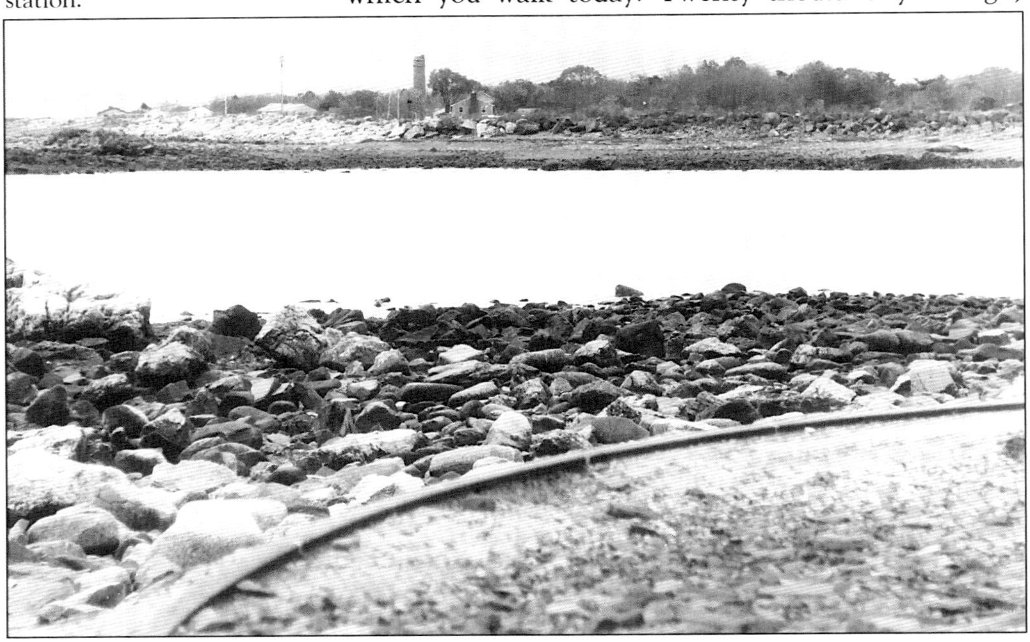

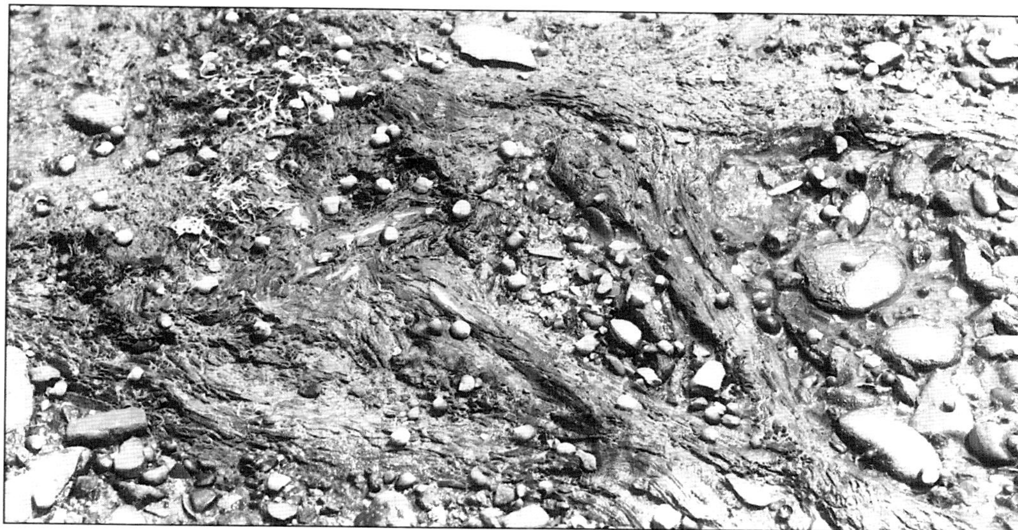

Roots of trees that lived some 3,500 years ago are exposed at low tide.

Odiorne Point was covered by a mile of ice, the weight of which pushed the land down some 1,300 feet. The glacier drew water from the ocean, lowering sea level by about 500 feet. This altered the shoreline so that about 13,000 years ago the shore was 20 miles west of Odiorne Point. If the coastline were there today, Route 125 near the Lee traffic circle would be ocean-front property. As the glacier retreated, the land rebounded, and terrestrial life returned. One fascinating piece of visual history here which helps us understand these changes is the "Drowned Forest". A forest of trees extended to the east from here to the Isles of Shoals and perhaps beyond. Using carbon dating, geologists have determined that 3,400 years ago the ice-age glaciers had melted enough that the sea had risen close to its present level, drowning the trees. Trunks and root systems of these trees may be seen today at low tide in the "Drowned Forest" at the southern rim of the park.

Gun Mounts to Battery 204

The history contained at Odiorne Point spans an almost unimaginable expanse of time. As the pathway bends to the west, you will jump ahead to another time: World War II.

On your right is a fairly well-preserved structure that appears very much like a large goldfish pond surrounding a sometime fountain. Actually it is a gun position, one of four in this part of Odiorne Point. With England under full assault and Germany on the verge of controlling all of the North Atlantic sea lanes,

The wheels of the 155mm guns rested on the center raised portion of the Panama mount.

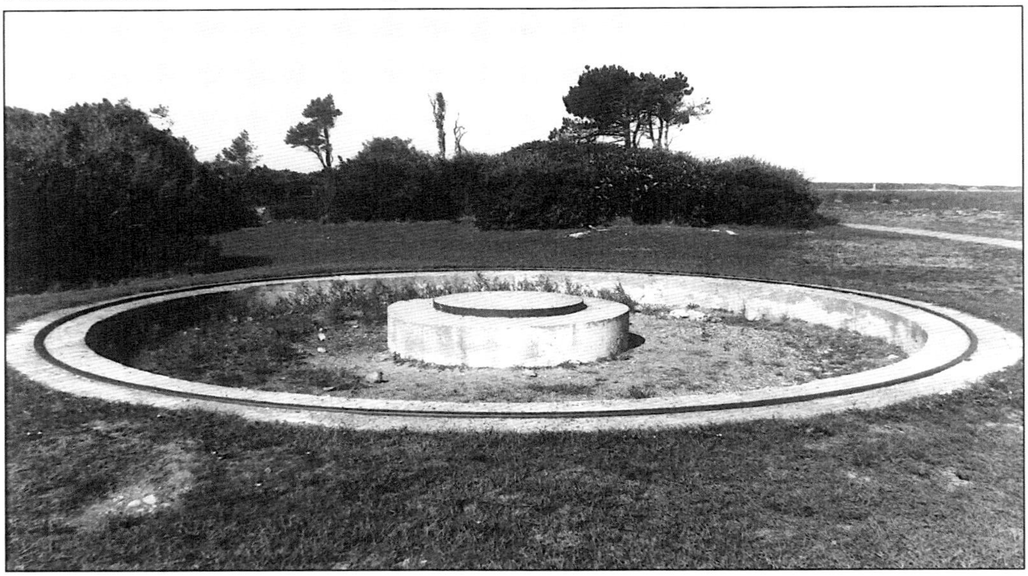

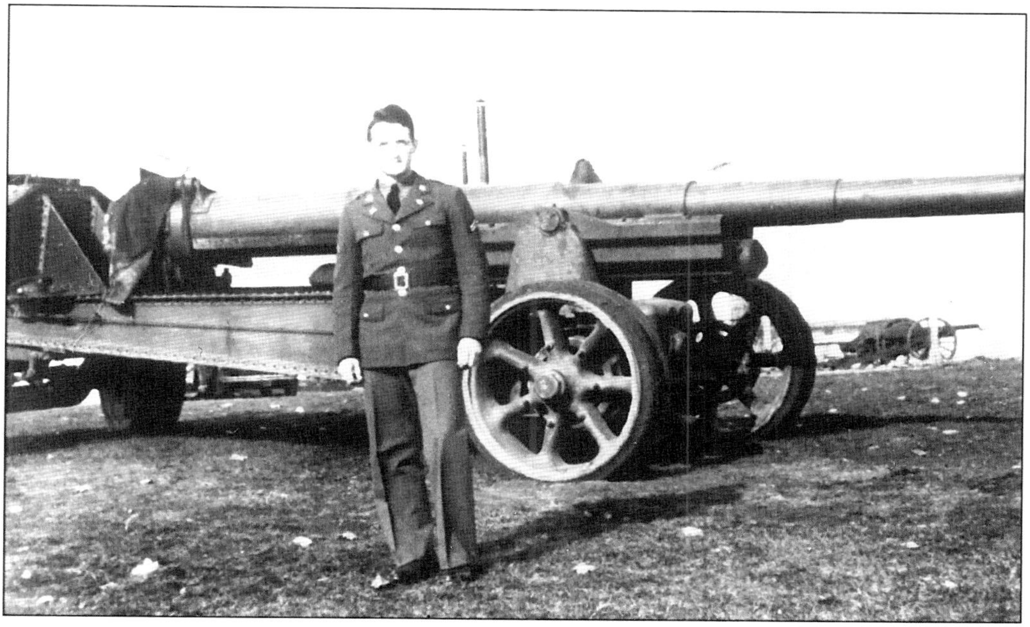

Although not taken here, this is a photograph of a 155mm gun. Four of these guns were mounted on the Panama mounts at Odiorne Point.

the US War Department formulated plans for US coastal defense in 1940. Upon the United States' entry into the war in December of 1941, these plans were implemented immediately. Odiorne Point was critical in protecting the Portsmouth Naval Shipyard, and Fort Dearborn was established here to defend the harbor at its entrance. The first installations were 155-millimeter (approximately 6-inch diameter) guns which were rushed to Odiorne's shore and installed here. Although these guns lacked the power to fire a shell the desired distance (they were designed in World War I as field artillery pieces), they were the only ones available for immediate installation in critical coastal positions. In the spring of 1942, four such guns were placed on these "Panama" mounts which were named for the place of their origin. Two more of these mounts directly ahead of you have been filled in. The fourth is completely obscured by vegetation.

This early defense installation was augmented quickly with underwater listening devices, three rows of mines and a submarine net across the mouth of the harbor. Waterfront searchlights, barbed wire and machine-gun positions on the shore also contributed to the defense system. Two additional gun positions were constructed at Odiorne Point: Battery 204 near the Science Center and Battery Seaman on the north side of the park. (You will see these later in your walk.)

From the gun mounts look south along the coast: you will notice a high tower about a mile away. It is an observation control tower for sighting enemy vessels. This tower is one of a string of high points which stretched from Halibut Point (Cape Ann), Massachusetts to Kennebunk, Maine. Not all of these were continuously manned, but could be activated if

The end of the patrol area for the lifesaving station at Wallis Sands was located near the Panama mounts. Using a key located at this station, lifesavers would 'punch' the time clock to record the time of their visit. Look closely to the left of the center of the photograph - the 'U.S.S. Constitution' is just visible.

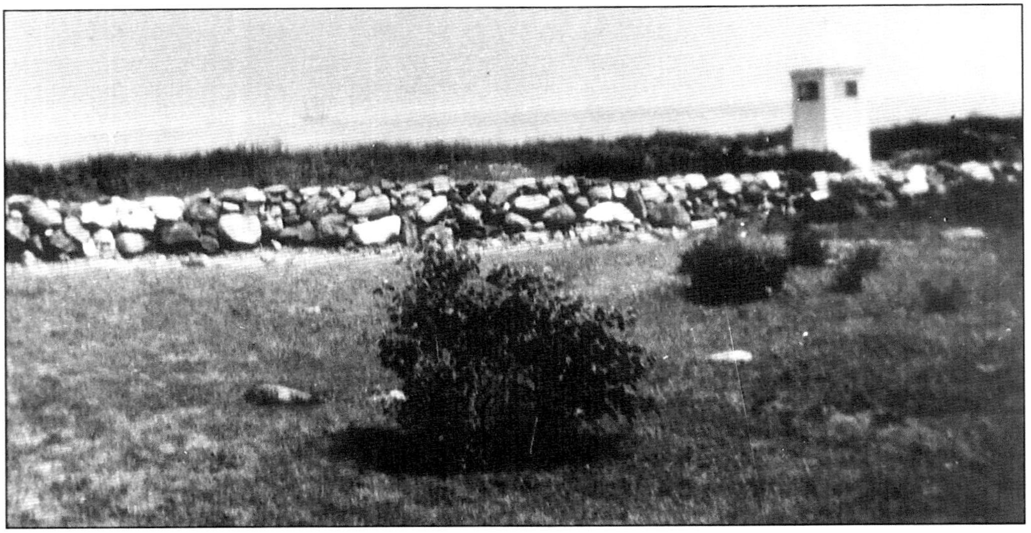

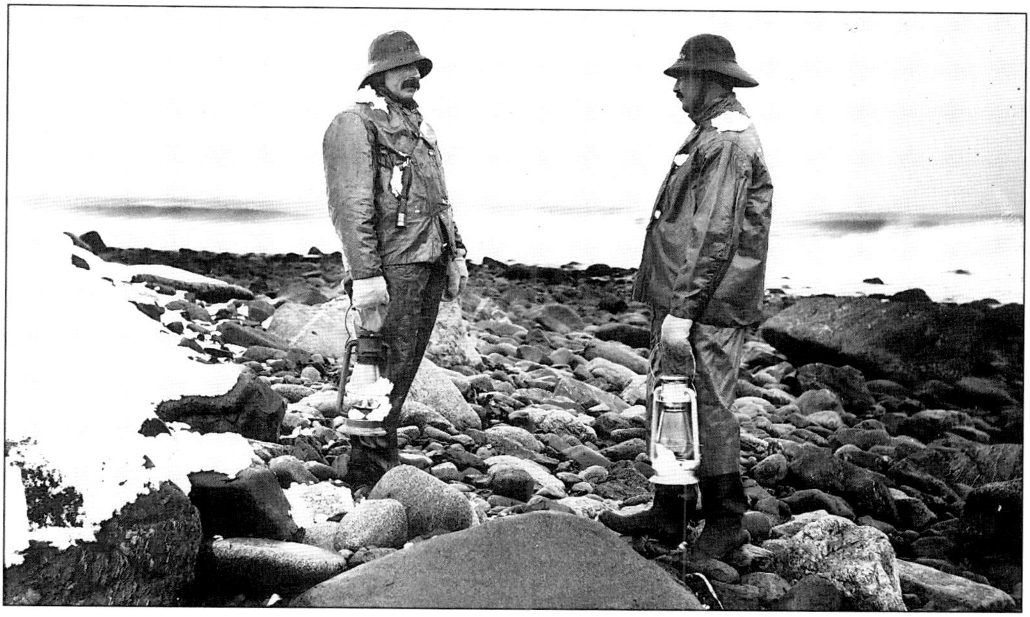

Lifesavers are shown meeting in this photograph from a glass plate negative. Note the snow on the men - it appears to have been placed here - perhaps to show how rigorous their duty was.

needed. As you look out to the Isles of Shoals, you will see another of these towers on Appledore Island (the largest island toward the left).

On the northern shore of this cove, a very small piece of ground was purchased in 1894 by the United States. On it a small check-in station was built marking the northern end of a foot patrol from a life-saving station at Wallis Sands Beach over a mile to the south. From 1894 into the 1930s, men walked this stretch of shoreline watching for "mariners in distress."

Take another turn on the asphalt path and as you head back toward the parking lot, you pass the site of the Eastman's house and barn.

Cyrus and Charles Eastman of Littleton, New Hampshire, built them here in the early 1870s and had a subdivision plan prepared in 1875. In that plan they proposed to sell small lots of land to potential summer cottage builders. However, they sold only one large plot, on which no building was ever constructed. The balance of the property remained undeveloped and was sold in 1906. The new owner, Charles F. Shillaber, realized no further sales of the subdivision and sold it fourteen years later.

In 1921, Robert Sugden purchased Shillaber's entire parcel. He had already bought the property immediately to the north and then had updated subdivision plans drawn for the "Shillaber" parcel. Sugden moved the old Eastman house and barn west to the edge of what is now Route 1A, remodeled the barn into a house and sold both. He also sold four lots to the Graves family, and his widow, Bertha Sugden, sold six lots to the Stevens,

On land bought in 1874, Mr. Cyrus Eastman built this Victorian house.

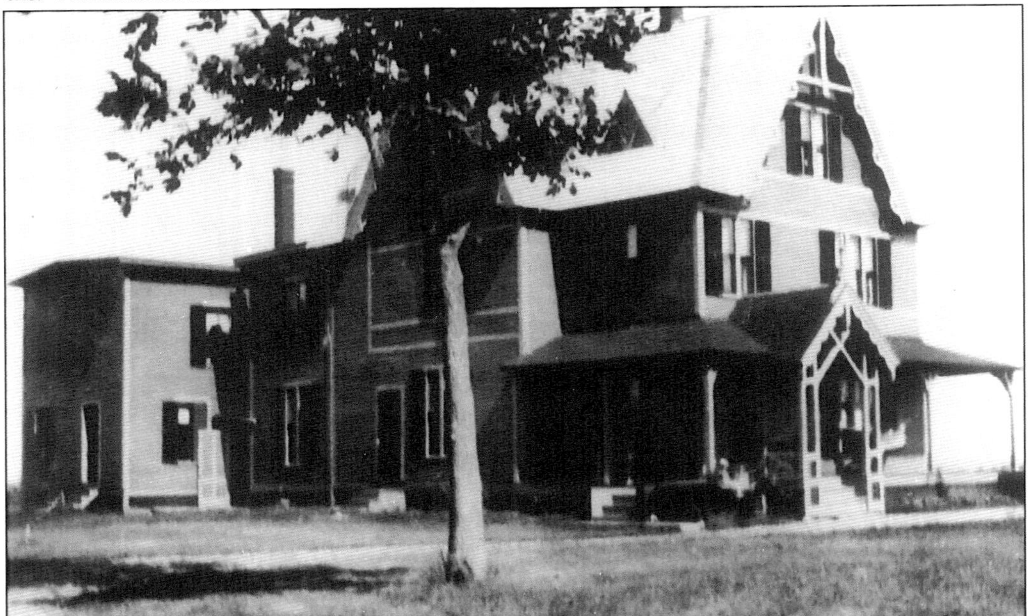

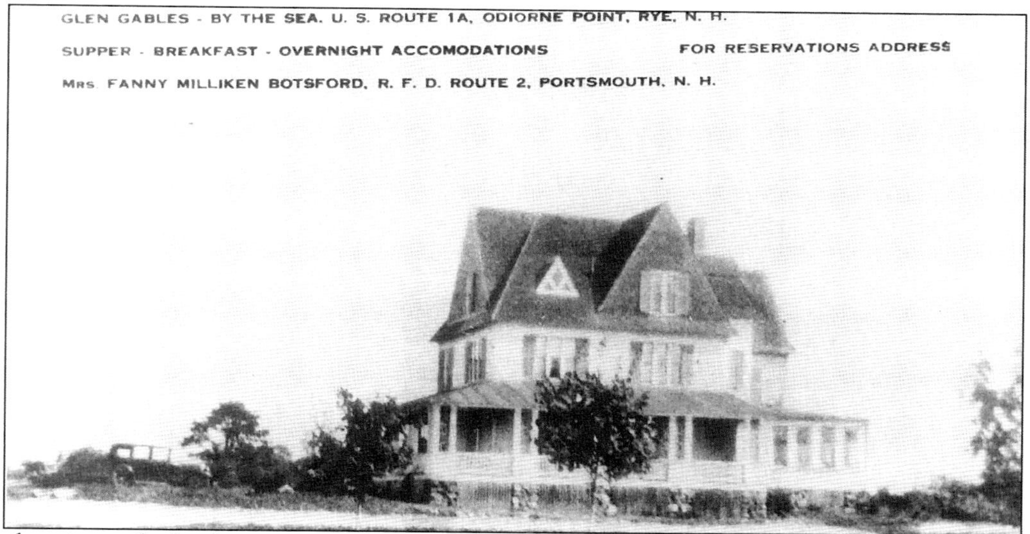

The Eastman House was moved to what is now route 1A and became'Glen Gables' when bought by Mrs. Fanny Botsford in 1933. This postcard is advertising accommodation for overnight guests. Note how open the area was then.

the sites of which you passed on your way to the gun mounts.

The Eastman house was purchased from Mrs. Sugden by Fannie Botsford in 1933 and opened to paying guests that summer as a tourist home called "Glen Gables." The renovated barn was bought from Bertha Sugden in 1927 by Florence Keller, who held it until 1939. She in turn sold it to Mary K. MacKinnon on behalf of George S. Howard, who established it as the 1620 Club, a reputed gambling establishment.

Walking along the asphalt path on the east side of the parking lot, you will notice you are approaching a high man-made mound overgrown by sumac and pine trees.

This mound did not exist before 1942: it is Battery 204, the second largest of Fort Dearborn's gun batteries. As you look about you, it is hard to believe that prior to World War II, there were flat open fields and continuous ocean views from almost any place on the peninsula.

Battery 204 to the Dolphin Fountain

Battery 204 was just one of many such batteries of a continuous coastal defense system. These batteries were all built from common plans and were positioned along the Atlantic coast from Maine to the Caribbean and along the Pacific coast from Alaska to Panama. Two 6-inch, "rapid-fire guns," one mounted on either side of the casemate (commonly called a "bunker"), could fire 138-pound shells about 15 miles out to sea, over twice the distance to the Isles of Shoals.

Under this mound of earth is World War II Battery 204. On the left side you can see one of its three ports.

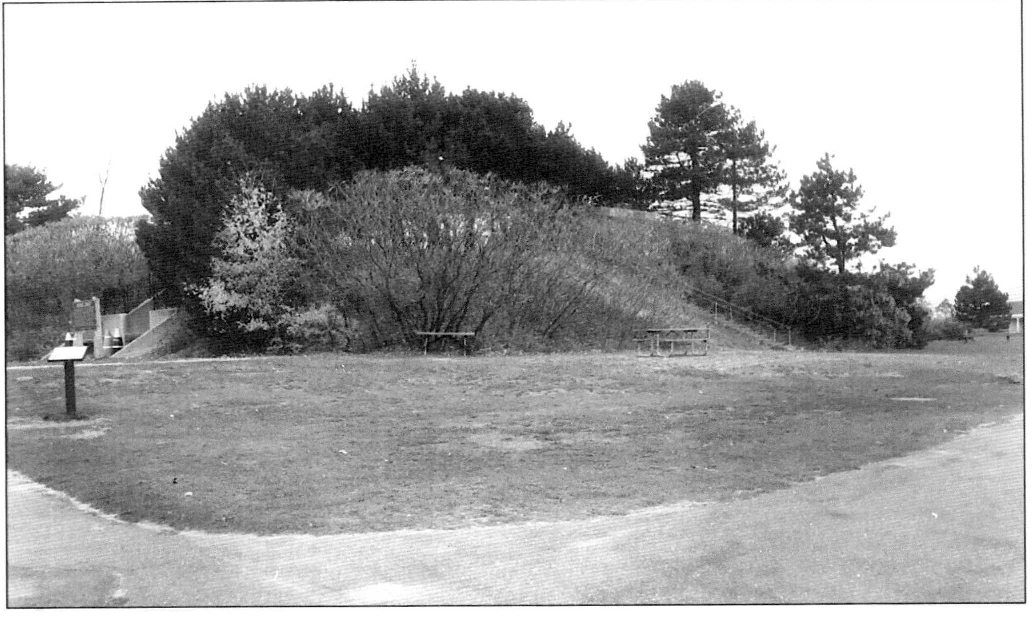

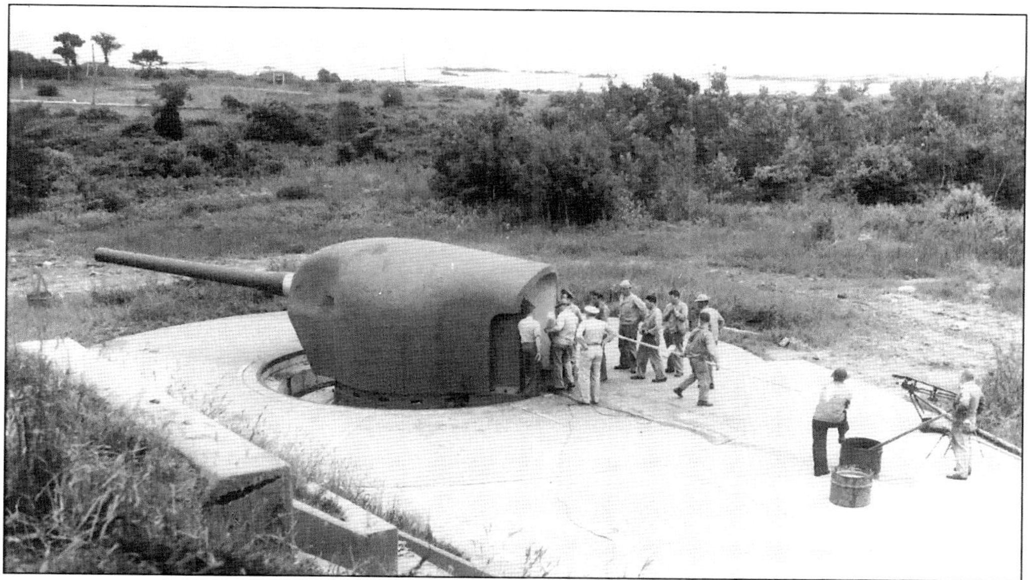

One of the two 6-inch guns of Battery 204. Note the two 'humps' along the shore by the trees on the left side of the photograph. That area is enlarged in the next photograph.

The observation post atop the bunker along with others from Cape Ann, Massachusetts, to Kennebunk, Maine, provided the "eyes" for the guns of Odiorne in the pre-radar years of the early 1940s.

The inside of the bunker was a honeycomb of rooms for shells, gun powder, and target plotting, plus a large electrical power room. Just recently it was learned that this battery may be unique. Unlike most other batteries, the coast artillery crew had direct, inside access from the bunker to the observation post.

The huge 16-inch shells that you see at this bunker are for the much larger gun position as we shall discover later.

Keeping the park toll booth to your left, proceed directly across the driveway. As you approach the woods on the far side of the field, a glance back will reveal the central port of Battery 204 through which

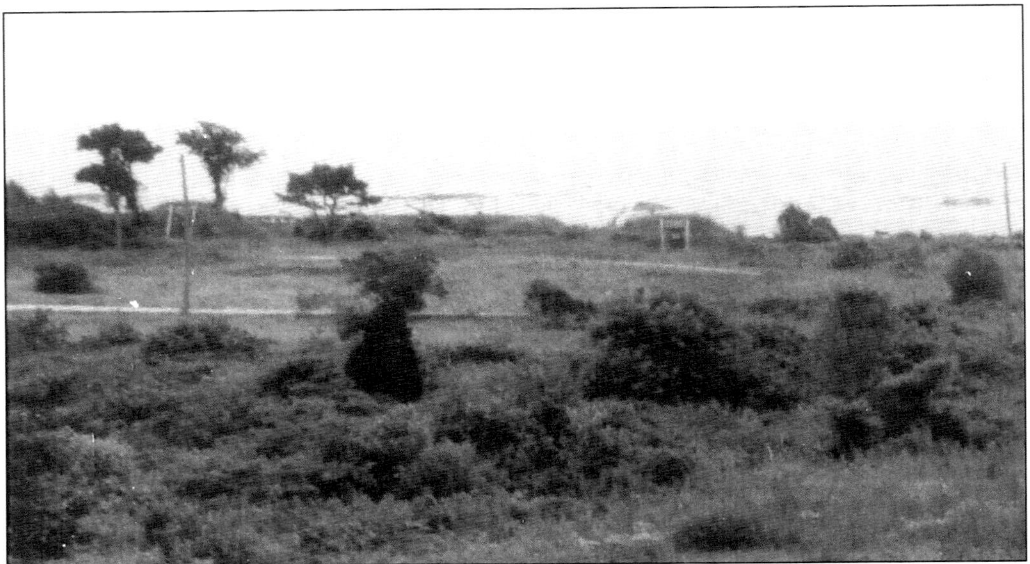

An enlargement of the previous picture shows the 155mm gun installation covered by camouflage netting and the ammunition magazines.

all materials were brought into the bunker.

In the meadow before you, as well as in many other open spaces throughout the park, an exquisite lacy flower may be found that has many interesting facts and legends associated with it. This abundant plant is

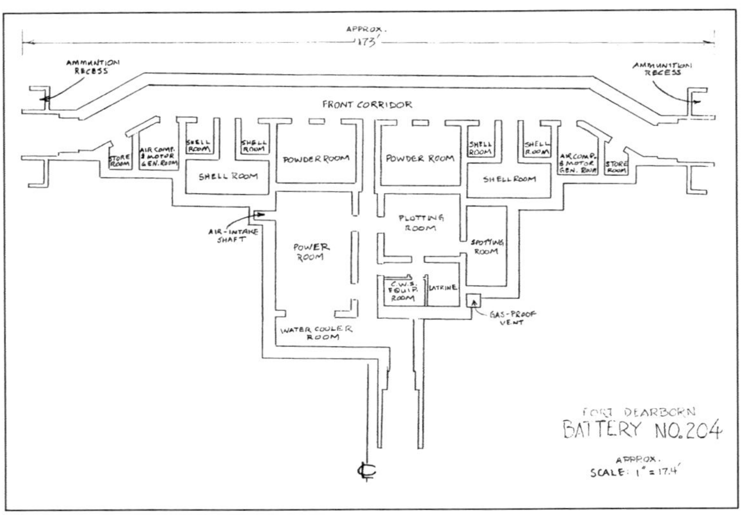

A sketch of the interior of Battery 204.

Queen Anne's lace, also called, and rightfully so, wild carrot. For centuries this species was eaten in Europe and early America, but was stringy and needed hours of cooking. During the early 1900s the value of vitamin A from these wild carrots was realized and scientists developed this stringy, bitter, tough plant into today's lush garden vegetable. As the legend goes, this plant was growing in Queen Anne's royal garden and being an accomplished lacemaker, she challenged her ladies-in-waiting to a contest of reproducing the flower in lace. Since it would only be proper for a queen to win her own contest, you can readily see why it is known as Queen Anne's lace.

The center entrance to Battery 204 today.

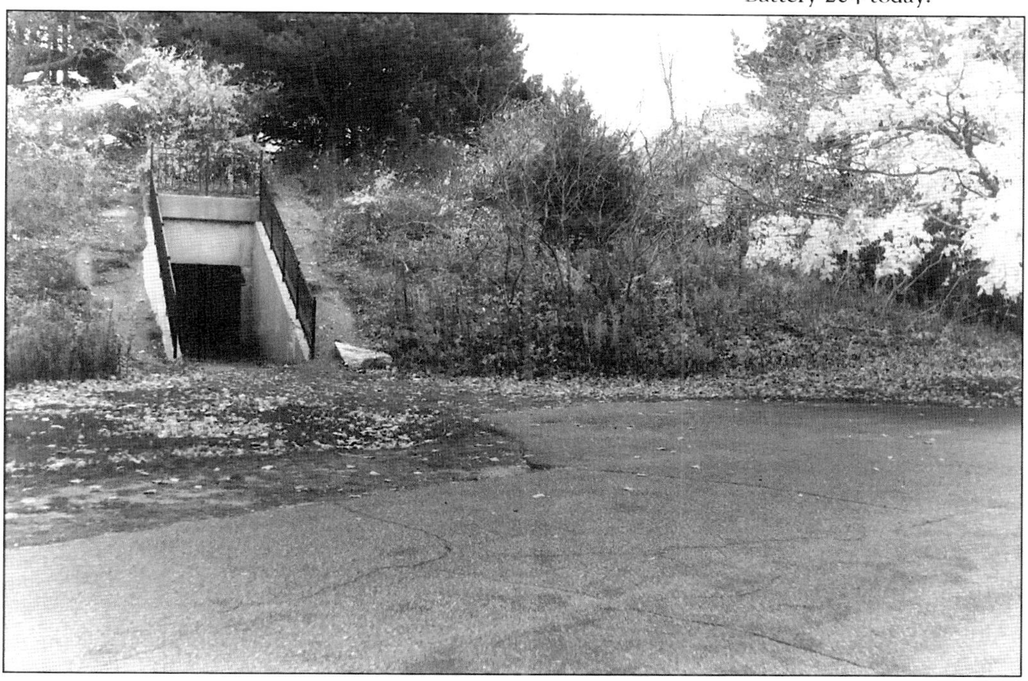

Dolphin Fountain to the Odiorne Homestead

Rounding the end of a low fence and curving to the right, you will follow a path through the field about 100 yards or so to a point where a second path diverges to the right. This path leads you to a masonry structure: the "Dolphin Fountain" of the Marvin/Straw estate.

Look closely at the center section and you will see a scallop shell and dolphin cast in relief. From the dolphin's mouth you see a metal pipe, which was the fountain portion of this structure. In the 1920s

The Dolphin Fountain as it existed prior to World War II. Water trickled from the mouth of the cement dolphin.

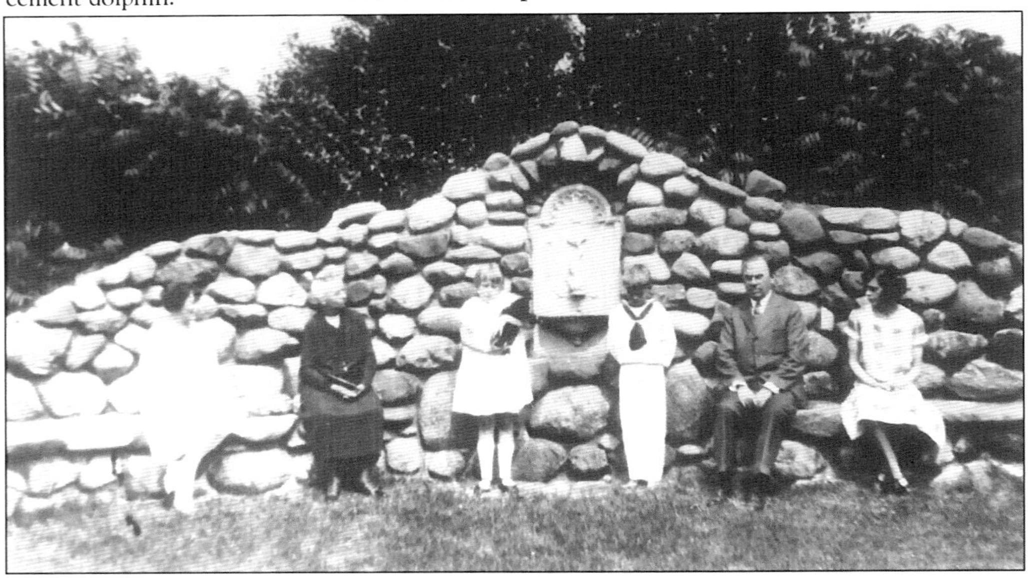

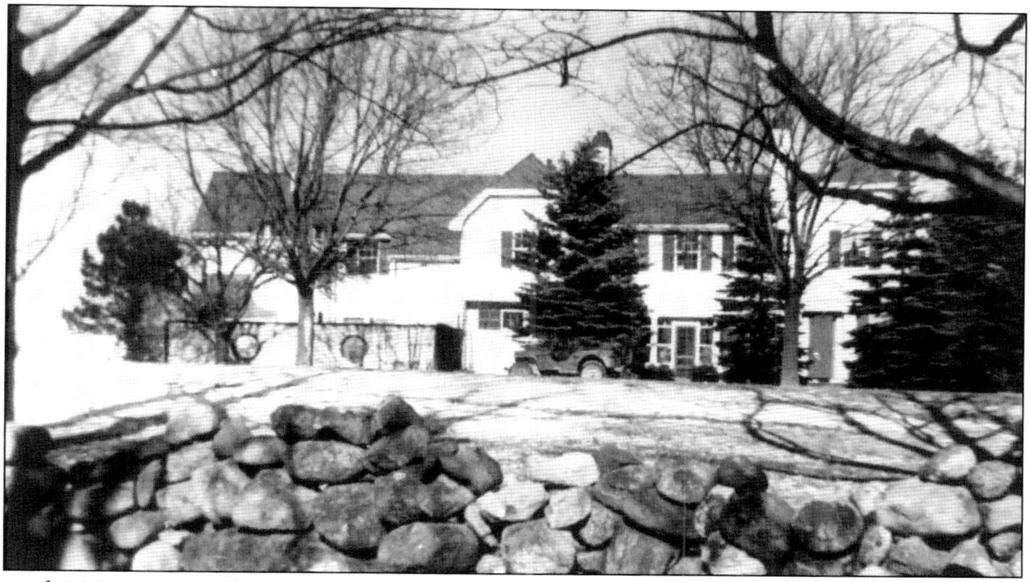

and 1930s, a small windmill some distance to its rear brought well water to the fountain: the stones flanking the fountain were benches.

To its left stood a stucco summer home that is called the Marvin/Straw house for the last two families to summer here. This house, built around the turn of the century on a reputed "old cellar hole," had five owners in all. We have come to know it best through the memoirs, written and oral, of Marjorie Marvin Hartford, who spent idyllic summers here with her family from 1920-37 in the house she called "Sea Acres." Just to the right of the Dolphin Fountain is a remnant patch of ancient roses. These "Apothecary Roses" could have been the earliest cultivated roses brought to New Hampshire. Though still surviving, the tree shade discourages their fragrant deep pink bloom.

Marvin/Straw house. This house passed through five owners. We now know it best by accounts and photographs by Marjorie Marvin Hartford who lived in 'Sea Acres' from 1920 to 1937.

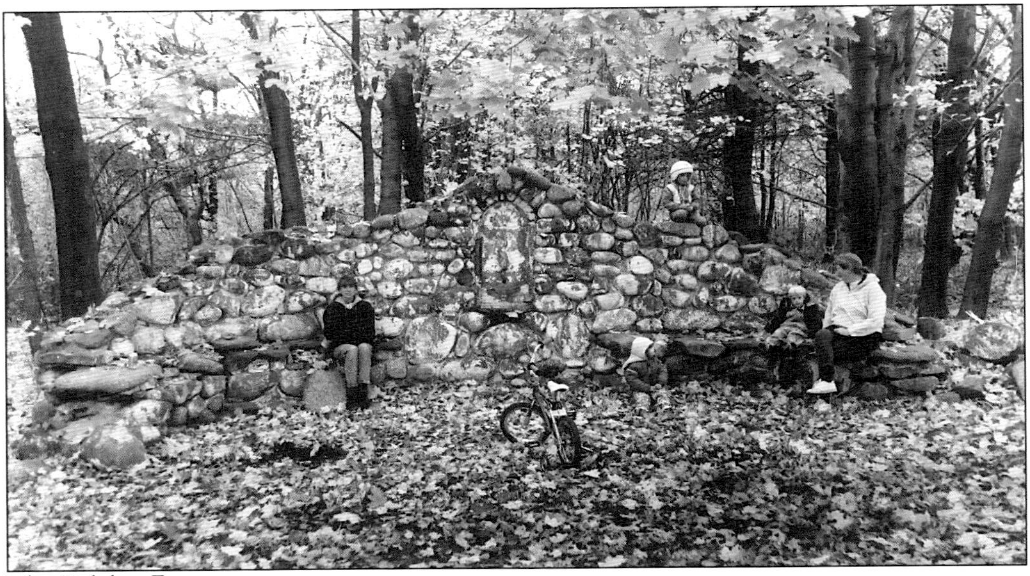

The Dolphin Fountain as it is today.

A 1937 real estate advertisement for the house described "Sea Acres" as a "desirable estate ... with spacious grounds attractively landscaped" and a long sun porch on the front, screened in summer and windowed the rest of the year. Its first floor had a large living room, dining room, butler's pantry, servants' dining room, kitchen, and laundry. Upstairs were five "master" bedrooms, a den, a bathroom, two servants' bedrooms, and their bathroom. Six large fireplaces graced the house, which had a separate garage, stable and "man's" room. The 1937 asking price was $17,000! The price had dropped during the Depression from $25,000 in 1920. It is interesting to note that the advertisement for the sale of the land also stated "The sanitary arrangements are excellent, there being a 500-foot sewer with a 7-foot drop leading beyond and emptying below the low water mark." The remains of

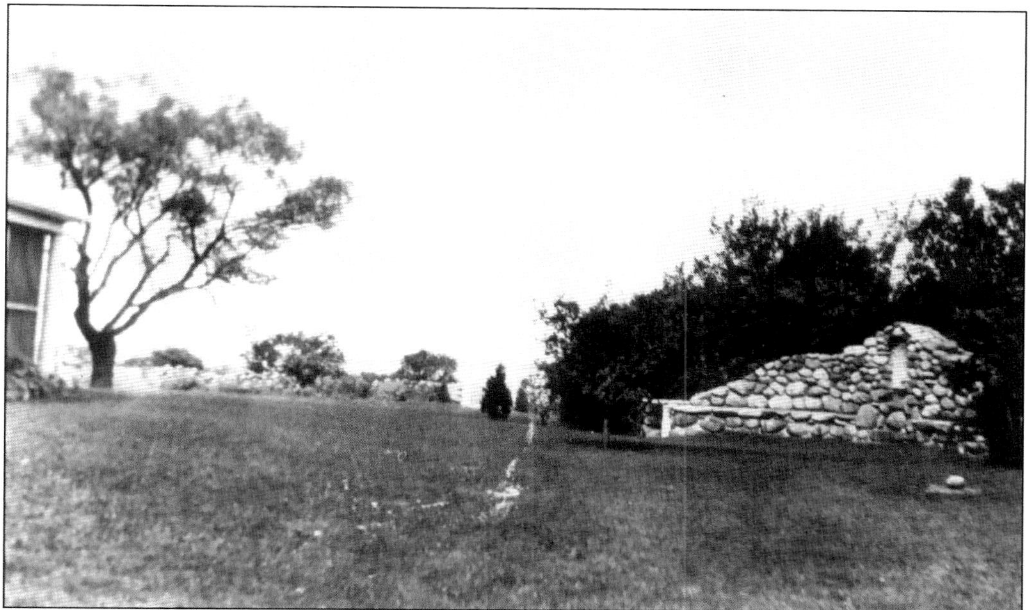

Standing by the fountain today, we are surrounded by trees. Prior toWorld War II mowed lawns and fields permitted sweeping views down to the sea.

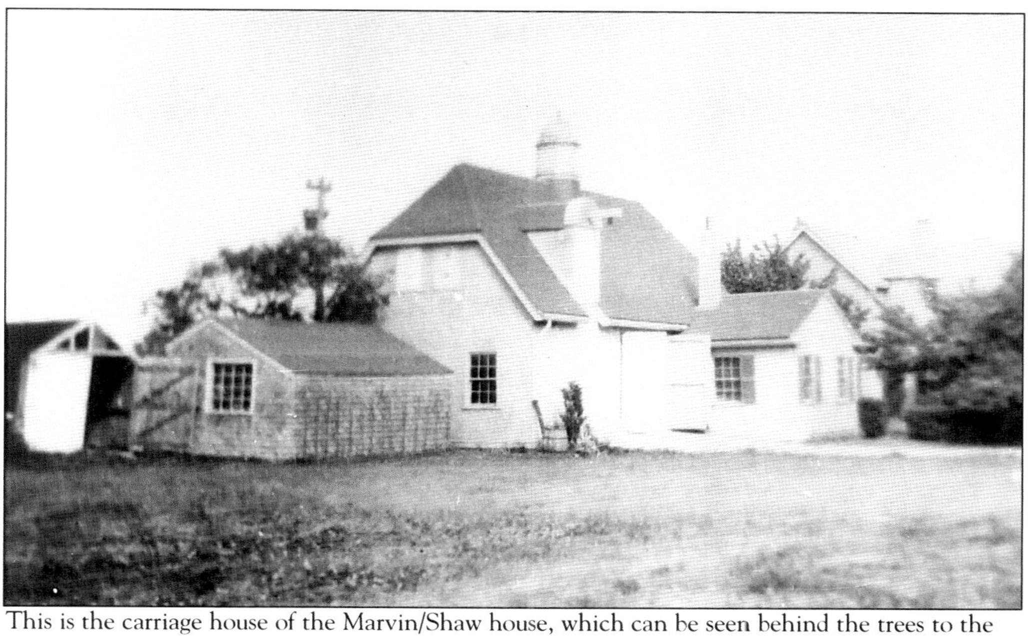

This is the carriage house of the Marvin/Shaw house, which can be seen behind the trees to the right. The carriage house, which included 'man's quarters,' was later used as a garage.

that pipe can be seen today along the shore. Before you leave the Marvin/Straw estate grounds, look at the dense growth of trees and brush behind the fountain. Most of that growth was not here in the 1920s and '30s and standing here during those decades, you would have had a clear view of the ocean.

Turning your back on the Dolphin Fountain, take the path that angles slightly to your right, and you will emerge onto the asphalt bicycle path. You will be following this path for several hundred yards. (Watch out for cyclists, and roller-blade skaters!)

Just as you reach the bicycle path, you will see twin masonry pillars at either end of the Marvin's Norway maple-lined, semi-circular driveway. Just as the Marvins did, volunteers plant geraniums and

One of the two sets of masonry gateposts which marked the entrance to the Marvin/Straw house from Route 1A. Volunteers plant flowers atop these posts every spring.

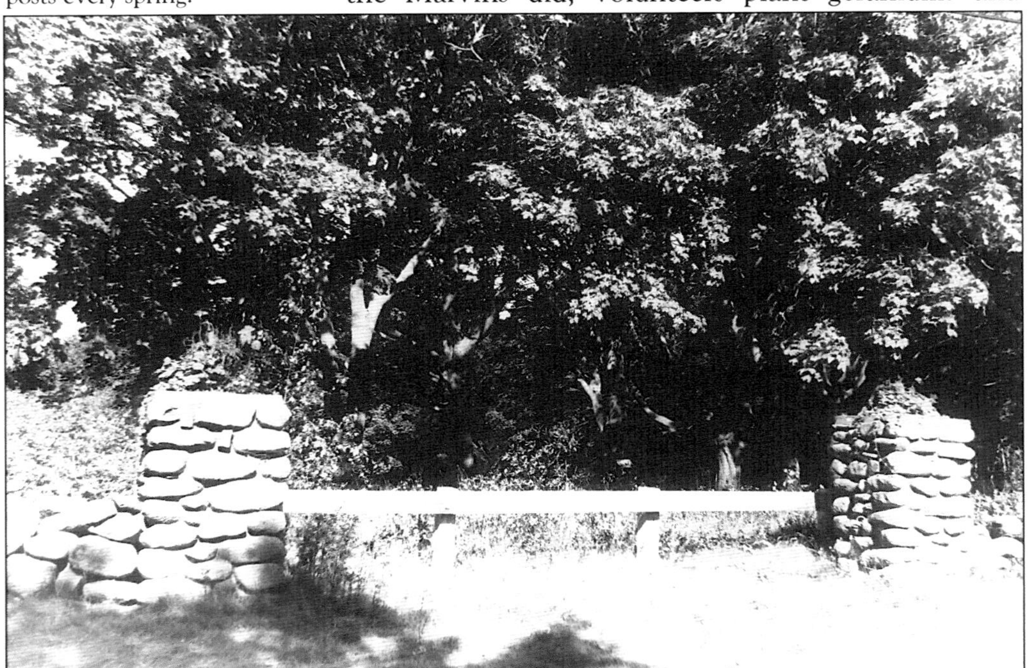

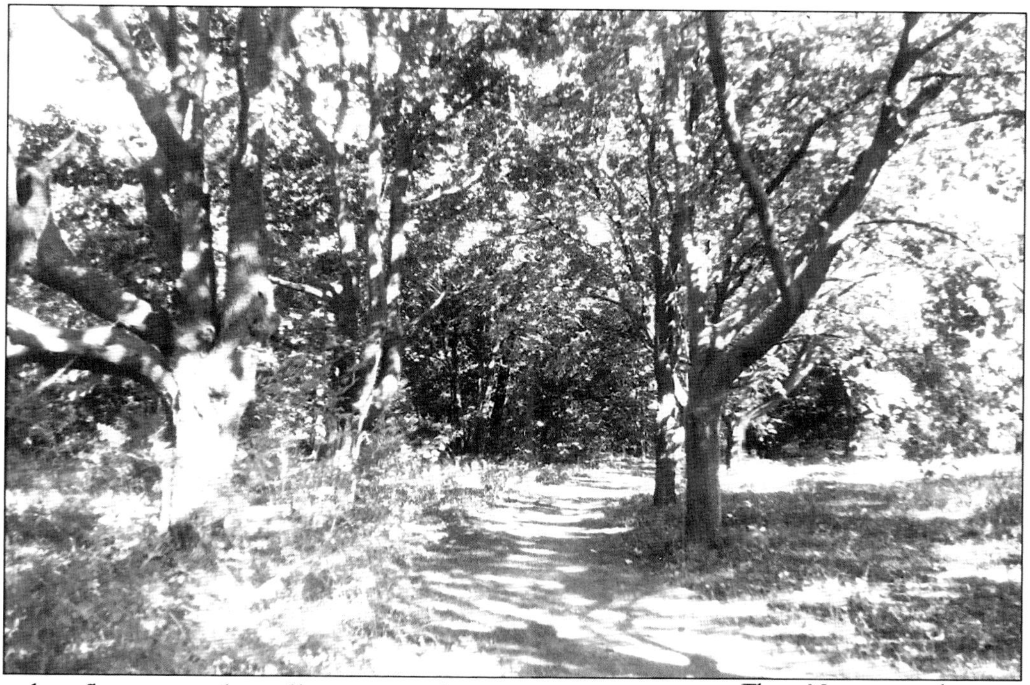

other flowers in the pillar tops each summer. Turn to the right onto the bicycle path on a slight downward grade, and stop when you are opposite the driveway in front of a white house across Route 1A.

These Norway maple trees line what was once the semi-circular drive for the Marvin/Shaw house.

The Odiorne Homestead to the Pond

The buildings here are those of the Odiorne Farm. The house, at least, dates from 1800. According to family history, this was the third house built by the Odiornes in an unbroken occupancy of 282 years, ending with the government's taking of the land in 1942 to build Fort Dearborn. In 1657, John Odiorne was a resident of Portsmouth. At that time Portsmouth included Great Island (New Castle) and much of Sandy Beach (Rye) as well as parts of other adjoining communities.

The 1800 Odiorne farmhouse as seen today from the bicycle path.

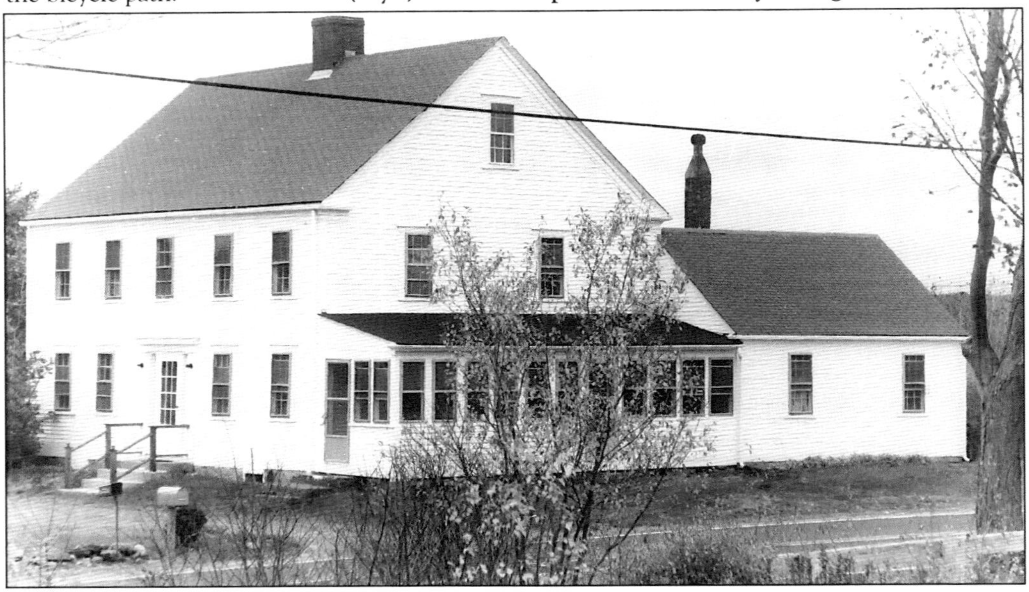

As a Portsmouth resident, John Odiorne could take part in a 1660 "division of public lands."

Whether the land he purchased then included all of today's park property or only some portion has not yet been determined. When his estate was divided after his death in 1707, no mention was made of land on the peninsula (he had previously deeded it to his son). However it did include 41 acres "in the Plains" (near the southern end of Islington Street in Portsmouth) and 3 acres "at Great Island." Creditors of John Odiorne received eighteen shillings and three pence for each pound (twenty shillings) due.

Born in Sheviock in Cornwall, England, Odiorne was said to be a fisherman on Smuttynose Island of the Isles of Shoals who "was granted" 42 acres on Great Island shortly before his purchase of land at Odiorne Point (according to the Odiorne genealogy). Hannah,

Ralph Edwin Odiorne, holding a pitch fork, at the Odiorne family farmhouse about 1903. Compare the front doors, aside porch and trees in the two pictures of the house.

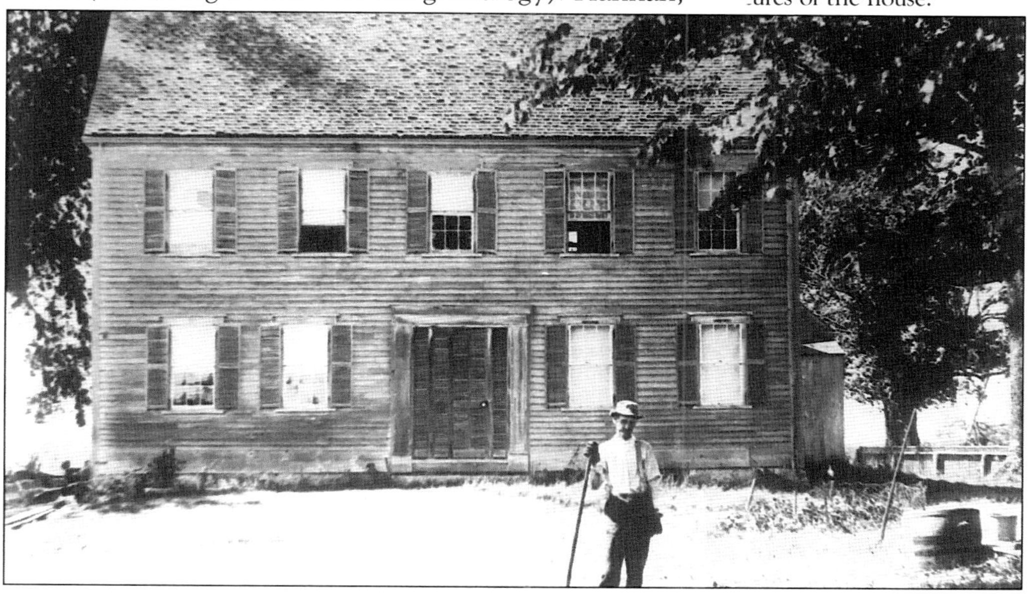

the first born of John and Mary (Johnson) Odiorne, married a Lt. John Batson of Saco, Maine. In an attack in Maine in 1703, American Indians captured the then-pregnant Hannah and her two children and took them to Montreal! Batson died in captivity in 1704. Two years later James Stilson, who had heard of Hannah, went to see her and purchased her release. They were married in October 1705.

At first, the Odiornes made their livelihood by commercial fishing, farming, haying the salt marsh, and trading with the American Indians. They later developed a more comprehensive farm which prospered enough so that, by 1800, fifth-generation Ebenezer was able to build the house you see across the road. Complete with a large barn, carriage house, shed and well, the house faces south over what then were gently

Odiorne carriage house, left, and shed, right. The shed, in disrepair, still exists today.

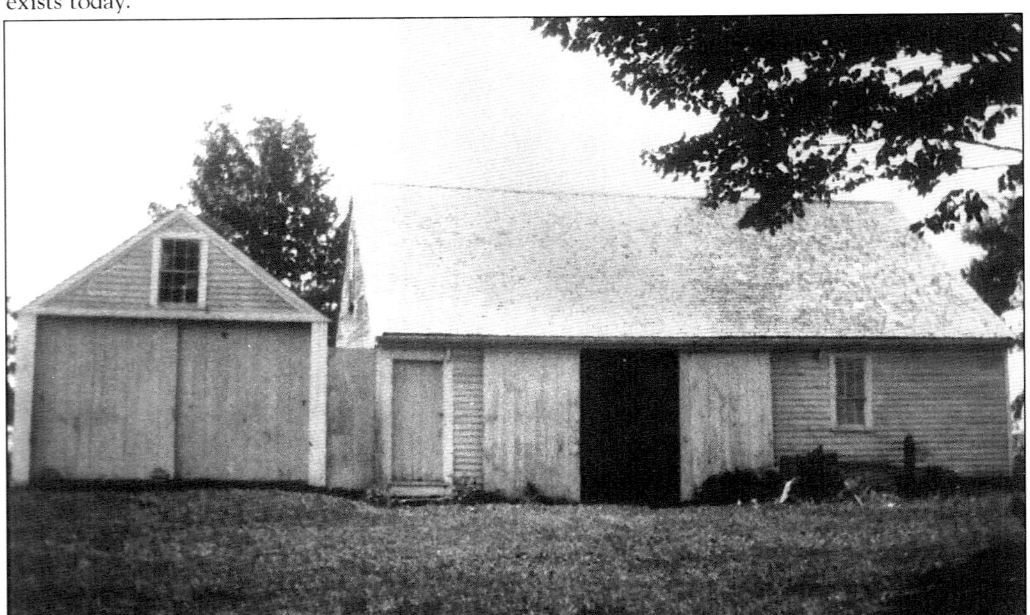

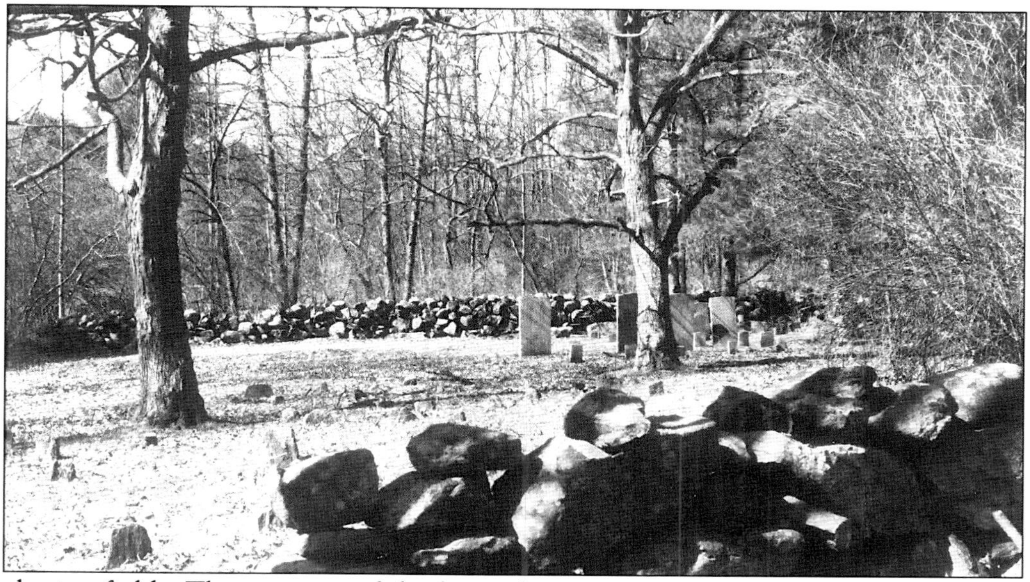

Members of the Odiorne family and other early settlers are buried in this cemetery to the west of the Odiorne farmhouse.

sloping fields. The position of the house kept winter's northeast blast to the rear wall. To the west of the house on a small rise, the Odiorne fishermen dried their catch on crude wooden platforms called flakes, giving that area the name "Flake Hill."

As the farmstead developed, the Odiornes needed more tools and built a blacksmith shop. A small family cemetery, possibly the oldest in New Hampshire, is still on the property and allegedly also contains the remains of early settlers and some American Indians with whom the early Odiornes had dealt peacefully. Many graves can still be found in the cemetery, which was deeded to the Colonial Dames of America in the State of New Hampshire. A granite monument to the first settlers was dedicated in 1899 by their organization. Originally the monument had been placed near the shore, but it was moved to the cemetery in 1955

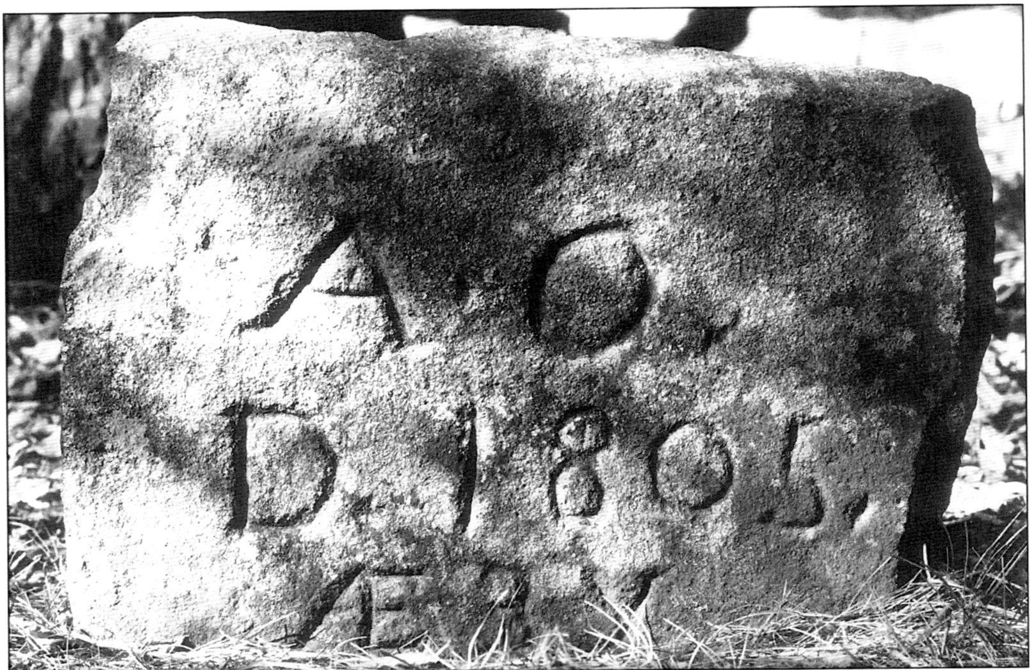

A gravestone in the Odiorne family graveyard.

to enable continued viewing while protecting it from vandalism.

In later years, parts of the farm were leased to others for haying, fruit orchards, potatoes, and other ground crops. The family had moved elsewhere and returned only in the summertime after 1915.

At the close of World War II, the federal government offered to sell back the property west of Route 1A to Ralph E. Odiorne. In his seventies, and settled in Massachusetts, Mr. Odiorne was unable to take advantage of the offer. By a sealed bid, the property and the entire marsh to the west were purchased in 1949 by Ralph Brown. An ardent conservationist and amateur historian, Mr. Brown restored much of the house and barn that had been unkindly altered by the military during World War II.

Well to the southwest of the farmhouse is a concrete-block structure, a powder magazine from World War II. This, the use of the farmhouse as a barracks, plus an infiltration training course comprised the primary uses of the farm as part of Fort Dearborn.

In the 1990s, Mr. Brown gave the western half of the marsh to the [Town of] Rye Conservation Commission and sold the balance to the State of New Hampshire. All of it is to be kept in a natural state. As of this writing, Mr. Brown still occupies the house, and has life-tenancy, so please do not go onto the farm property without his permission.

While few Odiornes still live in the Seacoast area, descendants of John Odiorne now live throughout the United States and Canada. The names of early

Business card for the Odiorne Point Tavern about 1925.

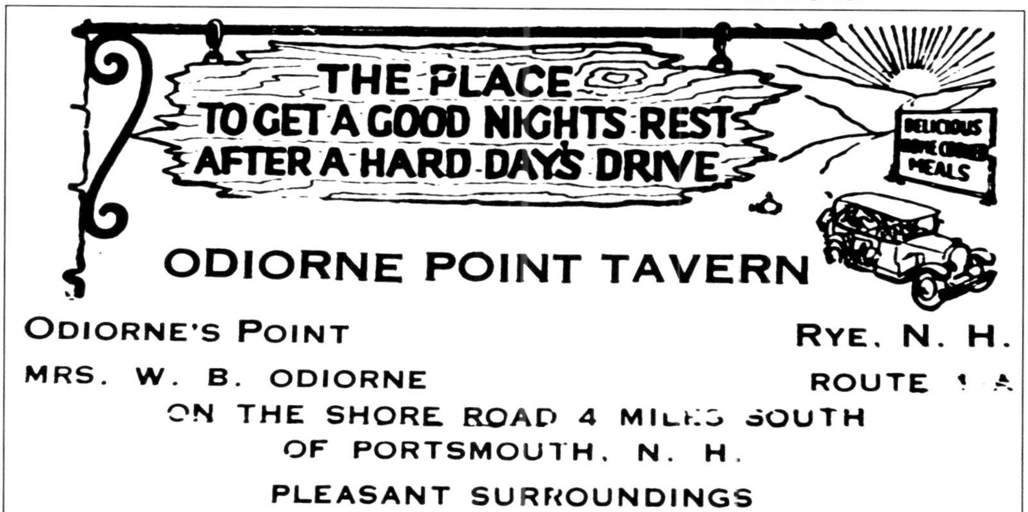

Odiornes echo in its history as farmers and fishermen, in foreign and domestic commerce, as ship owners and masters, sailcloth manufacturers, leaders in the colonial assembly and in the state legislature in the early decades of our Republic.

Turn away from the homestead and look along the shoulder of the cycle path to your right. You will see a narrow pit-like depression. From its center grows a small stand of quaking aspen: it is, in fact, a man-made pit.

In 1838, the Odiorne Point land owners petitioned the selectmen of Rye to construct Columbus Road to the sea just north of here. This road provided access to the shore for small-boat fishing and for inland farmers to collect seaweed as fertilizer for their fields and gardens.

Columbus Road as it appeared in the 1920s.

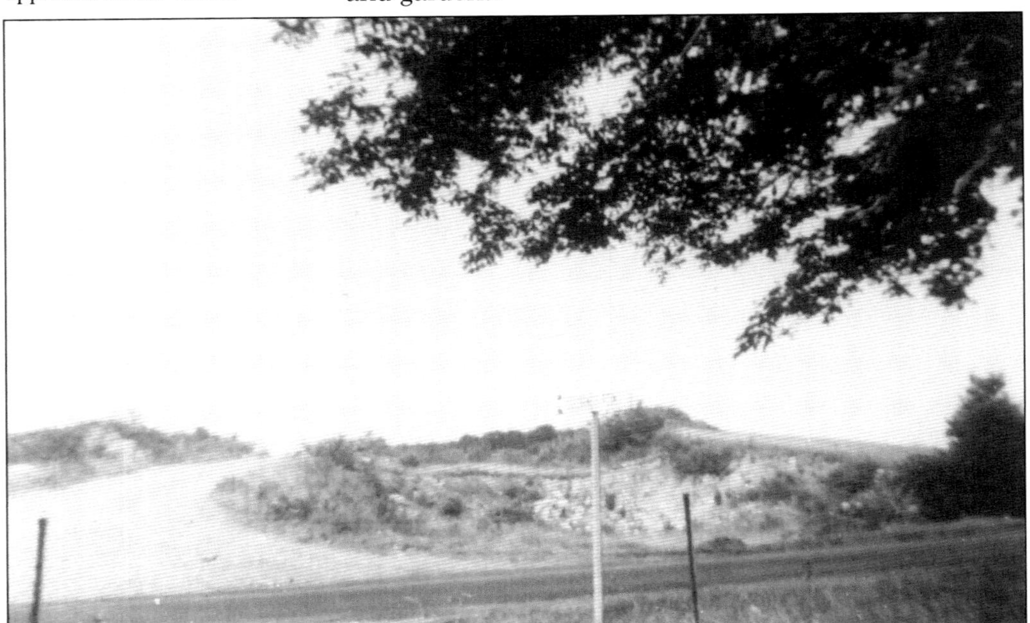

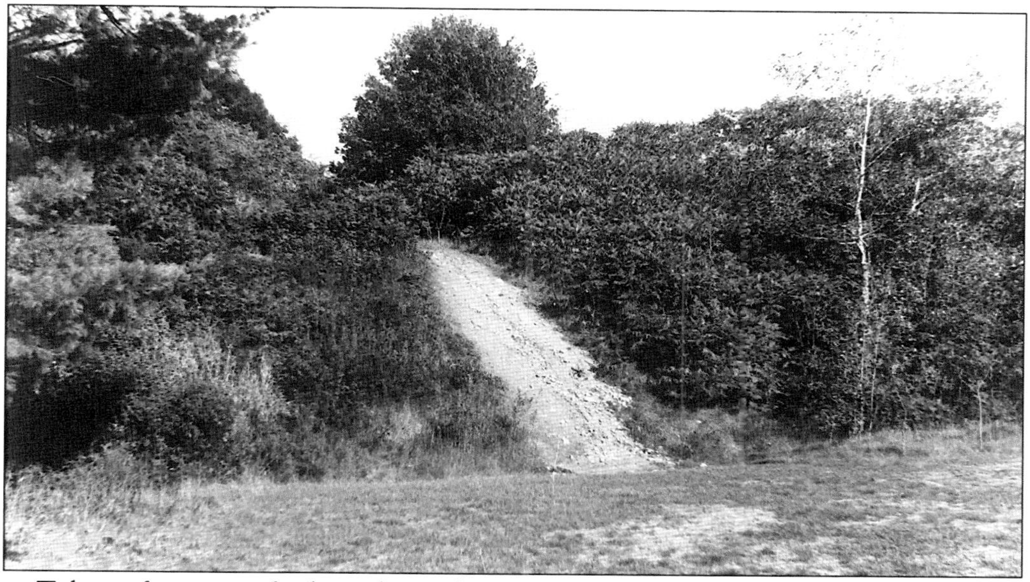

What remains of Columbus road today. Near this high point of land some believe that David Thomson built his 'Great House'. Gravel from this hill was removed at the turn of the century to construct what is now Route 1A.

Take a few steps farther along the path and, still on your right, you will see the scarred face of a hill, the highest natural elevation on Odiorne Point. This marks the site of a gravel pit. The Columbus Road of 1838 went over this crest, but in 1902 the state had mounted a project to extend the shore road (now Route 1A) to the south, cutting into this hill for gravel. Of itself, this was hardly a momentous event, except that the gravel pit is, by oral tradition, the site of the first house in New Hampshire. Unfortunately any traces of this dwelling probably would have been obliterated by this excavation.

Around 75 yards along the cycle path you will see a pond behind the fence to your right. Like the road builders before them, the builders of Fort Dearborn dug their gravel pit here in the 1940s; gravel from this pond was used to construct Battery Seaman (you

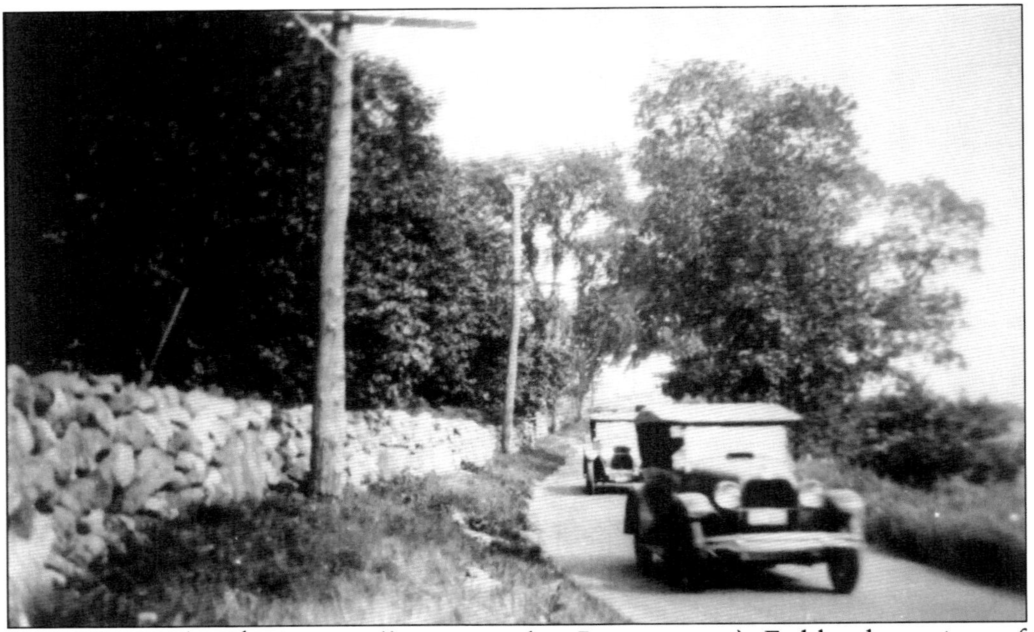

Cars on Route 1A in the 1920s.

will come to that Battery soon). Fed by the springs of Odiorne, this pond provides a freshwater habitat for wildlife and is an interesting place for study. Before its excavation this pond was a gentle slope on the farm of Mrs. Janette Gage. Mrs. Gage's son, Edward, was the friend of Arnold Whittaker who dreamed of owning a chicken farm, but needed a place to establish it. Through his friendship with Edward, Arnold was permitted to use part of a huge barn and the sloping land as his chicken farm. When the federal government descended on Odiorne in 1942, he was given only thirty days to remove his chickens, in spite of a wartime ban on interfering with food production. However, move he did to a farm he found in Stratham, New Hampshire, taking thousands of chickens with him.

Despite his efforts, Arnold's dream came to an

abrupt end in 1958. The chickens contracted a contagious disease, and he had to destroy the entire flock. Whittaker moved to an island in Yarmouth, Maine, where he acquired a captain's license and a reputation as a good navigator. In 1961, he was offered the contract for ferry service from Portsmouth to the Isles of Shoals' Star Island. Whittaker bought the M/V Viking in Long Island, New York, in order to carry out that contract. Today, Captain Bob Whittaker, Arnold's son, is the owner and principal captain of the Isles of Shoals Steamship Company.

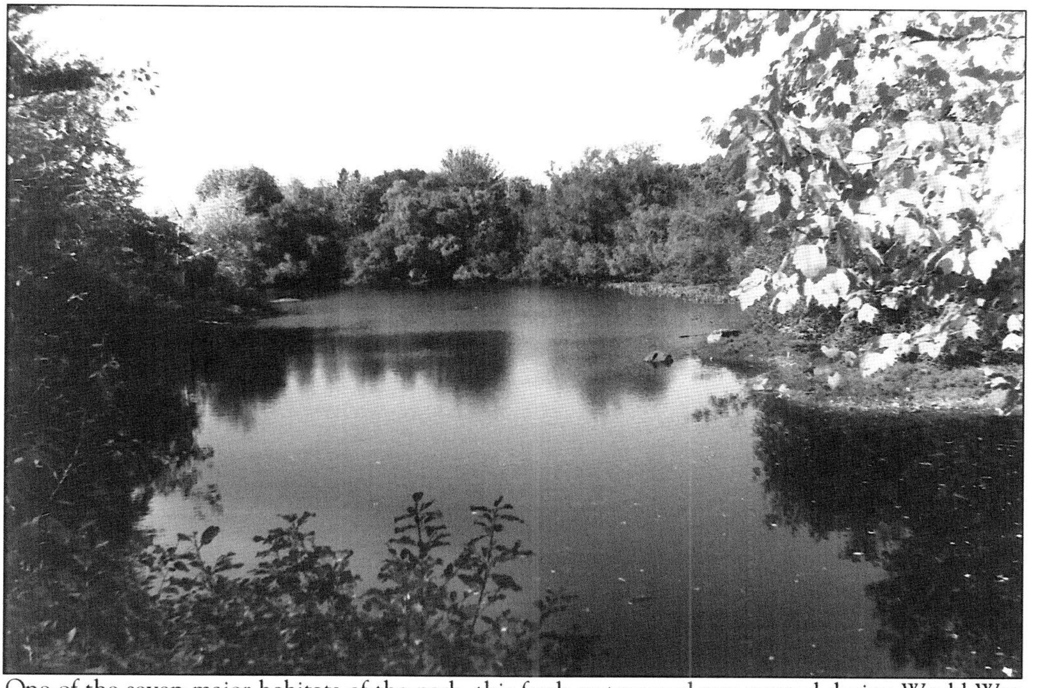

One of the seven major habitats of the park, this fresh water pond was created during World War II by excavating the soil for other purposes. Springs keep water in the pond.

Pond to the Salt Marsh

Odiorne Point is fascinating for its natural history as well as offering a visual representation of the earliest New Hampshire history. In some ways it is possible to see the area even as the first settlers would have seen it by looking at different natural features. If you are taking this walk between late August and early October you will see splashes of yellow blossoms in every open field. Look closely; in addition to goldenrod, you will see an abundance of tansy. Notice its cluster of button-like yellow flowers: it is a strewing herb. A native of Europe, this herb was brought here by early settlers and is now a common weed in North America.

This path, which parallels Route 1A, is enjoyed by bikers and walkers most of the year and cross country skiers in the winter.

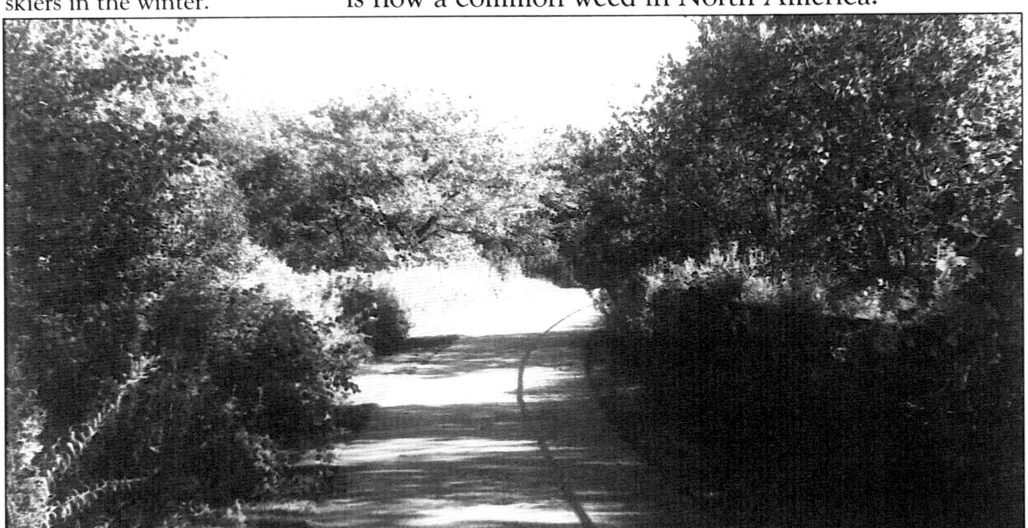

Settlers scattered tansy inside on their earthen floors and outside along their foundations because it was a deterrent to lice, mosquitos, and other insects. Break off some leaves and crush them. Its pungent odor is another attribute: it is a deodorant! Since the early colonists washed their clothes infrequently, an odor fighter of any degree was no doubt welcome.

Tansy leaves may be steeped to make tansy tea, but since it is a sedative, too strong a brew can be dangerous. If you have an itchy mosquito bite, rub the crushed leaves on it, and you can experience the sedative value of this very useful plant. By rubbing your face and arms with the leaves, it will help repel mosquitos.

Salt Marsh to Heritage Garden

Continuing along the bicycle path look across the marsh to where, toward the right, Route 1A crosses Seavey Creek at the wooden bridge. Try to picture a working tidal mill there. The Pine Tree Mill had been operated by William Seavey and John Foye until they sold it to the Odiornes as a grist and saw mill in 1842. Operation continued until 1863, when the mill burned and was not restored. As you continue along the path, you will see expanses of open salt marsh to your left. This marsh played an important role in the settlement of the area, and continues to be an important marine

Salt water marsh seen from bicycle path. The western side of the park is almost completely bounded by saltmarsh. The Odiorne family operated a tidal mill near the bridge in the 1800s.

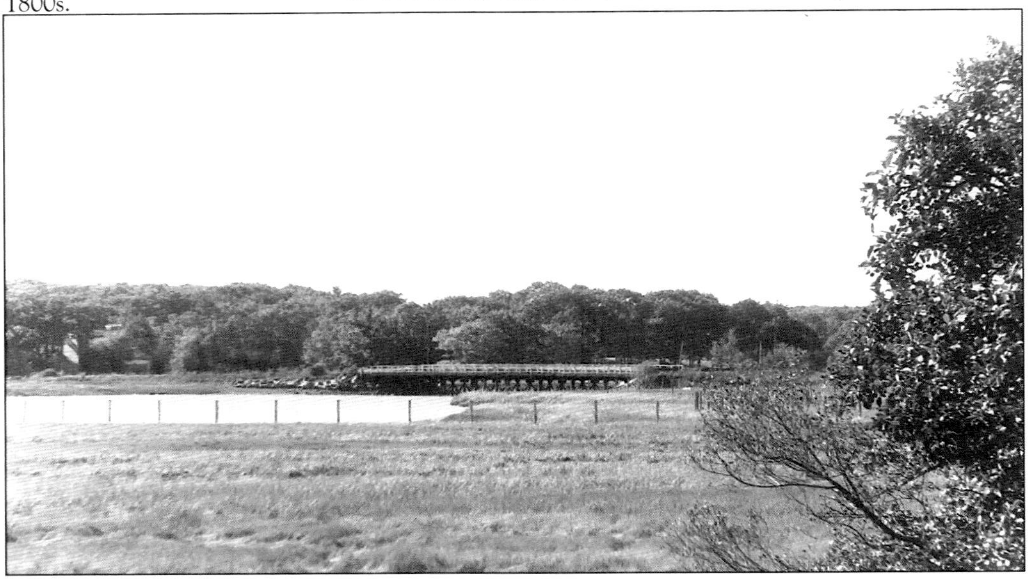

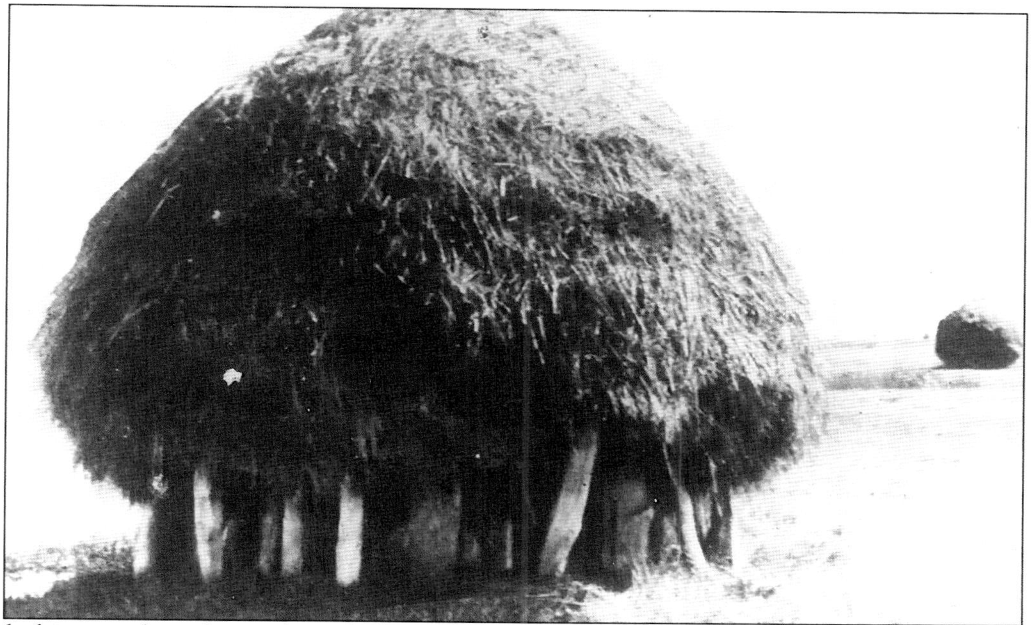

Salt marsh hay was stacked upon wooden posts called staddles to keep it dry at high tide and to allow its removal by boat or by wagon when the marsh was frozen.

habitat within the park and along the coast. The first settlers chose Odiorne Point for many good reasons. There was plenty of stone and wood for building and, in the surrounding marshes, rich marsh hay for their animals and for roof thatch. Just as important were the many fresh water springs of Odiorne Point. As the demand for hay increased, new approaches were required to move the harvested hay out to market. For this, gundalows were utilized and bog shoes for horses and oxen were designed.

At first, the gundalow was nothing more than a "dumb barge," no rudder, no sail, no deck, no deck house, all of which were added in later years. These water-going carriers were pressed into all sorts of service until roads were cut through the forests. Marsh hay was harvested and piled to dry on circles of pilings called

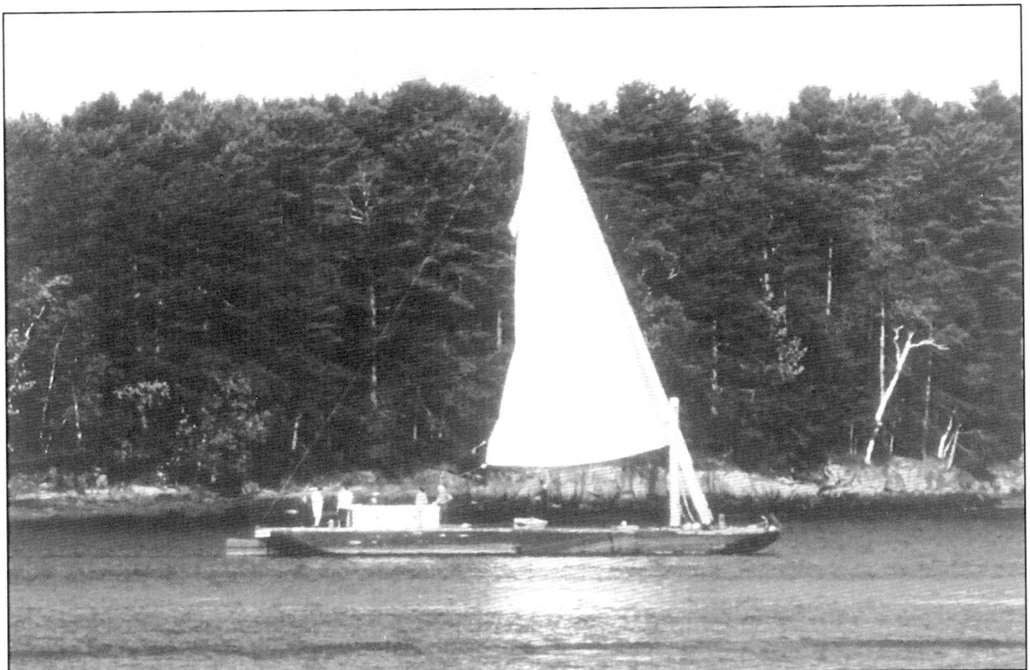

Flat bottomed boats, called gundalows, were used in the Odiorne Point area to haul salt marsh hay and supplies.

staddles, remains of which can still be seen in some marshes along the New England coast. Transferred to a gundalow and brought to the soggy shores of creeks, the hay was pitched onto wagons pulled by horses or oxen wearing bog shoes. They served as a kind of "snowshoe" and were fastened to the animals' hooves to spread their weight and prevent them from sinking into the marsh.

You can see strings of old fence posts along the edge of the marsh creeks. These cedar posts mark the "Dead Line" at the rear of World War II Fort Dearborn. Any intruder found inside that line was to be shot! A former soldier mused if the fencing here were not primarily devised to keep the military in rather than intruders out.

As you continue along the path, you will pass a gravel road with a (usually) closed gate to Route 1A.

This is Frost Point Road. Residential estates once lined this road, and the estate owners used it to get to the northernmost point of Odiorne. For now, your walk passes this road: we'll rejoin it later.

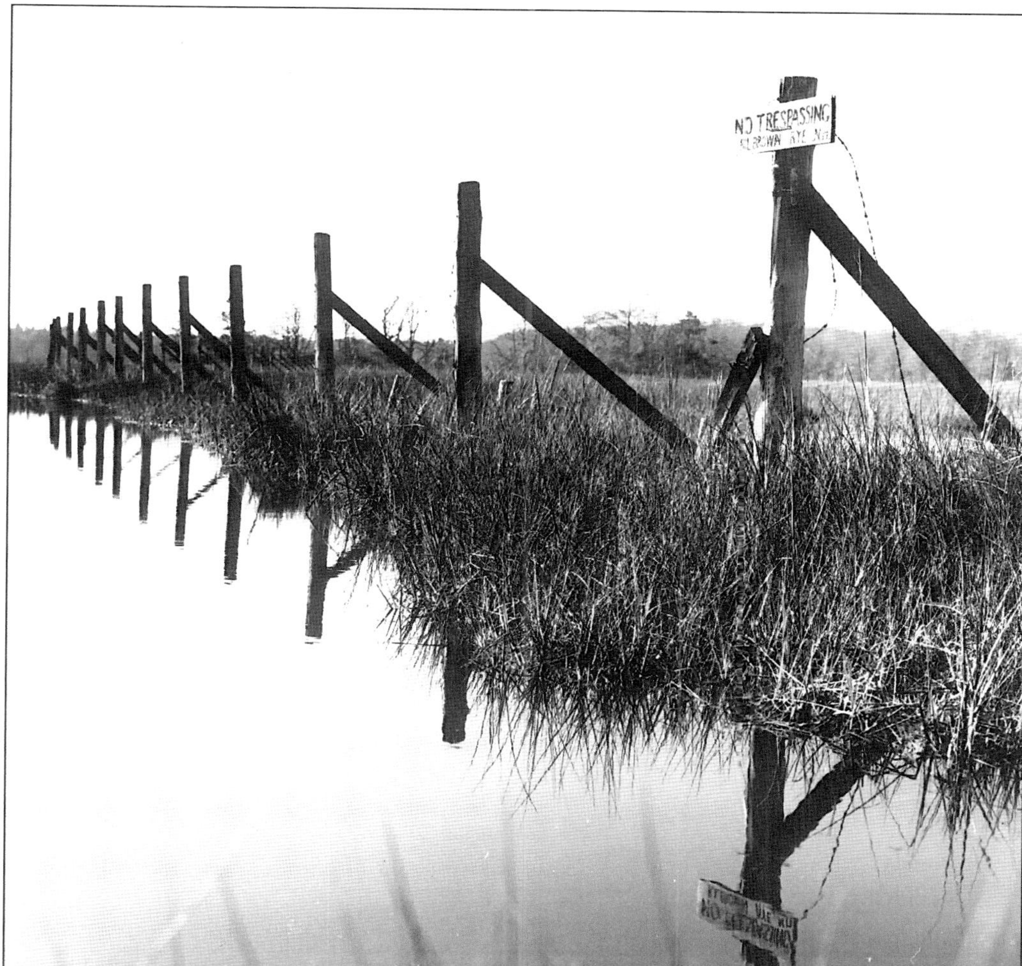

During World War II, the salt marsh perimeter of Fort Dearborn was enclosed by these posts strung with barbed wire to prevent the entry of unauthorized personnel. This photograph was taken after Mr. Brown purchased the property; his name, R.L. Brown, appears on the post sign.

Heritage Garden to the Plotting Room

Continue north on the bicycle path just over 100 yards, past one narrow path on your right to a much broader, well-defined lane on your right. Flanked by stone walls, this was the private driveway to the Foye/ Whitcomb House. As you begin the walk up the drive, a clearing on your right marks a flower garden.

The roses here were once famous: people would drive past the garden just to smell the resplendent blooms. Today, park volunteers have lovingly restored much

In several areas of the park you will notice meadows such as this. They are created by controlled mowings to provide a habitat for plants and animals.

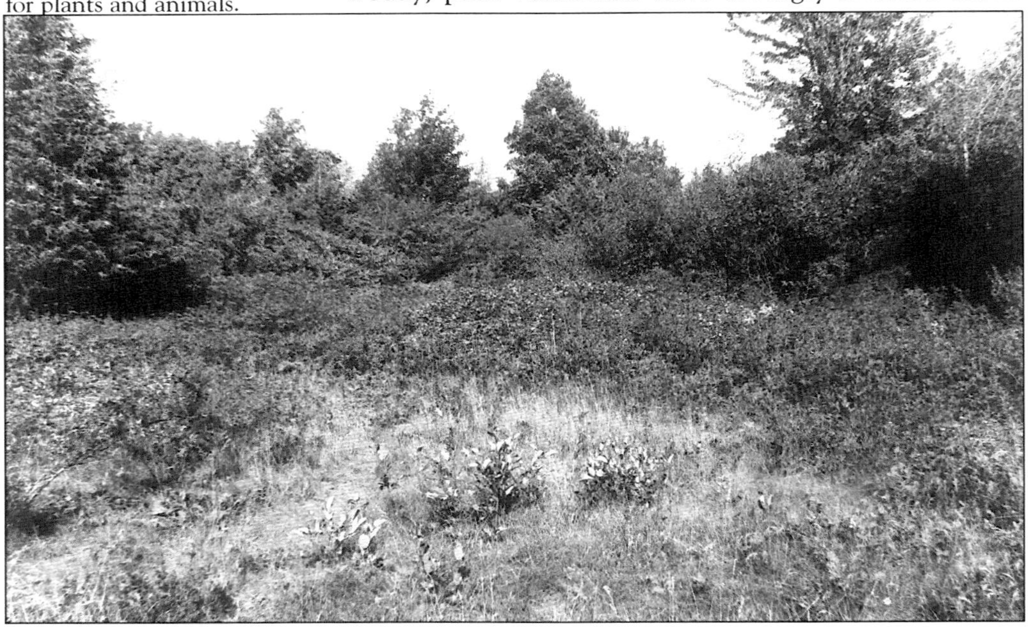

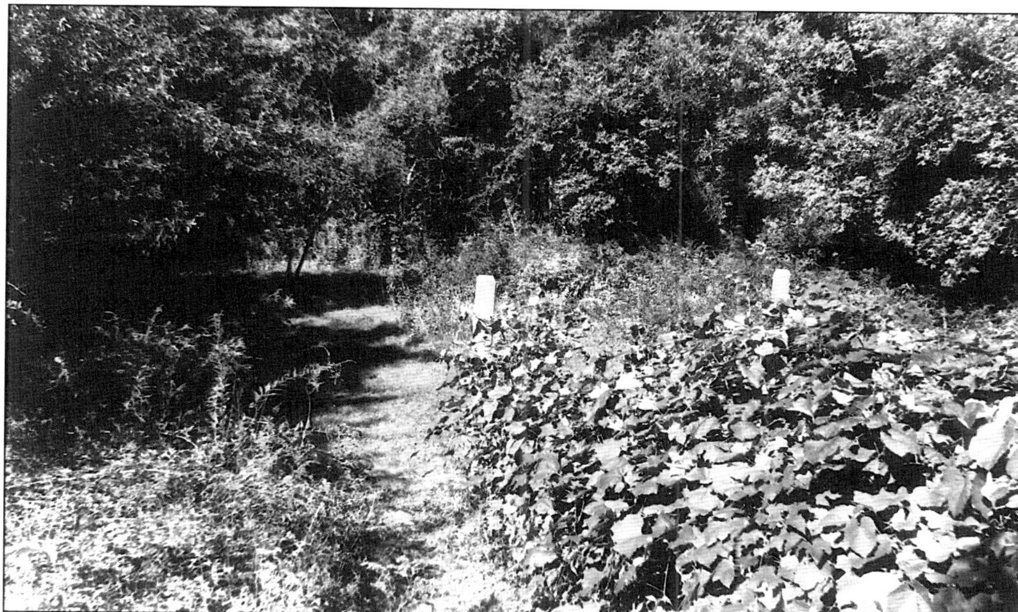

Foye/Whitcomb garden today. Volunteers have maintained Mrs. Whitcomb's garden. The rows of tall trees on three sides of the garden demonstrate what happens to a privet hedge if not clipped.

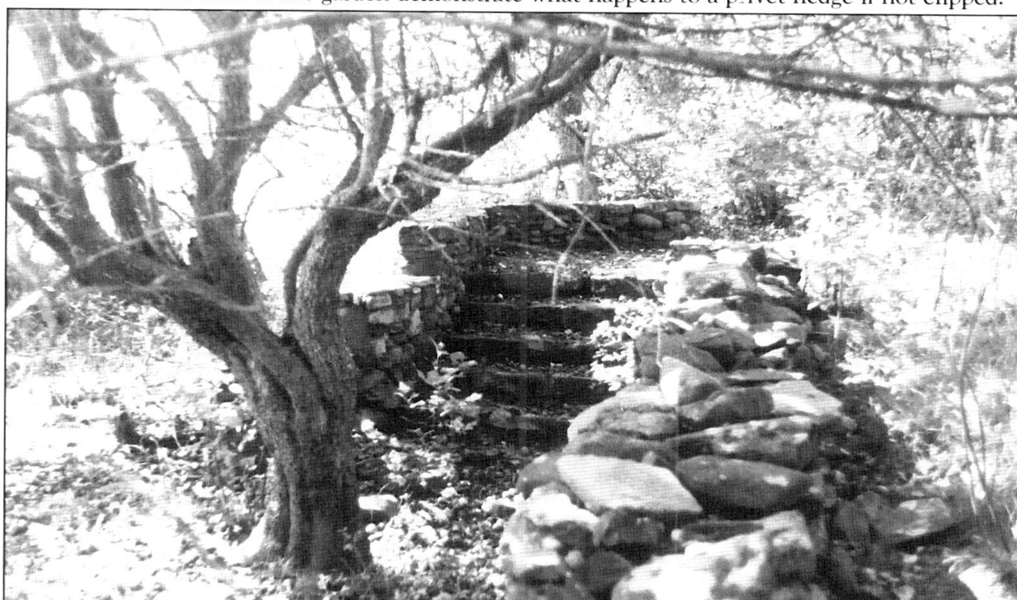

Steps in Whitcomb stone wall. These steps and the garden are the only evidence of the Whitcomb home that remain today.

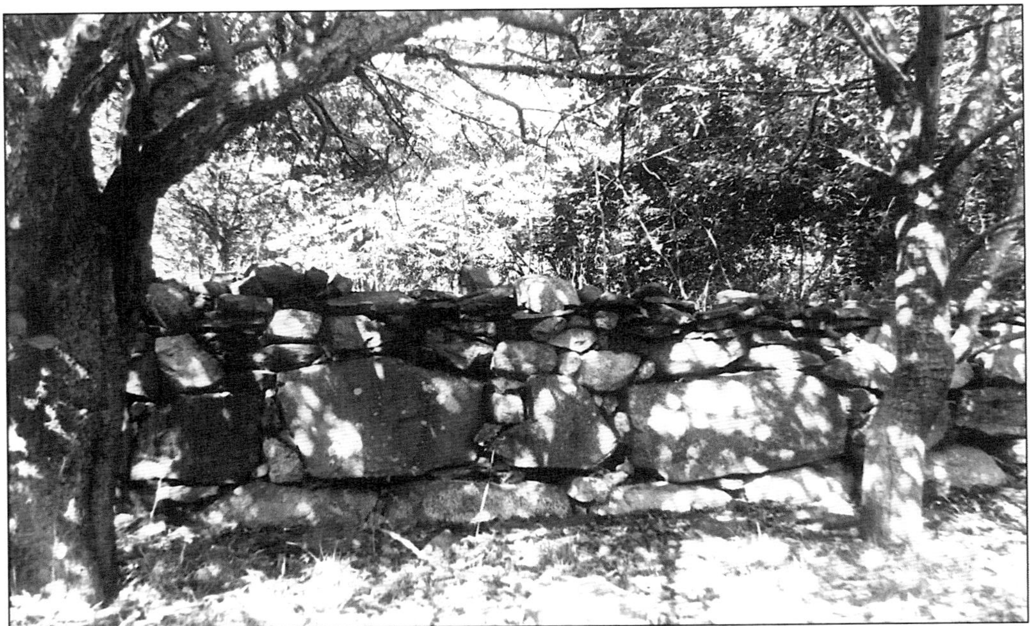

At the foot of Whitcomb steps are these huge rocks that were put into the wall to retain the terrace.

of the garden, and named it the (Foye/Whitcomb) Heritage Garden.

The drive ends in some broken asphalt left from World War II. Directly ahead are some foundation stones hidden in the grass and brush which are fun to explore. At first just a small farm house; buildings, sheds, and barns were added by the Foye family over the decades. Paul and Kathleen Whitcomb purchased the property and named it "Pioneer Farm." When the government descended in 1942, "Pioneer Farm" was a twenty-four room estate and it served as an example of the undervalued payments received from the government by the eleven home owners of Odiorne. The elegant home and over 41 acres of land were purchased at the price of only $23,500!

Mr. Whitcomb and his mother (his father had died

earlier) owned a chain of restaurants, "The Baltimore Dairy and Lunch", with (allegedly) locations in New York, St. Louis, New Orleans, Minneapolis, and other metropolitan areas. At least some of the seats in these eateries were like the school chairs with one enlarged, desk-like arm. This feature, probably not unique to the Whitcomb diners, gave rise to the epithet "one arm lunch."

A wealthy man, Paul Whitcomb would arrive for the summer with two Locomobiles, a phaeton and a limousine: very expensive cars. In the later '20s and '30s his wife, Kathleen, (who suffered from epilepsy) and her brother, Luther Robie, both from a Nashua, New Hampshire building supply family, began to live here year-round with one "Denny" Driscoll as caretaker.

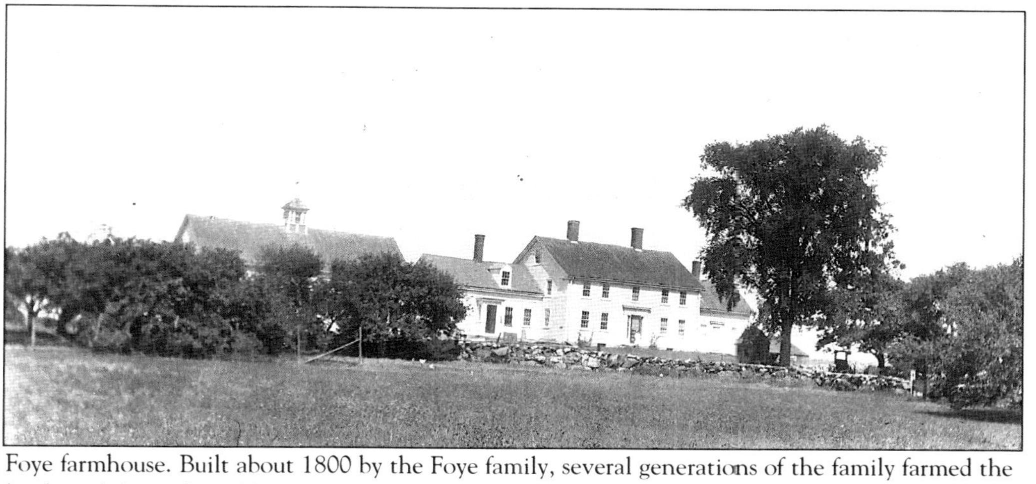

Foye farmhouse. Built about 1800 by the Foye family, several generations of the family farmed the land until the early 1920s.

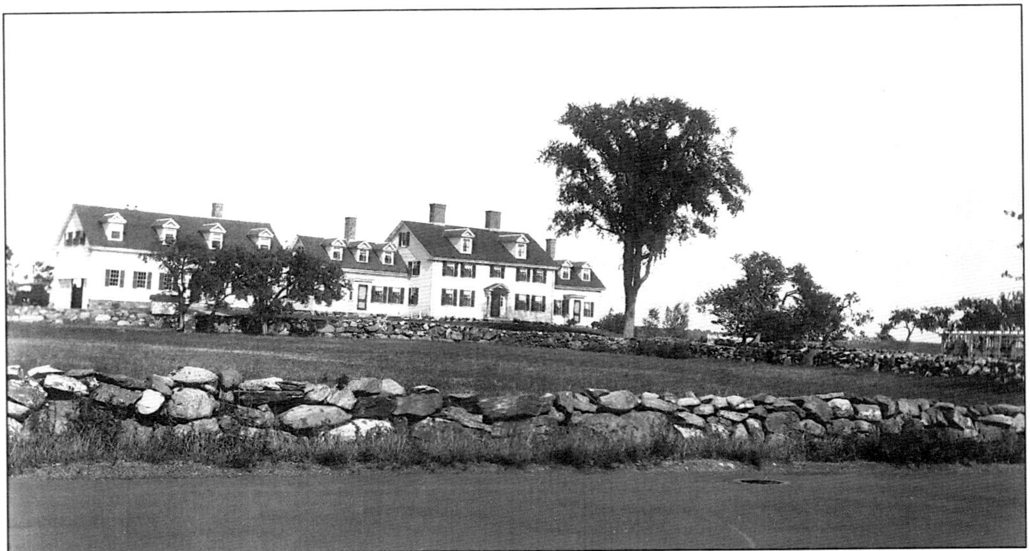

Whitcomb Home. The Foye house was bought by the Whitcombs in the early 1920s and many modifications were made to the house and the barn.

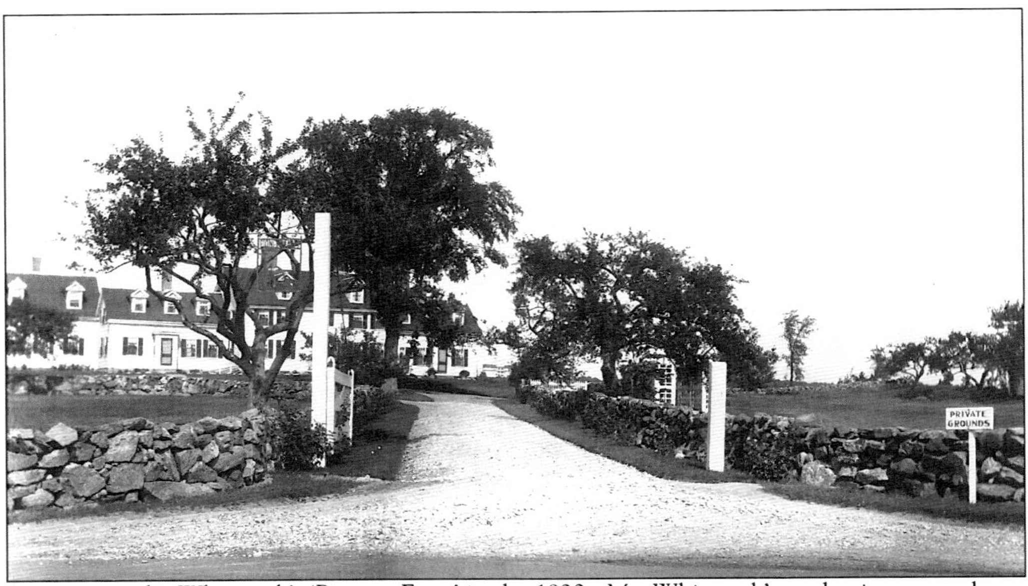

Entrance to the Whitcomb's 'Pioneer Farm' in the 1930s. Mrs.Whitcomb's garden is seen to the right of the driveway.

Plotting Room to Battery Seaman

At this point you should turn toward your right and as the broken asphalt becomes a dirt path, another man-made hill looms up on your right. Although bunkers for smaller guns included a self-contained room for plotting targets, sensitive targeting instruments could be damaged by the earth-shaking concussions from the firing of the huge 16-inch guns. For these larger guns, a separate plotting room was needed several hundred feet away, and such a plotting room was built within this bunker. Telephone land lines from the 50-mile web of observation posts to the north and south converged here. Target coordinates were called in and the plotter would calculate the correct aiming points for the guns. The ports of this bunker are now barricaded with huge stones.

Due to their historic interest the New Hampshire Division of Parks would like to open all of the bunkers to the public, but the twin problems of vandalism and of funding to make them safe have thus far prevented such an undertaking.

The stone walls that you can see here were built with the rocks and stones unearthed as the then-open fields were developed and houses built.

At a slight rise in the path as it circles to the northerly end of the plotting room, you will see on your left the junction of stone walls and a large area of trees. This is a miniature upland forest habitat, the fourth habitat type you have encountered on your walk. Deer and fox have been spotted here as well as in other wooded areas of the park. If you are quiet you might see one, especially in the fall when there are fewer park visitors to frighten them away from open areas and paths.

On your right, a path leads to the top of the plotting room bunker where air vents from the rooms below are still in place.

During your walk you may discover a unique plant growing in the meadows that looks like a rosette of very furry leaves. As the summer progresses, a tall stalk covered with small yellow flowers will develop and may grow several feet tall. Mullein was brought to North America from Europe and was well established by 1800. You may know this fuzzy plant as "quaker rouge." Because Quakers were not allowed to use makeup to enhance their complexion, they rubbed their cheeks with Mullein leaves. The little barbed hairs caused an irritation that reddened their skin and gave the desired effect of rouge without breaking any rules. Local Indians quickly discovered that lining their moccasins in the winter with this naturally occurring "fur" was a great way to insulate their feet against the cold.

Continue along the well-trodden path around the

bunker as it dips and begins a slight rise into a group of very rough-barked trees. At the largest of these shagbark hickories, around 100 yards along, the path you should follow makes an abrupt left turn. After another dip and rise, the nearly straight path will deliver you back to Frost Point Road about 100 yards east from the bicycle path.

Turn left on Frost Point Road. A small hill along the left side of the road was the cover over pumping equipment for an underground reservoir, which was built to provide fire-fighting water to hydrants located in and around Battery Seaman.

After 100 steps or so the southerly port of the two

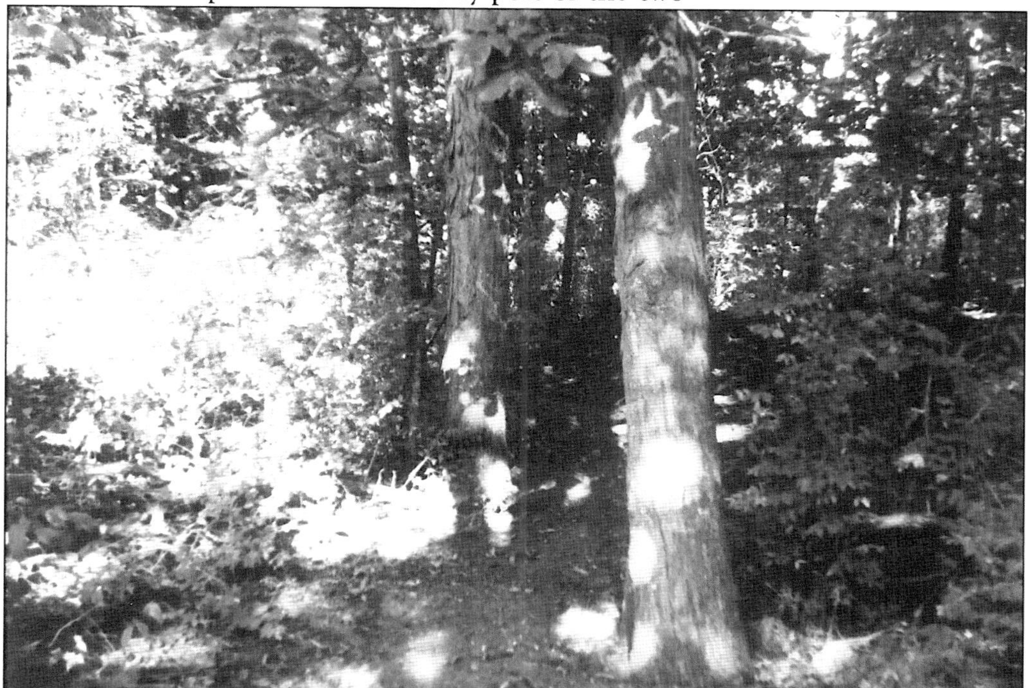

Just beyond the blocked-up command post entrance you pass through woods that contain many shagbark hickory trees.

16-inch gun positions will come into view on your right. You will return here, but for now proceed along the road. Note the heavy growth of bittersweet on the bunker. This plant, along with all the other fast growing shrubs and trees, was planted here by the U.S. Army Corps of Engineers to camouflage the bunker .

The raised banking on the left side of the road covers a series of end-to-end foundations which can be seen on a Corps of Engineers map. It is believed that this series of foundations accurately locates "the farm that grew." Property and a small house built by George Frost in 1759 was purchased by Stephen Foye in 1799: the cottage is shown on an 1805 map. John Seavey Odiorne bought the small farm in 1842, but his early death led to its sale to Captain Thomas R. Clark only eight years later in 1850. Capt. Clark enlarged the house to two stories, and opened a boarding house. Boarders were taken in, and sleighing parties were entertained in winter. However, neither Clark nor his successor, Captain George W. Towle, were able to make a financial success of the boarding house.

George Pierce purchased the property in 1868. He and his brother James, both of whom had experience on a Vanderbilt yacht and at the Rockingham Hotel in Portsmouth, further expanded the house by adding a "substantial" wing. They opened the "Sagamore House" as an elaborate country inn. Their enterprise flourished and a second wing of three stories was built for the 1870 season, during which Cornelius

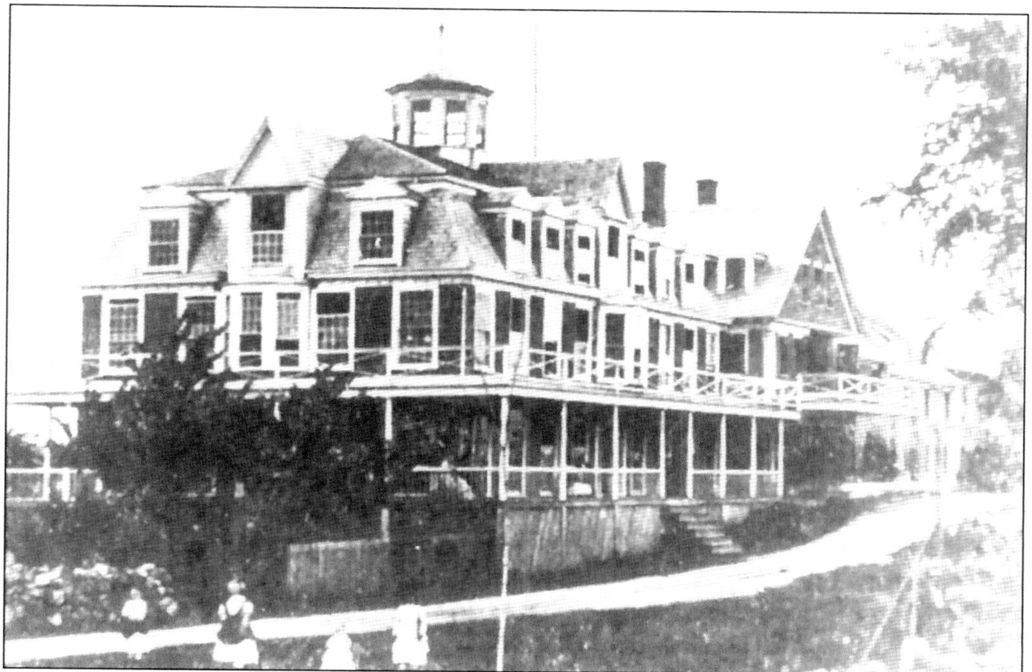

Elegantly appointed Sagamore House attracted notables in the early 1870s.

Vanderbilt was a guest. While they prepared for the 1871 summer, a fire broke out in the kitchen and, accompanied by much confusion with the Portsmouth Fire Department and a breakdown of its equipment, the hotel was gutted by the fire, except for a separate bowling alley.

Only partially insured and deeply in debt, the Pierces were unable to rebuild. James moved to San Francisco, while George remained on the property, living in all that was left of their once-prosperous inn, the bowling alley. Finally, in 1889, the property was sold to Dr. W. Duncan McKim of New York.

Battery Seaman to Frost Point

The large port to the bunker on your right is the central port for Battery Seaman. Into this port shells, gunpowder, and other supplies were moved; half to the right, half to the left. A little farther on the northerly gun position will come into view, but you will pass it by for now. Continue until you emerge into an open area with a panorama of Little Harbor on your left. From here you can see the town of New Castle, Fort Stark and the Wentworth Hotel straight ahead, Whaleback Light on your right, and Kittery Point,

Taking the path to the top of Battery Seaman gives spectacular views on a clear day. Here are Little Harbor and the Wentworth Hotel.

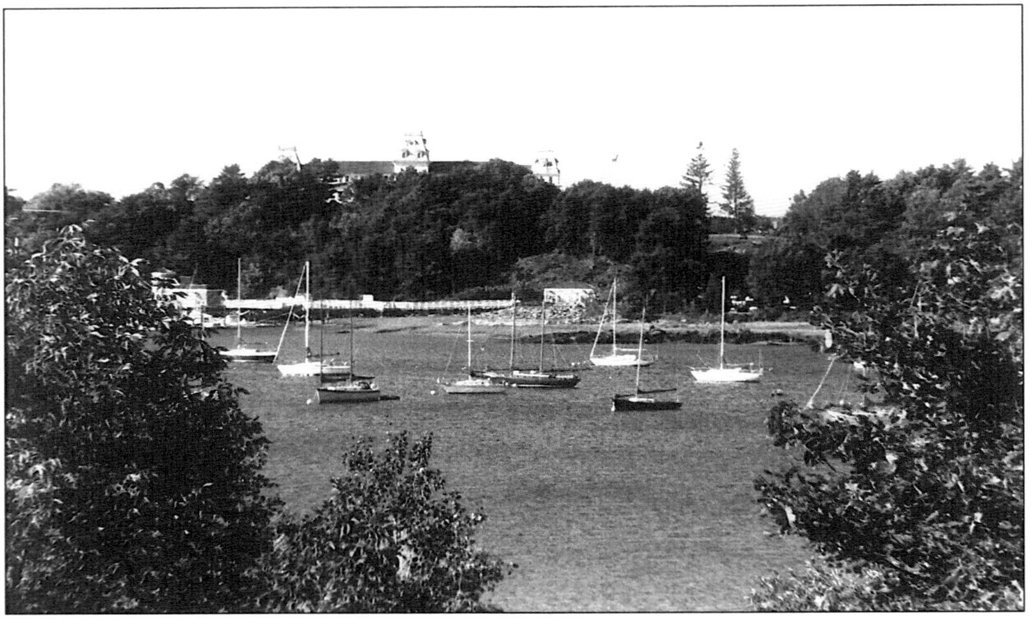

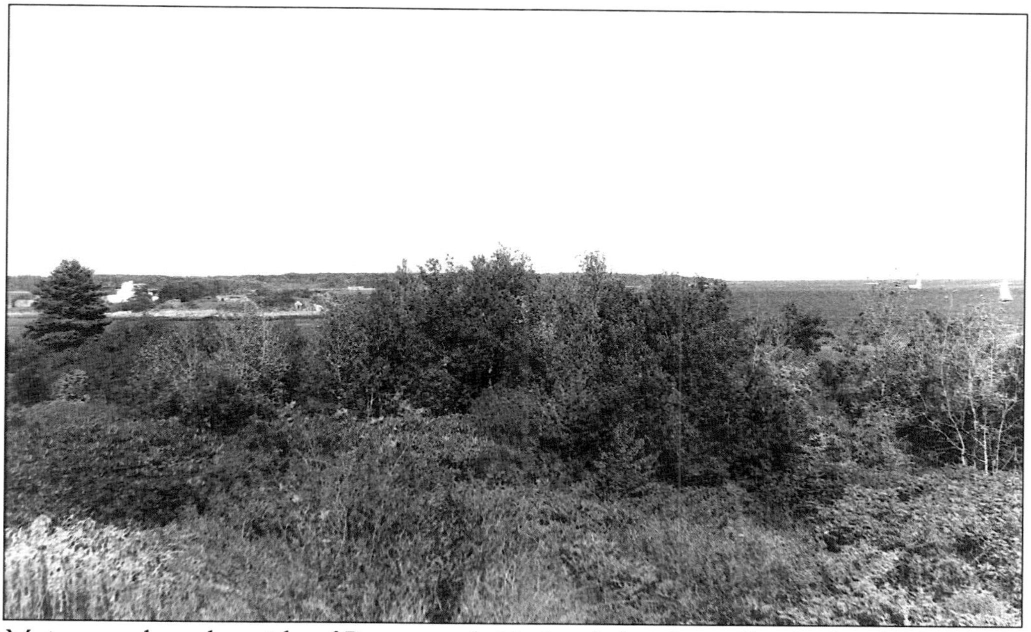

Maine on the other side of Portsmouth Harbor behind Whaleback Light.

Fort Stark and Whaleback Lighthouse. The white building to the left was the World War II Harbor Entrance Control Post. To the right is Whaleback Lighthouse.

This is Frost Point, named for the family who owned and squabbled over it during the last half of the eighteenth century. The farm, including some marsh, was acquired during the mid-1700s by George Frost. Leaving others to farm his property, Frost moved in 1770 to Durham, New Hampshire, where his children were raised. The first judge of Strafford County, he suffered a stroke in 1794. A few months later, he deeded the entire farm at Odiorne to his younger son, John. When the judge died in 1796, an older son, George Jr., his sisters and their husbands joined in a suit to have the deed voided. The trial ended with John still in possession of the property.

George initiated a second suit contending that the

stroke had left his father with unsound judgment. In the end, the court directed John to sell the land to satisfy the interests of the others. In deeds of March, 1799, John sold segments of the land to John Foye, Stephen Foye and Ebenezer Odiorne. Although John lost all of his property, the land kept his family's name: Frost Point.

Walk down the path on your right to a point, marked by a breakwater completed in 1903 by the US Army Corps of Engineers. Together with a second barrier from the shore of New Castle's Fort Stark (on the opposite side of the harbor), this breakwater protects the entrance to Little Harbor. Today dozens of pleasure boats find sheltered moorings here in the summer. The breakwaters have created the sandy shore

Frost Point breakwater. Completed in 1903, this breakwater protects Little Harbor. If you walk along it, note the shallow sandy bottom on the harbor side and the deeper rocky bottom water on the seaward side.

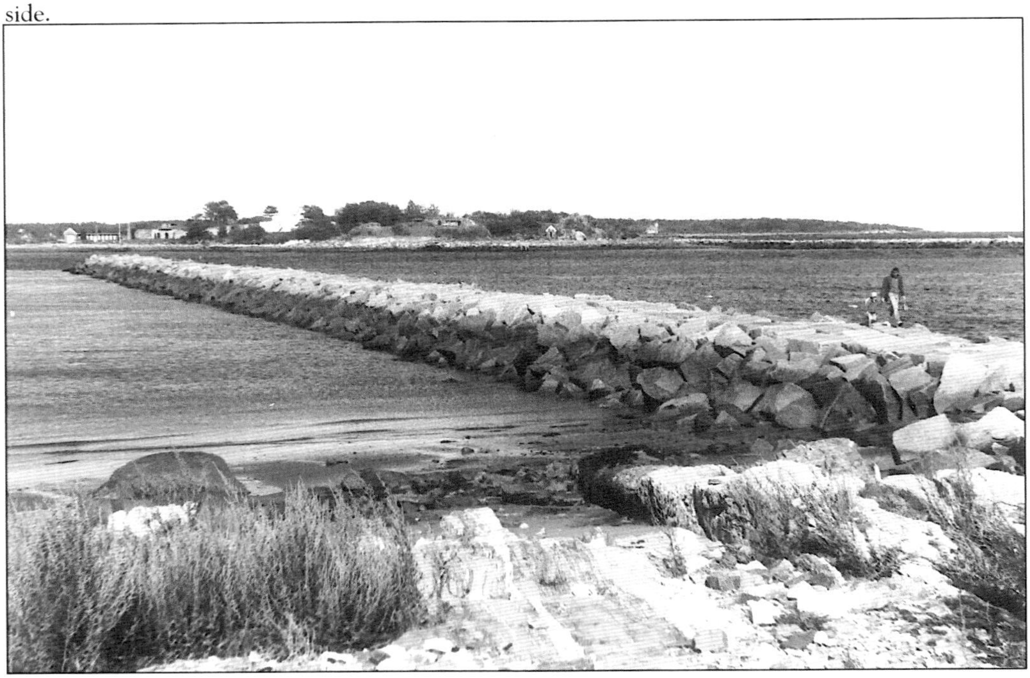

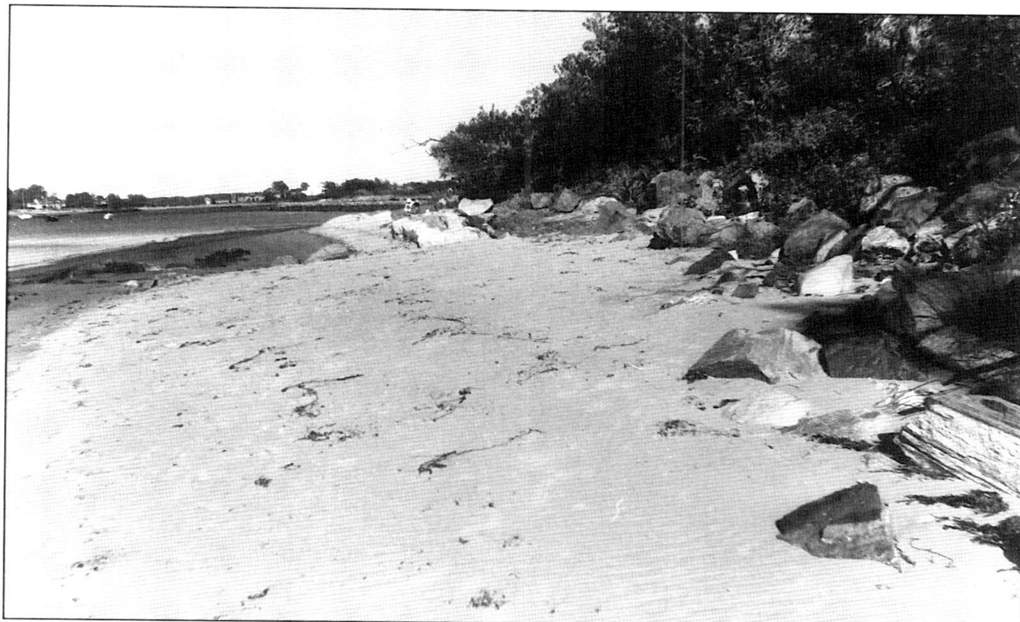

stretching several hundred yards to the left on this side of Little Harbor. The sandy shore is the fifth different habitat you have encountered in your walk.

Frost Point sandy beach. Probably formed and protected by the Little Harbor breakwaters, this sandy beach adds to the varied habitats of the park. Many family picnics were held here before the war.

Sheltered only by the natural "breakwaters" of the land in 1623, this haven is the accepted anchorage of the ship "Jonathan" early in that year. The arrival of this ship marks the beginning of the first European settlement in what is now New Hampshire by thirty-one-year-old David Thomson. Thomson led the small band who arrived on the "Jonathan" to establish a settlement and trade with the local Indians. The fishing vessel "Jonathan" made several voyages to the settlement as did the "Providence," bringing additional settlers, provisions and news from England.

David Thomson's story is told in two versions, the first of which is a narrative blending the works of

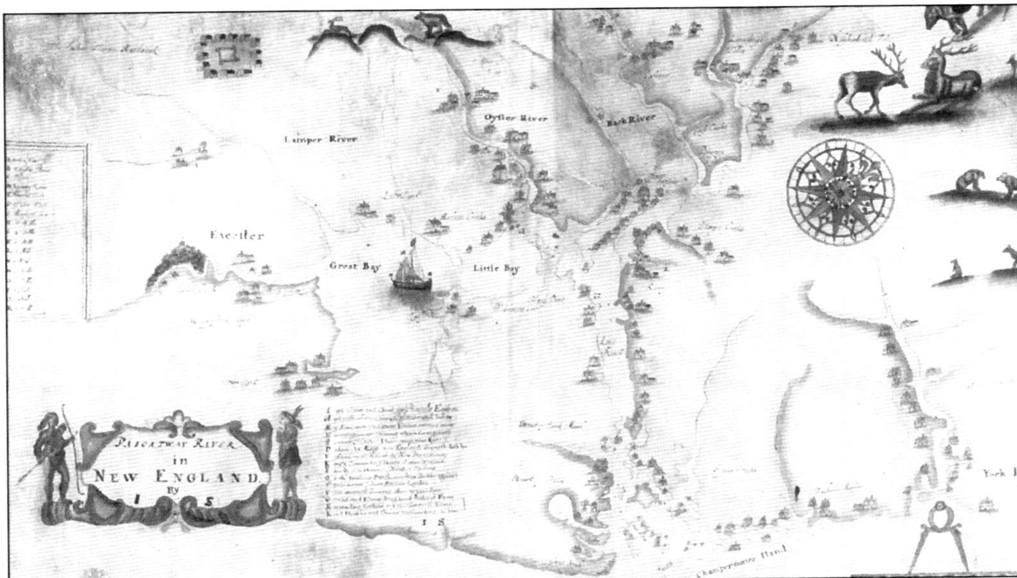

The earliest known map of the Piscataqua River, c.1660. European explorers found friendly American Indians in this area. (Courtesy British Museum Library)

chroniclers of early New Hampshire. In these accounts, Thomson worked as a young clerk in the Plymouth (England) offices of the Council for New England. Two council members, John Mason and Ferdinando Gorges, gained a joint grant to the area from King James I. They conferred a patent on Thomson for 6,000 acres presumably including today's Odiorne Point, New Castle, and perhaps the area which would become Strawbery Banke and later Portsmouth. For his part, Thomson was to fulfill for Mason and Gorges terms of their grant from the King: that they "... shall and will before the expiration of three years ... have in or upon the said portions of lands or some part thereof, one part with a competent guard and ten families of his Majesty's subjects resident and being in and upon the said premises ...."

Exactly where Thomson's settlement and trading

post was located probably will never be known. As you recall, one site suggestion is near the pit-like depression across from the Odiorne homestead you passed earlier in your walk. It is, by oral history, the site of the first European house in New Hampshire although there is no proof that is the site. Unfortunately, that place was disturbed when the gravel pits were dug for road and World War II fort construction. It is now unlikely that even a proper archaeological dig would produce any evidence to confirm the location of New Hampshire's first house.

The second account of Thomson's settlement was published by two descendants of Thomson in 1979. This newer account contends that Thomson came here more than once before 1623, first in 1607 as an apprentice to a seagoing apothecary, Dr. Richard Vines, and later as a representative of the Council of New England to build a fortified position as a foothold for England in "Northern Virginia".

Also by this account, Thomson's building, Pannaway Fort, served as a haven for fishermen of the Isles of Shoals in the "off season." (Pannaway is an American Indian word meaning "place where the waters [of the ocean] spread out" into the marshes.) Samuel Maverick wrote in 1666 of his alleged visit in 1623, that the fort was "... a strong and large house, enclosed with a large and high palizado and mounted gunns ..." Some have argued that this fort was actually at New Castle, not Odiorne. That argument is weakened by accounts of guns later being hurried from England to protect a fishing community at Fort Poynt (New Castle). The guns were needed to protect the community following a raid by the pirate Dixie Bull in 1632. Further, if Pannaway Fort were built before 1623, it is reasonable to believe that it was built on the ocean-facing shore of Odiorne rather than inland. A coastal position would enable them to bombard Spanish or French ships that might attack the "Northern Virginia" settlements of England.

Further, through several decades of the settlements around the Piscataqua basin, Pannaway acquired the name "Rendezvous Point." This epithet referred not to the land here, but to the practice of mariners along the northern coasts to form into convoys; the better to protect themselves from pirates, privateers and the Spanish and French. It is possible, of course, that both accounts of the first settlement bear elements of truth: that the first construction was of a "fort," and that, when Thomson brought his family to Pannaway, he built a separate home, or a "great house" for them. This home may also have served as a trading post for commerce with local Indians with whom he was known to have been friendly. Although we do not know exactly where it was, we do know from their accounts that the settlement was begun and was visited by a number of contemporaries. Miles Standish came to Pannaway Fort in its first year. He sought much-needed supplies to sustain New Plymoth until the next

English ship arrived there with additional provisions. David Thomson returned with Standish to Plymoth, only a day's sail in good weather.

Perhaps it was on this trip or in the course of earlier exploration of the coast with the apothecary, Dr. Vines, that Thomson spotted an island in Massachusetts Bay. In 1624, he was charged by his English "masters" with helping Samuel Maverick build at present day Chelsea "... a small fort ... placing four murtherers (cannon) to protect him from the Indians ..." This task reintroduced Thomson to Massachusetts Bay and its "planters."

England was once more preparing for war with Spain, and support by the Council of New England for Pannaway sagged. Thomson's interest was renewed for the island he had seen in Massachusetts Bay, and he began building a trading post there in 1625. The following summer he moved his family and a few servants there, leaving his 6,000-acre patent behind.

In 1627 and early 1628, the "old planters" around Massachusetts Bay were alarmed by the antics of one Thomas Morton. Trading guns and liquor with the Indians for furs, Morton turned Mt. Wollaston into the unbridled rowdyism of Merry Mount. "... drinking and dancing about many days together, inviting the Indian women for their consorts ..." according to New Plymoth's Governor Bradford. Scandalized, the "old planters" prevailed upon Bradford to suppress Morton. The cost of the action to seize and deport Morton was shared by the settlers, and Mrs. Thomson was listed as a contributor in the amount of fifteen shillings from Thomson's Island, a name the Boston Harbor isle retains today.

The time and place of David Thomson's death are unknown, but Amias' name on the list to deport Morton presumes that she was a widow at the time of Morton's extradition. New Hampshire's first settler had led an active and adventurous life in the short span of only thirty-six years. Thomson's widow subsequently married Samuel Maverick and kept house for him, their three children, and his mother. They moved to Noddle's Island (East Boston) in 1633 and remained there until 1650. Subsequently, the Mavericks lived in Saco, Maine, and in New York City, where Maverick finally was able to escape the "life-long tension between his Church of England loyalty" and "the grim and forbidding mien of the separatist Puritans."

Frost Point to Battery Seaman

Now you should turn away from Frost Point, and retrace your steps to the flat ground on the road. As the dirt path begins to change to a gravel road, take the less frequently used trail to the left in front of the bunker. This path takes you along the shore-side of Battery Seaman to the northerly position of the two 16-inch guns which were contained in this battery.

With the success of the Allies in Europe by 1944, a July moratorium was declared on coastal-defense construction. Test firing of the guns of Battery Seaman

Photograph of a 16-inch gun taken at the Aberdeen Proving ground.

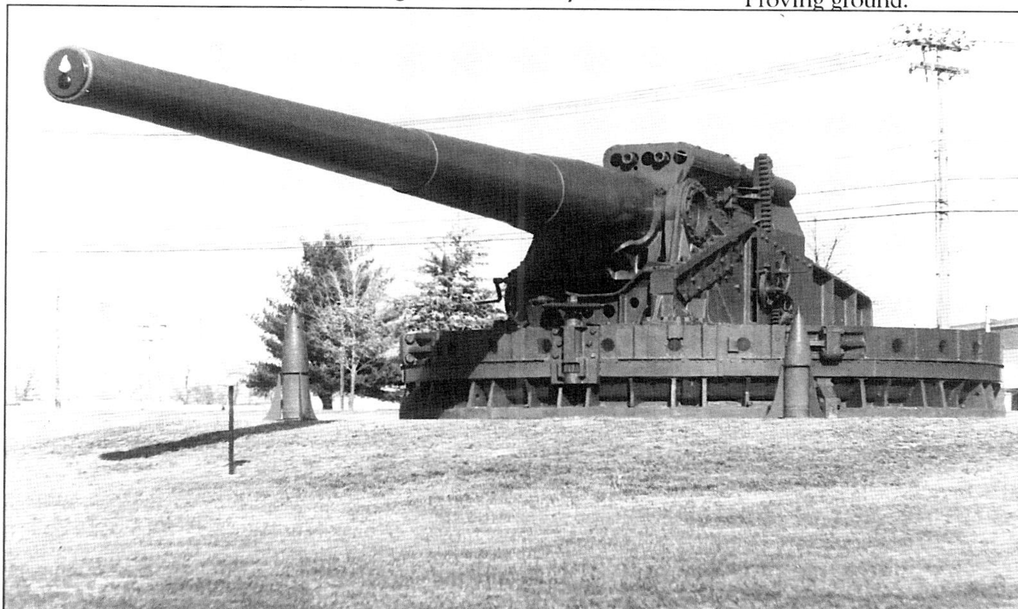

(Battery 103) was scheduled on June 19, just short of this moratorium. Bad weather postponed the test until June 21 because the concussion of the huge guns would be amplified by "heavy" weather. A contingent of the 22nd Coast Artillery Regiment was sent to the Wentworth Hotel in New Castle to open windows and remove art and statuary from vulnerable spots! Perhaps you saw the hotel on the other side of Little Harbor, a large white building with two faded red-roofed towers. Three shells were fired from each gun and the sound and vibration were "plainly felt in Portsmouth and Kittery." According to one unsubstantiated report, tradesmen spent many days replacing window glass at the Wentworth in spite of precautions to protect them.

Walk past this northerly gun position to its twin

One of the Battery Seaman guns firing in 1943. Note the camouflagepaint and lack of vegetation.

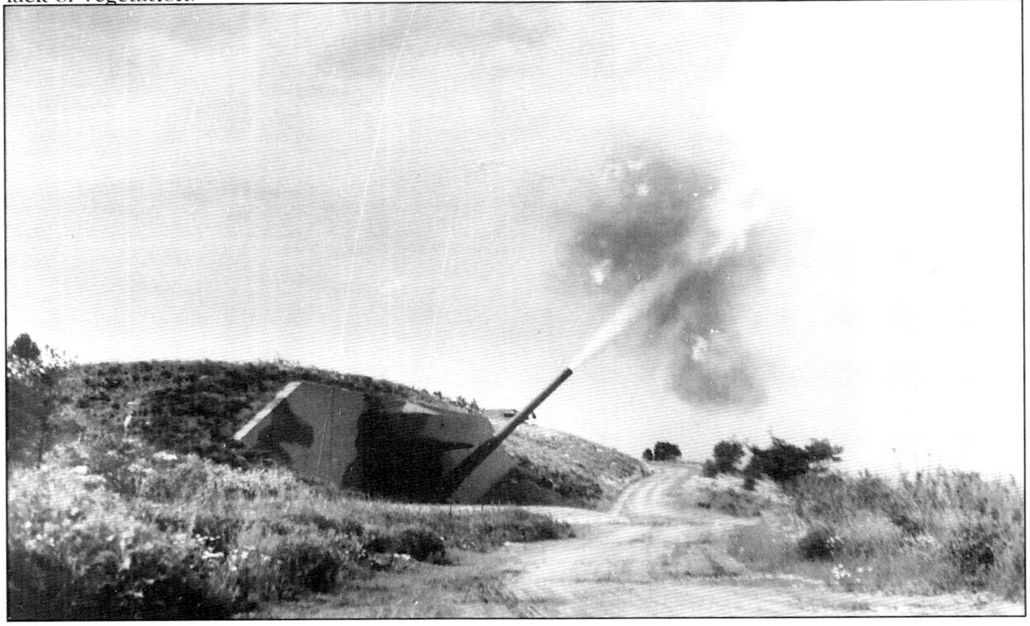

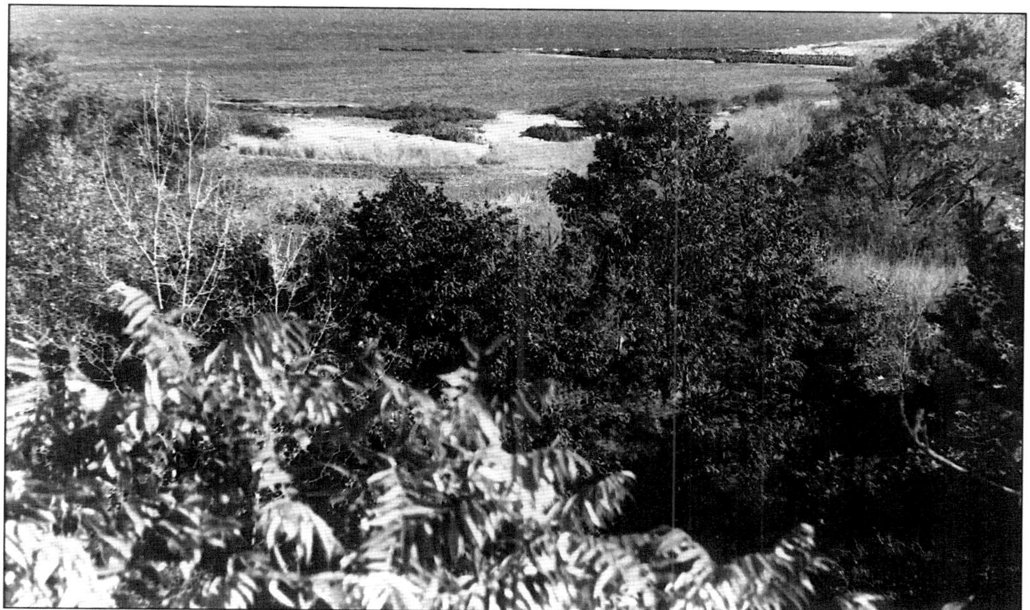

Fresh water marsh from on top of Battery Seaman

in the south. A small path on the right of the bunker leads up onto the top of this casemate, and the magnificient view from the "summit" make the detour very rewarding! The view from the top is one of the best of land and sea, from the salt marshes that feed into Little Harbor, Portsmouth Harbor, up the Maine coast and out to the Isles of Shoals. You will also have a full view of the enclosed fresh water marsh which is in front of you on the ocean side. This is an unusual habitat to be so close to salt water. During the spring and fall it is alive with migrating birds, providing a source of fresh water for shore birds and a home for fresh water marsh plants and animals throughout the year.

Proceed into the gun port. The circular rails you see in the ground mark the gun's actual position. The

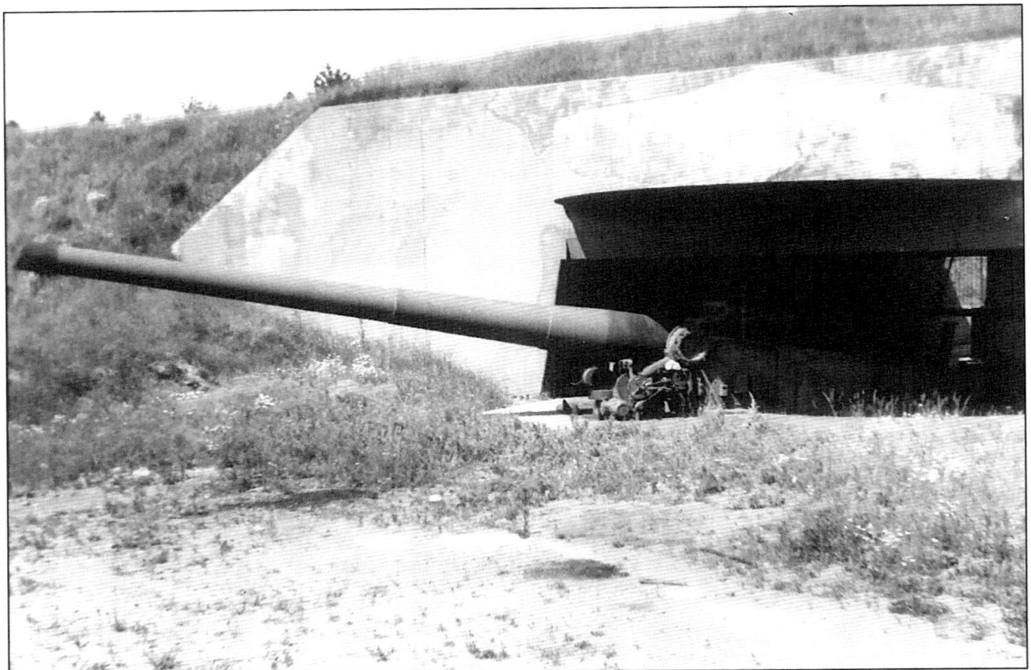

One of the two guns at Battery Seaman.

thick roof and overhang above you were designed to withstand a considerable bomb or shell strike. The ceiling still has some rusting cleats from which a monorail hung to bring the 2,240-pound shells from storage to the guns. As you continue on through the port, stop at the metal door on your right and peer through the openings. The subdued light you see filtering through is from the northerly gun position 500 feet away.

Battery Seaman to the McKim/Gage Property

When you emerge from the battery you will return to Frost Point Road. Turn left and retrace your earlier steps about 100 yards. There a triangular patch of grass on the left marks the entrance of the driveway to a house built around the end of the nineteenth century by Dr. W. Duncan McKim. He was the one, you will remember, who bought all the land from the

Fresh water marsh. In severe northeast storms this fresh water marsh, located to the southeast of Battery Seaman, will turn brackish due to salt water intrusion.

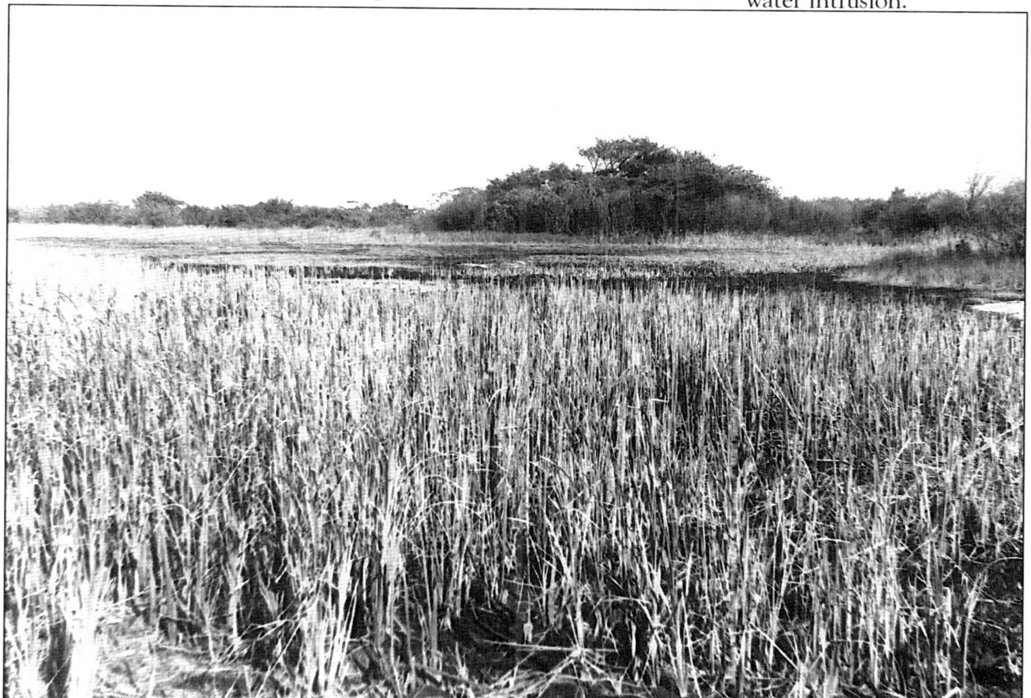

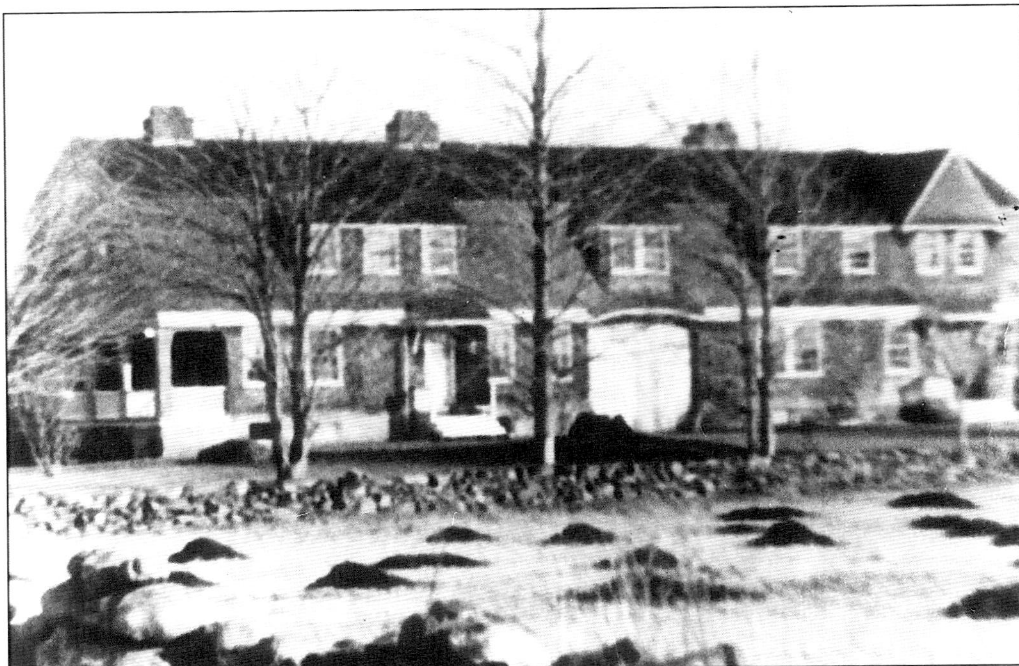

Dr. W. Duncan McKim built this sixteen room house in 1892 which he called "Sagamore Farm."

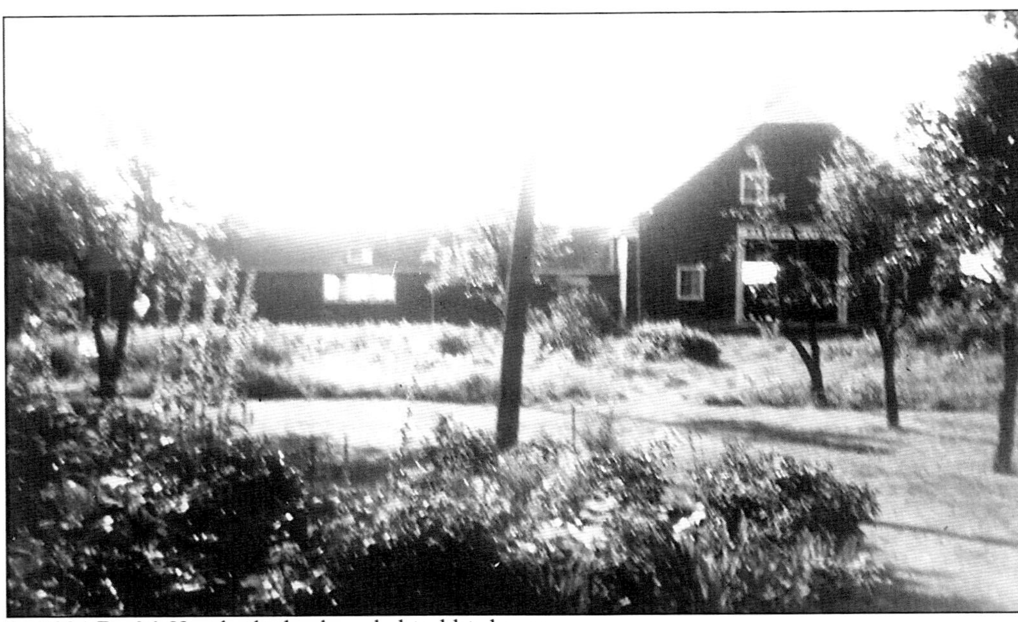

In 1894 Dr. McKim built this barn behind his house.

Pierces after the "Sagamore House" burned down. This was a large house with two matching sides separated by a porte cochere (a carriage drive-through) which went through the house to the large barn behind. The barn itself had two ells, one of which was large enough to house Dr. McKim's 40-foot pleasure boat in winter. Down at Little Harbor he built a 100-foot pier and a house nearby. With an organ valued at several thousand dollars, his wife, Rogé, an accomplished musician, gave organ recitals in this lovely "Organ House."

Proceed up this driveway, noting the parallel rows of sugar maples which line the drive. Farther up, look carefully and you will see gateway posts of stone. If you take a detour to the right you will find the house and outbuilding foundations, but it will take a thorough

A closer view of Dr. McKim's barn.

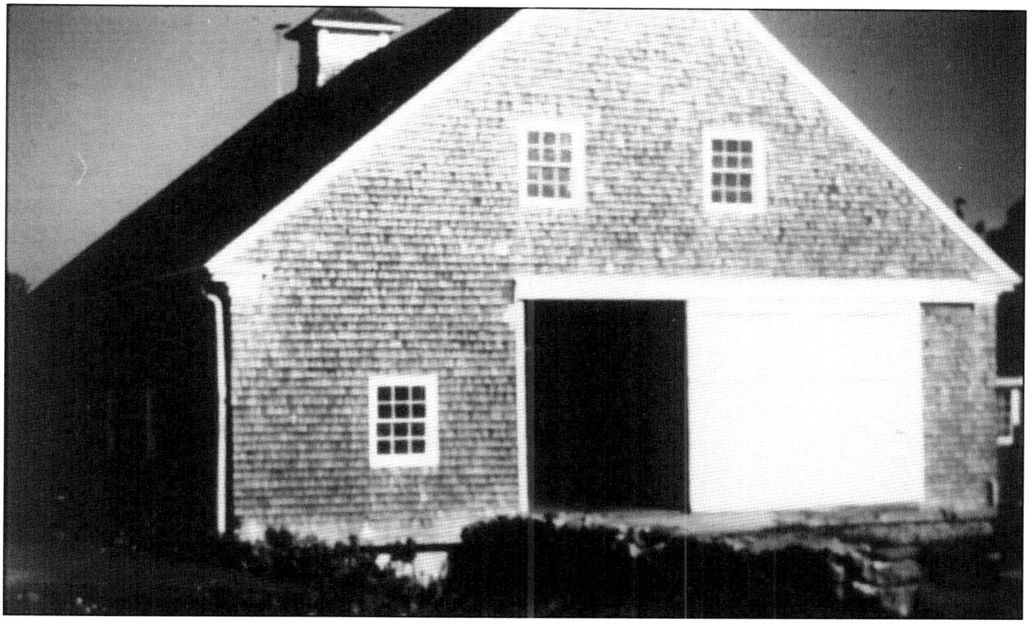

search to find these ruins. The McKim house and property were sold in 1918 to Mrs. Janette W. M. Gage.

It was Mrs. Gage, who in 1924, had the large piece of acquired property subdivided for sale. She sold all the lots along the shore of Little Harbor from Frost Point to the Whitcomb property.

In addition to the McKim/Gage house, other summer homes stood on two of the subdivision lots. At the harbor end of Frost Point, a handsome two-story masonry and wood house was built by retired Chief Justice (New Hampshire Supreme Court) Robert J. Peaslee. A lot with Mrs. McKim's "Organ House" was purchased (excluding the organ) and expanded somewhat by Mrs. Helen M. Waldron. The Peaslee house survived during the war as (according to one unconfirmed report) the residence of the commanding officer of the 22nd Coast

In the late 1800s, Dr. McKim built this cottage to house an organ for his wife. An accomplished musician, she gave many recitals here.

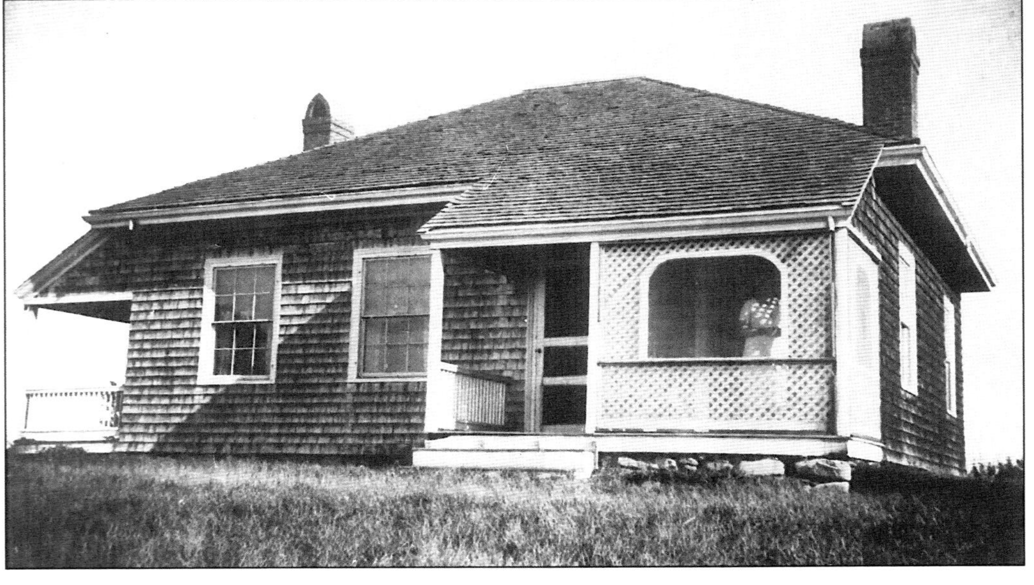

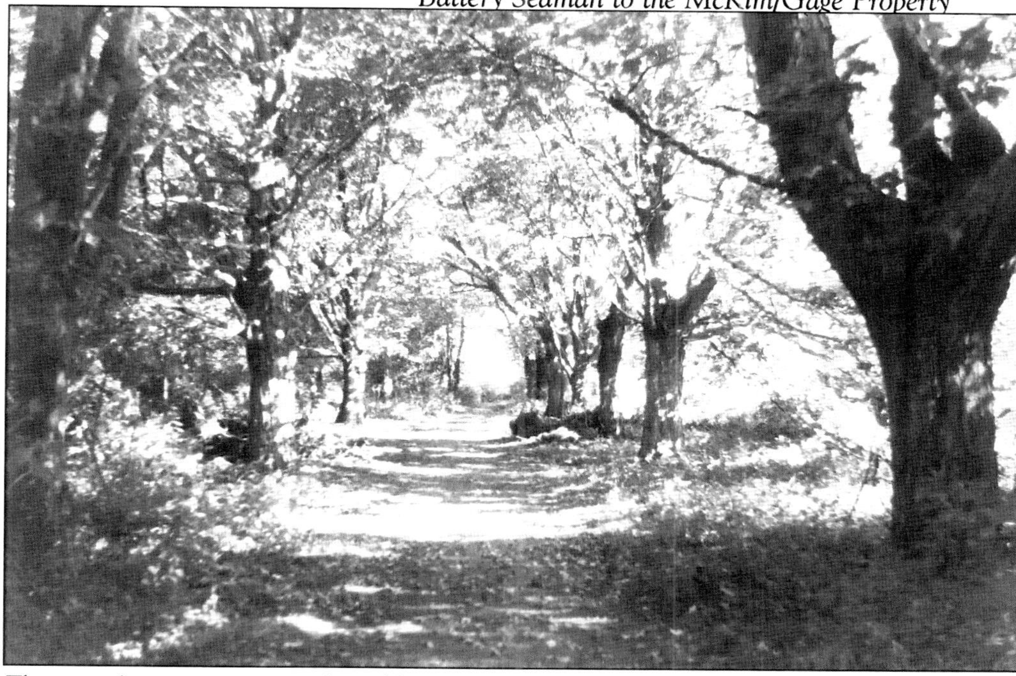

These maple sugar trees were planted by Dr. McKim along his driveway.

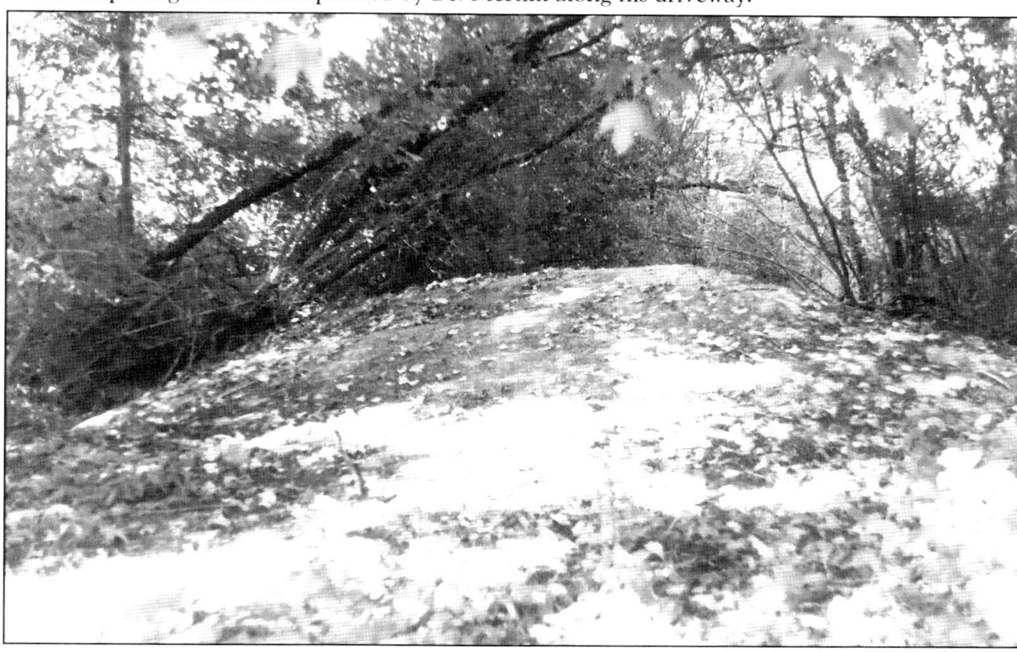

This huge stone near the sugar maples shows the polishing action of the glacier that covered the area during the last ice age.

Artillery Regiment. Dilapidated, it was razed after the war as a safety precaution. The Waldron cottage had stood near Battery Seaman and it had to be razed after the war since the concussions of the test firings had ruined the "Organ House".

The story of how Odiorne Point became a state park is an extremely interesting one. The large Gage house had been one of eleven homes taken by the government at the outset of World War II. At that time, both the written laws and verbal representations of federal agents promised the landowners the opportunity to re-acquire their properties when the government no longer needed them. The Government continued to use the land until 1959, when all the acreage east of Route 1A was declared surplus.

However, in 1949, a federal law had been enacted outlining new rules for disposition of federally acquired

The Waldrons converted the organ house into a cottage with a new wing, running water, and electricity. The family's cat appears to be welcoming the photographer.

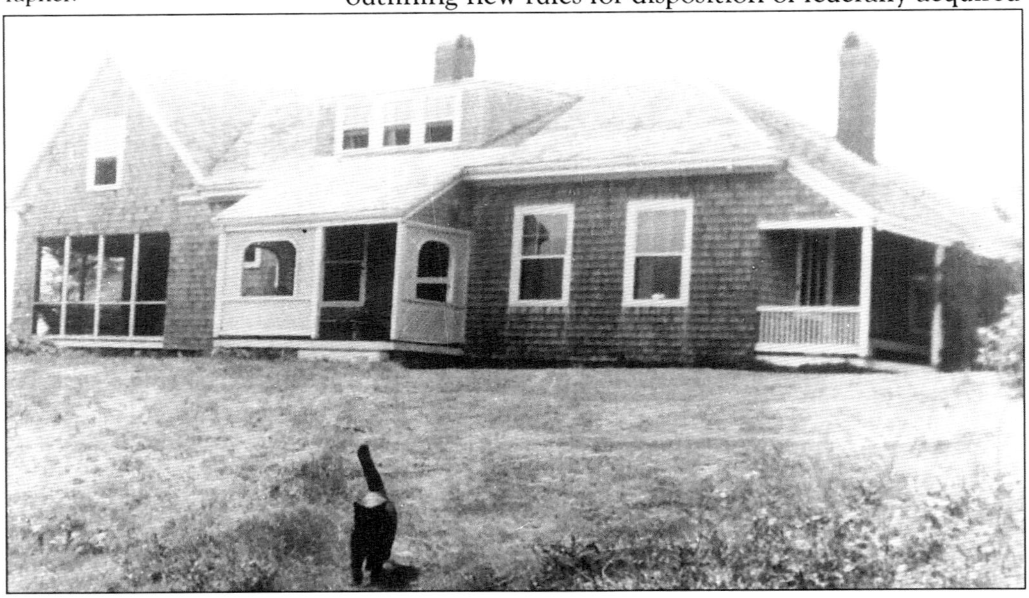

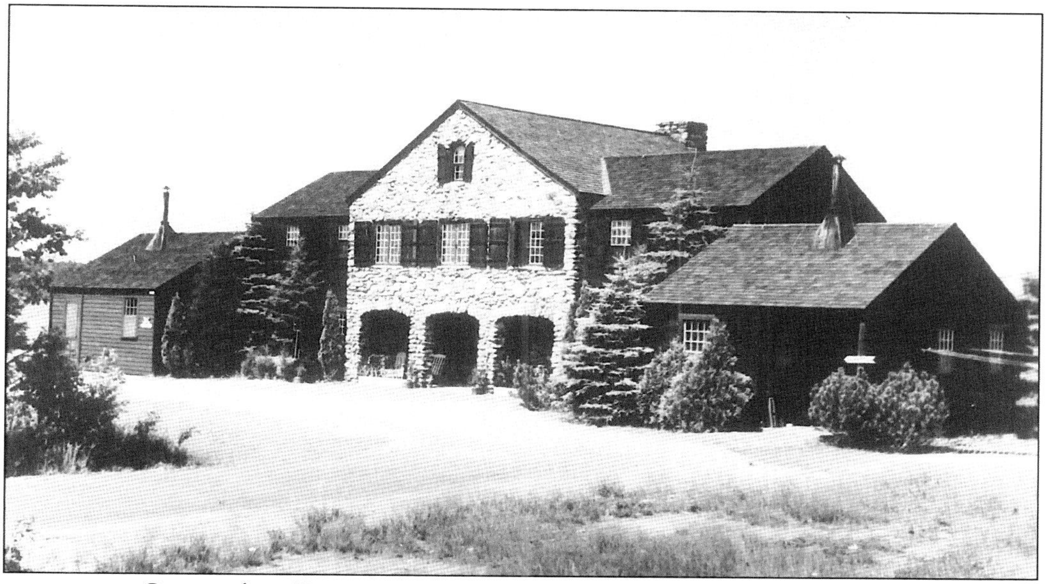

In 1933, retired Chief Justice of the New Hampshire Supreme Court, Judge Peaslee, built this stone and wood house at Frost Point.

property. Once the Department of Defense had no further need for such properties, other federal departments were offered the land. If the land was of no use to the federal government, it was then made available to state governments and municipalities, in that order. Only after all public agencies declined the properties was it offered at auction to the public, including but not limited to the original, private owners. Although a number of bills were passed in Washington D.C. to override this law for the properties in various other areas around the country, one to favor the Odiorne Point landowners passed the Senate but failed to be reported out of committee in the House of Representatives.

The landowners of Odiorne waged the Battle for Odiorne under the strong leadership of Edward Gage (by then a lawyer). Despite valiant efforts to get their

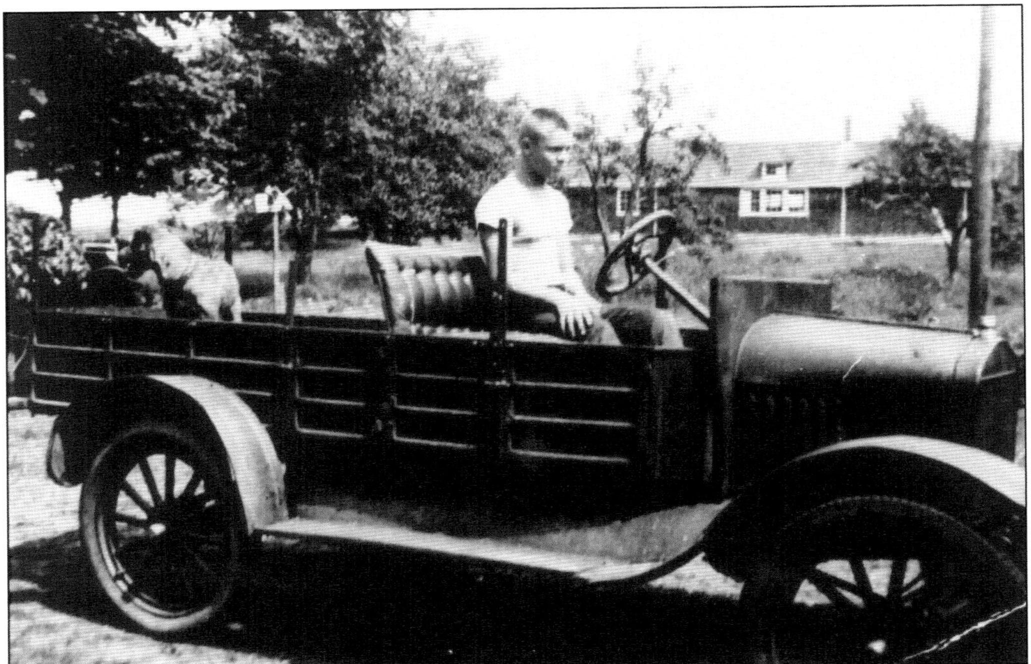

Edward A. Gage II and his dog, Ski, in a 1918 Model T Ford depot wagon in 1935. Edward Gage later played an important role in trying to get the government to sell Odiorne land back to its pre-war owners.

homes back, they failed in their challenge of more powerful interests. Their properties were sold to the State of New Hampshire in 1961 for $91,000 with the proviso that the land be used as a park. After a decade of inactivity the state was prodded by a group of private citizens to do something about the natural and historic promise of Odiorne Point. Led by conservation activist Annette B. Cottrell, a series of studies was prepared and, in 1972, Odiorne Point was dedicated as a state park. The park was going to be named Fort Dearborn State Park. However, just before it opened the name was changed to Odiorne Point State Park to recognize that family's long association with the land.

The years of World War II began badly for the twenty-four families who owned property at Odiorne

Point. There had been rumors, of course, but no one who knew the quiet elegance of living here could quite believe that this land would be needed to defend the Portsmouth Naval Shipyard. After all, there were Fort Constitution, Fort Stark and Fort Foster: that should be enough.

Unfortunately, the shipyard was far more important to defense planners than Odiorne families realized. Especially hard hit were those eleven families who owned homes at Odiorne; even more so the few who lived here year around. Within a few weeks after the December 7th attack on Pearl Harbor in 1941, the landowners of Odiorne Point knew the worst. They received notice that they had to vacate their properties and remove all their goods: they were given only a month to do so! Some furnishings of absentee owners were removed to an old warehouse in Portsmouth, where subsequent ravages of leaking roofs and vandalism reduced them to ruin. It cannot be said that any property was surrendered happily! Many owners, in fact, were so shocked by the low valuation placed on their estates that the government was forced to go to court to have their properties condemned. This slowed the transfer process so much that some properties were not legally owned by the government for over a year after the families had been ousted.

Having commandeered the land, the Army Corps of Engineers and private contractors immediately set about converting Odiorne Point into the primary defensive position guarding the approaches to the shipyard. Route 1A was closed from Brackett Road on the west nearly to Wallis Sands on the south. The "Dead Line" barbed wire fencing was strung in the marsh and along the shore (you saw fence posts in the marsh), and machine guns were placed at critical points. Building of the fortification began at a frantic pace.

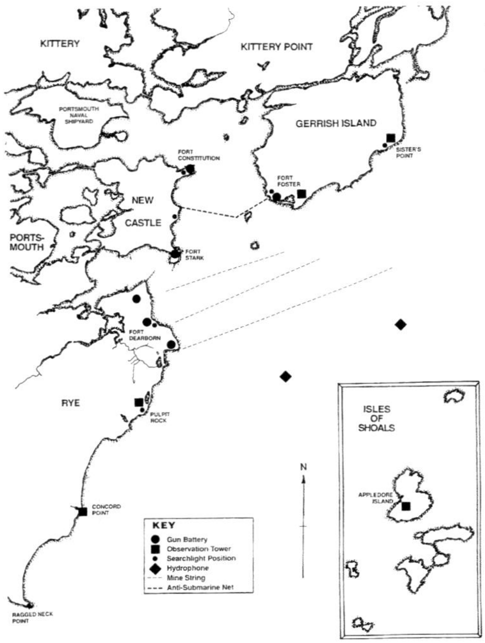

A sketch of the World War II Portsmouth Harbor defenses. Fort Dearborn was a key element in those defenses.

As the fort went up, houses went down: among the first to go were several summer homes. Meanwhile, construction proceeded with deliberate speed on additional gun positions. Together with the 155-millimeter guns placed near the Drowned Forest, two 6-inch guns and two 16-inch guns were to be placed on the peninsula. In May 1943, the Odiorne Point area had a new name: Fort Henry Dearborn, in honor of a distinguished Revolutionary War general from nearby Hampton. One of the stories of the construction period highlights an ironic conflict between civil defense directives and the military's need to meet fort construction schedules. During the war, coastal and strategically important towns were instructed to "black out" by covering windows, painting the top half of car headlights black and a number of other ways to prevent any light from showing the enemy where land and targets were at night. The Portsmouth area was no exception. Army troops patrolled the waterfront of Portsmouth and civilian defense wardens saw to it that even the narrowest shaft of light was put out. Meanwhile Fort Dearborn was ablaze with lights for round-the-clock construction!

Fort Dearborn construction was completed in three years. Ironically, the guns of Odiorne were never fired at the enemy, and were obsolete as defensive weapons by the time of their completion in June of 1944. Perhaps only one of the 16-inch coast artillery guns (originally designed as naval guns) survived post-war scrapping. If you are ever near the Aberdeen Proving Grounds in Maryland, you can find a lone survivor there.

Park visitors often question the necessity for building these fortifications. Was the threat of coastal attack in the early days of World War II great enough to justify the large expenditure of money and manpower? Although the Germans had no aircraft capable of crossing the Atlantic to bomb the Portsmouth Naval Shipyard in early 1942, they did possess surface ships that were capable of shelling the coast from well offshore. Because most of the U.S. fleet was in the Pacific, these coastal guns became an important means of defense. Even in mid-1943 the Germans still possessed two major naval warships that could cross the Atlantic and shell the coast. By the end of that year, however, the threat no longer existed, but by then Fort Dearborn's fortifications were well on the way to completion.

Fort Dearborn certainly would have been a powerful deterrent to enemy naval forces had it been needed, and the Portsmouth Naval Shipyard proved well worth protecting. The shipyard constructed eighty-five submarines between 1939 and 1945. With a maximum employment in 1943 of over 22,000, the shipyard succeeded in launching three submarines in a single day, January 27, 1944!

With the end of the hostilities in 1945, the colors of the 22nd Coast Artillery Regiment were struck, and Battery Seaman (16-inch guns) and Battery 204 (6-inch guns) were dismantled, and the mines and submarine net were removed from the port entrance. Observation posts from Cape Ann to Kennebunk were abandoned, like hundreds of similar installations on the Atlantic and Pacific coasts.

Before 1900 this was the end of the road from Portsmouth. Horsedrawn carriages brought people here to enjoy the seashore. This was the site of the "Parking Lot" for the carriages.

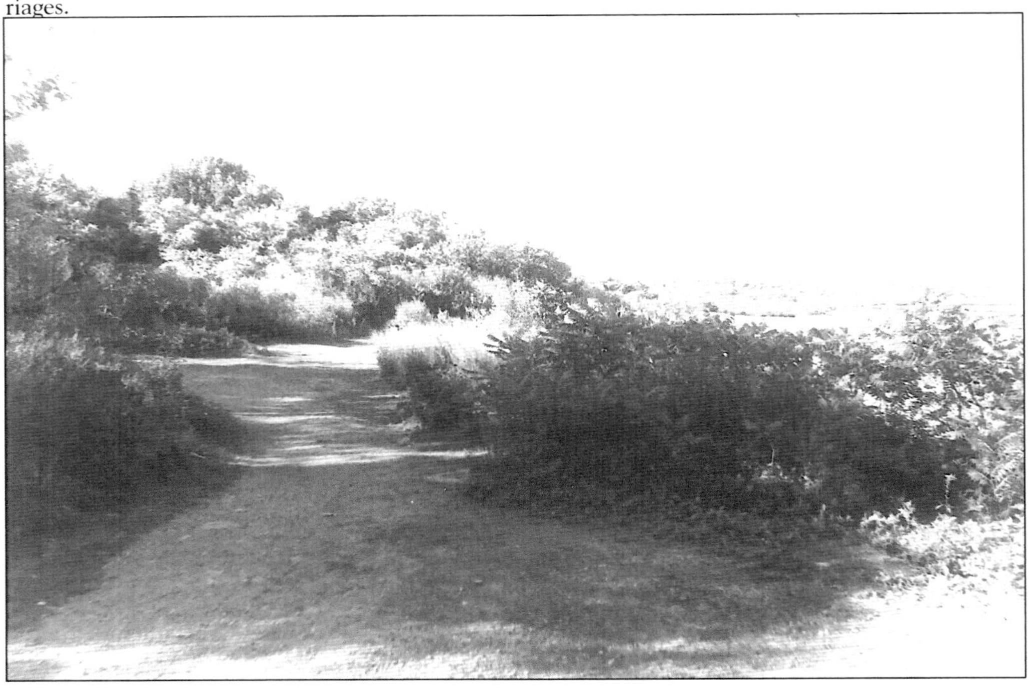

The McKim/Gage Property to Columbus Road

As you proceed beyond the avenue of sugar maples the path winds over a ridge and eventually emerges from the woods to a magnificent view of the mouth of the fast flowing Piscataqua River. This overlook was the ocean-side end of Columbus Road, the 1838 road which you passed earlier in your walk, across from the Odiorne farm. It is now protected from erosion by the huge rocks placed here by the Army Corps of Engineers.

Taken in the early 1900s this photograph is of the monument erected by the Colonial Dames at the end of Columbus Road. It was later moved to the Odiorne family cemetery. The large white buildings on the left are the Wentworth Hotel.

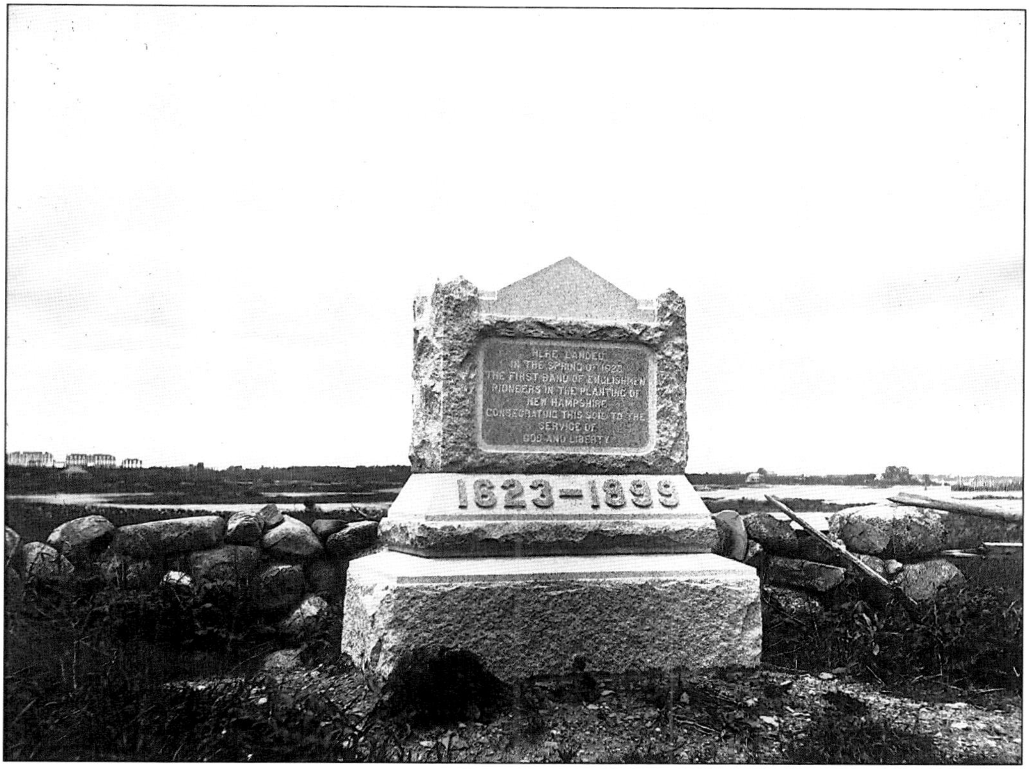

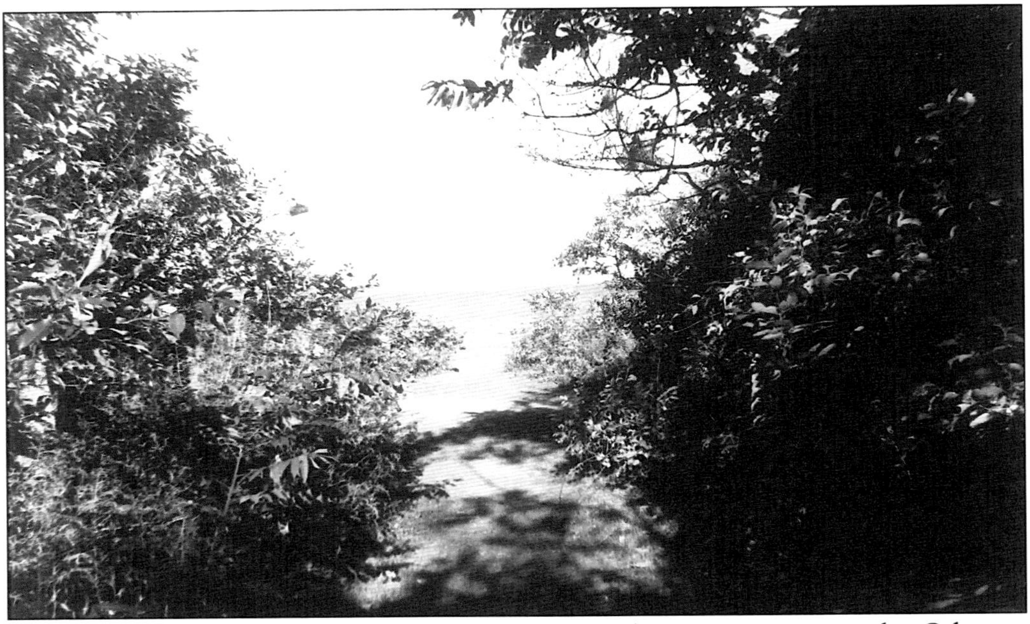

Seaward end of Columbus Road. The road from Portsmouth turned towards the ocean on Columbus Road.

There are many fresh water springs on the Odiorne peninsula, but none in a more unusual spot than the one among the rocks near the high-tide line, below and a few yards to the right of this overlook. Early fishermen from the Isles of Shoals probably had to come to the coast to replenish their water supply. If they found this spring, it certainly would have been more convenient to get to than those inland.

This beach is fascinating to explore. As you walk farther along the path, look for the remains of the sewer pipe from the Marvin/Straw house. Another quarter mile along the edge of the rocky shore returns you to the rear of Battery 204, and, on your left, the Seacoast Science Center.

In 1973, the Audubon Society of New Hampshire sent a naturalist to conduct nature programs in a building the military had used as a fire station. This was the first public/private partnership at Odiorne. Audubon, a private, non-profit organization worked with New Hampshire Parks and Recreation in opening a summer nature center. When that building was removed, the Sugden House, which had been used, it is said, as a war-time officers' quarters and later as a park manager's residence, became the Park's visitor center in 1976. This center was managed by a third sponsor, the University of New Hampshire Cooperative Extension/Sea Grant Program. In 1985, a fourth sponsor, The Friends of Odiorne Point State Park, Inc., joined the other three to help oversee the programs at the Visitors' Center and in the Park. The Friends spearheaded a fund-raising effort which

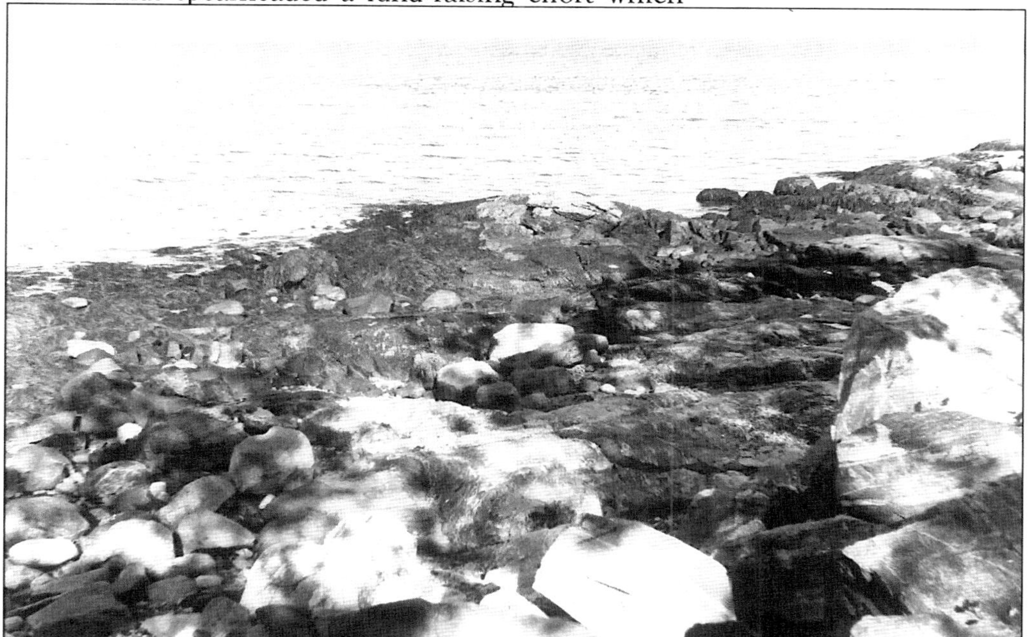

Amongst these rocks runs a fresh water spring that is submerged at high tide.

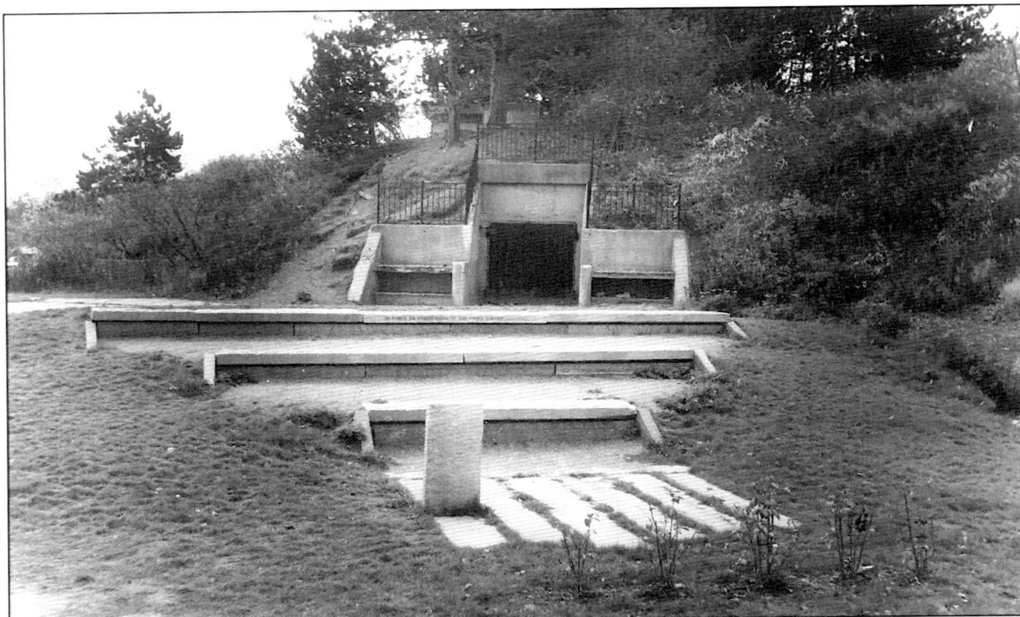

Annette Cottrell Teaching Steps. Teaching steps constructed in honor of Mrs. Annette Cottrell recognize her many contributions to the establishment of the Odiorne Point land as a state park. It incorporated the landscape of Battery 204 in its design.

raised $1.2 million dollars to build the Seacoast Science Center. It opened its doors June 13, 1992. Retaining the Sugden House as its primary exhibit was a prerequisite of all designs for the Center. As the last private residence on Odiorne Point, it has a prominent place in the story of the park.

In 1920, Robert I. Sugden, a prominent Portsmouth businessman, purchased nine acres from Mary J. Foye. There he built a handsome masonry summer home, employing local artisans. A rarity for those days, the house had electric lighting and appliances, although an early electric refrigerator apparently failed and had to be replaced with a traditional icebox.

The home had nine rooms on the first floor, including a large living room across the front facing the ocean flanked by three sitting-room porches. From a central hall were three bedrooms on the north side, while a dining room, kitchen, and bathroom lined the south side. A recessed stairway could be lowered to lead to an additional pair of bedrooms and a sitting room on the second floor. The upper level, plus a two-car garage and some interior walls on the ground level were removed when the Science Center was built. When you go inside the Center's meeting room, look at the stone fireplace: you will see the Sugden's initial, S, in the masonry above the mantle. The fireplace still works and today is used during special programs and events.

Outside, wide lawns and flower beds surrounded the house. Because of the rocky shore, Sugden built a saltwater swimming pool. The pool was right at the

Mr. Robert Sugden's summer home built in 1920. Note the power pole behind the house.

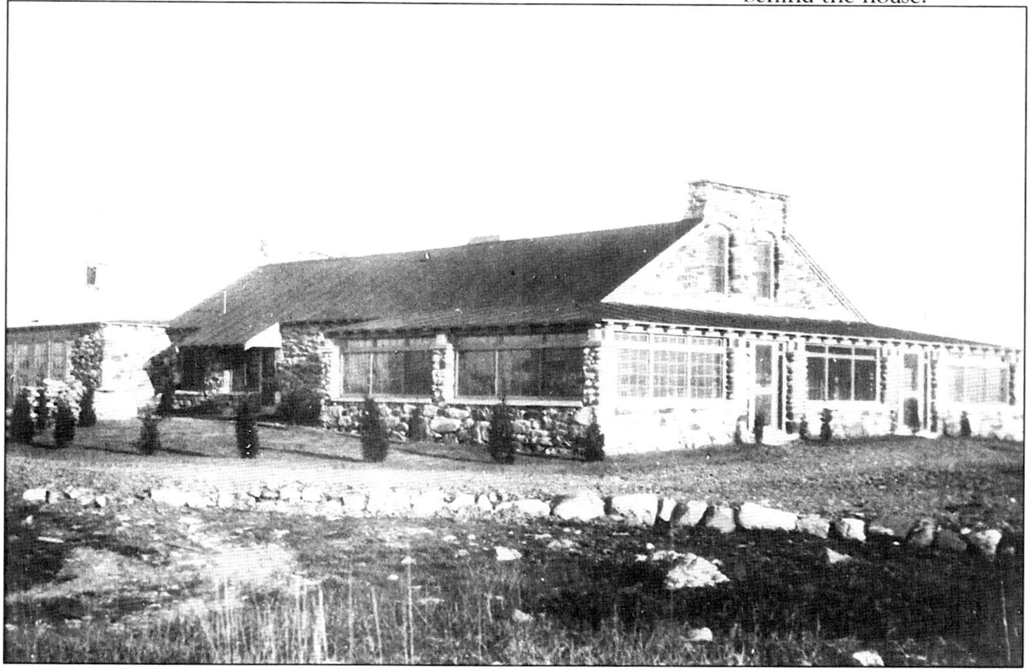

water's edge and was filled by the incoming tide: the water retained by a shut-off valve as the tide ebbed. Enclosed porches running along the east, north, and south sides gave the Sugdens a grand view of the harbor approaches, lighthouses, islands and boating activity. There was excitement during prohibition when rum runners tried to land illegal liquor in the cove north of the Sugden House. A United States Coast Guard chase forced the smugglers to dump their cargo at sea, some of which later washed up south of Odiorne Point.

As a finale of this historical walking tour of Odiorne, you are invited to share the Sugden's sea view from the porches of the Sugden House, along with the history exhibits to be found there. Also, don't forget to visit

Mrs. Phyllis Sugden Frink, with her daughters Barbara and Madeline, sitting on the edge of the family pool.

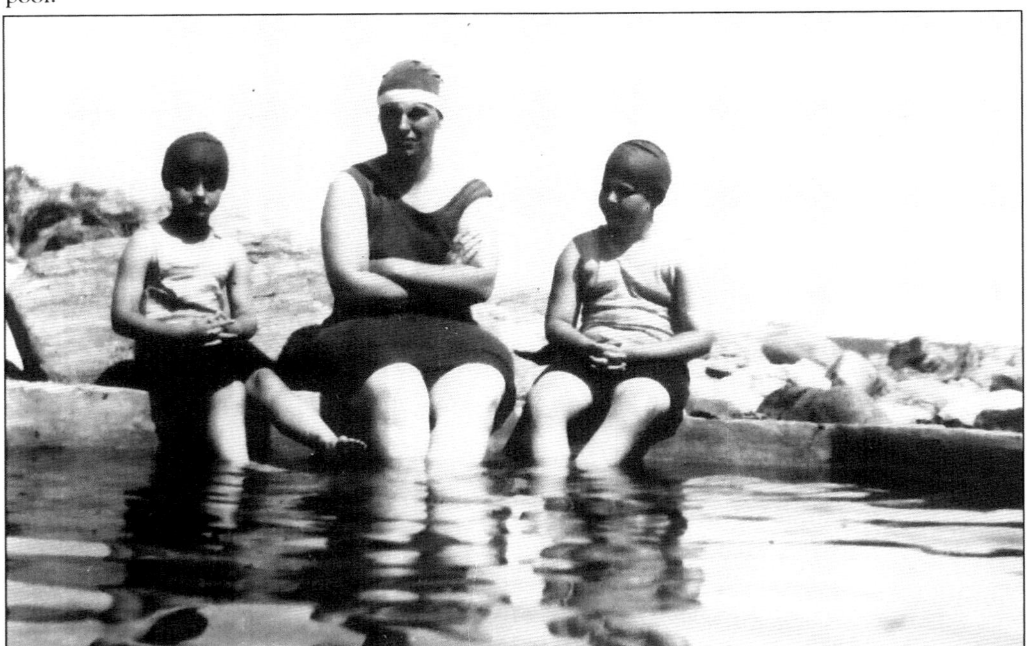

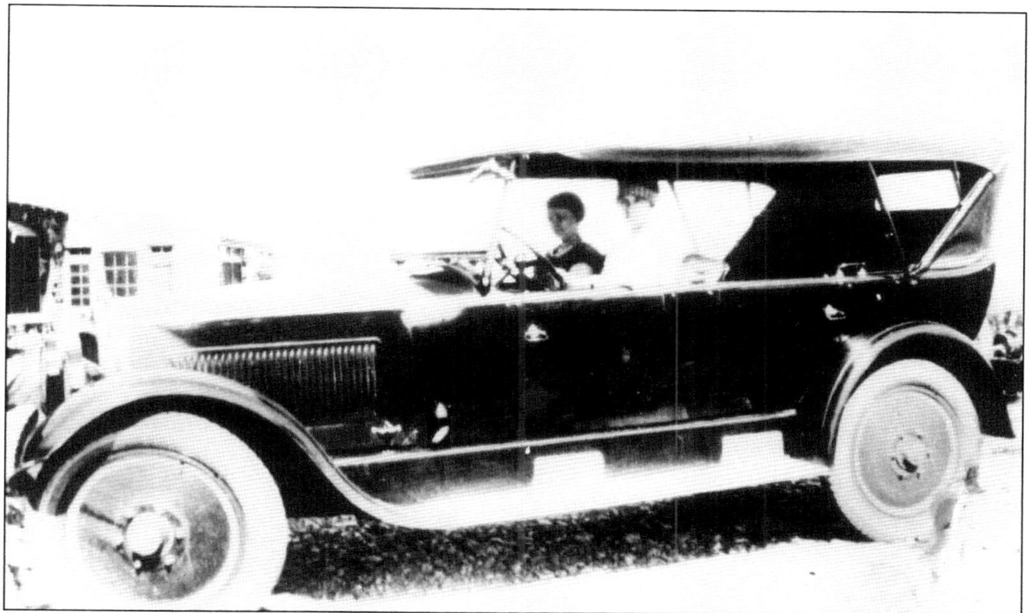

Phyllis Sugden Frink, a progressive woman of the 1920s, at the wheel of the family's touring car.

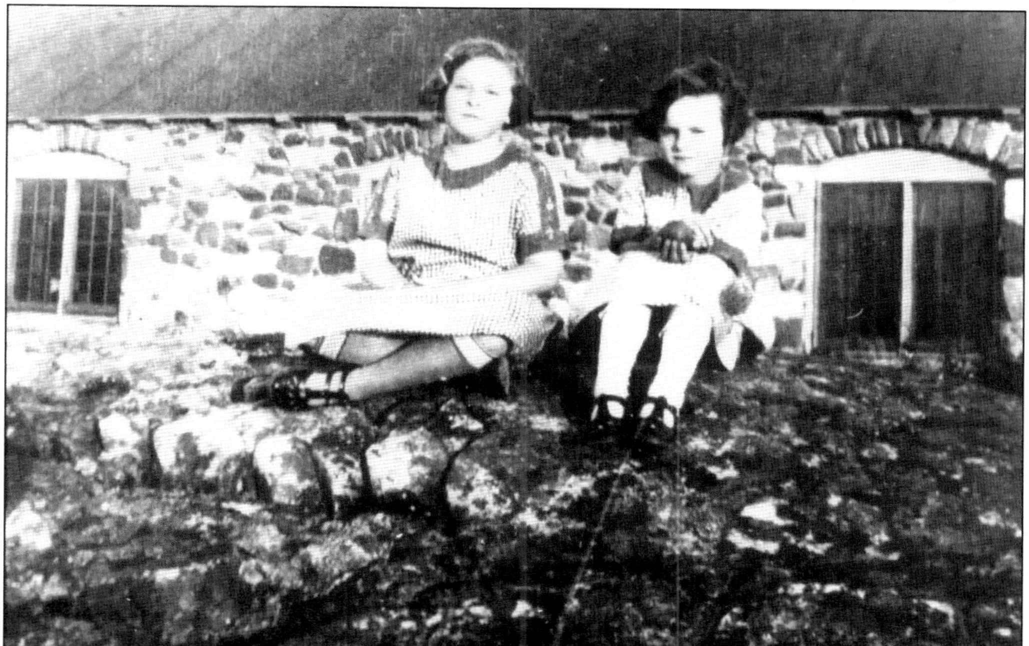

Madeline and Barbara Frink, ages eight and five, outside their grandfather Sugden's house where they spent their summers.

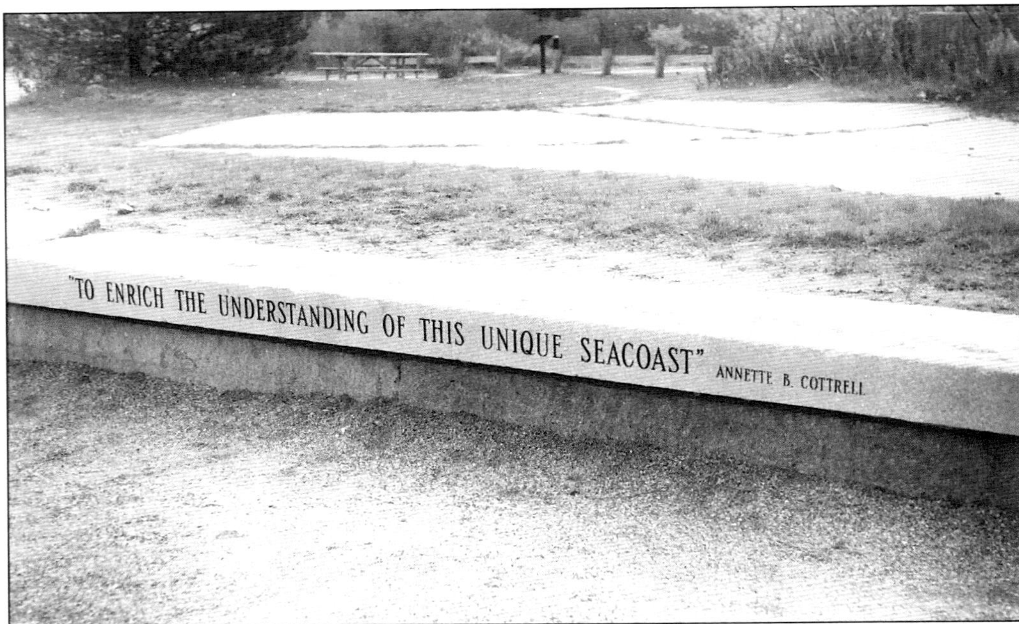

Annette Cottrell Teaching Steps inscription. Mrs. Cottrell used these words to argue that the land we now know as Odiorne Point State Park should be preserved. Note the remnants of one of the 6-inch gun mounts by the picnic table.

the habitat exhibits in the Brown Exhibit Hall, to get a closer view of the many habitats you saw along your walk. We hope that this guide has helped you appreciate the many facets of Odiorne Point's cultural, natural and military history.

Bibliography

Brewster, Charles W., *Rambles About Portsmouth*, First Series, Portsmouth, N.H., 1859, Second edition 1873. Second Series, Portsmouth, N.H., 1860.
Brighton, Raymond A., *They Came To Fish*, Portsmouth, N.H., 1973
Clark, Charles E., *The Eastern Fronteer*, New York, N.Y., 1970.
Deane, Charles, *The Indenture of David Thomson*, paper written 1876. Text reprinted 1895 in New Hampshire State Papers, vol. 25, pp. 713-739.
Gurney, C.S., *Portsmouth, Historic and Picturesque*, Portsmouth, N.H., 1902.
Jenness, John Scribner, *Notes on the First Planting of New Hampshire*, Portsmouth, N.H.,1878. Reprinted 1895 in New Hampshire State Papers, vol. 25, pp. 663-673.
Levett, Christopher, *A Voyage Into New England and the Severall Townes Therein*, believed written in 1660. Text reprinted in N.E. Historical and Genealogical Register, vol. 39, 1885.
Odiorne, David W., Editor, *Genealogy of the Odiorne Family*, Revised Edition, Ann Arbor, Mich., 1967.
Parsons, Langdon B., *History of the Town of Rye, N.H.*, Concord, N.H. 1905. Reprinted 1962 and 1970.
Raymo, Chet and Maureen E., *Written in Stone*, Chester, CT, 1988.
Saltonstall, William G., *Ports of Piscataqua*, Harvard Univ. Press, 1941. Re-issued by Russell and Russell, New York, N.Y., 1968.
Tallman, Louise H., *Odiorne Point: Highlights of History*, One of a series of educational pamphlets, Concord, N.H., 1973. Revised 1992.
Thompson, Ralph E. and Matthew R., *The First Yankee*. Privately printed, Salem, Ore., 1979.
Varrell, William M., Jr., *Rye on the Rocks*, Boston, Mass., 1962.
Whittaker, Robert H., *Land of Lost Content*, Dover, N.H., 1993.
Winslow, Ola Elizabeth, *Portsmouth, Life of a Town*, New York, N.Y., 1966.
Historical New Hampshire, New Hampshire Historical Society, Apr. 1948.

Articles:

King James and His Council of New England.
The First Planting of New Hampshire, J.S. Jenness (excerpts).
Notes Relating to David Thomson, Charles Deane (excerpts).
New Hampshire State Papers:
Vol. 1 - Early years, miscellaneous papers.

Vol. 17 - Transcripts of early documents.
Vol. 25 - Complete text of papers by Deane and Jenness.
Rockingham County Records, Court Records, Series A, Frost vrs. Frost; 1797 and 1799.
Register of Deeds, various deeds and plans.

Other Sources

Hassel-Shearer, Christi, *Odiorne Point Oral History*.
Project of Rye. Co-sponsored by Rye Historical Society, Rye Library, and the Friends of Odiorne Point, 1988.

Interviews on audio tape with:

Elizabeth *Howe*, Edward A *Gage*, Marjorie *Marvin* Hartford, Barbara Frink Hauck (*Sugden*), Paul *Hobbs*, Robin *Graves* Howe, Barbara *Odiorne* MacGregor & Priscilla *Odiorne* Newcomb, Ann *Waldron* Almendinger, Arnold *Whittaker*.

Ralph L. Brown, Nancy Odiorne Condon, Barbara Frink Hauck, Lt. Col. Wilbar Hoxie, U.S.A. Ret., Nelson Lawry, Arnold Silverstone, Annette Cottrell.

Friends of Odiorne Point State Park; History Committee: Howard S. Crosby, Chair, Nancy O. Condon, Bonnie Goodwin, Barbara F. Hauck, Richard T. MacIntyre, Stephen C. Miller, Lester Stevens, Louise Tallman, Phyllis Wilcox.

Photography:

Charles West
Howard Crosby
Thomas Arter
Wendy Lull

Nature drawings:

Sylvia Jones

Trail map:

Patrica Miller